GHOSTS
OF 42ND
STREET

ANTHONY BIANCO

wm | *William Morrow*
An Imprint of HarperCollins *Publishers*

GHOSTS
OF 42ND
STREET

A History of America's
Most Infamous Block

HarperCollins books may be purchased for educational, business, or sales promotional use. For information please write: Special Markets Department, HarperCollins Publishers Inc., 10 East 53rd Street, New York, NY 10022.

FIRST EDITION

Designed by Judith Stagnitto Abbate

Printed on acid-free paper

Library of Congress Cataloging-in-Publication Data

Bianco, Anthony.
    Ghosts of 42nd Street : a history of America's most infamous block / Anthony Bianco.
      p. cm.
    ISBN 0-688-17089-7 (alk. paper)
    1. Forty-second Street (New York, N.Y.)—History.   2. Times Square (New York, N.Y.)—History.   3. New York (N.Y.)—History. I. Title: Ghosts of Forty-second Street.   II. Title.

F128.67.F7B53   2004
974.7'1—dc22   2003066533

04 05 06 07 08 WBC/QW 10 9 8 7 6 5 4 3 2 1

For Marissa,
with love and pride

Our relationship with the places
we know and meet up with . . . is a
close bond, intricate in nature, and
not abstract, not remote at all: It's
enveloping, almost a continuum
with all we are and think.

—TONY HISS, *THE EXPERIENCE OF PLACE*

CONTENTS

GHOSTS OF 42ND STREET

Overture

Before Hollywood, there was 42nd Street, birthplace of American mass-market entertainment. Beginning in 1899, a burst of construction on the mid-Manhattan block of West 42nd Street between Broadway and Eighth Avenue created the greatest concentration of theaters America has ever seen or likely will see again. It was 42nd Street's pioneering dazzle that transformed today's Broadway theater district into the Great White Way. On 42nd Street John Barrymore played Hamlet, George M. Cohan introduced "Give My Regards to Broadway" ("Tell all the gang at 42nd Street/That I will soon be there") and the Marx Brothers made their Broadway debut. Here, George Gershwin began his long and fruitful collaboration with his lyricist brother Ira, Fred and Adele Astaire first starred on an American stage, Bob Hope caught his big break, and Florenz Ziegfeld Jr. glorified several generations of American girls in his eponymous *Follies.* On 42nd Street, too, film began to evolve from flickering novelty to art form with the premiere of D. W. Griffith's racist masterpiece *Birth of a Nation* at the Liberty. Vaudeville reached its madcap zenith at Hammerstein's Victoria, where Charlie Chaplin conspired with Stan Laurel in the invention of pie throwing and the likes of Buster Keaton, Will Rogers, and Harry Houdini made a name for themselves.

No city in America has as many famous thoroughfares as New York

City. Who does not know Fifth Avenue, Madison Avenue, Park Avenue, Wall Street, or Broadway? But 42nd Street in its heyday was the quintessence of the quintessential American metropolis—excessive, expensive, unpredictable, loud, fun, and a bit dangerous. No place in America has ever evoked the glamour and romantic possibilities of big-city nightlife as vividly as did 42nd Street in its Golden Age.

From the first, with an eclectic mix of amusements high, low, and in between, 42nd Street attracted pleasure seekers from all economic classes. The beauty of the street was not only that it democratized entertainment, but that it also struck an artful balance between catering to middle-class proprieties and flouting them. No one walked this tightrope more skillfully than Oscar Hammerstein I, 42nd Street's pioneering impresario (and grandfather to the famous Broadway lyricist of the same name). Instead of simply parading seminude women around the stage of the Victoria, Hammerstein posed them as famous statues from antiquity. Hammerstein and his son, Willie, also hired Evelyn Nesbit, the wife of millionaire Harry Thaw, to perform on a velvet swing after Thaw had made them both into celebrities by murdering her lover, the architect Stanford White. But 42nd Street's trademark brand of titillation was most famously exemplified by its chorus shows—*The Earl Carroll Vanities, George White's Scandals,* and, above all, *Ziegfeld's Follies*—with their ornately stylized displays of perfect chorine flesh. The street may have prided itself on being "naughty, bawdy, gaudy," as the title song from the 1933 film *42nd Street* put it, but it was far too commercial a venue to deliberately offend the paying customers.

From the successive use made of the theaters of 42nd Street, a cultural paleontologist could deduce the entire history of popular entertainment before television and rock and roll. But show business was not the street's only founding claim to fame. In 1903–4, the *New York Times* built itself a slender twenty-five-story tower on an odd, triangular site formed by the convergence of 42nd Street, Broadway, and Seventh Avenue. In the newspaper's honor, the city named the square facing the tower Times Square. Times Tower's completion was commemorated on December 31, 1904, with fireworks—the first of the annual New Year's Eve celebrations for which Times Square became world renowned. The newspaper additionally promoted itself by hanging makeshift banners from tower windows announcing the results of elections and sporting contests. Times Square quickly became New York's favorite gathering place during all important civic events, not just on New Year's Eve. On August 14, 1945—V-J Day—750,000 people packed the place in anticipation of the end of World War II. When the news of the Japanese surrender finally moved across Times Tower's Motogram zipper, the roar of the crowd could be heard all the way to the middle of Central Park.

The Golden Age of 42nd Street entertainment ended by 1930. Many theater producers failed in the Great Depression, and 42nd Street was particularly hard hit. By 1934, only the grandest of its ten theaters—the New Amsterdam—was still functioning as a playhouse, and its days were numbered. Before live entertainment passed from the scene, 42nd Street afforded "class" burlesque its ultimate, national showcase. At Minsky's Republic (originally Hammerstein's Republic), Gypsy Rose Lee perfected the art of sly, slow-motion striptease while Georgia Sothern, "The Human Bombshell," shimmied through her routines in a blur of ferocious athleticism. Undeterred by police raids ("I wasn't naked," Gypsy once protested. "I was completely covered by a blue spotlight"), Minsky's and 42nd Street's two other burlesque houses offered ever more daring shows as the Depression deepened. Meanwhile, down the block at the Rialto Theater, a new proprietor named Arthur L. Mayer, the Merchant of Menace, added what he called the *M* Product—mystery, mayhem, and murder—to the 42nd Street mix. Instead of glorifying the American girl à la Ziegfeld, Mayer's goal was "to glorify the American ghoul." The Rialto was 42nd Street's first movie "grinder"—that is, it offered discounted admissions to second- and third-run features and played them virtually twenty-four hours a day. By the early 1940s, when crusading Mayor Fiorello La Guardia finally succeeded in putting 42nd Street's burlesque houses out of business, every one of the old theaters had been made over into grinders, with a single family—the Brandts—owning most of them. Forty-second Street would remain New York City's great B-rated movie belt for the next five decades, longer even than it had been the city's definitive theater street.

Forty-second Street's fame soured into infamy as it devolved from the nation's first show business capital into its first retail porn center. Its denizens rechristened 42nd Street as "Forty Deuce" or simply "the Deuce," as the place became the ultimate in film noir stage sets. By the mid-1970s, 42nd Street and the rest of Times Square had become so extreme in their degradation, so utterly despoiled, that they were perversely alluring. Busloads of German and Japanese tourists routinely disembarked at the Pussycat Cinema, prepaid tickets in hand, to take their carefully chaperoned walk on the wild side. Twice a week, Women Against Pornography took suburban housewives on tours of 42nd Street's fleshpots. Meanwhile, elements of the intelligentsia embraced 42nd Street as one of the last outposts of urban "authenticity" in a country that seemed increasingly to consist of look-alike shopping malls and retail chain outlets laid end to end. "Times Square has all the mystique of another age," Marshall McLuhan observed in the late 1960s. "If they were to dispose of it now, they'd probably rebuild it, like Williamsburg, in fifty years."

Through all of 42nd Street's transformations, there was this constant: the place was packed day and night. For most of the century, the heavily trafficked intersection of 42nd Street and Broadway was known far and wide as the Crossroads of the World and the 24-Hour Corner. Many out-of-towners came to Times Square just to gawk, for by the early 1920s its colossal electronic signs and billboards were a world-class attraction in their own right. Above all, 42nd Street was where tourists and locals alike went to mix with the moving crowd, to feel New York's erratic, racing pulse. No place in the city was as vividly present tense as 42nd Street and yet so redolent of nostalgic associations, especially for the native New Yorker. Each of the street's successive incarnations was deeply imprinted on the public consciousness and lived on in the city's collective memory—in the 42nd Street of the mind—long after its day had passed.

Schemes to rebuild 42nd Street were first floated in the 1920s, when plans were hatched to tear down some of the theaters and replace them with hotels and office buildings. The Depression snuffed out these private initiatives and preserved 42nd Street's historic theaters in the amber of hard times. Even as New York and most of the country boomed after World War II, West 42nd Street continued to languish, an increasingly brackish economic backwater wholly deprived of capital investment. By the late 1960s, the downtowns of most U.S. cities of a certain size and demographics had given rise to blighted "tenderloin" districts subsisting off rough trade in pornography, drugs, and prostitution. But 42nd Street and the adjoining precincts of Times Square were the ghastliest tenderloin of them all, if only because it attracted runaway teenagers by the thousands. In such cities as Detroit, Newark, and St. Louis, the essential urban problem of this benighted era was that of a city center hollowed out by white flight and a shrinking commercial tax base. However, this was not the fate of Manhattan, where the rest of the borough's Midtown quarter exploded with office tower development even as 42nd Street fell into the gutter. A conspicuous property-value sinkhole amid the world's costliest stand of skyscrapers, the Deuce affronted the custodians of New York's economy no less than its guardians of civic safety and public morality.

The redevelopment of West 42nd Street was a tortuous process, filled with stops and starts, detours and dead ends, false promises and true lies. The beginning of the end of decades of failure came with an effort so small and so inwardly directed as to be virtually invisible except to its small band of participants. In 1975, the prolific Off Off Broadway theater company Playwrights Horizons opened a tiny, bare-bones theater in a run-down tenement on far West 42nd Street between Ninth and Tenth Avenues. The Walt Disney Company's restoration of the New Amsterdam Theater, the begrimed jewel of 42nd Street's Seventh Avenue block, in the mid-1990s was the great milestone in the Deuce's transformation into the New 42nd Street. But it was the unheralded Playwrights Horizons—not mighty Disney—that brought the theater back to 42nd Street to stay. The troupe's pluck inspired Fred Papert, a retired advertising millionaire seeking personal redemption through civic improvements, to form Forty-Second Street Development Corporation. This not-for-profit company acquired a ragged honky-tonk strip of porn stores and abandoned tenements and joined with Playwrights Horizons to fashion from them eight additional small theaters, rehearsal halls, restaurants, and other amenities. This improbable cultural oasis was called Theater Row, and it took deep, lasting root on one of America's worst blocks.

The success of private citizens practicing an organic kind of urban renewal, one small-scale project at a time on the far west end of 42nd Street, contrasted with the blundering and bullying efforts of government to redevelop the Seventh Avenue theater block, off Times Square. After much backroom maneuvering, in 1982 the city and the state fell in behind a $1.6 billion plan that would have bulldozed most of the Deuce, leveled the Times Tower, and turned the Crossroads of the World into a colossal office complex while making a token effort to convert the movie grinders back into playhouses. To further this draconian, politically cynical scheme, New York State was prepared to use its powers of eminent domain to condemn two-and-a-half square blocks and evict hundreds of tenants, most of them small businesses that had nothing to do with smut. This, the largest urban renewal project in New York history, was bitterly opposed in many quarters, establishing the contours of a debate that went beyond aesthetics to basic issues of governance. Whose voices would be heard? Whose interests would be served and whose harmed in the remaking of 42nd Street? As Michael Sorkin put it in *Variations on a Theme Park,* "The struggle to reclaim the city is the struggle for democracy itself."

As originally conceived, the 42nd Street Development Project never did get off the ground in a decade of groaning attempts. Virtually everything that could go wrong with it did go wrong. It was almost as if the ghosts of 42nd Street's fabled past—Oscar Hammerstein, Flo Ziegfeld, Billy Minsky, Arthur Mayer, and the rest—conspired at every turn to save their ancient haunts from vanishing into the great Midtown corporate complex. These restless spirits found an ally in government, an urban planner and state redevelopment official named Rebecca Robertson, who had not grown up in New York City—or in the United States, for that matter—but was deeply attuned to the spirit of old 42nd Street nonetheless. "That's the magic of the place—the feeling of time. You can't wipe that away," Robertson rhapsodized in a press interview. "The ladies in bustles. The fat old men with their gleaming tuxes and cigar smoke. The chorus girls. You've got to be able to feel its ghosts."

The charming, relentless Robertson appeased the ghosts and rescued the 42nd Street Development Project by reversing its priorities. Her mantra was: "Do right by the old theaters and the rest will follow." In the end, the Crossroads of the World was indeed transformed by an office tower on each corner of Seventh Avenue's intersection with 42nd Street. However, the Times Tower, now officially known as One Times Square, was spared the wrecking ball, and five of 42nd Street's theaters were rehabilitated as beautifully appointed playhouses. In addition, two new multiscreen movie theaters were built. Among them, the five restored playhouses on the old theater block, plus the eight on Theater Row, have only one-third of the seating capacity of the ten playhouses that lined 42nd Street in 1920. On the other hand, the theater block now has more movie screens—thirty-eight—and more movie-house seats—8,100—than it did in the heyday of the grinder. On Friday and Saturday nights the place is so thronged with fun seekers of all description that it is virtually impassable to the passive pedestrian.

The fate of the "New 42" is a matter of more than local interest. Its redevelopment is emblematic of one of the most basic demographic trends of contemporary America: the rebirth of downtown. All across the country, central cities are hanging their hopes for the future on what is known in the planning trade as Urban Entertainment Destinations—complexes that combine entertainment venues with stores and restaurants. The idea is not to re-create the suburban shopping mall in a central locale but to outdo it, to become "the exotic 'nearby gateways' for consumers who desire a fleeting escape from the homogeneous suburbs." West 42nd Street is far and away the largest such experiment, and its fate will go a long way toward determining whether the Urban Entertainment District is in fact the salvation of America's downtowns or merely a costly fad.

In the Cyber Age, no locale will ever again dominate popular culture the way that 42nd Street did from the turn of the last century through the 1920s. But the 1990s revival of New York's historic central entertainment district is proof that even in the brave new world of the World Wide Web, man cannot amuse himself by computer screen alone. Forty-second Street's tumultuous passage from the two-balcony playhouse and the lobster palace through the heydays of the burlesque hall, the movie grinder, and the adult bookstore and massage parlor brought the definitive New York thoroughfare back in a general sense to where it began. At the beginning of the twenty-first century, 42nd Street is again what it was at the outset of the last century: the most entertainment-intensive block in the city that is America's once and future cultural capital.

Fathers of Times Square

By all rights, Times Square should have been called Oscar Hammerstein Square. Hammerstein opened the first theater in what would become Times Square—the magnificent, doomed Olympia—in 1895, a full nine years before the *New York Times* moved into the neighborhood and bestowed its name upon it. In fact, by the time that the newspaper occupied its slender tower on 42nd Street in 1904, Hammerstein had completed two more theaters in the area, the Theatre Republic and the hugely successful Victoria. Times Square would have become the new theater center of America even if Hammerstein had never left Berlin; geography *is* destiny. But the fact is that the German-born impresario got there first, years ahead of his rivals, and planted the flag of glamorous fun in a part of Midtown Manhattan that had been defined by its many odiferous horse stables and brazen pickpockets and prostitutes. The mad brilliance of Hammerstein's genre-spanning pioneering went a long way toward establishing 42nd Street's intersection with Seventh Avenue and Broadway as the hub of the liveliest and most celebrated entertainment district the world has ever known. Hammerstein was hailed during his lifetime as the "Father of Times Square," but awareness of his seminal contribution faded after his death in 1919, and today he has been all but forgotten. He not only was denied the immortality that "Hammerstein

Square" would have vouchsafed him, but he even lost pride of place within his own family as his fame was eclipsed by that of his grandson and namesake, Oscar Hammerstein II, who wrote the lyrics to many of the greatest Broadway musicals of the 1940s and 1950s.

That Oscar the elder could ever have been consigned to anonymity would have astounded his contemporaries. "In his heyday," wrote one biographer, "he was perhaps the best known man in the United States after the President." This has the ring of hyperbole, but coverage of Hammerstein's exploits was indeed a front-page staple of journalism in New York City for three decades. Hammerstein was not a modern celebrity, which is to say that his fame was solidly grounded in accomplishment. In his day, he was far and away the city's leading theater builder. Between 1888 and 1914, Hammerstein constructed ten theaters in Manhattan, most of which were spectacularly grand, yet all but one were located on the outer edge of established entertainment districts. Hammerstein also was New York's most daring and versatile impresario during this span. At a time of increasing segregation between high and low culture, he ranged across the full spectrum of entertainment, flouting category and classification with impunity while providing performers of all sorts with their proverbial big break. Hammerstein's passion—his obsession, really—was grand opera, and yet he also was acclaimed as the greatest vaudeville promoter of the 1890s. A more polished and family-friendly version of the ribald variety shows that had long been staged in saloons, vaudeville emerged in the 1870s and 1880s as America's most popular form of entertainment until the advent of the Hollywood movie in the 1920s.

In contrast to most rival impresarios, who were businessmen first, last, and always, Hammerstein was a polymath who put profit second. Conservatory-trained in violin and piano, he was a prolific if undistinguished composer, adept in many different musical genres. On a bet, he once wrote a three-act comic opera—*The Kohinoor*—in forty-eight hours and presented it onstage to hilarious effect. The opening-night audience "laughed themselves blue in the face" at the opening chorus, which consumed a third of the first act, one critic observed. "Two comic Jews, alternatively for half an hour, sang 'Good morning, Mr. Morganstern, Good morning, Mr. Isaacstein,' while the orchestra shifted harmonics to avoid too much monotony." Hammerstein collected on his $100 wager but happily lost $10,000 on the production. Although Hammerstein had no training in architecture, he designed all of the theaters that he built, displaying a particular talent for the nuances of acoustics. He also was a prolific mechanical inventor who seemed able to devise some clever new contraption at will—or at least whenever he needed a big chunk of money. In 1895, an exceptionally fruitful year, Hammerstein was awarded thirty-eight patents, most of them related to the construction of the Olympia theater complex.

In business, Hammerstein had the Midas touch. He was an instant success both as trade journal publisher and real estate speculator, as well as vaudeville promoter. But money per se meant nothing to Hammerstein. Three times he made his fortune, three times he blew it on impossibly ambitious opera schemes, dying penniless at seventy-three. When Oscar II, who was born in 1895, was a boy he rarely saw his grandfather but felt his influence hanging heavily. "Members of the family had referred to him always as 'the old man.' They spoke of his predilection for grand opera as if it were a sickness. They told funny stories about him," the lyricist recalled. "To my child's ear, sensitive more to inflections than to the specific meaning of words, it was evident that my father, my aunts and uncles, and my stepgrandmother, his second wife, were all afraid of him. That made me afraid of him, too. It was equally evident to me that in a shy and guarded way they loved him."

Hammerstein endeared himself to the New York masses by adopting egalitarian admission and seating policies at many of his venues and by pricing his attractions to the working-class budget. He also did flamboyant battle with many of New York City's most powerful and elitist cultural institutions, refusing most notably to pay truck either to the Metropolitan Opera or the Theatrical Syndicate, which was to entertainment at the turn of the century what Standard Oil was to petroleum. In sum, Hammerstein vividly personified the American dream for several generations of European immigrants. As his most recent biographer, John F. Carroll, put it: "Because of his determination to work independently in order to achieve his ambitions on his own terms, he became a modern-day folk hero to the thousands of immigrants, who, like himself, had come to America believing that every man could create his own opportunities for advancement."

Hammerstein attracted attention beyond what even his impressive accomplishments warranted, for he was both a true eccentric and a masterful self-publicist. For years, he slept where he worked: in two large rooms situated over the marquee of the Victoria Theater on 42nd Street furnished only with a workbench, a piano, a few ragged armchairs, and a cot. After an evening's performance, he often wandered Manhattan alone late into the night, lost in his private reveries. Hammerstein was so heedless of personal luxury that he often forgot to carry money with him and yet rarely appeared in public except in evening wear—swallowtail coat with velvet lapels, striped pants, French silk top hat—as if perpetually garbed for opening night. He adopted this look in his middle years, and his biographers agree that it was at least partly contrived to pique the interest of the newspapers and their readers. The giveaway was the top hat, which Hammerstein rarely removed in company indoors or out and which Oscar II described after his grandfather's death as "a conically shaped topper favored by Frenchmen at that time or, at any rate, by stage comedians impersonating Frenchmen." The fact that it also was a couple of sizes too tall for Hammerstein's portly five-foot-four frame added to the effect. The big cigar that protruded pugnaciously through his meticulously trimmed (and old-fashioned) goatee also undercut the elegance of his getup. The Hammerstein persona, complete with German accent, was imprinted so indelibly on the public consciousness that it continued to define the popular image of an opera impresario for many decades after his death.

Born in 1847 in Stettin, Germany, Hammerstein was the eldest son of a Jewish building contractor turned stock trader. Just after his twelfth birthday, Oscar entered a music conservatory, where he studied violin and piano and swooned over opera. Oscar was fourteen years old when his mother died, leaving him to the untender mercies of his father, a troubled man who played the violin himself and who beat his son so severely after he skipped practice one afternoon to go ice-skating that he needed stitches in his forehead. Oscar ran away from home the next day, fleeing first to Hamburg by train, then by boat to Dover and to New York City. Landing in America in 1864, in the middle of the Civil War, the fifteen-year-old soon found a $2-a-week job in cigar making, an industry dominated by German immigrants.

Oscar quickly rose in the cigar trade on the strength of his diligence and inventiveness. Within a year of arriving in New York, he produced the first of many moneymaking inventions, a new kind of cigar mold, which he quickly sold for $300. Oscar not only attended the theater at every opportunity, but also soon began dabbling in the business, investing in a couple of small theaters and writing one-act plays and incidental music for the stage. He was able to add handsomely to his net worth just the same by founding a trade journal for cigar makers, the *United States Tobacco Journal*, in 1874. With Hammerstein acting as both editor and publisher, the *Journal* became required reading in the tobacco business, thanks in large part to its proprietor's strong-armed approach. "Any tobacconist who refuses to advertise with him is likely to find a caricature of himself, clinging precariously to a lamp post, captioned 'On another drunk' in the paper."

Soon, Hammerstein also moved into property development in Harlem, then a lightly populated village on Manhattan's far northern fringe. Many of the homes on 125th Street, Harlem's main east-west thoroughfare, were still wooden shacks when Hammerstein began buying land in the area. Anticipating Harlem's emergence as a prosperous middle-class residential community by at least a decade, Hammerstein built twenty-four apartment buildings and fifty houses in Harlem during the 1880s. He and his wife moved into one of his creations, a town house on 120th Street. In 1888, he put a small theater into the basement of a colossal new apartment block that he built way up on 136th Street. Its popularity helped convince Hammerstein that booming Harlem was capable of supporting a first-class entertainment venue of its own. He sold the *Tobacco Journal* for $50,000, borrowed as much money as he could, and erected the Harlem Opera House on 125th Street between Seventh and Eighth Avenues. It had a grand entryway, massive arches, gilded moldings, and plenty of red plush to go with its 1,375 seats. But it lacked something crucial upon its opening in 1889: a box office; Hammerstein simply forgot to include one in his design.

The Harlem Opera House was ninety blocks due north and a world apart from "the Rialto," New York's vibrant center of theater and nightlife. Extending north up Broadway from 14th Street all the way to 41st Street, the Rialto was home to two dozen playhouses, concert halls, and variety theaters, as well as several grand hotels and innumerable restaurants and brothels. During the afternoon, the sidewalks of the Rialto's center section—from 23rd to 34th Streets—were so thick with actors and other performers that it was said that a producer could cast a show merely by perusing from his office window the passing parade of talent. After sundown, no part of Manhattan owed a greater debt to the ingenuity of Thomas Alva Edison than the Rialto. "The great thoroughfare is ablaze with the electric light, which illuminates it with the radiance of day," marveled the author of *New York by Sunlight and Gaslight*, published in 1882. "Crowds throng the sidewalks; the lights of the om- nibuses and carriages dart to and fro along the road-carriages like myri- ads of fireflies; the great hotels, the theatres and restaurants, send out their blaze of gas-lamps, and are live with visitors."

The Rialto was the floodlit center stage of a great national enterprise. After the completion of the transcontinental railroad in 1869, large the- atrical booking agencies emerged in New York that made a lucrative busi- ness out of bringing plays, operettas, and variety shows originating within the Rialto to every American city and town with a good-size theater. In the mid-1880s more than 100 such touring or "combination" companies were crisscrossing the nation; by 1904, the number would have soared to 420. As the traditionally local enterprise of theater was centralized in New York, news and gossip from the Rialto became an essential feature of American journalism nationwide, establishing this feverishly active few blocks of Midtown Manhattan as the nation's first celebrity incubator of popular style and fashion. The Rialto "was a street of legend, and it had a romantic attraction for all Americans across the continent," wrote one his- torian. "If you visited New York during the 1880s, you inevitably went to the theater, for certain playhouses were nationally famous and you could scarcely face your friends at home unless you could talk about them."

Hammerstein built his Harlem Opera House both to stage his own operas and to host touring productions of the Rialto's classiest offerings. But to lure the city's leading opera performers and Shakespearean actors into the wilds of Harlem, the budding impresario had to overpay, saddling his new theater with substantial operating losses. Hammerstein soon ar- rived at a characteristically headlong solution: he built a second, even larger theater—the Columbus—just five blocks east of the opera house on 125th Street. During the summer of 1890, he sold all of his apartment buildings to concentrate wholly on the theater business. Two theaters did indeed prove better than one. The 1,649-seat Columbus thrived from the moment it opened in 1890 as a venue for less highfalutin Rialto fare than featured down the street at the Harlem Opera House. "With an unexpect- edly sure 'feel' for commercial reality, he promoted a series of highly profitable popular shows at the Columbus—vaudeville, thrillers, even minstrel shows—while concentrating on opera at the Harlem."

But running a couple of "out-of-town" combination houses did not satisfy Hammerstein for long. The Rialto beckoned. In 1891, he began excavating a site on 42nd Street and Sixth Avenue, on the theater district's northwest fringe. After a legal dispute over the title to the land arose, Hammerstein sold the site and bought another smack in the heart of the Rialto at Broadway and 34th Street. Here, where Macy's flagship department store now sits, he built the Manhattan Opera House. It opened in 1892 with great fanfare. There was no denying the grandeur of this ornately decorated hall, which contained 2,600 seats, 52 boxes, and a foyer that rivaled that of the Palais Garnier in Paris or the Staatsoper in Vienna. The problem was that ordinary theater proved all but inaudible in this cavernous space; in between opera productions the great hall remained dark most of the time. Hammerstein's losses quickly mounted, exceeding the profits he was making in Harlem and threatening him with ruin.

In mid-1893, he swallowed his pride and went into business with Koster and Bial, saloon owners who had made a pretty penny doubling as producers of down-market variety shows. Every other row of seats was removed from the Manhattan Opera House's orchestra section to make room for dining tables and a large bar, transforming it into "Koster & Bial's Music Hall." With Hammerstein booking the talent and Koster and Bial handling the sale of food and drink, the new venture was a huge commercial success. Hammerstein paid top dollar to bring many of the leading variety stars of Europe to New York for the first time and was rewarded with enthusiastic capacity audiences night after night. Yet the music hall's success grated on Hammerstein, who resented the artistic compromises forced upon him by his association with a pair of philistines like Koster and Bial. They, in turn, resented their partner's hauteur and flair for self-promotion. Push came to shove in the fall of 1894, when Koster and Bial insisted on hiring a no-talent French singer as a favor to George Kessler, a prominent champagne merchant who fancied her. Hammerstein retaliated by standing up in his box to loudly hiss the singer's entrance on opening night, much to the audience's amusement. He and Kessler ended up in a fistfight that spilled out of the music hall onto Broadway, where the police arrested both combatants and took them to a nearby precinct house. Hammerstein sued Koster and Bial, who were so eager to part ways with their cantankerous partner that they paid him $650,000 for his interest in the theater in an out-of-court settlement. Hammerstein vowed to take revenge on his former associates. "When I get through with you, everyone will forget that there ever was a Koster & Bial's," he declared. "I will build a house the like of which has never been seen in the whole world."

———

Hammerstein's search for a building site large enough to make good on his vow took him up Broadway a few crucial blocks past 40th Street, the Rialto's de facto northern boundary. In the early 1880s, two landmark structures had opened on Broadway at 39th Street. The grandest of them, the yellow-brick Metropolitan Opera House, served as a kind of high-culture clubhouse for the city's emerging social elite of super-rich industrialists, men such as J. P. Morgan, William Rockefeller, and Jay Gould. Facing the Met directly across Broadway was the Casino Theater, one of the most architecturally distinctive buildings in the city, with its elaborate, Moorish-inspired facades and interiors. Built as a concert hall, the Casino found a highly fashionable niche both as the city's preeminent venue for light opera and burlesque and as its "most elegant display-case for feminine beauty." In 1883, the Rialto's frontier had been nudged a bit farther uptown by the opening of the Empire Theater on the corner of Broadway and 40th Street. The Empire was the artistic home of producer Charles Frohman, one of the Rialto's greatest starmakers. Despite this northward drift, the prevalent view when Hammerstein went scouting for sites was that 42nd Street was a street too far for respectable entertainment. Never mind that theater builders had been leapfrogging one another up Broadway in search of lower-cost sites ever since the city's first theater district had coalesced around 14th Street at Union Square just after the Civil War. The uptown migration had to end sometime, and producers and theatergoers generally presumed that the Rialto was the New York theater district brought to completion, if not quite to perfection.

This was a misconception strongly reinforced by the sheer ugliness of Broadway above 42nd Street. This particularly unappetizing stretch of cityscape was dominated by the horse and livery trades and had been named Long Acre Square, after the center of London's carriage-making industry. Stables, blacksmiths, harness shops, carriage dealers, and the occasional riding ring lined both sides of Broadway and Seventh Avenue, all the way up to 59th Street. The streets were clogged with landaus, broughams, tradesman's carts, and other vehicles waiting to be repaired. The stench of manure was overwhelming. Developed haphazardly over the previous two decades, Long Acre Square had taken on the aspect of a slum by the mid-1890s. After nightfall, scores of prostitutes, pickpockets, and miscellaneous thugs emerged from the many cheap boarding-houses on side streets to perform their nefarious deeds under the cover of near darkness. By this time, most of Manhattan south of 42nd Street had been illuminated by electric streetlights, but only a single gas lamp lit Long Acre Square, known then as "Thieves Lair."

Hammerstein was not the first theater entrepreneur to breach the 42nd Street barrier. This distinction fell to T. Henry French, who was a veteran Rialto producer and a partner in Samuel French and Son, an important play publishing company. Like Hammerstein, French dreamed of building big and had to venture outside the bounds of the Rialto to locate an affordable site of sufficient size. He found it along Eighth Avenue between 41st and 42nd Streets. This was not wilderness exactly; the Franklin Savings Bank occupied the corner across the street, and a major pharmacy was close by. But French's half-acre property was a long block west of Broadway, the Rialto's main stem, and its sidewalks were deserted after sundown except for the customers of the many brothels in the vicinity. Here, French built the American Theatre, the third-largest theater in New York and the first on 42nd Street. The American's 1,900-seat auditorium was located on 41st Street, but a narrow carriage entrance gave the theater a 42nd Street address.

The American Theatre opened in May 1893 with *The Prodigal Daughter,* a melodrama that had appeared under the Samuel French and Son banner in London the previous season. French slavishly re-created the successful West End version of the play, importing from London not only all of its scenery and costumes, but also nine racehorses, ten hounds, and five jockeys. For the horse race that featured in the play's climactic scene, French built a replica of the Grand National Steeplechase course at Aintree, complete with a hurdle and water jump. Ten horses raced diagonally across the American's enormous stage on treadmills, creating the illusion that the beasts were headed right for the audience. (The horses were rehearsed at Tattersall's, a horse exchange at Seventh Avenue and 50th Street, in the upper reaches of Long Acre Square.) This unnerving spectacle became the talk of the Rialto, convincing many of its denizens to give French's annoyingly out-of-the-way 42nd Street theater a try. Originally scheduled for a short run, *The Prodigal Daughter* packed them in for twenty-nine straight weeks. However, it was followed by a circus-based spectacular complete with live elephants that flopped resoundingly, providing a more accurate forecast of the American's fate than the smash hit that preceded it.

Hammerstein undoubtedly attended *The Prodigal Daughter* but left no record of his opinion of the play, or of the American Theatre. In any event, he chose not to follow French to the Rialto's western edge but instead homed in on Long Acre Square to the north. Hammerstein stood for hours where Seventh Avenue and Broadway crossed just above 42nd Street, trying to conjure a vision of a glorious future from Long Acre's befouled present. He found all the encouragement he needed in the constant clang of passing streetcars. As one of the busiest transfer points in the city, Long Acre Square was easily reached from most anywhere in Manhattan. Hammerstein's was an essential insight, for Times Square's emergence as the prototype of the modern urban entertainment district was largely a function of its accessibility by mass transit. "Historically, the center of the city had always been either City Hall or the central market, the forum or the agora. Times Square, located in the transportation hub of New York, was neither," wrote urban historian William Taylor. The modern American city "developed an unanticipated inclination to locate its entertainment and amusement industries where they were most accessible to the most people."

Forty-second Street had been established as Manhattan's intercity rail nexus as early as 1854, when the Common Council enacted a law prohibiting steam-powered locomotives entering the city from the north from venturing beyond it. At a switching yard on Fourth Avenue (now Park Avenue), railcars bound for locations in the settled city were uncoupled from their noisy, fire-spewing steam engines and hitched to teams of horses. So much traffic was passing through here by 1871 that the New York Railroad built Grand Central Depot, the precursor of the even larger Grand Central Terminal. Elevated passenger trains, or "els," were introduced for intracity use in 1876 but were too slow to qualify as "real rapid transit" and did little to spur Midtown's further development. Underground rail service was feasible—London had introduced the world's first subway in the 1860s—but its sponsors made little headway until 1894, when New York's corruption-wary voters at last authorized the use of public funds for subway development. Business interests throughout the city applied heavy pressure on the special commission authorized to set the route of the inaugural line. The plan that eventually would establish 42nd Street as its geographic linchpin was first floated in 1895—just as

Hammerstein was closing on a purchase of a large property in Long Acre Square—and did not win formal city approval in 1898. For all of Hammerstein's impetuousness, his move into the heart of disreputable and dangerous Thieves Lair was brilliantly timed, heralding the huge run-up in land values that preceded the opening of the 42nd Street subway station in 1904.

Hammerstein spent all of his Koster and Bial settlement money and then some—about $1 million—to buy the entire frontage on the east side of Broadway between 44th and 45th Streets. Most of this immense site had once been occupied by the 71st Regiment Armory, which had been destroyed by fire. "My theater will make a place for itself," Hammerstein declared, "because I will give the public what they have never had before." The impresario was as good as his word, erecting the Olympia, which consisted of three opulent auditoriums under a single roof—a huge, 2,800-seat music hall and a smaller playhouse and concert hall—as well as a glass-enclosed roof garden theater up top. Clad in a thick limestone that made it seem even bigger than it was, the ten-story Olympia complex was appointed in the style of a French Renaissance palace and cooled by Hammerstein's own patented system of air-conditioning. The Olympia was honeycombed with promenades, elegant lounges, smoking rooms and bars, though Hammerstein's plans for an "Oriental" café, a Turkish bath, and several billiard halls and bowling alleys went unrealized. For fifty cents—a bargain price even then—you could enter the Olympia through one of the four massive oak doors that marked its entrance on Broadway and wander at your leisure from venue to venue without additional charge. The electric sign over the entryway put greater emphasis on Hammerstein's name than on the name of his new complex, reflecting the man's superior drawing power.

Unlike Koster & Bial's New Musical Hall and the other vaudeville halls in the Rialto, the Olympia did not style itself as a family entertainment venue. Content to leave the middle of the road to others, Hammerstein experimented with provocative new acts and formats that expanded vaudeville's boundaries. He blended drama and opera into his bills to such crowd-pleasing effect that even the Metropolitan Opera was compelled to follow suit, to a point. The Met stopped well short of imitating Hammerstein's "Living Pictures," which featured a degree of nudity never before seen on a respectable New York stage. Presented between scenes from miscellaneous operas, the Living Pictures used live actresses to create facsimiles of classical paintings depicting unclothed women. "There was a tremendous uproar," and Hammerstein "took full advantage of it by means of polemics in the press about censorship. The public flocked to see his 'Living Pictures,' whether they cared anything for the interludes of opera or not." In 1897, Hammerstein broke the Broadway color barrier by booking Isham's Octoroons, a troupe of black singers and dancers, into the Olympia roof garden. "Hammerstein's originality, in this as in so many other things, did not arise from principles," concluded biographer Vincent Sheean, "but from the persistent attempt to provide novelty for his public."

In presenting the Cherry Sisters, vaudeville's first great "lemon" act, Hammerstein vaulted even further into the future, prefiguring the postmodern conceit of entertainment that's so bad it's good. These four sisters from Iowa were not horrible looking. No scandal had enlivened their name, just as no achievement had elevated it. They were distinguished only by their awfulness as performers and their seeming incapacity for shame and embarrassment, as here documented in the *New York Times'* review of their Broadway debut at the Olympia in 1896:

> It was a little after 10 o'clock when three lank figures and one short and thick walked awkwardly to the center of the stage. They were all dressed in shapeless red gowns, made by themselves almost surely, and the fat sister carried a bass drum. They stood quietly for a moment, apparently seeing nothing and wondering what the jeering laughter could mean. Then they began to sing, in thin, strained soprano . . . the ancient "Ta-Ra-Ra Boom de Aye." People listened in amazement as one senseless verse followed another, accompanied at rare intervals by a graceless gesture and intermittent thumps on a big drum.

The reviews were uniformly terrible, but the Cherry Sisters drew standing-room crowds to the Olympia for five weeks running. A perverse form of audience participation, apparently started by Hammerstein himself, enhanced their popularity. One night Oscar armed his sons Arthur and Willie with formerly fresh produce and stationed them in opposite corners of the music hall's gallery. Effie, the eldest Cherry, was halfway through a wretched ballad when a small head of cabbage flew at her, unleashing a barrage of rottenness that apparently included a fish or two. According to one account, Oscar hurried backstage afterward and explained to the "bewildered bucolics that fruit-and-vegetable throwing was a symbol of success in New York. 'Other stage stars,' he said to Effie, 'are jealous of anybody who has outstanding talent and they hire people to throw things at girls like you.'" The next night, and for the rest of their run at the Olympia, the sisters performed behind a net.

The Olympia's success took a satisfyingly ruinous toll on Koster & Bial's New Music Hall, but Hammerstein's victory ultimately proved hollow, for it ended in his own downfall. Had he displayed the same sure touch in selecting plays and other productions for the Olympia's Lyric Theatre that he did in programming vaudeville venues the complex might at least have lived out the nineteenth century. As it was, though, he had spent too lavishly in building the Olympia to survive the numerous flops that he booked into the Lyric. Hammerstein's desire to be recognized as a serious composer contributed greatly to his undoing. He spent far more on vanity productions of his own composition than was necessary and kept them running long after attendance had dwindled to nothing.

In June 1898, Hammerstein ran out of money and closed the Olympia. The president of New York Life Insurance, which held the mortgage on the building, wrote Hammerstein a polite note urging that he work with a company representative to rework the Olympia's finances. Hammerstein's reply was impetuous and provocative. "I am in receipt of your letter, which is now before me," he wrote, "and in a few minutes will be behind me." New York Life promptly foreclosed on the Olympia and also took title to both of his theaters in Harlem and his town house on 120th Street. Utterly broke, Oscar had to borrow $500 from son Arthur to buy food. The elder Hammerstein seemed to take a certain perverse pride in the totality of his ruin. Meeting a friend on Broadway, he offered him a cigar. "I have lost all my theaters, my home, and everything else," he said. "My fortune consists of two cigars. I will share it with you."

By the time that New York Life sold the Olympia at auction for $967,000 in mid-1898, Hammerstein had started building a new theater in Long Acre Square. Walking on Broadway one day with the comedian Louis Harrison, he pointed to some run-down buildings on the corner of 42nd Street and Seventh Avenue. "You see those old shacks and stables?" he said. "That, Louis, is the finest site in New York for a theater. I am going to build one there." Development of the property had been blocked for years by disagreement among its owners, the battling heirs to an estate administered out of Albany. Hammerstein borrowed the money for a roundtrip train ticket upstate. "He encountered flat opposition at first: it was too commonly known that he was 'irresponsible,'" Sheean wrote. "But he persisted and was able to go back to New York the same day with a twenty-year lease" on highly advantageous terms—$18,000 a year and no money down. Hammerstein borrowed small sums from various friends and raised about $25,000 by patenting and selling two new inventions: a contraption for shortening men's suspenders so that they could be made of linen rather than elastic and a machine for recycling tobacco stems, traditionally discarded as waste.

The Victoria would become the most famous and profitable of all of Hammerstein's theaters, but it was the least impressive looking of the lot. By necessity, its construction was an exercise in artful penny-pinching overseen by Arthur Hammerstein, who, at his father's insistence, had trained as a professional plasterer. Although the Victoria was planned from the start as a theater, the Hammersteins engaged in a protracted charade designed to convince city officials that the 1,250-seat venue would be a concert hall, and thus subject to less stringent and costly building code requirements. Much of the brick and timber taken from the demolished buildings on the site was recycled. Mounds of rubbish were used as filler in the walls of the new theater rather than carted away. All of the 42nd Street theater's fixtures were secondhand, and the red carpeting was taken from an old ocean liner. Even the Victoria's gold and white color scheme was a product of parsimony. "We had no money for paint," Arthur explained. "The 'white' was only the unpainted plaster." But Oscar was unbowed. "I have named my theater the Victoria because I have been victorious over mine enemies—those bloodsuckers at New York Life," he announced.

Modeled after the Folies-Bergère in Paris, the Victoria was considered New York's most unconventional playhouse upon its opening in March 1899. Its seating capacity was less than half that of the Olympia music hall, but the orchestra was unusually large and surrounded on three sides by a promenade that could accommodate another 2,000 patrons. Admission to the promenade was only fifty cents and smoking and drinking were allowed, further enhancing its appeal to common folk. The Victoria's enormous stage, the second largest in the city, could accommodate any theatrical genre. Perhaps the most surprising aspect of Hammerstein's comeback was his decision to operate the Victoria not as a vaudeville house but as an uncommonly versatile playhouse offering everything from Shakespearean drama to musical comedy and verse tragedy. He did a much better job of programming the Victoria than he had the Lyric Theater, wisely refraining from producing anything of his own other than waltzes and other incidental music between performances. One of the greatest European actresses of the era, Eleanora Duse, made her American debut at the Victoria, but Hammerstein scored his biggest hit with a gloomy dramatization of Leo Tolstoy's *Resurrection*. Hammerstein also kept his hand in as a vaudeville promoter, presenting twelve-act bills during the warm weather months at the Victoria's roof garden—the Venetian Terrace—which featured two separate stages and two simultaneous shows.

Like the Columbus in Harlem, the Victoria was profitable right from the start, enabling Hammerstein to promptly lease a small adjoining lot. He demolished the ill-famed McGory's Dance Hall and in its place built the Theatre Republic at 207 West 42nd Street. Making the best of the site's diminutive dimensions, he created a lavishly decorated, intimate 900-seat auditorium, or "drawing room of the drama," as he called it. Hammerstein envisioned this, his second theater on 42nd Street, not merely as a pure playhouse, but also as a national showcase for serious, refined dramatic works by America's best playwrights. In his curtain speech at the Republic's opening in the fall of 1900, he compared his elegant but undersize new theater to the great, state-subsidized theaters of Europe's capitals. According to a newspaper account, Hammerstein said "simply, and no doubt truthfully, that he wished to devote the new house to pure and noble things. The Parisian, he declared, spoke proudly of 'our Comédie-Française,' the Berliner called the Imperial Opera House 'ours,' and he wished the New Yorker to learn to say 'our Theatre Republic.'" However laudable, Hammerstein's ambitions were impractical to the point of grandiosity. In 1900, the American theater's relationship to England and the Continent remained essentially colonial. Most of the Rialto's shows either were direct foreign imports or Americanized versions of British musical farces or Continental operettas. Producers aspiring to prestige presented revivals of classics or iconoclastic foreign pieces rather than original American plays, which would be a long time measuring up to their European forebears.

By connecting the roofs of the Victoria and the Republic, Hammerstein was able to replace the Venetian Terrace with the larger and more elaborate "summer resort" called the Paradise Roof Gardens. With a fully equipped stage and a seating capacity of 1,000, the Paradise was nearly the size of the Victoria itself. It had to be, because in the summer Hammerstein preferred to present his top acts on the roof, forsaking the sweltering confines below. On especially warm nights, windows in the glass walls that encased it were opened to let breezes blow through. "The roof was a wonderful place in the summer," recalled Loney Haskell, the Victoria's longtime master of ceremonies. "We could fill it up when the hot, unventilated houses on the street level would be practically empty. Partly because it was cool and partly because we gave everybody his money's worth in entertainment."

The Paradise was instantly successful, and Hammerstein added to its popularity by creating a miniature Dutch village on the Republic side of the roof. A working windmill perched atop a hill, beside a quaint clay cottage with a stork's nest on its chimney and an attached stable. A rustic bridge led over a duck pond and down into a valley, where a fisherman's hut, a gristmill, and a tavern were situated on the banks of a river. The wall fronting 42nd Street was built up above the roofline and made to look like a ruined castle. The Paradise was not just an elaborate stage set, but also an interactive entertainment animated by real ducks, chickens, two cows, and a live milkmaid who offered fresh milk to underage patrons. "Realizing that its main appeal lay in its novelty, Hammerstein made constant changes in the farm so that there was always something new for his customers to see," theater historian Margaret Knapp observed. "Coupled with the excellent vaudeville show on the Victoria roof, the farm became an irresistible attraction to summer theatergoers."

By 1902, the revivified New York Times had outgrown its musty old quarters on Park Row in lower Manhattan. Adolph S. Ochs, the ambitious former printer's apprentice who'd bought the newspaper in 1896 at a court-run bankruptcy auction, initially planned to build an attention-grabbing new tower nearby. But when the deal he struck to buy the property unraveled, Ochs cast his gaze uptown to 23rd Street, site of the Flatiron Building, the city's celebrated new skyscraper. The Flatiron's fame was a product not just of its height but of its strategic location within Manhattan's street grid. Because mid-Manhattan is laid out in a checkerboard pattern, the utmost distance at which most buildings can be viewed is the width of an avenue. In Midtown there are only four points where the pattern is interrupted by irregular-shaped openings that allow for a longer view: where Broadway intersects with Fifth, Sixth, Seventh, and Eighth Avenues in its meandering across the city. Straddling the intersection of Broadway, Fifth Avenue, and 23rd Street, the Flatiron could be seen for long distances on each thoroughfare. A building site near the Flatiron was for sale, but a businessman friendly with Ochs talked him out of buying it. "He told the publisher that he had chosen the wrong site; that the business center had already passed 23rd Street and was moving north." One of Ochs's smartest competitors, James Gordon Bennett, recently had stolen the march on the *Times* by moving his *New York Herald* to the Sixth Avenue equivalent of the Flatiron Building's site (which was promptly renamed Herald Square in the newspaper's honor). Determined to outdo Bennett in attracting public attention, Ochs turned his attention to the Seventh Avenue anomaly in the grid: Long Acre Square.

The combination of Hammerstein's pioneering and the city's decision to locate a key subway station at 42nd Street and Seventh Avenue had brought Long Acre's redevelopment to the tipping point. Several au courant dining establishments called "lobster palaces" had recently opened, and the Astor family was putting the finishing touches on a grand first-class hotel. In July 1902, Ochs bought the little trapezoid of property that floated in the middle of Long Acre between 42nd and 43rd Streets and Broadway and Seventh Avenue. He demolished the Pabst Hotel and Restaurant, which occupied most of the site, and, at a cost of $1.7 million, built a slender twenty-five-story tower, New York's second-tallest skyscraper. It was modeled after Giotto's campanile for the cathedral in Florence, which the publisher had admired during a trip to Italy.

The Times Tower did not rise easily. The odd dimensions of the site—20 feet wide at its northern end, 58 to the south, and 138 and 143 feet on the long sides—gave Ochs's architects fits. Worse, the Times Tower had to be erected directly atop the new subway tunnel; indeed, the tower and the 42nd Street subway station were constructed simultaneously, with separate but intertwined foundations and steel frameworks. To give the subway its "supreme" right-of-way, as mandated by the state legislature, many of the tower's steel columns had to start from the subway roof. However, Ochs put his printing presses in a deep basement carved into the bedrock *beneath* the subway floor, allowing the *Times* to boast in its own columns that its new headquarters was literally "founded upon a rock." The Times Tower established itself as a prime tourist attraction when it was still a hole in the ground—a very deep hole—inspiring breathless feature articles in European publications, as well as more grudging coverage from Ochs's New York competitors. "The excavation is highly interesting by night," noted the *New York Herald*. "The brilliant illumination of Broadway scarcely reaches to the well-like depths of the great shaft. . . . The great throng which surges along the brightly illuminated sidewalks of Broadway looks down at an abrupt angle into what appears to be a bottomless abyss."

Cost overruns bedeviled the project from the start, totaling $600,000 in the end. As the project neared completion, the *Times'* mortgage lender, the Equitable Life Assurance Society, insisted that Ochs economize by dispensing with what the publisher envisioned as the tower's crowning glory—an observatory topped by a lantern and flagpole. The assemblage added six stories of height. "The tower makes the building monumental and . . . differentiates it from the usual skyscraper type and avoids it being termed 'The Little Flat Iron,' a term that I think would be harmful," protested Ochs in a letter to the Equitable, which refused to relent. Ochs borrowed the extra money needed from another source and added the extension. In early 1904, the publisher set sail for Europe from a Midtown pier on the Hudson and was transfixed by the site of his nearly completed tower, visible for a distance of twelve miles. "The new building loomed up in all its beautiful and grand proportions, out of mid-New York, as we sailed away, and my heart swelled as I thought of association with its erection," the publisher wrote in a note to his mother. "Then it stood foremost and most conspicuous among the best buildings in the Metropolis of the World—and I grew really sentimental."

Renaming Long Acre Square after the *Times* was not Ochs's idea—at least not officially. The proposal was formally presented to the municipal government by August Belmont, a prominent Wall Street investor who ran the company that was building the subway for the city. Belmont also was a shareholder in the *New York Times,* though he had used a trust to mask his ownership. "No station on our route is liable to be more active or important than that at Forty-Second Street and Broadway," Belmont wrote in a letter to the city's transit board. "We are planning, in connection with the Times Building, to have access to it from Seventh Avenue. Owing to the conspicuous position which the *Times* holds, it being one of the leading New York journals, it would seem fitting that the Square on which its building stands should be known as Times Square, and the station named Times Square. Long Acre, the present name of the Square, means nothing, and is not generally known throughout the city." A resolution to this effect passed the Board of Aldermen in April 1904, and the signature of Mayor George B. McLellan made it official: Long Acre now was Times Square. Among the city's newspapers only the *Times* reported this development, downplaying the news not out of modesty but its opposite. The newspaper so deserved this honor that "very likely the name would have been conferred by the speech of the people without official action," declared a gloating editorial, probably written by Ochs himself.

Five months later, the first Independent Rapid Transit subway opened amid great fanfare. New York's inaugural underground train line ran from a point near City Hall in lower Manhattan straight up Fourth Avenue to Grand Central on East 42nd Street. There, the tracks turned due west and ran under 42nd Street to its intersection with Broadway, where they took a sharp right and headed north through the Upper West Side up to the Bronx. A look at the map made it plain: 42nd Street was the pivot of the new subway system. Instead of simply diverting passengers from the elevated and surface railways, the speedy new subway encouraged New Yorkers to travel more often; mass transit patronage in the city would soar by 60 percent from 1904 to 1914. Designed to carry no more than 600,000 riders a day, the subway had reached its theoretical capacity limit after just a year of operation and by 1908 was averaging 800,000 people per day. The IRT's traffic was denser than that of any rail line in the world, topping the Paris Metro by some 23 percent, the Berlin railway by 41 percent, and the London Underground by 50 percent. A greater percentage of this great mobile throng passed through Times Square than through any other place in the city. In the IRT's first year alone, an astounding five million riders passed through the station at 42nd Street and Broadway, making it the busiest station in the whole system.

As a newspaper plant, Times Tower was a disaster. The exceptionally narrow office floors were the least of it. Accessible only through a single, undersized freight elevator and hemmed in on all sides by the subway, the basement chamber that housed the printing presses could not be expanded to keep pace with soaring circulation. By 1913, the paper would move into a vast new horizontal building less than a block away, at 217–229 West 43rd Street. Even so, Ochs would give no thought to selling Times Tower. As an advertisement for the *Times*, the building was a great triumph for reasons that had nothing to do with the fleeting novelty of its height. Ochs shrewdly delayed the formal dedication of the Times Tower until December 31, 1904, in order to combine his own commemoration with the public celebration of New Year's Eve. Hundreds of thousands of people gathered round the tower for a raucous street party that climaxed with a thunderous fireworks display. "A final burst of fireworks wrote '1905' in flames against the heavens, and the throng screamed and shouted themselves hoarse," exulted Meyer Berger, the *Times'* official historian. "It was one of the greatest promotion projects of the age." But it wasn't until the 1906 celebration that Ochs added the pièce de résistance. As the final seconds of the expiring year were counted off, an illuminated glass ball was lowered from the tower's flagpole. The crowd went wild, as it still does today. In appropriating New Year's Eve for his own promotional ends, Ochs not only outdid Bennett and every other rival publisher in the city, but he also went a long way toward establishing Times Square as New York's de facto town square.

The Great White Way:
Pleasure Zone Supreme

The large crowds attracted by the Victoria, the Republic, and the Paradise Roof Gardens not only established 42nd Street as a viable new theater address but also turned it into a central battleground in a war for control of the American theater. In 1896, seven preeminent New York producers and theater owners led by Abraham Erlanger and his partner Marc Klaw had banded together to rationalize the chaotic process of booking Rialto road shows throughout the country. By 1900 their Theatrical Syndicate had matured into a monopoly as noxious as Standard Oil or any of the other infamous industrial trusts of the robber baron era. Because it controlled so many of the important theaters in the United States—some 700 at its peak—the Syndicate was able to dictate bookings nationwide at exorbitant fees and force virtually every major stage star to submit to its self-enriching dictates.

Abe Erlanger, the Syndicate's dominant personality, was the most hated person in show business at the turn of the century. A squat, blocky man with a bulldog face and a personality to match, Erlanger was odd and even a bit mad. He kept a loaded revolver on top of his desk, though there is no record of him actually brandishing it during negotiations. Imagining himself the Napoleon of Broadway, he was inordinately proud of his collection of Bonaparte paraphernalia, which filled his office and home with busts, paintings, and uncut first editions. Erlanger walked the streets with an overcoat thrown over his shoulders like a cape, a brooding scowl fixed on his face. During interviews, he liked to slip a pudgy hand inside his vest. The writer P. G. Wodehouse, who worked for Erlanger early in his career, referred to him in his autobiography as "a bit of a Tartar. That's our expression. The Tartars, meeting a particularly tough specimen, would say that he was a bit of an Erlanger."

The Theatrical Syndicate avidly courted Oscar Hammerstein, who was one of a handful of producers with the talent and the nerve to resist its threats. But even Hammerstein had his moment of weakness, forming an alliance with Klaw and Erlanger in 1899 in hopes of ensuring a steady supply of productions for the Victoria. However, his innate independence quickly asserted itself as the fledgling Victoria thrived. Hammerstein severed ties with the Syndicate in 1900, just before the Theatre Republic opened, prompting Erlanger to blacklist both of his 42nd Street theaters. Although Hammerstein was unable now to book enough first-class productions to keep his 42nd Street theaters lit, he refused to succumb to the Syndicate's bullying. Instead, in 1902 he leased the Theatre Republic to a fellow independent, David Belasco.

A director and playwright as well as a producer, Belasco was as floridly theatrical in his manner as the bombastic melodramas in which he specialized. A notorious rake and a Jew, Belasco nonetheless was known as the "Bishop of Broadway" because he affected the appearance of a priest, complete with clerical collar. He molded many star actresses, taking charge of every aspect of their lives and rehearsing them remorselessly, sticking pins in their derrieres and dragging them around by their hair to fire their passion. Brooks Atkinson of the *New York Times* was as evenhanded a drama critic as ever covered Broadway, but he loathed Belasco, whom he variously damned in print as "the master of mediocrity" and as "a showman masquerading as an artist." However, Atkinson conceded that Belasco was "a pioneer in stagecraft" whose technical innovations—many of which were introduced on 42nd Street—did much to modernize the American stage. "He measurably improved the standards of stage décor by his ingenious use of lighting and his meticulous attention to the detail of scenery," Atkinson wrote.

When Belasco leased the Theatre Republic from Hammerstein in 1902, he was just emerging as an important producer in his own right, having served a long apprenticeship to Charles Frohman, the most benign of the Theatrical Syndicate's founders. Even so, after splitting with Frohman, Belasco was squeezed hard by the Syndicate and was so eager to secure a house of his own that he agreed to pay Hammerstein a rich rental of $30,000 a year, plus 10 percent of the Republic's revenues over the five-year term of the lease. In exchange, Belasco demanded a free hand to remake the Republic to his own taste and technical requirements. He gutted the two-year-old building, leaving only its walls and roof, and blasted a new subbasement out of the bedrock beneath the theater. Belasco installed Broadway's most elaborate lighting system, and a stage comprised wholly of close-fitting trapdoors through which scenery could be precisely hoisted into place. On the top floor, Belasco constructed a plush suite of rooms for himself and another for his current star and protégée, the notorious divorcée Mrs. Leslie Carter. The theater's new color scheme made generous use of Mrs. Carter's favorite hue, rose du Barry. On the back of each chair, Belasco embroidered a Napoleonic bee, which the producer intended as a symbol of his industry as well as of his surname.

It was on 42nd Street that Belasco produced many of the hits that made him a Broadway legend. At the Victoria, meanwhile, Hammerstein's defiantly expansive booking policies helped other independent producers, directors, and actors to defy the Syndicate and still make a living. Thoroughly annoyed, Erlanger exerted escalating pressure on Hammerstein. Having already blackballed the Victoria and the Republic, he and Klaw bought the Olympia complex in 1902, turning Hammerstein's own creation against him. At the same time, the Syndicate's leaders broke ground on a spectacular new theater of their own, the New Amsterdam, the first theater on the south side of 42nd Street. Klaw and Erlanger sunk $1.9 million into what was the block's grandest theater— some twenty times what Hammerstein had spent to build the Victoria— and miraculously got their money's worth. The New Amsterdam actually was two theaters in one: an 1,800-seat, ground-floor theater and a 680-seat roof garden theater. Entirely decorated in the Art Nouveau, a Beaux Arts variant that was the rage in Europe but rarely seen in the United States, the New Amsterdam was dubbed "The House Beautiful" by drama critics. "The New Amsterdam Theatre is beyond question the most gorgeous playhouse in New York," gushed the *New York Dramatic Mirror.* "Architecturally it is near perfection." Klaw and Erlanger moved their offices into the ten-story building, effectively establishing the New Amsterdam as the Syndicate's national headquarters.

The New Amsterdam was one of two magnificent new theaters that opened on 42nd Street in the fall of 1903. The other, the Lyric Theatre, was built by the Shubert Brothers, the Syndicate's emerging archrivals and eventual vanquishers, directly across the street at 213 West 42nd Street, right next to the Belasco Theater. The Shubert brothers—Sam, Lee, and Jacob—set up their offices in the 1,543-seat Lyric, the first of many theaters that they would build in the greater Times Square area.

Runtish, poorly educated Jewish immigrants who had gotten their start as theater operators in Syracuse, the Shubert brothers had hardly seemed a threat to anyone when they first insinuated themselves into New York City in 1900 by leasing the run-down Herald Square Theater near 34th Street. Sam, the eldest, was just twenty-five years old, and so high-strung and twitchy that "even his hair looked as if it might crackle and emit sparks at a moment's notice," as the *New York Sun* put it. The Syndicate gladly supplied attractions to the Shuberts at first, only to freeze them out after they made a surprising success of their first season at the Herald Square and acquired two more theaters, including the Casino, a former Syndicate stronghold at 39th and Broadway. Sam chose 42nd Street as the site of the Lyric both because he considered it the emerging center of the "New Rialto" and because he wanted to stand shoulder to shoulder with Belasco, his boyhood idol. In 1885, Belasco had put on a play in Syracuse and had given Sam, then in grade school, a bit part. Sam was so taken with the Bishop of Broadway that he tried to look and act like him when he first embarked on his own career as an impresario (though he wisely stopped short of wearing the collar) and later enlisted Belasco's support in his war against the Syndicate. For his part, Belasco was flattered by Shubert's admiration and needed all the allies he could attract.

Not to be outdone by the upstart Shuberts, Klaw and Erlanger built a second 42nd Street theater, the Liberty, in 1904. The Liberty was the new professional home of the Rogers Brothers, major musical comedy stars of the era and one of the Syndicate's stalwart acts. The Liberty (234 West 42nd Street) was much smaller than the New Amsterdam, consisting of a single 1,200-seat auditorium. At the top of its facade was a relief carving of the Liberty Bell surmounted by an American eagle with outspread wings. Inside the gilded auditorium, scores of gold eagles and Liberty Bells were affixed to the proscenium arch and box seats.

The leaders of the Syndicate and New York's top independents now faced one another across 42nd Street like generals atop their battlements. "From their rooms in the New Amsterdam, Klaw and Erlanger could look out their front window at the Independent theaters across the street," wrote theater historian Margaret Knapp. "Perhaps they could see David Belasco standing at the window of his office in the playhouse which now bore his name, or their newest and ultimately their strongest adversaries, Sam and Lee Shubert, in their offices over the entrance to the Lyric. Klaw and Erlanger must also have known that Oscar Hammerstein spent a good deal of his time in his workshop and office over the Victoria. . . . The close proximity of the leading contenders in the theatrical wars, which no doubt intensified their enmity, served to concentrate the attention of the theatrical world on the 'theater block' of West 42nd Street."

Forty-second Street's rising stature was most memorably expressed in a song from *Little Johnny Jones,* the Liberty Theater's second production. This early George M. Cohan musical introduced both "I'm a Yankee Doodle Dandy" and "Give My Regards to Broadway" to the lexicon. Cohan's first two Broadway plays had stiffed, and *Little Johnny Jones* would not fare much better, on its first go-round anyway. Yet in "Give My Regards" the twenty-six-year-old Cohan presumed to write in the voice of an established star:

> *Tell all the gang at 42nd Street*
> *That I will soon be there.*

After *Little Johnny Jones* ended its disappointingly short Broadway run, Cohan rewrote it and took it on the road, playing Syndicate houses throughout the country. The musical's return engagement on Broadway was a big hit. Cohan was on his way. His next offering, *Forty-Five Minutes from Broadway,* opened at the New Amsterdam and was the city's greatest musical comedy success since the 1860s. The absurdly prolific Cohan wrote eleven musicals (in addition to a few straight dramas) from 1905 to 1911, most of which were staged on or near 42nd Street. Oscar Hammerstein had pioneered 42nd Street as a theater location, but more than any other performer, Cohan made the place synonymous with the big, brash

American musical. "His shameless flag-waving, his sentimentality, his electricity, his rhythm, his noisiness, his brash personality, were the essence of show business. . . . He invented a type of musical show in which everybody talked at the top of his voice, everybody sang full out and danced ferociously."

During his rise, Cohan played the Syndicate's game, shrewdly and grudgingly. One evening, Cohan was chatting with Hammerstein and his stage manager on the sidewalk outside the Victoria when Abe Erlanger materialized at his side.

"George," Erlanger growled, "how can you stand on the same street so close to these rats, the scum of the earth, the Shuberts?"

Cohan eyed Erlanger carefully and replied, "And what are you, my good friend?"

In May 1905, Sam Shubert died in a horrible train wreck in Pennsylvania that claimed twenty-two lives all told. Lee was so distraught over his brother's death that he had to be hospitalized and, by some accounts, may have attempted suicide.

A few weeks after Sam's funeral, Lee crossed the 42nd Street divide for a private audience with Erlanger in his office above the New Amsterdam. Erlanger made some perfunctory remarks about how sorry he was about Sam, but Lee came right to the point. Admitting to exhaustion, Lee said that he was prepared to open negotiations on the sale of all thirteen of the Shuberts' theaters in the United States and England. However, Lee said, he and Jake would sell only if Erlanger honored their contracts with Belasco, which guaranteed the producer bookings in various Shubert venues.

After chewing on his cigar for a time, the Napoleon of Broadway growled, "I don't honor contracts with dead men."

Lee turned pale with rage and left without a word. He walked back across 42nd Street and returned to the Lyric, where Jacob and the brothers' lawyer were anxiously waiting to hear what had transpired. Jake, the most pugnacious of the Shuberts, was livid over Erlanger's disrespect. "We'll kill the son of a bitch," he said. Sam's defiant brothers would indeed do mortal damage to the Syndicate, building a national network that would encompass a hundred theaters by the end of the 1920s.

However, neither the boys from Syracuse nor Klaw and Erlanger were involved in the construction of 42nd Street's eighth theater, the

Eltinge, which opened in 1912 at 236 West 42nd Street. This elegant 889-seat house was named after Julian Eltinge, Broadway's most celebrated female impersonator. Drag had been a staple of the respectable theater for years, but it was not until Eltinge emerged in 1904 in his first starring role on Broadway that "America really took a female impersonator to its heart." Eltinge was so popular that he started his own magazine and line of cold cream, but his gender-bending act did not play with everybody. "Women went into ecstasy about him," W. C. Fields once said. "Men went into the smoking room." A closeted homosexual who disdained the term "female impersonator," Eltinge also played male roles and labored to cultivate a virile off-stage image. His publicists circulated stories of brawls with stagehands, fellow actors, and even audience members who dared cast aspersions on his masculinity. In 1911, the actor opened at the Liberty Theater in his biggest hit, *The Fascinating Widow,* which played for four years. Early in the play's run, Eltinge decided to join with his manager, the prolific Broadway producer Al H. Woods, and invest a portion of his burgeoning fortune in building a new theater just down the street. Although Eltinge never played the Eltinge himself, the portly star apparently saw to it that its orchestra seats came in three different widths instead of the uniform size. "For the obese theater lovers this will be a genuine treat," commented the *New York Times.*

While the great 42nd Street theater war still raged in 1903–4, Oscar Hammerstein was mainly occupied with building a second Manhattan Opera House on 34th Street near Eighth Avenue. He did manage to fire off one return salvo, though, building a new theater of his own at 254 West 42nd Street, just a few doors down from the Liberty. The strain of these overlapping building projects proved too much for Hammerstein, who collapsed in the street one summer day and was taken to a hospital for a month of enforced rest. Upon his release, he resumed his exhausting routine. "I lead a life of great simplicity," he famously protested. "I eat little and drink nothing and smoke only twenty-five cigars a day." With just 770 seats and a tiny lobby, the newest 42nd Street theater was a re-creation of the elegant, undersize Theatre Republic in many respects. But its most distinctive feature was a new automatic fire-fighting system designed by Hammerstein himself. Activated by a chain hanging backstage, it consisted of a maze of pipes connected to a pair of 5,000-gallon water tanks on the roof.

Hammerstein had no intention of going toe to toe on 42nd Street with either Abe Erlanger or the Shubert brothers. He had built the new play-house—his fourth in Times Square—intending from the start to lease it to the comedian Lew M. Fields, who named it after himself. More important, while putting the finishing touches on the Lew M. Fields Theater, Ham-merstein made what proved to be the shrewdest commercial move of his career, changing the Victoria from a playhouse to the first pure vaudeville outlet in Times Square. The impresario erected huge electric signs that spelled out HAMMERSTEIN'S in letters over four feet high on both the 42nd Street and Seventh Avenue facades. Nicknamed "the Corner," Hammer-stein's Victoria not only marked the center of the budding Times Square theater district but also quickly established itself as the new national cap-ital of vaudeville. As one historian put it, "Vaudeville audiences across the nation accepted the phrase, 'direct from Hammerstein's,' as proof that a vaudeville artist had reached the pinnacle of success."

New York's vaudeville houses were scattered throughout its most populous neighborhoods. "Small-time" halls tended to cluster in working-class or immigrant areas and featured four to six shows a day on a contin-uous performance schedule. "Big-time" venues offered just two shows a day—like a playhouse—but their bills were much larger, often including twice as many acts as small-time houses. The city's small- and big-time theaters alike were cogs in the great regional and nationwide circuits as-sembled by a handful of dominant vaudeville promoters operating out of New York. Benjamin F. Keith and his business partner, Edward F. Albee, built the most powerful combine and cowed the owners of the other cir-cuits into booking through their United Booking Office (UBO), which ruled vaudeville nationwide from a modest office building on Broadway, midway between 42nd and 43rd Streets. The UBO was the vaudeville equivalent of the Theatrical Syndicate, and Albee wielded his power with a callousness that embittered even many of vaudeville's biggest stars. As Groucho Marx put it, "Albee was the owner of a large cotton plantation and the actors were his slaves."

For all of its fame, the Victoria was not 42nd Street's first vaudeville venue. Not long after he'd opened the American Theatre along Eighth Avenue in 1893, William French had put a vaudeville show into its spa-cious roof garden. The American's small-time vaudeville policy proved moderately successful, despite a 1896 bust for public indecency (the first of many to come for 42nd Street establishments). A police inspector took exception to a vaudeville sketch called "Ten Minutes in the Latin Quartier; or, a Study in the Nude" and hauled its featured actress and the roof garden's manager off to jail. The resulting surge in attendance was not sufficient to save the overextended French, who in 1897 lost his theater in a foreclosure that mirrored Hammerstein's unhappy experience with the Olympia. Rooftop vaudeville survived under new ownership, which also restored the American's main auditorium to profitability by presenting bastardized English-language versions of great Italian and German light operas.

Hammerstein considered the American a minor competitive annoyance and succeeded in keeping the mighty Keith-Albee combine at arm's length until 1907, when the great contretemps known as "the second vaudeville war" erupted. Unlike the first war, in which Hammerstein's Olympia had vied with the New Koster and Bial's Music Hall for artistic as well as financial supremacy, this second skirmish was all about money. It started when Klaw and Erlanger and the Shuberts temporarily set aside their enmity and joined forces to set up a new circuit—called "Advanced Vaudeville"—to challenge the Keith-Albee monopoly in the East and Midwest. Advanced Vaudeville formed an alliance with the booking agent William Morris, who had worked closely with Hammerstein for years but now abruptly stopped supplying the Victoria with talent. Hammerstein made the best of a perilous situation by negotiating an uneasy alliance with Keith and Albee and the UBO. Hammerstein agreed to put UBO acts into the Victoria. In return, the vaudeville trust effectively granted Hammerstein the exclusive right to present big-time vaudeville within the greater Times Square area, extending from West 37th up to 56th Street and from Fifth Avenue to the Hudson River.

The second vaudeville war proved short-lived, leading to Advanced Vaudeville's demise within a year. But Hammerstein's pact with the victors, Keith and Albee, would hold until 1913, when the fabulously upscale Palace opened at 47th and Broadway. Neutralizing vaudeville's most powerful combine worked to the great benefit of the Victoria, but Hammerstein's Victoria did face formidable competition right on 42nd Street. In 1908, not long after Advanced Vaudeville bit the dust, the agent William Morris, a diehard foe of the UBO, created a New York showcase for his stars by leasing and renovating the American, which he renamed the American Music Hall. Now, both the American's main stage and its roof garden were given over to two-a-day, big-time vaudeville bills that often gave the Victoria a run for its money.

Hammerstein's deal with the devil did not cost the Victoria its soul. To the contrary, the Corner remained an idiosyncratic venue with an ambiance all its own. Vaudevillians nicknamed the Keith-Albee wheel the "Sunday school circuit" because the promoters imposed so many restrictions on what performers could say and how they dressed. At houses controlled by Keith and by the E. F. Proctor circuit, even audience members were reprimanded for bad behavior, including booing. But at Hammerstein's, almost anything went, including drinking and smoking, both of which were prohibited at most other vaudeville venues. Not only did the Victoria not censor performers, but it also encouraged them to try out new, unproven material. At the same time, patrons were free to express their displeasure as loudly as they wanted. The Victoria's bills often included acts that explicitly encouraged rowdy audience participation in the tradition of the Cherry Sisters, who, as seemingly nonplussed as ever, returned to New York in 1905 for a successful run at the Victoria. Hammerstein's son Willie devised a sketch called "Hanged," in which the warden refused to spring the trap as he loudly avowed his opposition to capital punishment. A volunteer from the audience was called up to finish the job. "Hanged" evolved into "Electrocution," in which a volunteer pulled a switch that sent sparks flying from a simulated electric chair.

By doubling the length of the Victoria's bills to as many as sixteen performers, Hammerstein could honor his pact with the Keith-Albee circuit and maintain a large measure of independence by continuing to book acts of his own choosing. Oscar increasingly relied on Willie to run the Corner while he invested his own time—and the Victoria's profits—in opera projects. Willie was twenty-seven years old when he began working at the Victoria in 1901, moving up to manager upon its conversion to full-time vaudeville in 1904. Many vaudeville performers and scholars regard Willie as the greatest showman in vaudeville history, eclipsing even his father. "If E. F. Albee owned the body of vaudeville," wrote Abel Green and Joe Laurie in *Show Biz,* "Willie Hammerstein owned its heart and soul." Yet in terms of personality, Willie was Oscar's opposite—a diligent, placid, even lugubrious man who seemed mystified as anyone by his showman's flair. "Whenever he had engaged a potential new headliner for the Victoria, he was wont to discuss it with a dour disparagement that might have discouraged an advertising department not familiar with his mental makeup," recalled Anna Marble Pollack, a veteran Hammerstein press agent. "However great his faith in his 'find,' he always presented it with so many qualifying apologies that it was difficult at first hearing to know why he had booked the turn."

Unlike most vaudeville promoters, Willie and his father worked hard at showcasing new talent. Among the many emerging stars who played the Corner early in their careers were Eva Tanguay, Harry Houdini, W. C. Fields, Al Jolson, Buster Keaton, and Charlie Chaplin. "That grand old showcase . . . was in its day everything—and perhaps a little more—than the Palace became later," recalled Keaton, who was still in his teens when he first appeared at the Victoria. "Any old-timer will tell you, Hammerstein's Victoria was vaudeville at its all-time best." Pie throwing, a staple not only of vaudeville but also of silent films, seems to have been introduced at the Victoria during an appearance by Fred Karno's English Comedy Troupe, which included Chaplin and Stan Laurel. "When the Karno company worked for Willie Hammerstein, he loved the act, and he gave us a bit of business," Chaplin recalled. "We had a boy in the box with me, and I used to knock him over. One day, Hammerstein said, 'Why don't you do it with a pie?' So we did. The *goo* of it. The laughter we got lasted two minutes, which was a long time. Willie Hammerstein had such a sad face. But the acts he had. The big time."

The Corner figured importantly in Will Rogers's rise. America's favorite cowboy/philosopher made his vaudeville debut at Keith's Union Square Theater in June 1905, billed as "The World Champion Lasso Manipulator." Just two days later, Willie effectively stole Rogers away (this was a full two years before the Hammersteins struck their mutual nonaggression pact with Keith-Albee), signing him to play the Corner for the whole summer at $140 a week, double what Keith was paying him. Rogers, whose act at the time consisted mainly of dazzling rope tricks delivered with minimal commentary, played a matinee at the Victoria and an evening performance on the roof, transporting his horse, Teddy, from one venue to the other by elevator. For his opening-night finale, Rogers mounted Teddy and twirled an eighty-foot rope overhead until it was a giant crinoline spinning and hissing over the heads of a gasping audience. The applause was deafening, but Rogers took a quick bow and headed to his dressing room. In his autobiography, Rogers recalled that he was intercepted by Ernest Hogan, a black comedian and singer, who shoved him back out in front of the curtain. "As I came off, he apologized and said, 'Boy, don't overlook any of them. They aint bows,' he says, 'thems curtain calls and there is damned few of them up here.'"

After his breakthrough appearance at the Corner, Rogers had plenty of opportunities to perfect the curtain call at theaters throughout the United States and Europe. Rogers's "dumb," or nonspeaking, act had made him one of vaudeville's most popular acts, but he was only getting started. In 1907, he returned to the Victoria to unveil a new "talking" wise-hick act and deliver the first of the ad-libbed, topical wisecracks that were eventually to transform him into the populist seer of American political life. "Rogers attains classification as a comedy talking act, with a great deal more certainty than a host of others who bill themselves that way," wrote the critic for *Variety*. "His incidental remarks are fresh and breezy as can be and the act runs along entertainingly." Rogers would vastly outstrip his vaudeville fame as a star in the Ziegfeld Follies (playing across the street at the New Amsterdam) and on the silver screen, but he always remained grateful to the younger Hammerstein in particular. "We have never produced another showman like Willie Hammerstein," he declared.

Harry Houdini's career in vaudeville reached its peak with an eight-week run on Hammerstein's roof in the summer of 1912. By this time Houdini had no trouble selling out theaters in New York, but the city's newspapers still had not warmed up to the great escape artist, treating him with a reserve that bordered on disdain. Early one morning, Houdini invited reporters to a pier on the East River to witness the daring new stunt that he planned to unveil that evening on Hammerstein's roof. The pressmen followed Houdini onto a tugboat. At the escape artist's request, some of them manacled his hands and feet with irons and locked him into a lead-weighted packing box. The box was lowered over the side of the tug and dropped into the depths of New York harbor. The reporters took out their watches. After fifty-seven seconds, Houdini surfaced, and the scribes burst into cheers. The box was hauled up and found to be intact and closed tight, with the manacles inside. That evening, a wildly enthusiastic audience watched as Houdini repeated the stunt in the large pool that was a permanent feature of Hammerstein's roof.

At the end of the first week, an exultant Houdini demanded his $1,000 salary in gold coins. Willie was taken aback but accommodated his star. Houdini took his bag of gold and drove straight from the theater to his mother's house uptown. He asked his mother to hold out her apron and poured the coins into it, in fulfillment of the vow of support he had made to his father on his deathbed. "Houdini always described this incident as the greatest thrill of his life," wrote a biographer. "Probably he did not exaggerate."

Willie Hammerstein was a bona fide star-maker, but it was his ennoblement of the freak act as Broadway fare that defined the Victoria as vaudeville's great "nut house." To Willie "drawing power was more important than talent," recalled Loney Haskell, the Victoria's most celebrated master of ceremonies. "That theory brought a lot of people to the vaudeville stage who never would have been on it otherwise." The Victoria trafficked in the sorts of classic freaks displayed in dime museums and circus sideshows—midgets, giants, exotic dancers, mind readers, and the like. A particular favorite at the Victoria was Unthan the Armless Wonder, who used his feet to play cards, fire a rifle, and play the violin. Willie even contracted with Barnum and Bailey to supply acrobats and animal acts during the circus off season. But at the same time, the younger Hammerstein enlivened and enlarged the freak genre by pulling stories about the famous and the merely notorious from the pages of the yellow press and turning them into stage acts. "In a sense, Oscar and his son, Willie, were the fathers of the modern tabloid," Haskell claimed. "They began to present at the Victoria . . . the most lurid news items of the day in a graphic form. Anything that would draw a crowd was meat for a Victoria bill."

The Victoria became the most topical theater in America, with boxers, polar explorers, and bicycle and running champions appearing alongside bejeweled divorcées and accused killers. When two comely girls shot a well-known Manhattan hotelier in the leg, Willie bailed them out and put them onstage as "The Shooting Stars." Their inability to sing, dance, or act did not prevent them from packing the house for a week, as they simply stood onstage while a monologuist recounted their exploits. A famous comedian of the day was asked what he thought of their act. "They'll have to *kill* someone to get another week," he replied. Florence Carman, the wife of a Long Island doctor, went from wounding one of her husband's female patients with a pistol directly to the stage of the Victoria, where she performed a touching rendition of the song "Baby Shoes."

Like his father, Willie excelled at hyping acts by manipulating the press and was perfectly willing to perpetrate outright hoaxes in pursuit of box office advantage. In one of his most effective stunts, Hammerstein succeeded in transforming a Swiss quick-sketch artist who performed with his wife, daughter, and sister-in-law into the court artist of the Turkish Empire and his three wives. Willie tried the act out first in Paris, where it caused a sensation, and then filled the New York papers with news of the performers' imminent arrival to play Hammerstein's. When the sketch artist and his entourage arrived from Europe, they were detained at Ellis Island on grounds of bigamy. Willie rushed to their well-publicized rescue even as he was secretly arranging for the Waldorf-Astoria Hotel to refuse lodging to his quartet, which he billed as "Abdul Kader and His Three Wives in an Exhibition of Rapid Painting." Finally, the immigrant impostors were taken to the apartment that had awaited them the entire time. Abdul and family drew standing-room-only crowds at Hammerstein's and then embarked on a national tour.

For members of the Hammerstein family, the Victoria was more than a rich source of income. It was where they went to see and perhaps speak with Oscar, who slept most nights in his rooms above the theater and generally kept his distance from his relatives. As the Victoria's manager, Willie was the Hammerstein most frequently in his father's company. Even so, Willie's eldest son, Oscar II, was seven years old before he even laid eyes on his namesake, standing in the lobby of the Victoria. Thereafter, Oscar and his brother, Reggie, spent nearly every Sunday afternoon of their childhood in a stage box at the Victoria watching the matinee. Once or twice a year, on their way into the show, Willie would lead his sons over to a corner of the lobby, where the "old man" stood. "Reggie and I would shake hands dutifully, but neither of us would have the courage to meet our grandfather's eyes for very long," the lyricist recalled. "He never said anything, not even volunteering the stale observation 'What big boys you're getting to be!' He seemed as relieved as we were when these short and pointless meetings were adjourned."

In the mind's eye, viewed in retrospect through the mists of a century of history, 42nd Street's theaters stand alone in the foreground, as if carved in bas-relief from an indistinct, shadowy streetscape. But Golden Age 42nd Street looked much different through the eyes of its contemporaries, the men and women who nightly packed the one dozen theaters lining the street and Times Square when these showplaces were shiny and new. To the turn-of-the-century New Yorker, 42nd was not a mere theater row but center stage of an after-dark pleasure zone nonpareil. "Broadway from 34th to 47th Street has been for the last few years the locality where the gay life of the metropolis has been most readily seen," Stephen Jenkins observed in his 1911 Broadway travelogue, *The Greatest Street in the World.* "Here are congregated great hotels, famous restaurants, and theatres; and the brilliant illumination by the countless electric lights has caused this section of the avenue to be called 'The Great White Way;' and no stranger has seen New York who has not traversed it." By 1910, if not earlier, Brooks Atkinson concurred, "The phrase '42nd Street and Broadway' stood for revelry and delight."

The new theater district's nightlife scaled a peak of bacchanalian excess every New Year's Eve. "The celebration of New Year's Eve in this neighborhood has become . . . a grand orgy after midnight, putting the blush to the wildest capers of the Moulin Rouge, Maxim's, and other notorious places in Paris," Jenkins wrote. "For this occasion it is necessary to engage tables a long time ahead, and in the way of drink nothing but champagne is served." Rector's, the preeminent Broadway lobster palace, took the precaution of boarding over its big windows with wooden planks on New Year's Eve and on election nights, which were similarly mobbed. "Demand for tables on these nights was so great that we could have used Madison Square Garden as an annex for our overflow and filled it," boasted George Rector, the restaurant's proprietor.

The Great White Way was the old Rialto relocated, enlarged, and pitched to a higher frequency of social adventure and self-indulgence. If New York had never seen anything quite like the "lobster palace society" nurtured by the new theater district's many grand restaurants and hotels, it was mainly because the city's monied elite had never before allowed itself to come into such thrillingly intimate contact with Broadway celebrity—Mrs. Astor and her famous Four Hundred be damned!

Caroline Webster Schermerhorn Astor, the iron-fisted queen of Gilded Age society, would sooner have jumped from the roof of her Fifth Avenue mansion than have put in an appearance at any of the hot spots along the Great White Way. In Mrs. Astor's view, the restaurant, the hotel banquet hall, and other places of public amusement lay far outside the ambit of polite society, which entertained privately and formally, or not at all. The very notion of the Four Hundred was rooted in this privacy imperative. Mrs. Astor invited only four hundred people to her famous balls because only four hundred people could fit within the stately confines of the Astor mansion ballroom.

Ironically, it was another Astor, nephew William Waldorf Astor, who struck the first telling blow against Mrs. Astor's oppressive social sovereignty. In the early 1890s, William tore down his father's mansion on Fifth Avenue at 33rd Street and replaced it with the Waldorf Hotel, the first public establishment in the city to rival the city's great private houses in the quality of its cuisine and the sumptuousness of its decor. William despised his aunt Caroline, who lived right next door, and was delighted when she decamped to new quarters uptown to escape the massive new hotel, which opened in 1893. A few years later, Caroline's son, John Jacob IV, tore down his mother's house and built a second hotel, the Astoria. Designed by the same architect, the adjoining hotels were combined to form the Waldorf-Astoria, whose elegant public rooms provided the more adventurous members of high society with all the cover that they needed to venture out and search for amusement beyond their own walls. The liberating effect of the Waldorf-Astoria's resounding success as a setting for society banquets and parties came as a shock even to its proprietor. "I never dreamed that it would be given to me to gaze on the face of an Astor in a public dining-room," William Waldorf Astor said.

In the Waldorf's wake a dozen other ultraposh society hotels and restaurants popped up along Fifth Avenue. But if places like Delmonico's, Sherry's, and the Savoy were much livelier than Caroline Astor's ballroom, they still were rooted in snobbish Fifth Avenue notions of propriety and exclusivity. The new restaurants and hotels that opened more or less simultaneously on Broadway were no less expensive but far gayer and showier than their Fifth Avenue counterparts. Broadway was *the* place to celebrate, and presidential elections, World Series victories, and heavyweight championships were toasted with as much verve as an opening-night smash hit. The doors of the lobster palaces were open to everyone with an appetite for luxury—and the means to pay for it. The charter members of lobster palace society included, by one account, "Wall Street financiers, industrial magnates, gilded factions of the Four Hundred, gaudy playboys, journalists, celebrities from the Bohemia of the arts, the greatest stars of the theater, gamblers, jockeys, pugilists, professional beauties, chorus girls, kept women."

The Astor family also pioneered in Times Square, building two of its most prominent hotels. The Hotel Astor replaced a whole row of theatrical boardinghouses between 43rd and 44th Streets on the west side of Broadway, a site that one Astor or another had owned since the 1700s. Built by William Waldorf Astor, the enormous 700-room Hotel Astor was solidly in the society-party mold of the Waldorf-Astoria; in fact, the new hotel, which opened in 1904, was so similar functionally that it was perceived to some degree as its replacement. More than half of the Astor's floor space was given over to enormous banquet halls and ballrooms, the largest of which sat 2,500. At the same time, the Hotel Astor defined a new Times Square style of hotel architecture in its emphasis on "scenographic" interiors resembling elaborate stage sets. "The Astor's interiors were a catalogue of historical styles, with evocations of the past and exotic locales which reflect the influence of theme restaurants."

John Jacob Astor, William Waldorf's erstwhile partner turned arch rival, tried to counter the success of the Hotel Astor by building a Times Square hotel of his own—the Knickerbocker—two blocks south at Broadway and 42nd Street. To create the feel of luxury at a comparatively modest cost, the Knickerbocker's architects commissioned a series of mural paintings. The most notable of them, *Old King Cole* by Maxwell Parrish, hung above the Knickerbocker's main bar. Financially, the smaller Knickerbocker was never a match for the Hotel Astor, but it quickly became a social landmark in its own right. George M. Cohan lived in the Knickerbocker for years, as did the great Italian "tenor of tenors" Enrico Caruso, who maintained his own chef and staff of servants there and periodically serenaded passersby from the balcony of his suite. The Knickerbocker's bar was such a popular meeting place for the men of lobster palace society that it was nicknamed the Forty-second Street Country Club.

One could dine sumptuously at the Astor, the Knickerbocker, or any of a half dozen other new hotels located within a block or two of 42nd Street and Broadway. Mrs. Leslie Carter, the Belasco Theater's resident star, preferred the Criterion at Broadway and 41st Street, dining there around midnight after most every performance. But the after-theater scene burned brightest at the stand-alone restaurants from which lobster palace society took its name. David Belasco occasionally joined his protégée Mrs. Carter at the Criterion but preferred the table perpetually reserved for him at Shanley's, which was just a half a block north of the

Belasco Theater and where, according to a 1903 restaurant guide, the famous producer might "be seen at the same hour every day."

Rector's, Shanley's, Murray's Roman Gardens, Bustanoby's, Churchill's, Reisenweber's, Healey's, and the other lobster palaces did indeed serve lobster—along with most every other delicacy imaginable—but they set themselves apart from ordinary restaurants by the plush theatricality of their decor even more than the lavishness of their menus. "A Broadway restaurant must necessarily be magnificently gorgeous at any cost," *American Architect* noted in 1910. Every top Broadway restaurant prided itself on its carvings, its fixtures, and especially its glittering crystal chandeliers—a fixture of the aristocratic Fifth Avenue home. Imperial imagery was pervasive, especially of the French variety. Rector's was done up in green and gold furnishings of the Sun King, while the Knickerbocker bar sported a Louis XIV design. The Hotel Martinique featured a main dining room modeled after the Apollo Room of the Louvre, with panels depicting Maurice de Saxe, Ronsard, Voltaire, Louis XV, the ladies of the court, and other great figures of the eighteenth century. Maxim's outfitted its waiters in cutaway coats, ruffled shirts, black satin breeches, silk stockings, silver buckled pumps, and powdered wigs.

Murray's Roman Gardens, which opened in 1906 at 228–232 West 42nd Street, adjacent to the Liberty Theater, was a virtual theme park of imperial civilizations. The exterior of the building was a two-story imitation of the ancient *hôtel* of the Cardinal de Rohan in Paris, elaborated by additional niches filled with heroic-size reproductions of allegorical figures and casts of classic sculptures from Paris. A huge doorway marked the entrance. The inscription it bore—*Les chevaux du soleil*—was copied from the cardinal's stables. Inside, the fantasy was more distinctly Roman, although the interior also incorporated Egyptian, Syrian, and Gothic motifs. Through a black and gold mosaic-lined foyer, patrons entered the enormous main dining room, which occupied three acres and was elaborately done up to resemble the atrium of a grand Roman house. High above, electric stars twinkled on the deep-blue ceiling. In the middle of the room was a huge fountain, surrounded by vines and trees. Diners gazed out from their tables on a replica of an ancient barge that fronted a terraced foundation crowned by a classical temple that rose virtually to the ceiling. Lavish mirrors were strategically placed throughout, heightening the spectacle while allowing diners to study one another covertly.

Murray's was hugely popular, but too theatrical by half, in the view of some critics. "They even have lights under the tables, at Murray's, so that a pink glow comes up through the cloth. Quite thrilling!" wrote Julian Street in the drolly satiric article "Lobster Palace Society," published in *Everybody's Magazine* in 1910. "It makes a good place to take your friends who come from afar and wish to gaze about, for dining there is like dining on a stage set for the second act of a musical comedy. You half expect a chorus of waiters to come dancing with property lobsters glued to property plates."

Rector's was the first and greatest of the palaces, opening in 1899, when Times Square was still Long Acre. Housed in a low-slung, yellow building on the southeast corner of 44th Street and Broadway, a bit south of Hammerstein's Olympia, Rector's featured two dining rooms, with a hundred tables on the main floor and another seventy-five upstairs—as well as New York's first revolving door. The restaurant's only identifying mark was the electrically illuminated griffin, the family's trademark, which hung from its facade. Oscar Hammerstein and Sam Shubert were counted among Rector's regulars, as was Abe Erlanger. Rector's "was the great Bohemian place where one met all the charming actresses and smart young men after the theater," recalled E. Berry Wall, a well-known society figure who moved with ease between Fifth Avenue and Broadway, helping popularize the tuxedo in the process. "This was certainly the 'Hollywood' of that period, for all the stars of theaterland congregated at Rector's." Rector's was a name often dropped not just in Broadway's theater lobbies—"Meet you at Rector's" was a catchphrase of the era—but also from its stages. "If a Table at Rector's Could Talk" was the big hit song from the first of Florenz Ziegfeld's famous revues, *The Follies of 1907.*

There were no Astors, Vanderbilts, or Goelets among the lobster palace proprietors. Like Oscar Hammerstein, their contemporary, most of them were self-made European immigrants who had started out as busboys, waiters, and bartenders. By contrast, tubby, jovial George Rector was a third-generation *American* restaurateur and awfully proud of his forebears and of himself. "I found Broadway a quiet little lane of ham and eggs in 1899, and I left it a full-blown avenue of lobsters, champagne and morning-afters," he boasted in his entertainingly self-serving memoir, *The Girl from Rector's.* "I brought Paris to New York and improved it by the transplanting."

George and Charles Rector, his father and mentor, scoured the world for exotic fare, importing wild boar ham from Spain, artichokes and endives from France, quail and partridge from Egypt, alligator pears from the West Indies, and bamboo from China. "Like Sherry's and Delmonico's, the Rector menu was based more on the vanity than the palate of our diners," George confessed. "We utilized foreign dishes as bait for the vanity of the snobs—and they bit fast and often." Rector's imported strawberries from southern Europe, for one female customer who dined at the restaurant every night, charging her fifty cents apiece. She ate just one a night. "As she held the fruit aloft on her fork she looked all around the room to make sure that everybody saw her," Rector recalled. "She didn't care any more for hothouse berries than a leopard cares to chew a wet whisk broom. She ordered them just to make her neighbors jealous."

Rector was as admiring of the gourmets among his clientele as he was contemptuous of the poseurs. His memoirs included a minutely detailed recounting of the eating habits of James Buchanan "Diamond Jim" Brady, the single most conspicuous consumer of the Gilded Age. The son of a lower West Side saloonkeeper, Diamond Jim made his fortune as a supersalesman of railroad equipment. He luxuriated in his money, ordering the finest custom suits by the dozen and spending $2 million on some thirty matched sets of diamond jewelry. "When Diamond Jim had all his illumination in place," Rector marveled, "he looked like an excursion steamer at twilight."

Diamond Jim did not invent expense account entertaining but did raise it to Olympian heights of excess. Brady, who was perhaps the most avid theatergoer in theater-crazed New York, patronized all of the lobster palaces, but Rector's held a special place in his heart—and gut. The three-hundred-pound, triple-chinned Brady was "the best twenty-five customers we had," Rector quipped. Rector's employed four bartenders, one of whom did little more than squeeze oranges to supply the three or four gallons of juice that Diamond Jim consumed at the start of every pretheater dinner. Next, he would eat two or three dozen Lynnhavens, the largest of oysters, and a dozen hard-shell crabs, claws and all. A half dozen lobsters followed. Brady was a seafood specialist but did not mind chasing the lobster with a steak or two. Then came dessert. "When he pointed at a platter of French pastry he didn't mean any special piece of pastry," Rector recalled. "He meant the platter." Next he ordered a two-pound box of candy from the restaurant's "candy girl" and passed it around the table. If any of his guests took a piece, Diamond Jim ordered another box for himself. "Whenever I sit down to a meal, I always make it a point to leave just four inches between my stummick and the edge of the table," he once said. "And then, when I can feel 'em rubbin' together pretty hard, I *know* I've had enough." But not for long. En route to one of the theaters nearby, Brady often stopped off to buy another two-pound box of candy, which he usually finished before the curtain went up. "It was nothing unusual for him to buy another box between acts," Rector added. "After the show he would return to Rector's for a midnight snack."

The Broadway restaurants, like their Fifth Avenue counterparts, were places to see and be seen. But the presence of Broadway actresses and chorus girls gave the palaces a frisson of sexual electricity all their own. "These restaurants were artfully contrived showcases for feminine beauty. . . . A liberal tip, and appropriate advance notice, persuaded the gypsy fiddler to meet you at the door, to play to your fair companion as she walked slowly to the table in time with the music, while forks were suspended in the air, conversation ceased, and all eyes were fixed upon her. This was known as making an entrance. To see it carried off with the greatest éclat, you had only to watch the progress to her table of any star of musical comedy."

However, the real drama took place offstage in the private dining rooms that many of the lobster palaces maintained to facilitate trysts between wealthy sporting gentlemen and the chorus girls and kept women who beguiled them. The menus of these *chambres separées,* many of which were helpfully outfitted with sofas, were said to feature "a hot bird and a cold bottle." The Rectors did not approve of these interclass dalliances and saw to it that their four private dining rooms were in fact used for dining, as well as the occasional stag gambling party. Such was Rector's renown as a haunt of theater folk that the legend of the hot bird and cold bottle attached to it like a barnacle just the same. The music hall team of Weber and Fields always got a knowing laugh with a bit in which a chorus girl is asked if she had ever found a pearl in an oyster. "No," she coyly replies, "but I got a diamond from a lobster over at Rector's last night."

Flush with profit, the Rectors decided in 1910 to build an entirely new restaurant on the site of the existing one and to encase it within a deluxe hotel, the Hotel Rector. Rector's was as popular as ever, but as the oldest of the lobster palaces it no longer seemed so palatial. Scores of new restaurants had opened, each seemingly grander and gaudier than the last. Louis Martin, owner of the popular Martin's restaurant on 26th Street, set a lofty new standard of excess in spending $2 million—a bit more than it cost to build the New Amsterdam—on his Café de l'Opera, which opened at the corner of Broadway and 42nd Street just as Rector's closed for remodeling.

The Café de l'Opera "at this writing, is the newest, the gold-and-bluest restaurant in Babylon, though they are building others faster than type can possibly set type," quipped Street in "Lobster Palace Society," published soon after the Café opened. "There is a black marble stairway that is quite the most magnificently heathen-looking thing in town. At the bottom of it stands a gigantic winged lion, with a man's head in bas-relief. The broad stair landing, visible from the main dining room, would be a fine place for a priest to make burnt offerings to barbaric gods," Street continued, his populist dudgeon rising. "On the large expanse of back wall of this stair landing the largest and most startling addition to New York's Lobster Palace Art Collection is displayed, in the form of an immense painting by [George] Rochegrosse, of the Fall of Babylon. . . . To place such a picture in a New York Lobster Palace would be daring if Lobster Palace society had brains or used them. But why have brains? Aren't sweetbreads just as good? So the elite of Lobsterdom have sweetbreads, and, eating, fail to see the writing on the wall."

Flo Ziegfeld and the Cult
of the Chorus Girl

The glamour of the Great White Way was a kind of stage effect that flicked on and off with the marquees of the theaters and the facades of the lobster palaces in the early 1900s. During the daylight hours, before the big spenders descended, Broadway and 42nd Street was a gray, workaday sort of place. When Charlie Chaplin landed in New York City for the first time one summer morning in 1910, he immediately took a streetcar to Times Square. "It was somewhat of a letdown," he recalled. "Newspapers were blowing about the road and pavement, and Broadway looked seedy, like a slovenly woman just out of bed. On almost every street corner there were elevated chairs with shoe lasts sticking up and people sitting comfortably in shirtsleeves getting their shoes shined. They gave one the impression of finishing their toilet on the street. Many looked like strangers, standing aimlessly about the sidewalk as if they had just left the railroad station and were filling in time between trains." Chaplin's mood brightened as he realized that many of these strangers were itinerants of a particular and appealing sort—his peers and colleagues. "Everyone on Broadway seemed to be in show business; actors, vaudevillians, circus performers and entertainers were everywhere . . . all talking shop," Chaplin continued. Even the civilians that he encountered in Times Square sounded like showmen. "One heard snatches of conversation in the streets, motherly old women looking like farmer's wives saying, 'He's just finished three-a-day out West for Pantages.' "

Broadway headliners might have been making a beautiful dollar, but most theater industry employees were barely scraping by, no matter whether they worked in front of the stage lights, or behind them. As a fledgling member of Fred Karno's traveling troupe, Chaplin could only afford to rent a back room above a laundry in a dirty, foul-smelling brownstone on 43rd Street. Chaplin had his choice of scores of unequally unappealing accommodations in the area, for Times Square was at once a burgeoning luxury entertainment district and a ghetto for the low-paid workers who serviced its affluent patrons. As a result, the pattern of Long Acre's gentrification into Times Square was wildly patchwork. For every rooming house or brothel that was demolished to make way for a new theater or restaurants, five or six remained. Many would even survive in derelict form into the 1980s.

As West 42nd Street was debauched into the retail pornography capital of America in the late 1960s, champions of reform would argue their case by contrasting the squalors of the present with the grandeur of the street's Golden Age in the early decades of the century. There is no question that 42nd Street in 1910 was a more benign and refined place than it would be in 1970—or in 1935, for that matter. But the Great White Way was steeped in sex from the outset, onstage and offstage—*especially* off. In Times Square's foundling years sex was not merely a vicarious pleasure experienced from an orchestra row seat, but a fully interactive amusement to a far greater degree even than in the notorious era of the peep show in the 1960s and 1970s. In 1901, investigators found that prostitutes were working out of no less than 132 buildings in the thirty-three-block area spanned by 37th and 46th Streets and by Sixth and Ninth Avenues. Very little undercover sleuthing was required to compile these statistics, for prostitution was as blatant as it was rampant. On Saturday and Sunday nights, customers stood in long lines outside the most popular of the theater district's brothels, which were "frequented by all classes, 'silk hat' roisterers, college boys visiting the city for 'a time,' businessmen out for a night of gayety, clerks and working men."

Like the theater and hotel industries, its boon companions, the sex trade had migrated over the decades from lower Manhattan to Midtown. Prostitution was much in evidence in and around West 42nd Street by the mid-1880s, a good decade before the theater established its twin beachheads—William French's American Theatre and Oscar Hammerstein's Olympia. In 1892, one hapless citizen named Dean Osgood somehow bought a residence on 39th Street, not far from the Metropolitan Opera House, without realizing that his block was thick with prostitutes. The scales fell from his eyes when he looked out his rear window one night and saw women dancing naked in the window of a building across the street, one of a dozen brothels in the vicinity. This cluster of bordellos on West 39th was known as "Soubrette Row" and was notorious throughout the city for its French madams and Parisian-style decor. (A *soubrette* was a coquettish young woman featured in many stage comedies of the era.)

By 1901, the appellation of Soubrette Row had moved uptown to West 43rd Street, where "The Little Tramp" had the misfortune of lodging and where almost every brownstone was a brothel. In 1896, the state of New York had inadvertently encouraged prostitution by enacting a new law that attempted to throttle the proliferation of saloons by restricting Sunday liquor sales to hotels with ten or more beds. Saloon owners simply divided their upstairs quarters into little rooms, thus adding about 10,000 bedrooms to Manhattan's total. This not only entitled them to continue selling booze on Sundays but also enabled them to diversify into the prostitution racket. Madams of upscale brothels disdained these so-called Raines Law hotels as "charity cases," but they attracted plenty of business. In addition, many of the Great White Way's cut-rate tourist hotels were operated as thinly disguised whorehouses. The Garrick, Valko, and Metropole Hotels—all of which were situated at the confluence of 42nd, Seventh Avenue, and Broadway—housed from sixteen to twenty prostitutes apiece. The Delevan down on 40th Street, a favorite of "sporting men and race track toughs," employed thirty prostitutes.

Once the sun set, all of the theater district's principal thoroughfares—42nd Street, Broadway, and Sixth, Seventh, and Eighth Avenues—crawled with streetwalkers. "Broadway was the avenue favored by streetwalkers, but only of the most expensive kind, and it was *de rigueur* not to solicit. The woman would linger at a shop window and wait for a man to approach with the formulaic come-on, 'Anything doing tonight, dearie?'" Meanwhile, less affluent ladies of the evening were blatantly on the make on the margins of the Great White Way. At the Hotel Lyceum on 45th Street, the resident hookers could be seen leaning half-naked out of the windows to solicit business. The Eighth Avenue end of the 42nd Street theater block was part of a red-light subdistrict known for its black prostitutes, many of whom were aggressive to the point of intimidation in soliciting trade. As one resident of the area complained, "Numerous colored women walk up and down the street, blocking the passage of white men and boys, and in some cases force them into the gutter."

The theater industry had expanded greatly as it progressed up Broadway from 14th Street to 42nd Street and Times Square, feeding an ever-expanding, ready-made supply of new johns to the city's appreciative pimps and madams. Broadway also inadvertently supplied the sex trade with an increasing number of prostitutes, thanks to the "cult of the chorus girl," which took hold just as the theater frontier was reaching 42nd Street. In the 1890s, a group of talented and ambitious Rialto producers and choreographers led by Rudolph Aaronson, George Lederer, and Julian Mitchell had created elaborate productions featuring chorus girls that had been primarily selected for their beauty. Broadway's press agents saw to it that the collective fame of Aaronson's "Casino Girls" and Mitchell's "Weber and Fields Girls" rivaled that of such individual stars as Lillie Langtry and even the great Sarah Bernhardt. "More than any figure on the American stage at the turn of the century, it was the chorus girl who fascinated the American public. . . . What particularly dominated all discussions of the chorus girl was the world of glamour in which she lived." Or, as press agent Nellie Revell noted, "The words 'chorus girl' evoke in the average mind outside the profession visions of limousines, diamonds, gorgeous furs, champagne parties, and wealthy admirers."

The Casino Theater on Broadway at 39th Street became the central shine of the chorus girl cult with the opening of Lederer's *Florodora* in 1900. The enormous popularity of this lavish trifle of a musical comedy was the product of a single scene in which six handsome swains serenade six fashionably attired beauties. "Tell me, pretty maiden, are there any more at home like you?" the men sang in unison while they paraded the ladies around the stage. "There are a few, kind sir, but simple girls, and proper, too," they responded, with a coquettish twirl of their parasols. Before exiting, each girl tossed a nod, a smile, and a wink to the audience. This last bit was "the fire that provides the flame," according to one student of the *Florodora* phenomenon. "Intimate formality of this kind has heretofore been unknown in musical comedy—usually girls of the chorus smile brightly over the heads of the audience."

Celebrated men-about-town like Diamond Jim Brady, Frederick Gebhard, and Stanford White ordered standing tickets and often used them during *Florodora*'s five-hundred-performance run. White, whose notoriety as a Broadway playboy nearly equaled his fame as an architect, attended the musical forty nights in a row. Each of the famous six were deluged with flowers, jewelry, and dinner invitations from wealthy admirers, as were many other lesser members of the *Florodora* chorus. "Outside the stage door, they waited in droves—old roués, young blades, romantic college boys down from New Haven and Cambridge, and even staid businessmen," recalled Evelyn Nesbit, who was just fifteen years old when she joined the *Florodora* chorus in 1901. "Leaving the theater to reach a waiting conveyance, a girl had to run the gauntlet of admiring males. . . . Need I hesitate to confess that I loved the adulation of the stage door 'johnnies'? All the girls got a kick out of it."

All of the original members of the *Florodora* sextette played the field avidly, appearing nearly as often at Rector's as they did at the Casino. Marie Wilson parlayed a stock market tip from one of J. P. Morgan's partners into a $750,000 windfall and then married Gebhard. Within a year of the show's opening, all six girls had married millionaires, a nephew of Andrew Carnegie among them. They were easily replaced, for their roles required an abundance of beauty but not a lot of talent, and pretty young girls by the hundreds were pouring into New York from the provinces in hopes of landing a job in a Broadway chorus line.

Needless to say, most of these would-be Cinderellas never made it to the ball. As Theodore Dreiser wrote in *Sister Carrie*, the story of an ingenue's rise from the chorus to stardom, "Girls who can stand in line and look pretty are as numerous as laborers who can swing a pick." For every aspirant who made it into *Florodora* or a less-celebrated Broadway chorus line, there were hundreds more who failed their every audition. Only some of them returned to Dubuque or Walla Walla or Tallahassee or wherever it was they had come from. By 1904, some 10,000 unemployed would-be chorus girls thronged the theater district. An unknown but no doubt substantial percentage of these young women found themselves turning tricks in Times Square rooming houses and hotels as they dreamed their wasting dreams of stage glamour and lobster palace romance. The theater's loss, if a loss it was, was the Churchill Hotel's gain. Operated by a former police sergeant, this 130-room establishment on

46th Street near Broadway employed some twenty underemployed actresses and chorus girls as prostitutes.

Not that a place in the chorus line and a table at Rector's guaranteed a happily-ever-after either. Prince Charmings were in short supply among the Lotharios of the lobster palace society. What wealthy men-about-town sought along the Great White Way was not love and marriage (many of them already *were* married) but a good time. Most of the wealthy socialites who seduced young actresses and chorus girls in the private dining rooms of the lobster palaces would not have dreamed of bringing their Broadway paramours back with them as they made the rounds on the Fifth Avenue side of Manhattan's great social divide. In this sense, the quintessential turn-of-the-century 42nd Street chorus girl was not Marie Wilson nor any of the other lucky *Florodora* Cinderellas, but Evelyn Nesbit, the ill-starred "Girl on the Red Velvet Swing." Nesbit starred in a 42nd Street love story for the ages, a sordid tale of money, madness, and murder—and a whole lot of lobsters.

Nesbit had grown up in Pittsburgh, the daughter of a lawyer. She was eight years old when her father died. His widow, Elizabeth, tried to make a go of it by taking in boarders but soon lost the family home and was reduced to begging alms at the doors of mansions. Evelyn was an exceptionally pretty girl, with delicate features, olive skin, and a perfect oval face framed by a cascade of thick, copper-colored curls. She so perfectly embodied the age's ideal of feminine innocence that at age fourteen she found herself in demand as an artist's model. In 1900, mother and daughter moved to New York, where Elizabeth hoped to find work as a seamstress. The widow Nesbit struggled, but young Evelyn was busier than ever posing. Soon she attracted the attention of a theatrical agent, who arranged for her to try out for a part as a Spanish dancer in *Florodora*.

Backstage at the Casino, the other girls nicknamed Evelyn "Baby" and "The Kid" and censored their conversations when she was in the room, shielding their underage colleague from the Broadway facts of life. "A girl my age *had* to possess the virtue of sex ignorance or she was not respectable," Nesbit wrote in her memoirs. Evelyn's ignorance survived her first visit to Rector's, though her innocence seemed to be fraying. The precocious chorine could not decide which was the greater thrill, "supping at Rector's, or having so many men of the world regarding me with evident admiration. For you see, I was beginning to take a keen delight in such adulation and the pleasurable knowledge that men considered me a theatrical beauty." Mrs. Nesbit allowed her daughter to accept the occasional luncheon or yachting invitation but always accompanied her as chaperone, until the fateful day that Evelyn met Stanford White.

At forty-seven, White had cut a wide swath through Gilded Age Manhattan. A prominent figure in civic affairs and high society alike, he was a tall, powerfully built man with flaming red hair and a boundless supply of energy. He had built many mansions and private clubs for the rich as well as such public landmarks as Washington Square Arch and Judson Memorial Church. The architect's signature creation was Madison Square Garden on Fifth Avenue at 26th Street. Completed in 1890, the original Madison Square Garden, like Hammerstein's Olympia, was a colossal amusement palace for the masses, with a theater, a concert hall, and a roof garden to go along with its 14,000-seat arena. Atop the Garden, White built an enormous tower containing seven private offices, one of which he commandeered for use as a personal party pad. "Stannie" White was a gregarious and generous man who routinely donated large sums to the needy, but he also was a voluptuary who exploited the double standard of lobster palace society with ruthless profligacy. Securely if not quite happily married, White maintained his wife and son in a mansion on Long Island while making use of his Madison Square Garden lair and the lobster palaces to romance Broadway ingenues by the dozen.

White's conquests included Edna Goodrich, a *Florodora* girl who took Evelyn Nesbit under her wing. One day in August 1901 Goodrich convinced Mrs. Nesbit to let Evelyn come along with her to lunch with a society gentleman. To Evelyn's surprise, Edna took her to a dingy commercial building on West 24th Street, where White maintained a luxurious studio hideaway. After lunch, Stanford took Edna and Evelyn upstairs to a studio with etchings of nude women on the walls and a red velvet swing hanging from a vaulted ceiling. "Let's put the little kid in the swing first," White said.

Smitten, the architect met with Mrs. Nesbit and offered to take mother and daughter under his wing. At White's expense, the Nesbits moved out of their rooming house and into the Audubon Hotel, conveniently located across Broadway from the Casino Theater. White sent flowers daily and opened a bank account for the Nesbits, depositing a tidy sum each week. One afternoon, with Evelyn's mother conveniently out of town, White brought the girl to his 24th Street loft, filled her with champagne, and raped her in a room with mirrored walls. Back at the Audubon, Evelyn sat up in a chair all that night and into the next afternoon, trying to reconcile the conflicting emotions that assailed her. In the end, she convinced herself that she had fallen "head over heels" in love with White and naively assumed that the feeling was mutual. White moved the Nesbits into a finer hotel a bit uptown and decorated their suite himself, swathing it in white satin. For Christmas—which also was Evelyn's seventeenth birthday—White gave her a pearl necklace, a set of white-fox furs, a ruby-and-diamond ring, and two solitaire-diamond rings.

Nesbit attracted many other admirers. A half dozen millionaires proposed marriage to her, including producer George Lederer himself. After *Florodora* ended its long run, Lederer cast Evelyn as a gypsy girl in *The Wild Rose*, telling her that she had inspired the musical's title. In a futile attempt to make White jealous, Nesbit dated several of the "Racquet Club boys," including Monty Waterbury, a dashing polo player. One night, several of the boys entertained her in a private room at Rector's, complete with a "coloured" orchestra. "It was loads of fun," Nesbit recalled. Waterbury "sat me on a chair behind a screen, stood on a chair on the other side, and fed me blue points over the top."

Nesbit's most persistent pursuer was Harry Thaw, a nouveau riche playboy from Pittsburgh who was infamous in lobster palace society for his extravagant presents to chorus girls, his hair-trigger temper, and his sadomasochistic proclivities. Thaw had sent flowers anonymously to Nesbit but first approached her at Rector's, glaring at her wild-eyed. "Why does your mother permit you to know that beast?" Thaw demanded.

"That beast?" she replied. "What on earth are you talking about?"

"Stanford White."

Nesbit came to understand that "hatred of Stanford White burned in [Thaw's] twisted brain" long before she met the architect. White had crossed Thaw off his guest list after he had behaved boorishly at one of his parties at Madison Square Garden, and also had blackballed him at a club. Just before Thaw had begun his pursuit of Nesbit, he had suffered a fresh humiliation that he blamed on White. A group of *Florodora* girls had agreed to join Thaw and some society chums at Sherry's only to stand him up and go to a party at White's instead. The gossip columns added to his humiliation. "*Florodora* beauties sing for their supper in White's studio," read one headline, "while Thaw's orchestra fiddles to an empty room at Sherry's."

As White gradually lost interest in Nesbit, Thaw redoubled his efforts. When White the architect failed to invite Nesbit to his annual Christmas Eve party in the tower in 1903, she let Thaw take her to Rector's to celebrate. Thaw and Nesbit made a grand tour of Europe in the summer of 1904 and were wed the following spring.

Nesbit retired from the stage and lived—unhappily—with her husband and his domineering mother in the Thaw family mansion in Pittsburgh. By the end of the first summer, Harry was back to biting his nails and railing against White. In June 1906, the Thaws decided to sail to England and moved into a New York hotel for a two-week stay prior to their departure. As usual, Harry was having his wife followed by detectives at all times. On the morning of June 25, Evelyn went to see a doctor for a sore throat and happened to bump into White, who hugged her and wished her well. That evening, Harry surprised Evelyn by suggesting that they take in "Mamzelle Champagne" at the roof garden of Madison Square Garden, after dining at Café Martin on Fifth Avenue. In the middle of dinner, Nesbit saw White walk through the restaurant and take a seat on the balcony. Thaw, whose back was to the room, did not see his nemesis. But as soon as White departed, Nesbit slipped her husband a note. "The B——— was here, but has left."

By the time that White arrived at the roof garden, "Mamzelle Champagne" was well under way. To the appropriate strains of the song "I Could Love a Thousand Girls," White made his way up the aisle to his front-row table, recalled one biographer. "His passage to his table was typical of him, half-ramble, half-stride, nodding to his friends on the way, a personal word to a group along his path, a wave to another table too far to reach, a star of Broadway brighter than any of those performing on the stage." Sometime during the second act, Thaw materialized at White's table. He pulled a revolver from under his coat, waited until the architect looked his way, and pumped three bullets between his eyes. Later, when Evelyn was allowed in to see her husband at the police station, she kissed him frantically, saying, "My God, Harry, you killed him!" and "Kiss me."

The Manhattan district attorney wanted to indict Evelyn along with Harry, reasoning that by inciting her deranged husband to violence she had conspired to rid herself of him and take revenge against White in one fell swoop. But as Nesbit became an object of fervent public sympathy, the DA decided he might well lose at trial. Thaw was acquitted in 1908 but locked away in an asylum for the criminally insane. Although Evelyn had testified on her husband's behalf, his mother soon cut off her allowance. Mrs. Thaw's lawyer told Evelyn that her mother-in-law hoped that "you will land in the gutter and thereby gain sympathy for her son."

The tactic almost worked. There is no indication that Nesbit ever resorted to prostitution to make ends meet. But by 1912, she was drinking heavily and living in a scuzzy apartment on Broadway, just a few blocks from Rector's. She was twenty-seven years old and seemingly without prospects. But if 42nd Street had conspired in the ruin of The Girl on the Red Velvet Swing, now 42nd Street raised her up again.

At a party at the Café de l'Opera given by *Follies* producer Flo Ziegfeld, godfather of Broadway chorus girls, Nesbit met a lawyer who invited her to sail with him to Paris on an extended business trip in the spring of 1913. On the boat, Nesbit met a top theatrical agent, who signed her to appear in *Hello, Ragtime!*, a hit revue at the London Hippodrome. Nesbit was not much in either the song or dance department, but she still had her looks, and her notoriety as "the woman in the case" played at the box office. Arthur Hammerstein, Oscar's son and now a producer in his own right, saw *Hello, Ragtime!* and signed Nesbit to appear at the Victoria Theater, leaving it to brother Willie to figure out how to contrive a solo act from her paltry talents.

As usual, Willie started with the publicity, planting stories about Nesbit's return to 42nd Street at the stunning salary of $3,500 a week. For the second time in six years, her photographs appeared in newspapers all over the country. Was Nesbit a "vamp" or a "damsel in distress"? Enquiring minds had to know. Her act, consisting of three routine dances performed with a professional hoofer named Jack Clifford, lasted a mere eight minutes, but *Variety* was kind: "She was dressed in a filmy, transparent, yellow ankle-length dress, her hair hanging down her back. . . . Clifford lifted Miss Nesbit above his head and whirled about a few times. After the third number she clung around his neck while he swung her. It's a nice little act if you don't stop to analyze it too closely."

Two weeks into Evelyn's Broadway run, Harry Thaw provided Willie with one of the great promotional opportunities of his career. Through a plot hatched at Shanley's, the 42nd Street lobster palace, a West Side gangster arranged for Thaw to escape from the Matteawan insane asylum in upstate New York. Willie promptly issued a press release announcing that Thaw had sent him a telegram threatening to kill Nesbit, to whom he was married still. (The couple would not divorce until 1915, when Mother Thaw got her son declared sane and released from Matteawan.) To give credence to the ruse, Hammerstein hired security guards to accompany his star, who was genuinely alarmed until the police informed her that they had tracked her husband to Canada. Ziegfeld had champagne waiting for Nesbit in her dressing room on opening night. "Though he and [Oscar] Hammerstein were not friends," she recalled, "they forgot their differences for the time being while we celebrated." Nesbit drew sell-out crowds for six weeks, establishing her as the most profitable freak act ever to appear at Hammerstein's. On the strength of her run at the Corner, Nesbit toured America as a vaudeville headliner for two years and went on to win a series of silent film roles, usually playing a beautiful but tragically misunderstood ingenue.

Nesbit's appearance at the Victoria was one of Willie Hammerstein's last triumphs. In June 1914, he died at age forty of Bright's disease. Hammerstein's Victoria perished soon after, a victim not only of Willie's passing, but also of intensifying competition from motion pictures and from the Palace, a colossal new vaudeville house on 47th Street. In a bizarrely tragic twist of fate, Arthur Hammerstein, who briefly succeeded Willie as the Victoria's manager, was the only one of Oscar's four sons to live out the year 1914. Oscar's youngest, Abraham, was found dead in a hotel room in mysterious circumstances never explained. Harry, the eldest, died of complications caused by diabetes. Oscar, sixty-eight years old now and afflicted with diabetes himself, had never been a family man; his children had barely known him until they were grown. But he was devastated just the same. The day after Willie's funeral, a reporter encountered a dazed-looking Oscar in the Victoria's lobby. "In my life I have experienced every great joy, every triumph, every success, every honor that can be won by a man single-handed. But I have also experienced every disappointment, every grief and every tragedy. But this. . . ."

About a year before he died, Willie had clashed bitterly with his father after Oscar sold the family's exclusive vaudeville booking rights to Times Square—the bulwark of the Victoria's prosperity—back to B. F. Keith and E. F. Albee. Oscar got $250,000, which he desperately needed for his latest opera project. Buying out Hammerstein enabled Keith and

Albee to wrest control of the Palace from its builder, Martin Beck of the Orpheum Circuit, before the theater opened in March 1913. The Palace was far larger than the Victoria and more elegantly appointed, in crimson and gold. Even so, the Keith Circuit's new flagship got off to a dismal start. The Palace's top ticket price of $2 was double Hammerstein's and yet its bills were considerably shorter and, in the consensus view, of lesser quality as well. But Keith and Albee persisted in their attempts to take vaudeville upscale, and in the Palace's second season it began attracting the same genteel crowd that patronized Broadway's theaters and also started cutting into the Victoria's gate. Arthur Hammerstein, whose forte as a producer was operetta, did not care much for vaudeville and had no feel for what played at the box office. "Arthur tried to keep it going for awhile, but it wouldn't work," recalled Loney Haskell, the longtime Victoria master of ceremonies. "The old-timers missed the hand of Willie."

In 1915, Oscar sold the Victoria to the Rialto Corporation, which planned to tear the theater down and build a movie palace in its place. Oscar finally retired from show business, moving out of his studio in the Victoria—his "machine-shop," as he called it—into a newly purchased house in New Jersey. Oscar billed the acts for the Victoria's final week as "Willie's Old Favorites." Attendance for this farewell tribute to Willie and the Corner was only "fair," *Billboard* noted in its review. "The customary crowd that gets up during the last act, from force of habit, didn't get up, and the reason for this was the thirteen-minute Charlie Chaplin film"—*Twenty Minutes of Love.*

Movies were 42nd Street's future, but they had coexisted with vaudeville and the theater from the beginning of the street's emergence as New York City's new entertainment hub. Like other vaudeville venues, the Victoria initially had used short films as a "chaser" to clear the house after the show had ended. But as advances in filmmaking technology gave birth to the "photo play," or story film, movies became an attraction in their own right, and the Victoria gave motion pictures a standard "turn" of fifteen or twenty minutes on most every bill. The eight-minute movie acclaimed as the first story film, *The Great Robbery,* made its New York debut at the Victoria in 1903. Later, the Hammersteins also presented a documentary film about the 1908 New York–Paris auto race, which had begun in front of the Victoria.

The first theater on 42nd Street expressly designed for movies was the Bryant, which opened in 1910 at 223 West 42nd, on the site of what had been a coal and wood yard. The Bryant had just three hundred seats and fell far short of the new standards of movie house elegance set by other theaters opening in the city and around the country. The new theater fared poorly until its owners began interspersing feature films with small-time vaudeville acts. The same policy was applied on a much larger scale at the American Music Hall after Marcus Loew, the king of "small-time" vaudeville in New York, gained control of 42nd Street's first theater in 1911. Loew presented at least three shows a day, charging bargain-price admissions of just five cents to twenty-five cents. Unlike Loew, who went on to build a major chain of movie theaters, the Hammersteins did not give movies equal billing with live acts. But in the winter of 1910–11, they did rent out the Victoria's roof garden to film exhibitors for use as a temporarily winterized movie theater.

In 1912, the film mogul Adolph Zukor rented the Lyceum Theater at Broadway and 45th Street for the premiere of *Queen Elizabeth,* which was the film debut of the great stage actress Sarah Bernhardt and the first feature-length film seen in America. This event legitimized the motion picture in the eyes of many Times Square and 42nd Street theater owners and producers, who increasingly showed special feature films to plug the gaps in their play schedules. Meanwhile, the rise of the movies brought a new group of managers and producers thronging to 42nd Street. They came to scout talent of all kinds—writing, directing, designing, and performing—on display before the live audiences of the theater district. Famous Players-Lasky and some other film production companies produced live shows in their own Times Square theaters and then made them into films in studios located in the Hell's Kitchen industrial district west of Eighth Avenue. Although the locus of film production would shift to Hollywood before the decade's end, many movie companies would maintain offices in the Times Square area for years. Scores of new film companies moved into the Candler Building, a handsome terra-cotta skyscraper that opened in 1914 at 220 West 42nd. At twenty-four stories, the Candler towered over every other building on the 42nd Street theater block.

By the mid-1910s, eight theaters on Broadway had converted into movie houses. In 1914, David Belasco infuriated Oscar Hammerstein by subleasing the Republic Theater to a movie production company for what was to be a short run of films. Hammerstein sued Belasco, arguing that exhibiting movies at the Republic would have "a deteriorating effect on the theater's reputation and value." Numerous films played the Republic as the two flamboyant impresarios fought a protracted legal battle. In the end, the court granted Hammerstein an injunction on the narrow grounds that motion pictures posed an additional fire hazard. Stung, Belasco gave up his lease, ending his twelve-year tenure on 42nd Street on a bitter note. Hammerstein had defeated Belasco but now understood that there was no beating back the popularity of motion pictures. He did not utter so much as a peep of protest when his new tenant at the Republic, theatrical producer Al Woods, subleased the theater to a film company.

Hammerstein's decision to close down the Victoria coincided with a landmark event in film history: the premiere of D. W. Griffith's *The Birth of a Nation*, at the Liberty Theater on 42nd Street. This twelve-reel, two-and-a-half-hour Civil War epic was the first cinematic blockbuster, the breakthrough film that caused movies to be taken seriously. (Of course, by today's standards, it also was a blatantly racist film.)

Out in Southern California, meanwhile, a handful of farsighted and ruthless film moguls was consolidating the disparate facets of film production and distribution into fully integrated studio companies of national scope. In the mid-1910s, these upstart Hollywood studios constructed dozens of palatial new movie theaters in New York and many other big cities across the country to build a mass audience. Technically speaking, the movie palace was a luxury theater with at least 1,500 seats that presented motion pictures in tandem with live stage entertainment. Movie palaces used a hodgepodge of classical architectural styles and design motifs in the service of deliberate visual overstimulation. Movie palaces were to the silent film what Broadway lobster palaces were to gourmet cuisine: entertainment venues of such overwhelming lavishness and theatricality that they were a show unto themselves.

The movie palace was largely a product of the fevered imagination of one man, Samuel Rothapfel. "Roxy," as he was known, took no interest in film as entertainment, as art, or as anything else except as a vehicle of his own razzle-dazzle showmanship. After founding his own little movie house in Pennsylvania and helping the nation's largest chain of vaudeville theaters incorporate motion pictures into its programs, Rothapfel came to New York in 1913. The city's first deluxe movie theater, the Regent, had just opened in Harlem on 116th Street. Roxy transformed the Regent from a white elephant into a money machine by refining the way it presented films in a hundred little ways, from lowering the projection booth to installing a red velvet curtain to cover the screen between features. Most important, he doubled the size of the theater's orchestra and expanded its repertoire in service of his revolutionary theory that musical accompaniment for a film should be tailored to fit the action on the screen.

But like Hammerstein before him, Rothapfel had ambitions larger than Harlem. In 1914, he was hired by the owners of a huge 2,800-seat theater under construction at Broadway and 47th Street and given carte blanche to devise what was to be New York's first true movie palace. This was the Strand and it was a sensation, attracting 40,000 patrons during its first week. After running the Strand for a year, the restless Rothapfel moved five blocks down Broadway to 42nd Street and helped create New York's second movie palace—the Rialto—on the corner made famous by Hammerstein's Victoria.

The Rialto opened in April 1916 as a showcase for the films of the Mutual Film Corporation. Touted by Rothapfel as a "Temple of the Motion Picture—Shrine of Music and the Allied Arts," the Rialto did indeed become a legend in its own right. The most distinctive of its features was what it lacked: a stage. "Even the Strand is built so that at very short notice it could be converted to the uses of opera or drama, but the Rialto is a motion picture house pure and simple," the *Times* noted. "It is stageless, the screen being placed boldly against the back wall of the theater."

A motion picture house it was indeed, but there was nothing "pure and simple" about Rothapfel's blending of film with live musical entertainment. The opening night's program began with a rendition of "The Star-Spangled Banner" and an overture performed by the Rialto orchestra and sixteen vocalists in white duck sailor suits. After a brief newsreel featuring the Rialto ushers drilling on the theater's roof, a female singer appeared on a platform flanking the movie screen and sang two songs. She was followed by a dancer who performed a classical piece on the opposite platform and a "scenic" film of a visit to Venice, site of the original Rialto. After a solo violin performance, the feature picture was shown, a western called *The Good Bad Man,* starring Douglas Fairbanks (who had acted in many a play on 42nd Street). When it finished, a noted baritone sang two classical songs and joined the Rialto Quartette in a musical comedy number. The show closed with a Keystone comedy, *The Other Man*, starring Fatty Arbuckle, accompanied at thundering volume on the Rialto organ.

With 2,000 seats, the Rialto was not as big as the Strand, but it was even better equipped. Its advertisements boasted of "The World's Largest Grand Organ—Superb Concert Orchestra—Most Wonderful System of Electrical Effects Ever Installed in Any Theatre—15c—25c—50c—No Higher." If anything, the ads underplayed the virtues of the Rialto's orchestra, which was the largest in New York City except for the Metropolitan Opera's, and its lighting system. Banks of light in rainbow hues were concealed in the ledges around the domed ceiling above the stage, behind columns, and behind translucent panels set in the walls and ceiling. Dimmers controlled them so that each scene of a movie could be given its own color scheme as well as its own music. This innovative system of "color harmonies" became one of the 42nd Street palace's most talked-about features, as did its corps of a hundred ushers attired in scarlet tunics piped in gold and looped across in front with thick gold braids and tassels. Each of the Rialto's ushers carried a swagger stick with a mother-of-pearl tip that lit up in the dark. The head usher carried a bugle, purely for show.

Oscar Hammerstein, who died in 1919, was the first of two towering figures who dominated 42nd Street's Golden Age. The second, Florenz Ziegfeld Jr., was a man of much narrower talent than Times Square's progenitor, but he achieved an even greater and more durable fame. Unlike Hammerstein, who was a good twenty-three years his senior, Ziegfeld did not build theaters, write music, or invent ingenious gadgets. He was all about "the Great Big Show." Working mainly out of the New Amsterdam, Ziegfeld embodied impassioned showmanship to a degree that has never been equaled in the American musical theater. Ziegfeld was "utterly devoid of intellect . . ." according to biographer Charles Higham. "His driving force was one of demonic sensuality and a passion for vivid artifice. From the very beginning his stage productions were direct expressions of his essentially primitive sexual character. He was at once witch doctor and organizer of tribal dances. The *Follies* were an astonishing demonstration of the mind of a man who sought to release his need for women in displays of adulation." The *Follies,* Ziegfeld's signature creation, completed the apotheosis of the showgirl into stage deity and stands to this day as the apogee of Broadway glamour.

Ziegfeld's avowed ambition was "to glorify the American girl." In a sense, though, the "Great Glorifier" was his own grandest creation. Inspired artiste and cold-hearted despot, incurable romantic and serial philanderer, showman and introvert, Ziegfeld was the Broadway mogul writ large as a 42nd Street marquee. With his narrow face, large nose, and overbite, he looked a bit rodentlike, and according to *Follies* star Fanny Brice, a superb mimic, he spoke in a "twangy, whiny voice—even I have never been able to imitate it." Yet Ziegfeld was the great Broadway ladies' man of his generation, at once irresistible and infuriating to beautiful women. He lived like a pasha, employing five chauffeurs to drive him in his five Rolls-Royce sedans, each a different color. He stockpiled Guerlain eau de cologne by the case, in bottles so large that they frequently were mistaken for bootleg liquor, and gave Patricia, his only child, a baby elephant and a diamond tiara. Ziegfeld had three gold telephones on his desk but preferred to communicate with lesser mortals— including actors at rehearsal—through the drama of the telegram. Ziegfeld feared a dwarf named Shorty, but considered thirteen his lucky number. Like Hammerstein, he made millions of dollars and died broke.

Born in Chicago in 1867, Ziegfeld grew up straddling the disparate realms of high and low culture. His father, Florenz Ziegfeld Sr., was a conservatory-trained pianist who had immigrated to the United States from Germany at age twenty-one and made his fortune as the owner-proprietor of Chicago's finest music school. A polished and dignified-looking man whose peremptory manner was leavened with flashes of charm, Flo Sr. was a shameless social climber who never earned a Ph.D. but called himself "Doctor Ziegfeld" anyway. An indifferent student himself, Flo Jr. went to work for his father after he finished high school, but he chafed under his father's Old World values and came to loathe the sound of classical music. He loved to dance and was good enough to win contests. Taking full advantage of his father's connections and his own glib charm, Flo Jr. romanced the daughters of the Chicago aristocracy at fancy balls and cotillions. But he also haunted the city's music halls and burlesque venues, developing a special fascination for Buffalo Bill's Wild West Show.

Flo Jr.'s talent at last began to manifest itself with the opening of the

Columbian Exposition in Chicago in 1893. His father was appointed chairman of the jury of piano and organ awards and helped book European performers into the Exposition. The elder Ziegfeld also tried to turn a profit by opening a music venue of his own, the Trocadero, to present some of the same acts performing at the Exposition. Flo Sr. sent his son to New York and to Europe to sign talent. At the Casino Theater (the future home of *Florodora*), Flo Jr. happened on the act that would make a financial success of the Trocadero and launch his own career in show business: "Sandow the Great," a German-born strong man. Ziegfeld bought out Sandow's contract and brought him to Chicago. Sandow was genuinely a man of Herculean strength, but Ziegfeld shrewdly spiced up his muscleman's act with sex appeal and novelty. Instead of the customary leopard skin, Sandow wore tight silk shorts and covered his body in bronze makeup to set off his blond hair in the spotlight. Dispensing with the usual flexing and barbell hoisting, the German lifted a man in the palm of his hand, bent an iron poker, and opened a safe with his teeth, among other crowd-pleasing stunts.

When the Exposition closed, Ziegfeld took Sandow and a troupe of second-string acts on the road, touring the United States and Europe through 1895. Flo's next discovery was Anna Held, the Dolly Parton of the European music hall circuit. Held was a French chanteuse of strong voice, outsized vivacity, and a voluptuous, hourglass figure. Ziegfeld first met her by bribing his way into her dressing room at the Palace Theatre in London. "It was like nitro meeting glycerin," wrote Held's biographer. Ziegfeld charmed the young singer into breaking a pending engagement at the Folies-Bergère in Paris and coming with him to New York to make her Broadway debut. Held was a hit, coyly singing such numbers as "Won't You Come and Play with Me?" and "I Just Can't Make My Eyes Behave" in heavily accented English.

Ziegfeld and his star fell in love but could not marry because Held already had a husband—a French playboy who would not give her a divorce. One night at a dinner party, Ziegfeld and Held rose, toasted each other with champagne, and declared that as far as they were concerned they were married. Under New York State common law, their marriage became legal in 1904, after seven years of cohabitation. By this time, Ziegfeld was in his midthirties and had staged a dozen Broadway plays, but he had attained no noteworthy success apart from Held, now firmly established as one of the brightest stars of the American stage. He was, in fact, "merely a dim satellite of Anna Held. His name was still misspelled in the press as often as not, and when he was mentioned, it was always as [Held's] husband and manager."

Ziegfeld's career did not gain traction until he aligned himself with the Theatrical Syndicate in 1906. The following year Abe Erlanger hired him at the modest salary of $200 a week to produce summer vaudeville shows in the roof garden of the New York Theater, formerly part of Hammerstein's Olympia. It was here that the *Follies* made its modest debut in July 1907. Ziegfeld was not the first producer to adapt the format of the Parisian revue to the Broadway stage, but he did so with panache. *The Follies of 1907* played through the summer on the roof, which was renamed the Jardin de Paris for the occasion, and then moved down to street level at the Liberty Theater on 42nd Street before going on the road. The show was a hit, returning a hefty profit of $120,000 on the $16,800 invested by Erlanger and two partners. For each of the next four summers, new annual editions of the revue (first called Ziegfeld's *Follies* in 1911) opened on the New York roof garden, an increasingly inadequate venue. Its stage was too small and shallow to contain Ziegfeld's theatrical imagination, and its glass-domed roof alternately leaked rain and concentrated the sun like a magnifying glass.

In 1913, Erlanger booked the *Follies* into his flagship theater on 42nd Street, the New Amsterdam, signaling its arrival as a big-time Broadway franchise. The show's move into the Great White Way's most technically sophisticated theater coincided with Ziegfeld's ascension from employee to co-owner of Ziegfeld Follies Inc. Ziegfeld held the top title of president in the new company and drew 50 percent of the profits, to Erlanger's 25 percent and Klaw's 25 percent. Between 1913 and 1927, thirteen editions of the Ziegfeld *Follies* would debut in the main auditorium of the New Amsterdam, contributing mightily to 42nd Street's racily glamorous image. At the same time, Ziegfeld made inspired use of its roof theater, turning it into an elegant posttheater cabaret featuring its own revue, *The Ziegfeld Midnight Frolic,* which ran year-round in seventeen editions from 1915 through 1922. The *Follies* and the *Frolic* were separate but overlapping shows, sharing many writers, choreographers, and performers along with "the Ziegfeld touch."

Most Broadway musicals started with a script or a score, but Ziegfeld usually began with a bevy of beauties and took it from there. He had a very precise notion of the ideal female figure: 36-inch bust, 26-inch waist, and 38-inch hips. But Ziegfeld girls came in three basic varieties, according to the writer J. P. McEvoy, who worked on the *Follies* for a time and described a typical rehearsal in his novel *Show Girl:* "Tall blondes with complexions like fresh cream and hair like twenty-dollar gold pieces and those yellow green eyes like tigers in the zoo have on Sunday when they don't feed 'em. And running all around under them little brunette dancers with legs like acrobats—and perched on a line of chairs against the wall, a lot of those slim, slender-legged young things looking boyish and silky at the same time."

Ziegfeld required his showgirls—the tall blonde contingent—to project a quality of reserve that bordered on hauteur. "Deliciously robotic creatures," they paraded to and fro using a special erect, sliding step, as if they were making their way across a tightrope. Smiling was frowned upon; the legendary Dolores, acclaimed as "the loveliest showgirl in the world" and whose last name Ziegfeld never disclosed, did not crack a smile once in her decade in the *Follies.* "A pretty girl is like a melody that haunts you night and day," Irving Berlin wrote in the ballad—"A Pretty Girl Is Like a Melody"—that Ziegfeld commissioned in 1919 and made the *Follies* theme song. "There are those today," a biographer observed in the late 1950s, "who never hear this hauntingly wistful tune without envisioning a woman of stately loveliness draped in chiffon and pearls, her long-legged beauty topped by a giant-size glittering headdress, moving slowly and beautifully across a stage or down a staircase."

The three thousand women who passed through the *Follies* and the *Frolic* over the years included such future stars of stage and screen as Louise Brooks, Ina Claire, Marion Davies, Billie Dove, Mae Murray, Irene Dunne, and Ann Pennington. But dozens of Ziegfeld's girls became the toast of New York at least fleetingly—feted, photographed, and pursued by latter-day Stanford Whites and Harry Thaws. After every *Follies* performance, limousines lined up outside the New Amsterdam's stage door on 41st Street, with Ziegfeld's chauffeur usually hovering at the back. Both of the producer's wives were actresses; he married Billie Burke in 1914, a year after he and Held divorced. He also had scores of indiscreet and often turbulent romances with *Follies* stars. When Ziegfeld first began seeing Burke, one of his mistresses pursued him up to the New Amsterdam roof wearing only a fur coat and threatened to flash the customers unless he dumped the actress. For her part, Burke couldn't help herself. "Even if I had known precisely what tortures and frustrations were in store for me during the next eighteen years because of this man, I should have kept right on falling in love," she recalled.

In Ziegfeld's hierarchy of theatrical values, clothes ranked just behind the girls who wore them. He worked much more closely with his costume designers than his writers or his choreographers in an effort to establish a distinctive look for each of the seventy-five to a hundred women who appeared in each edition of the *Follies*. "I have a natural knack of knowing what costume will be most becoming to each girl," he said. "I am able to design my own costumes and the girls learn that they attract more attention in my shows than in some others." In one of the most striking scenes in the Ziegfeld oeuvre, twelve showgirls paraded across the stage, each dressed as a different type of brightly plumed tropical bird. In the center was Dolores, who wore a pearl-trimmed white satin sheath with a ten-foot train embroidered with blue, green, and pink paillettes and bugle beads to resemble peacock feathers. For the finale, Dolores pulled on the sequined ropes attached to her train, which rose via a series of hidden pulleys to become an enormous fanned tail.

Ziegfeld spared no expense on costumes or on sets, which were often so dazzling as to provoke audiences to gasp upon first sight. The brilliant work of Ziegfeld's set designer, the Austrian-born artist and architect Josef Urban, was a revelation to New York theater audiences. Ziegfeld gave Urban free rein to design his sets before any other part of the production had been fixed. This allowed Urban to use visual leitmotivs and recurring patterns that brought unity to what otherwise might have seemed little more than a series of glorified vaudeville numbers.

The *Follies* and the *Frolic* closely mirrored Ziegfeld's personal taste in every way but one: the prominence they afforded comics. Understanding that audiences wanted their displays of pulchritude leavened with comedy, Ziegfeld grudgingly boosted the careers of many of the greatest comic performers of the era, among them Bert Williams, Leon Errol, Eddie Cantor, W. C. Fields, Ed Wynn, Will Rogers, and Fanny Brice. But he rarely joined in the laughter himself, unless it was Rogers onstage. "Half the comedians I've had in my shows that I paid a lot of money to and who made my customers shriek were not only not funny to me, but I couldn't understand why they seemed funny to anybody," Ziegfeld recalled late in his career. "But this Rogers, I never miss him if I can help it, though you'd be surprised how many of my expensive comics I've run out on and locked myself in my office when they were onstage." It was only when

Ziegfeld was talking about comics that he sounded like a cheapskate. In truth, he resented his comedians not because he had to pay them much more than the average chorine, but because they distracted the audience from its worshipful regard of his girls.

Ziegfeld took a particularly intense dislike to Bill Fields, a formidably irascible man in his own right. The comedian had a golf act that he wanted to use in the *Follies* of 1918. Ziegfeld reacted enthusiastically, predicting that it would be a hit. "There is only one little thing," the impresario added. "We have a beautiful yacht set, all full of beautiful girls. Now if you will only change your golf gag to a fishing gag it will be a sensation." Fields played along until the final rehearsal, when he did his golf act without alteration, marring Ziegfeld's magnificent set with its incongruity. "The act got over all right, but Ziggy was in tears," Fields recalled. "But he had to give in. He finally compromised. I could do the golf act, but he would have at least one girl in it. He would have one of his beauties walk across the stage, leading a Russian wolfhound. I knew that would ruin my part of the show completely, but I couldn't argue him out of it. To Ziggy, an act wasn't worth putting on unless he had one of his girls in it."

On opening night, Fields was halfway through his golf act when a gorgeous girl in costume walked on with a wolfhound. Fields waited until the intruders had exited, and said, "My, what a beautiful camel." The line got a huge laugh. Ziegfeld allowed the comic to keep it, much as it must have pained him to see one of his beauties made the butt of Fields's humor.

Ziegfeld sought revenge by assigning Harry Kelly, a famous *Follies* scene stealer, or "flycatcher," to fill the role of Fields's caddy for the golf scene. Fields tolerated Kelly's flycatching only briefly, literally punching him offstage after one performance at the New Amsterdam. "Give me anybody, anybody but Kelly," Fields roared, and then pointed at a stagehand named William Blanche, a dwarf with a huge head. "Shorty" Blanche nailed the caddy part and became Fields's onstage "stooge" and offstage assistant until the end of his Broadway days. It is unlikely that the comic selected Blanche knowing that Ziegfeld had a pathological fear of dwarves. But Fields realized soon enough that the best way to keep Ziegfeld at bay was to keep Shorty at his side. By some accounts, Ziegfeld screamed with rage whenever the dwarf came near his office.

Ironically, the greatest of all of the *Follies* stars was a woman who fell well short of Ziegfeld's ideals of female beauty: skinny-legged, thin-hipped, and plastic-faced Fanny Brice. Born Fannie Borach, daughter of a saloon keeper on Manhattan's Lower East Side, Brice is best remembered today as the subject of *Funny Girl,* the 1960s musical and movie that made a superstar of Barbra Streisand. In fact, Brice was more than Streisand's equal, being both an astonishingly expressive comedienne—"a cartoonist working in the flesh," as she put it herself—and a torch singer of the first rank.

Brice appeared in seven *Follies* from 1910 to 1923 and also starred on the New Amsterdam roof in several editions of the *Frolic.* Ziegfeld, ever the press agent, told reporters that he had discovered Brice selling newspapers under the Brooklyn Bridge. In truth, he found her in burlesque performing comic Yiddish songs. Just nineteen when Ziegfeld signed her to the *Follies,* Brice was overjoyed at her ascent into the rarefied realm of the Great White Way. After signing her first contract with Ziegfeld, Brice went to Broadway to "display it to the world," as she recalled. Standing either on the corner of 42nd or 47th Street, depending on the account, Brice showed her contract "to the cops on the beat, the professionals who passed, strangers." She thrust the paper into Irving Berlin's astonished face no less than five times and "before long it was in ribbons." Ziegfeld obliged her with another copy, which she also fondled to shreds.

Brice scored the greatest triumph of her long stage career in the 1921 *Follies,* with "My Man," a blues-tinged lover's lament that Ziegfeld had selected for her personally. "Do you think you can make them cry?" he asked, handing her the sheet music. As Ziegfeld well knew, Brice's rogue of a husband, the debonair gangster Nicky Arnstein, had just been sentenced to two years in Leavenworth Penitentiary. In rehearsal, Brice made her entrance in a red wig, wearing a black velvet dress and sparkling earrings. Complaining that she looked like a female impersonator, Ziegfeld sent one of his designers onstage with a pair of scissors. He cut Brice's skirt in half, tore it up the side, ripped her stockings, and smeared her with ashes. "Now, sing it," Ziegfeld commanded. Brice always sang "My Man" with her eyes closed, her right hand gripping her left arm. "Oh my man I love him so, you'll never know." Brice never cried, but many who heard her could not help but weep, the Great Glorifier included.

Last Suppers and Final Curtains

In commercializing sex to an unprecedented degree in the very heart of Manhattan, the creators of the Great White Way incited the city's self-appointed moral guardians to launch the first of many campaigns to "clean up" Times Square. Throughout the nineteenth century, New York's municipal government had made only token efforts to regulate public morality, periodically raiding the most disorderly brothels and saloons. Most high city officials simply did not see the prevalence of prostitution as a civic problem. But in 1905, the Committee of Fourteen, a citizens' association allied with the Anti-Saloon League, began the most successful antiprostitution drive in the city's history. The committee first took aim at Raines Hotels by successful agitating for new legislation that put most of these saloon-brothels out of business in short order. Reform groups took a different tack in going after the rest of Times Square's houses of ill repute, hiring private investigators to document violations of building codes and the Tenement House Law. By forcing the closure of scores of whorehouses on 40th and 41st Streets, the Committee of Fourteen and its allies finally shamed City Hall up onto the antiprostitution bandwagon. In 1910, Manhattan's district attorney impaneled a special grand jury chaired by John D. Rockefeller Jr. to prosecute all remaining "vice resorts."

By the start of World War I, prostitution had become a clandestine enterprise in New York. As a Bureau of Social Hygiene report put it: "In 1912, prostitution was open, organized, aggressive and prosperous; in 1916, it is furtive, disorganized, precarious, unsuccessful." All of the furnished rooming houses from 37th to 42nd Streets between Seventh and Eighth Avenues were effectively closed to prostitutes, and theater district hotels were required to report male customers who arrived without luggage and to require proof of marriage to any woman who accompanied them. Prostitution survived in more nefarious forms, of course, but as the Committee of Fourteen boasted, New York now had "less open vice than any other of the world's largest cities."

However, even as the vice reformers were drawing a bead on prostitution, they were caught flatfooted in 1911 by the eruption of a national dancing craze featuring exuberantly erotic "animal" dances lifted from African-American culture. The bunny hug, turkey trot, grizzly bear, the fish walk, lame duck, and so on were a revelation to white folks. As one observer put it, "Never before had well-bred people seen—much less performed—such flagrantly salacious contortions."

The surging demand for late-night dancing exceeded the capacity of the 42nd Street theater district's existing dance halls and ballrooms, prompting most of the big Broadway hotels and lobster palaces to install dance floors. By the "feverish, festive" winter of 1913, even the grandest of the lobster palaces now "were merely public dance halls of a more expensive kind than those frequented by the working classes." Reisenweber's turned over three entire floors to dancing. Murray's Roman Gardens differentiated itself by installing a huge revolving dance floor. The Café de l'Opera, on Broadway at 42nd Street, was the first of the new cabarets to hit upon the widely imitated business-building strategy of employing a professional dance team to demonstrate the latest steps to diners. At the same time, many theater owners turned their roof gardens into giant dance emporiums. Klaw and Erlanger opened the largest of Broadway's rooftop cabarets, the Jardin de Danse, on the roof of their New York Theater, after Ziegfeld's *Follies* decamped to the New Amsterdam.

Rector's, the oldest of the lobster palaces, perished for unrelated reasons just as the dance craze was taking hold. During the year that it took to build the Hotel Rector many of the restaurant's patrons shifted their loyalty to other establishments and never did return. The new hotel failed to drum up much business, leaving Charles and George Rector unable to meet their mortgage payments. Creditors seized the hotel and the restaurant in 1913. Charles died within a year, but George grudgingly swung with the times, opening a new Rector's as a restaurant cabaret a few blocks up Broadway near 48th Street. George would make good money in cabaret, but he smiled through gritted epicure's teeth the whole while. "I speak of the last years of Rector's with regret. Not that it was closed, but because it was ever opened," he lamented. "It was not a restaurant, but a madhouse. Nobody went into Rector's to dine. We had a kitchen, but the chefs were all out on the dance floor with the customers."

Like theater district brothels, the new Broadway cabarets drew their patrons from most every point of the social spectrum, from Fifth Avenue swells in evening dress to Tenth Avenue truck drivers and longshoremen in work boots. But the cabaret, unlike the brothel, was at least as popular with women as with men, even serving as an early vehicle of women's liberation, of a sort. Many cabarets offered special midafternoon dance programs for unescorted women. These events were known as *thés dansants* or "tango teas," though the beverage of choice was stronger. "It was a booze *dansant*," Rector confided, "even though the cocktails were served in fragile Dresden china teacups." Cabaret owners also supplied male dance partners, who typically were out-of-work actors. The silent film idol Rudolph Valentino got his start as a *thé dansant* gigolo.

The cabarets and the licentious "modern dances" that they promoted appalled the New York Commission on Amusements and Vacation Resources for Working Girls. Although most of the working girls the commission had sworn to protect did their dancing in cheap public dance halls, the group shrewdly advanced its reform agenda by announcing early in 1912 that it was going to begin sending investigators to society balls in Fifth Avenue hotels. Deeply embarrassed, social leaders in New York and other cities promptly banned the animal dances from their events. Soon, most of the city's posh hotels, lobster palaces, and high-end cabarets adopted rules designed to differentiate themselves from public dance halls: "Do not wiggle the shoulders. Do not shake the hips. Do not twist the body. Do not flounce the elbows. Do not pump the arms. Do not hop—glide instead. Avoid low, fantastic and acrobatic dips."

The counterreformation in social dancing worked to the advantage of Vernon and Irene Castle, a young, white married couple (he was English, she was American) who had developed a repertory of eccentric dances in Paris at the Café de Paris. Returning to the United States in 1913 to work the Café de l'Opera at the unheard-of salary of $300 a week (soon doubled to $600), the Castles became big stars by tamping down the aggressive sexuality of the animal dances into a more respectable form. The refined couple and their followers replaced the turkey trot, grizzly bear, and bunny hug with the long Boston, the fox trot, and the Castle Walk. The Castles were well mannered but high-spirited in their own way, with a talent for inventing amusingly tricky steps. "It sounds silly and it is silly. That is the explanation of its popularity," Irene said of their signature step, the Castle Walk, which she and Vernon had created while fooling around at a party in their private apartment above the Café de l'Opera.

At the peak of their popularity, the Castles were Broadway's most pervasive performers, much in demand for stage musicals and vaudeville productions alike. "Nowadays we dance morning, noon and night," Mrs. Castle declared in *Modern Dancing*, the best-selling book that she wrote with her husband. She did not exaggerate. In 1914, the producer Charles Dillingham showcased the Castles in a spectacular revue at the New Amsterdam, commissioning Irving Berlin to write the tunes for *Watch Your Step*. (This was Berlin's first complete score, and it catapulted him from song-plugging obscurity to Broadway.) After the curtain fell at the New Amsterdam, the Castles would hurry over to the 44th Street Roof Garden, which was renamed "Castles in the Air" in honor of their extended engagement there. The busy couple hit the dance floor about midnight. The audience danced until 2 A.M., when a curfew law forced the roof to close. The Castles then went to Castle Club, a 400-seat, members-only club in the basement, where they performed until 4 A.M. They also frequently danced at Sans Souci, a small and very smart supper club of their own at 42nd Street and Broadway. It was literally underground, a T-shaped room accessible only through a stairway in the sidewalk. "The opening night was quite brilliant," Irene recalled. "People who do not commonly go out to supper came to Sans Souci."

But it was Flo Ziegfeld who brought cabaret to its artistic zenith high atop the New Amsterdam. The Aerial Garden, the New Amsterdam's roof theater, had closed in 1910 when an air-cooling system was installed in the main theater. In 1914, Ziegfeld reopened the garden as a makeshift cabaret called the Danse de Follies for people who wanted to take the elevator to the roof and go drinking and dancing after the *Follies* ended downstairs. The cabaret was such a hit that Ziegfeld had Josef Urban remodel the roof theater into a sleek nightclub with a movable stage, glass balconies, an open-air garden, and lighting that created remarkable rainbow effects. With the inauguration of *The Ziegfeld Midnight Frolic* in January 1915, the Danse de Follies began staying open year-round. An initial admission charge of $1 soon rose to $5, the highest on Broadway.

The *Frolic* was built around the Ziegfeld girl to a greater degree even than the *Follies*. As one reviewer said, the rooftop revues were "short on wit, long on leg." For one thing, the chorus was constantly onstage and much closer to the audience than in the theater downstairs. To discourage patrons from fondling the girls as they strutted about, Ziegfeld and director Ned Wayburn instructed them in what became known as the "Ziegfeld strut"—arms back, chin up, zero eye contact. It almost worked. In contrast to the *Follies* but in keeping with cabaret tradition, audience participation was encouraged. Each table was provided with noisemakers, including wooden mallets, and intertable telephones. Through several editions, actors dressed in period costumes led sing-alongs while the words were flashed onto a screen for the benefit of the audience. Another popular feature was Sybil Carmen and her "balloon girls," who walked through the audience tempting men to use their cigars to explode the balloons that covered their skimpy costumes. After two seasons, equally combustible miniature zeppelins replaced the balloons. Now, the girls were caught in a crossfire of searchlights as they paraded against an Urban background of a burning city.

The *Midnight Frolic* thrived against a backdrop of general decline in the cabaret business. By the time that Ziegfeld's new revue debuted, the moral reform movement was beginning to make headway against the cabarets. Its object was not so much to abolish public dancing as to ban it from restaurants. "It was dangerous, it appeared, to eat, drink and dance in the same place," scoffed one commentator. Yet another new citizens' committee headed by Mrs. Henry Moskowitz, a confidante of future governor Alfred E. Smith, turned an army of 125 private investigators loose on the restaurant cabarets in 1915. The information they gathered was turned over to City Hall, which promptly imposed a 1 A.M. curfew on every restaurant that sold liquor and offered entertainment. Rector's, Maxim's, Reisenweber's, and other popular establishments also were fined for presenting revues without a theatrical license.

All of this was bad enough for business, but by the end of 1915 the dance craze also was fading. Attendance at *thés dansants* fell into especially steep decline, thanks to newspaper coverage of women victimized by male dance instructors, now demonized as "tango pirates." The big roof garden cabarets were unable to make ends meet as the smart set tired of mixing with the hoi polloi and either retired from the scene or switched their allegiance to pricier, more exclusive cabarets. Vernon and Irene Castle's long run at the 44th Street Roof Garden ended unceremoniously in mid-1915 when the first couple of dance was replaced with an uninspired variety bill. The roof theater would remain open for a few more years but would never again succeed as a cabaret. The Jardin de Danse made a fleeting attempt to fill its half-empty dance floor with novelty acts, including an exhibition of Greco-Roman wrestling, before shutting down, too.

With America's belated entry into World War I in 1917, Broadway's surviving restaurant cabarets came under renewed attack. "Pep speakers and patriotic societies damned the cabaret as being wasteful, even sinful, and 'lobster palace' became a phrase to hiss." On the other hand, the specter of impending apocalypse "over there" inspired one last outburst of hard partying. "There was a weird aroma of patriotic hope and fear in the atmosphere," George Rector recalled. "In all my career as a restaurateur I have never seen such sincere drinking, such sustained jollity, such Marathon dancing."

In 1919, the temperance movement finally achieved the most radical of its aims with Congress's enactment of the Volstead Act. The new law criminalized the sale, though not the consumption, of beverages containing more than .5 percent alcohol. This ban then was chiseled into the nation's legal bedrock by the states' approval of the Nineteenth Amendment to the U.S. Constitution. Prohibition went into effect January 17, 1920.

In New York City, the national capital of booze, the last night of legal drinking was a second New Year's Eve, minus the good cheer. "New Yorkers crowded into corner saloons, into the cafes and supper rooms of hotels, into hot spots along Broadway's roaring Forties, joylessly awaiting the midnight hour that would inaugurate a future of deprivation and drought." At the bar of the Waldorf-Astoria, a man sang a mournful version of "Auld Lang Syne" and the oldest bartender wept bitter tears. The next night William "Bat" Masterson, the legendary former Dodge City sheriff, went alone to Shanley's near 42nd Street. Masterson, who was working as a columnist for the *Morning Telegraph*, ordered a steak and a cup of tea. But at many of the other lobster palaces the mood was more sardonic than solemn. At Maxim's the waiters shed their Louis XIV–era finery and came dressed as pallbearers, and Reisenweber's staged a mock funeral ball. The funeral imagery proved prophetic, though in a way no one foresaw at first.

The lobster palaces were particularly vulnerable to Prohibition because their outsize investments in real estate and furnishings were chiefly supported by liquor profits. In selling whisky at 40 cents per glass, Rector's had brought in $40 for each gallon sold—$38 of which was pure profit. On every barrel of whisky, the restaurant booked a profit of $2,000. Rival palaces were no less dependent on booze. "We can't go on at a profit on soft drinks," lamented Tom Shanley of Shanley's. "We obey the law and lose money, and we can't afford that." Most of the lobster palaces remained open for a few years, perishing by degrees. The story was told of an evening when a diner came into Shanley's and asked for a steak with a half a pound of butter sauce. "Why, sir," sighed the waiter, "if there was that much butter in the house, Mr. Shanley would eat it himself."

Attempts by Broadway restaurants and cabarets to defy the new law only hastened their demise. Speakeasies by the hundreds routinely violated the Volstead Act with impunity, but most of them were tucked away in the shadows of Midtown's side streets—in the cellars, basements, and back rooms of converted brownstones. There was no place to hide along the Great White Way. Broadway and 42nd Street offered a symbolic path of least resistance to the federal agents whose enforcement of Prohibition was notoriously selective. While gangster-owned speakeasies made a fortune from adulterated liquor and indifferent food, the city's finest restaurants and cabarets were repeatedly raided and padlocked, to the gloating delight of the president of the Anti-Saloon League. "Ask the big hotels and restaurants which laughed at the law, whether enforcement is a fizzle. Then hear the doleful chorus," he boasted. "Let the Paradise restaurant on 58th Street, New York, sing bass; let Shanley's, Murray's, and the Little Club sing tenor; let Cushman's and the Monte Carlo sing alto; let Delmonico's sing soprano, and the words of the music are, 'We have been padlocked, padlocked, padlocked.' The famous Knickerbocker Grill sings, 'Amen, padlocked, amen and amen.'"

The Knickerbocker was the first of the founding pillars of 42nd Street nightlife to crumble after Prohibition. Vincent Astor, Jack's son, closed the hotel in mid-1920 and converted it into an office building with retail stores on its lower two floors. Habitués of the "Forty-Second Street Country Club" raised a great hue and cry over the fate of the Old King Cole mural, which was crated and placed in a warehouse. Flo Ziegfeld's prestige kept the Danse de Follies open longer than any competing cabaret, but it shut down after the sixteenth edition of the *Midnight Frolic* ended in April 1922. There simply was no place left to make a grand night of it on 42nd Street after Murray's Roman Gardens, the last of the palaces, closed in 1924. Adding insult to injury, some of the shuttered cabarets and lobster palaces along the Great White Way were converted into cut-rate dance halls affiliated with cheap Chinese restaurants. These "chop suey joints," most of which had relocated from lower Manhattan's Chinatown, offered "dancing, a sort of show, and a dinner, all for a dollar and a half."

Prohibition may have fatally wounded the Broadway lobster palace and the cabaret, but it failed miserably in its attempt to legislate virtue. The debauched high life of the Roaring Twenties would make the excesses of the preceding decade seem tame by comparison. New Yorkers and Americans in general indulged themselves on an epic scale as the economy boomed, the stock market levitated, and traditional morality continued to crumble. Despite Prohibition, or even perhaps because of it, public drunkenness became a kind of badge of honor among the affluent young. This was the era of the flapper—she of the bobbed hair, short skirts, and promiscuous habits—and of the "boola-boola" boy, with his raccoon coat, hip flask, and sports car.

The lobster palace was dead, long live the speakeasy! In 1929, New York's police commissioner estimated the number of illegal drinking establishments, or "speakeasies," in the city at 32,000, double the number of legal saloons and "blind pigs" extant before Prohibition. Most speakeasies were little more than rudely furnished holes in the wall. Upscale nightlife survived in the form of the nightclub, which simultaneously flouted both the Volstead Act and local curfew laws. Nightclub entrepreneurs bought up the names and charters of antiquated societies and, under the flimsy cover thus provided, retooled the restaurant cabaret as an exclusive, members-only club. Many of the swankiest nightclubs sported French names—Palais Royal, Moulin Rouge, Bal Tabarin, Beaux Arts Café—but were brash, prosperous, and distinctively American. Unlike their lobster palace predecessors, the leading nightclub proprietors "knew little about cooking and didn't bother to learn, for their customers didn't care. The new children of the night wanted a gay show, swift dance music, and no curfew."

Most New York nightclub owners either were beholden to gangsters or were gangsters themselves. Prohibition not only forced fashionable Manhattan nightlife underground but also diminished its concentration within the Times Square theater district. The block of West 52nd Street between Fifth and Sixth Avenues was renowned throughout the country for its wall-to-wall illegal nightclubs and speakeasies, including the 21 Club, known to initiates as "Jack and Charlie's." The theater district's late-night cachet also was dimmed by the emergence of Jazz Age Harlem as an exotic uptown entertainment zone for white bohemians and slumming thrill seekers. From midnight on, "you saw throngs on Lenox and Seventh Avenues, ceaselessly moving from one pleasure resort to another. Long after the cascading lights of Times Square had flickered out, these boulevards were ablaze."

The throttling of the Great White Way's glamorous nightlife did not dim its appeal as an entertainment center. As the Roaring Twenties began, some 750,000 people were descending on Times Square nightly. Forty-second Street's intersection—now hailed far and wide as the "Crossroads of the World"—was busier than ever, at least until midnight. Many visitors to New York City came simply to gawk, for Times Square's colossal electronic signs and billboards had become a world-class attraction in their own right, a new and distinctively American form of public amusement: advertising as spectacle. "Hundreds of thousands of people are now thinking of New York in terms of the 'whiter light district' . . . centering around Times Square. To them, this is the spirit of New York," wrote the author of *Adventuring in New York*, published in 1923. Times Square is "the only New York possessing a thrill. It is . . . the carnival supernal."

Cliquot ginger ale set a new standard of dazzle in 1924 with a colorful sign featuring a three-story soda bottle in a giant sleigh driven by a smiling Eskimo boy in white furs. In flashing sequences, the youth snapped a six-foot whip, which in turn activated three other Eskimo boys who started running, pulling the bottle along behind them. Another crack of the whip sent the name Cliquot flashing in the sky, followed by GINGER ALE.

In the 1920s, the Broadway theater scaled peaks of popularity that it had never before approached and never would come close to again. The previous decade had been an excellent one for New York theater, with an average of 114 shows debuting each year. Yet from 1923 through 1929, the number of new productions exceeded 224 every single year and peaked during the 1927–28 season at an astounding 264. The outbreak of what can only be described as theater mania during and after World War I supported the construction of two dozen new theaters in greater Times Square, including three new houses on 42nd Street.

All three of them were built by the up-and-coming producing team of Edgar and Arch Selwyn. Their Selwyn Theater, at 229 West 42nd Street, was a 1,180-seat house decorated in the style of the Italian Renaissance. Its most novel feature was separate smoking rooms for men and women. Each dressing room was equipped with a shower and a telephone—another first. The Selwyn brothers moved their offices into a five-story office building adjoining the new theater. Even before their eponymous theater opened in 1918, the Selwyn brothers were working out a deal to build two more theaters nearby. The Times Square and the Apollo both opened in late 1920 at 219 West 42nd and 223 West 42nd, respectively. The theaters shared a single facade but had separate marquees. Designed with musicals in mind, the Apollo was the larger of the two, with a seating capacity of 1,194 to the Times Square's 1,057. The completion of the three Selwyn-owned theaters brought the number of theaters on 42nd Street between Seventh and Eighth Avenues to ten—a density unmatched anywhere else in the city.

Forty-second Street was home to the single biggest Broadway hit of the hyperactive 1920s: *Abie's Irish Rose*. An old-fashioned melodrama, *Abie's* survived a righteous thumping by the critics to become the longest-running show in Broadway history. It played the Republic (the original name of Hammerstein's showcase was restored after David Belasco had given up his lease) for 2,327 performances spanning more than five years—a record of longevity that would not be surpassed until *A Chorus Line* came along in the mid-1970s. *Abie's Irish Rose* was formulaic fun, but its formula was not easily replicated. *Kosher Kitty Kelly*, a ludicrous attempt at a Jewish version, closed after a single performance a few doors down 42nd Street at the Selwyn's Times Square Theater.

The success of *Abie's Irish Rose* notwithstanding, 42nd Street's forte during the 1920s remained sophisticated musical comedy. The years

1924 and 1925 were particularly rich with historically significant productions. At the Times Square, the English import *Andre Charlot's Revue of 1924* gave American audiences their first glimpse of the virtuoso actresses Gertrude Lawrence and Beatrice Lillie. The Liberty presented *Lady, Be Good,* the first musical to pair George and Ira Gershwin. This musical was no less noteworthy for giving Fred and Adele Astaire their first lead roles on the American stage. The Lyric scored big with *The Cocoanuts,* which featured a book by the reigning master of musical comedy, George S. Kaufman, and songs by Irving Berlin. *The Cocoanuts,* a madcap satire of the Florida land mania of the day, was first and foremost a vehicle for the Marx Brothers, vaudeville veterans appearing in their first major Broadway play. Groucho and his brothers improvised with abandon, convulsing audiences even as they drove Kaufman to distraction. The playwright salvaged a measure of immortality from the experience with one of the most famous quips in Broadway history. Pacing anxiously at the back of the theater one night, Kaufman suddenly stopped and touched his hand to his ear. "I may be wrong," he said acidly, "but I think I just heard one of the original lines."

Flo Ziegfeld put his stamp all over 42nd Street during the Roaring Twenties. During 1920 and 1921 alone he produced eight shows at the New Amsterdam—two editions of the *Follies,* five of the *Frolic,* and the book musical *Sally.* With songs by Jerome Kern and a glorious star turn by Marilyn Miller, this airy saga of a dishwasher's rise to fame in the *Follies* was the fourth longest-running musical of the 1920s. The divalike Miller was so overcome by emotion during one thunderous and prolonged ovation that she ran down a ramp to the aisle and left the theater. Much of the audience followed her onto 42nd Street, circled the block, and returned to their seats to continue cheering. After one matinee, Ziegfeld took his daughter, Patty, backstage to meet Miller, who was one of the impresario's more tempestuous mistresses. The six-year-old's doe-eyed innocence did not prevent Miller from aiming a tirade of profanity at her father. "I'd never seen anything that beautiful that angry," Patty later recalled.

In the early 1920s, the *Follies* faced serious competition for the first time from a half-dozen other flashy girl-based revues. Each worked its own distinctive variations on the Great Glorifier's formula. The designer-dominated *Greenwich Village Follies* stressed simplicity, wit, and taste. *The Music Box Revues* revolved around clever stage effects and exuberant scores by Irving Berlin. *George White's Scandals* were fast and snappy, with first-rate songs. *The Earl Carroll Vanities* was the most erotic of all the revues, just a step above burlesque. With the *Follies* ensconced at the New Amsterdam, the *Scandals* in residence at the Apollo, and the *Andre Charlot Revues* alternating between the Times Square and the Selwyn, 42nd Street was the theater district's center of girlie action in the 1920s, as it would be again in the 1970s and 1980s, albeit in less rarified form.

Under New York State law, nudity on the stage qualified as a legal "artistic exhibition" as long as the unclothed performer remained stationary. The motion barrier was broken in 1923 by the Shubert revue *Artists and Models,* which paraded twenty topless showgirls across the stage. Earl Carroll promptly raised the ante in the 1924 edition of the *Vanities,* which opened with the startling image of a nude actress hanging upside down on a pendulum. The show's highlight was a "peacock dance" in which 108 chorus girls strutted about waving huge feathered fans, intermittently revealing glimpses of their naked bodies. Carroll circumvented state law by the judicious use of flesh-colored tape but was arrested anyway and charged with corrupting the morals of children by displaying seductive posters in the theater lobby. The producer spent four days in jail but was acquitted at trial. In his *Vanities of 1925,* Carroll again pushed his luck by sending out "hostesses" in black tights to dance with patrons before the show and during intermission.

Imitation may well be the sincerest form of flattery, but Ziegfeld was plainly unnerved by the proliferation of competing revues. He worked longer hours than ever, bullying his minions with unreasonable demands and capricious changes. "He kept strands of colored ribbon in his pocket, which he played with. Often he would fish one out and redo an entire show in that color." At the same time, Ziegfeld's publicity stunts grew more frequent and elaborate. One of his showgirls played a golf tournament dressed only in a barrel, starting a craze for "strip golf." Another announced that she would "rather have dinner with a pig than some men I know"—and then hosted a swanky dinner party seated next to a pig in a high chair wearing violet silk ribbons. At a "surf jazz" party at Rockaway, *Follies* girls played saxophones as they danced in the ocean under a full moon and shadowy couples embraced under cover of rocks.

Ziegfeld's competition with the other revues also provided plenty of juicy copy for the press corps. Ziegfeld, who haughtily considered the

Follies above reproach, organized the Alliance to Reform the Stage, which took as its slogan "Back from Nudity to Artistry." In a telegram to the district attorney of Manhattan, the Great Glorifier urged City Hall to investigate the most brazen of *Follies'* rivals. "The baring of breasts to the youth of America to draw a few extra dollars and absolute nude figures dancing around the stage should be stopped," he declared. Ziegfeld's voice blended with a Hallelujah Chorus of complaint raised by the Society for the Suppression of Vice and other watchdog groups. Bowing to reform pressure, Mayor Jimmy Walker privately warned Broadway producers to clean up their act. It wasn't just the revues that were offending moralists, but also such risqué plays as Mae West's farce *Sex.* In 1926, Manhattan's beleaguered district attorney empaneled a committee of three hundred citizens "to pass on the moral content of theater productions." Even Earl Carroll took the hint; the 1926 edition of the *Vanities* contained not a single nude woman—and flopped at the box office.

Ziegfeld reviled Carroll as a smut merchant, but the *Follies'* most formidable rival was *George White's Scandals.* White had studied the Ziegfeld formula from the inside as a dancer in the *Follies* for four years, departing in 1919. In 1923 he started his own revue starring one of Ziegfeld's featured performers, Ann Pennington. Ziegfeld fired off a telegram offering White $2,000 a week to return with Pennington. White wired back a cheeky counteroffer: $3,000 a week for Ziegfeld and his actress-wife, Billie Burke, to appear in the *Scandals.* This exchange of telegrams marked the beginning of one of 42nd Street's longest and most intense feuds.

White was a dancer with a discerning eye and ear. He shrewdly denied Ziegfeld and other producers the services of Erté, the Russian-born illustrator, by signing him to a long-term contract. Erté's opulent designs added greatly to the prestige of the *Scandals.* White also had the foresight to make a very young George Gershwin his musical director. White had tumbled to Gershwin's genius when the aspiring composer was still a rehearsal pianist looking for a break. Gershwin wrote five scores for the series but quit in a huff in 1924 when White refused to pay him more than $125 a week. White's loss was the musical theater's gain, but the *Scandals* series continued to be celebrated for its music just the same, as Gershwin was replaced by the skilled songwriting team of DeSylva, Brown, and Henderson. They were best known for "Birth of the Blues,"

"Black Bottom," and "This Is My Lucky Day"—all of which debuted on 42nd Street. Meanwhile, White burnished his celebrity by playing himself in the hit *Manhattan Mary,* a Cinderella story in which a poor girl rose to become a star in the *Scandals.* The musical comedy, which played at the Apollo, included a scene set at the Apollo and another across the street at Hubert's Museum.

Hubert's, 42nd Street's newest amusement attraction, employed a few showgirls of sorts but certainly was no threat to Ziegfeld. It was an old-fashioned dime museum, a notoriously low-down form of amusement popularized by P. T. Barnum in the mid-1800s and closely identified in New York with the Bowery, the Lower East Side's den of iniquity. "Bowery museums were the true underworld of entertainment, and their compass could include anything too shoddy, too risqué, too vile, too sad, too marginal, too disgusting, too pointless to be displayed elsewhere," Luc Sante observed in *Low Life.* As the best of the dime museums had migrated uptown to the Union Square theater district along with more respectable forms of amusement, they came to specialize in the same sort of freak and magic acts found in circus sideshows and occasionally featured in vaudeville bills. Hubert's star attraction, Heckler's Marvelous Trained Flea Circus, had once played the roof of Hammerstein's Victoria. Descended from Hubert's Dime Museum, long a fixture on East 14th Street, Hubert's Museum moved into 228 West 42nd Street in 1926, filling much of the space vacated by Murray's Roman Gardens.

With the opening of Hubert's, John Barrymore, Noël Coward, and Fred Astaire now shared 42nd Street's spotlight with the likes of Lady Olga, the Bearded Lady; Henry Burton, Spider Boy; Amok, Philippine Headhunter; Andy Potato Chips, the Midget; and Sylvia-Chester, half-woman, half-man. Although many high-minded members of the Broadway community were offended by Hubert's presence, the dime museum successfully catered to theatergoers. Virtually every evening, Professor Roy Heckler, a second-generation flea trainer, gave three performances in quick succession before the eight-o'clock curtain at the playhouses. "After the theater we'd be jammed with everybody waiting until the traffic thinned out to go to the supper clubs," Heckler recalled in the late 1950s. "Nobody ever went home in those days. All the theatrical people used to come in, too, when they weren't working." Fred Allen, the Broadway comic and future radio star, was especially enamored of Stanley Berent, better known as Sealo, the Seal Boy, who had flipperlike hands in place of arms. "He used to get ideas from talking with Sealo," Heckler said. "Softest touch in the world Fred was—and this got about."

The New Amsterdam was ideally suited to Ziegfeld's brand of so-phisticated flamboyance. But it was Abe Erlanger's property and he never let the Great Glorifier or anyone else forget it. The Theatrical Syndicate had long since fallen apart, but Erlanger was the same nasty bully he had always been. Ziegfeld was tired of dealing with him and he was tired of his ninth-floor office quarters in the New Amsterdam, a little rabbit warren of rooms with bilious green walls. Right outside his window the marquee blinked intermittently, making it seem as if lightning illuminated his office.

In 1926, Ziegfeld finally decided to build a theater of his own on 54th Street between Sixth and Seventh Avenues, a site just outside the theater district. Designed by Josef Urban, the Ziegfeld opened early the following year with the sumptuous musical *Rio Rita,* launching its namesake on the greatest winning streak of his long career. After several off years, the *Follies* returned to dazzling form in 1927 at the New Amsterdam. Irving Berlin wrote the entire score of this latest edition, and Eddie Cantor returned from Hollywood to star. "It's Up to the Band" featured nineteen showgirls pretending to play nineteen white grand pianos, a spectacle that prefigured the extravagant choreography of Busby Berkeley. Ziegfeld followed this triumph with two massive hit musicals on 42nd Street: *Rosalie,* at the New Amsterdam, and *The Three Musketeers,* at the Lyric Theatre. But Ziegfeld reserved his pièce de résistance, *Show Boat,* for his own theater. With a score by Jerome Kern and lyrics and a book by Oscar Hammerstein II, this was a breakthrough that marked the birth of the modern American musical.

In the fall of 1928, Billie Burke threw a grand party at the Ziegfeld to celebrate her husband's phenomenal run of good luck. Actually, it was more of a by-invitation-only pageant, with eight groups of friends costumed to represent the casts of eight of Ziegfeld's greatest hits, *Show Boat* included. "Everyone had fistfuls of money to spend," Burke recalled. "The world was a place created just for fun, and Flo Ziegfeld of all people was the man best equipped for having that fun." Unfortunately, "fun," in the Ziegfeld lexicon, had come to mean not only producing blockbusters, but speculating heavily on the stock market and dropping $100,000 in a single night at a casino gaming table. Ziegfeld, in short, was the Roaring Twenties personified.

The cataclysmic stock market crash of October 1929 and the Great Depression that followed devastated every industry in America, the New York theater included. Broadway's fortunes had begun to sour in late 1926, even as stock prices continued their meteoric rise to unsustainable heights. Yes, new plays would continue to open in record numbers into 1929, but a steady decline in "theater weeks" provided a truer reflection of the theater's erosion. (One production occupying one theater for one week constitutes a theater week.) The steady decline in theater weeks from a record 2,852 in the 1925–26 season to 2,432 two years later meant that more and more new shows were closing with unexpected abruptness, darkening playhouses.

It was bound to happen, for the unprecedented levels of activity in the 1920s were a product not only of the American theater's artistic coming-of-age, but also of an influx of hot, dumb money that didn't know a quality show from a pork belly. Thousands of investors who had made a killing in the stock market decided to roll the dice on Broadway, convinced that they would be the one to pull off the next *Abie's Irish Rose*. The $10,000 that its author, Anne Nichols, had invested returned $2 million on the sale of movie rights alone and netted her a total profit of $10 million to $15 million. By mid-decade, mass pursuit of the pot of gold at the end of the theatrical rainbow had glutted the stage with amateurish work that sent audiences stampeding to the exits. Broadway produced a record number of plays in 1926, but 72 percent of them failed even to cover their costs—a sobering reminder of the steep odds against success in the theater.

Who wanted to risk an evening of bad theater when motion pictures were proliferating and easily accessible at a fraction of the cost of a play? Nowhere in America were there as many movie palaces built at such close quarters as along Broadway in Times Square. The Strand, the Rialto, the Rivoli, the Capitol, Loew's State, Loew's New York, the Criterion, the Paramount, the Embassy, and the Roxy had come to dominate Broadway from 42nd Street up to 50th Street with their enormous entryways and outsize marquees. The movie palaces literally cast the playhouses on Broadway into the shadows, advertising their attractions with a stridency that put even the likes of Hammerstein and Ziegfeld to shame.

In 1925, the Criterion cloaked its entire facade in a forty-foot display to advertise the Cecil B. DeMille epic *The Ten Commandments*. The pharaoh and six hundred warriors on chariots were shown swarming below a towering figure of a grim-faced Moses. This was not a painting but an assemblage of metal-cut figures that seemed, to one observer, to leap "madly toward the spectators" on the sidewalk. Every few minutes, the sign released 100,000 volts of energy in the form of a bluish steak of faux lightning that hit Moses's stone tablets with a blinding burst of light.

In opening the Roxy at 48th Street in 1927, Rothapfel elaborated his bigger-is-better philosophy to the point of absurdity. Touted by its namesake as the "Cathedral of the Motion Picture," the 6,214-seat Roxy was the city's grandest movie palace and one of the great monuments to vanity in the history of American entertainment. A veritable amusement village complete with its own hospital, barbershop, and gymnasium, the Roxy had a rotunda the size of a railroad station, an auditorium as lavish as a royal palace, and mechanical equipment suitable for the largest ocean liner. Actually watching a movie here was almost beside the point, as the architect Paul Morand pithily complained after a visit to Rothapfel's cathedral of bombast: "The overheated air is unbreathable, the din of the mechanical orchestra, which one failure in the electricity could bring to a standstill, is merciless. . . . I find a seat in a deep, soft fauteuil, from which for two hours I witness giant kisses on mouths like the crevasses of the Grand Canyon."

Broadway's theaters held their own against the movie palaces until the late 1920s, when the allure of the motion picture was immeasurably increased by the addition of sound. U.S movie attendance soared from 60 million per week in 1927 to 110 million in 1929, permanently diminishing the audience for theater as film took over the job of providing everyday entertainment in America. The theater's intrinsic disadvantages vis-à-vis the movies and radio—and television to come—were economic, not aesthetic. A play was a handcrafted, one-of-a-kind sort of thing. But hundreds, even thousands, of copies of a movie could be made at incremental cost while a radio broadcast was infinitely replicated by the simple act of turning on a receiver.

By 1928, if not earlier, it was evident that theaters were in much greater supply on Broadway than theatergoers. Forty-second Street's playhouses were especially vulnerable, not only because of their age but also because most of them had been designed in the outmoded style of nineteenth-century European theaters. That is, they were large, narrow rectangles with the stage at one end and two or three tiered balconies at the other. With their wide, fan-shaped orchestra sections and single low-ceilinged balconies, Times Square's newer theaters made more efficient use of increasingly expensive real estate even as they put the average patron closer to the stage. As attendance declined in the late 1920s, the theaters along 42nd Street tended to be vacant for longer periods than was the average Times Square playhouse, reflecting producers' preference for the newer houses that lined Broadway's side streets. In short, 42nd Street gradually lost its standing as the city's theater block as the locus of activity shifted to 44th and 45th Streets between Broadway and Eighth Avenue. These, the so-called Shubert blocks, have remained the center of the Broadway theater district ever since.

By the late 1920s most of the 42nd Street theaters were worth considerably less than the land they were built on. A real estate survey found that three of the ten most valuable properties in Manhattan were located along 42nd Street, at its intersections with Madison, Fifth Avenue, and Broadway. Modern office towers were springing up along the street from Second all the way to Sixth Avenue, and real estate mavens predicted that the redevelopment of the theater block was imminent, in part because the Eighth Avenue subway line had just opened. Developers and speculators drove up the price of theater block real estate as they maneuvered to lock up choice sites. The lot at 241 West 42nd Street, a typical midblock piece of property, had sold for $38,000 in 1905. By 1929, its worth was assessed at $150,000 and its market value was closer to $250,000. Virtually every theater on the block changed hands at least once as the Roaring Twenties built to a climax. A developer bought the Lyric Theatre and laid plans to replace it with a thirty-story office building. Bethlehem Engineering paid $12 million for the old American Theatre and readied plans to demolish it and erect a thirty-story office tower.

The riptide of speculation flooding down 42nd Street spilled over onto the comparatively nondescript block between Eighth and Ninth Avenues. From 1922 to 1925, an obscure developer named John A. Larkin quietly bought up more than a dozen of the run-down four- and five-story tenement buildings lining the south side of this block. Larkin had assembled the entire frontage from 320 to 346 West 42nd Street by 1926, when he announced a scheme to put up a 110-story office tower—the tallest building in New York and all of America—at the staggering cost of $22.5 million.

Redevelopment gained momentum right up until the moment that the stock market crashed. Many property speculators lost huge sums on the demise of their 42nd Street schemes in the early 1930s, but Larkin miraculously was not among them. The developer never came close to breaking ground on his colossus, but he did gracefully extricate himself from his outsized 42nd Street investment by swapping his property for a 13-story building owned by the McGraw-Hill Publishing Co. on Tenth Avenue near 36th Street. McGraw-Hill, a trade magazine and book publisher, had expanded greatly during the 1920s, launching *The Business Week* magazine in September 1929. Shrugging off the crash, the company hired a top-drawer architect, Raymond Hood, whose much-praised Daily News Building was rising on East 42nd Street. Completed in 1931 at a cost of $4 million, the 35-story McGraw-Hill Building would prove a financial disaster but won renown as one of the most distinctive Manhattan skyscrapers. Hood made bold use of Art Deco detailing, which included a sign spelling out "McGraw Hill" in letters eleven feet high on top of the building. But the architect departed from orthodoxy most radically in his use of color. Popularly known as "the Green Building," McGraw-Hill "looks as if [it] was cut with a palette knife out of blocks of green plasticene," one writer noted.

As the "Green Building" was rising at 330 West 42nd, the Broadway theater's decline turned into a rout. Producers cut ticket prices to the quick and still could not fill the theater district's sixty playhouses, one-third of which were dark on any given week by the fall of 1930. Three preeminent producers who had been active on 42nd Street—the Shubert brothers, Al Woods, and Arthur Hammerstein—went bankrupt in 1931, and the banks also foreclosed on scores of lesser operators. The next year Ziegfeld died in Hollywood at sixty-five. Despite ruinous losses in the stock market and a string of money-losing plays, the Great Ziegfeld lived large until the end, bequeathing one million dollars in debt to his widow.

The theater was dying on 42nd Street, but the abrupt circumstances of its passing would make possible its improbable rebirth on the block six decades later. Had the 1920s kept on roaring into the 1930s, every playhouse on 42nd Street, with the possible exception of the New Amsterdam, would have been demolished and replaced by a bigger commercial building as developers extracted full value from the huge run-up in land values. Instead, the street's theaters were spared the wrecking ball, with one exception. Badly damaged in a fire, 42nd Street's first theater, the American, was razed in 1932, and its remnants were carted off to the same swamp in which Hammerstein's Victoria had been interred two decades earlier. The American was replaced by a parking lot, which the Veterans of Foreign Wars leased to a carnival complete with a Ferris wheel, a harbinger of 42nd Street's honky-tonk future.

The Grind House Phoenix

Even at the height of its Gilded Age elegance, 42nd Street had never been homogeneously posh. Its playhouses and vaudeville venues had priced their gallery seats to the working-class budget, and the lobster palaces and cabarets sat cheek by jowl, as it were, with lunch counters and juice stands. But over time the economic underpinnings of luxury on 42nd Street had eroded, tilting its balance toward cheaper, mass-market fare. First, Prohibition doomed the lobster palace and the cabaret. Then, motion pictures and radio appropriated the job of providing everyday entertainment to the nation, diminishing the audience for theater, the foundation of 42nd Street's glamour. During the 1930s, the Great Depression drastically shrunk the nation's amusement dollar, steepening the amplitude of 42nd Street's down-market slide. Hard times would end, but 42nd Street never would be restored as an after-dark playground of the rich and famous. This was not all bad. What was generally mourned as the theater district's deterioration could just as plausibly be celebrated as its democratization. Even as the Depression impoverished millions of Americans, it stimulated the national appetite for entertainment. A new breed of 42nd Street promoter—heir to Oscar Hammerstein and Flo Ziegfeld—emerged to satisfy this craving with a flair and resourcefulness in short supply in 1930s America. At a time when both Wall Street and Main

Street were limping along at a fraction of their productive capacity, 42nd Street remained a vital, if increasingly raffish, amusement hub.

The Depression hit New York harder than most any other city in the country. Manufacturing businesses by the hundreds shut down, never to reopen. By 1933, more than 1.5 million residents were on the dole, and long lines formed daily at the soup kitchens operating out of the backs of army trucks parked in Times Square. Most of the theater district's first-class hotels closed or, like the Hotel Astor, lowered their rates and their standards to remain in business. Meanwhile, the cafeteria supplanted the restaurant as the characteristic Times Square dining establishment. The theater block of 42nd Street was particularly cafeteria-intensive, with Hector's Cafeteria, Chase's, Bickford's, Dixon's, and an Automat outlet all competing for customers. Horn & Hardart had opened the first of its famous nickel-in-the-slot Automat mechanized cafeterias in 1902, but the company enjoyed its greatest success during the Depression. In the first two years after the 1929 stock market crash, the three dozen Automats in New York City posted a 50 percent increase in volume and added 1,000 employees.

Mass supplanted class in the amusement trade, too. Broadway "has degenerated into something resembling the main drag of a frontier town," the longtime Broadway columnist Stanley Walker noted in 1933. Walker counted seventeen cheap dance halls from 42nd Street to 57th Street, with prices ranging from one cent to five cents a dance. "There are chow-meineries, peep shows for men only, flea circuses, lectures on what killed Rudolph Valentino, jitney ballrooms and a farrago of other attractions which would have sickened the heart of the Broadwayite of the period of even ten years ago," Walker continued. "The money-makers are the larger places, where as many people as possible may be taken care of with the greatest possible speed, whether it is a dance hall or 'the longest bar in the world.'" Ward Morehouse, another veteran theater writer, offered his own list of unworthy new Broadway attractions of the early 1930s: "shooting galleries, bowling alleys, guess-your-weight stands, gypsy tea rooms, rug auctions, electric shoeshines, dance halls—fifty beautiful girls—chop suey, beer on draught, wines and liquors, oyster bars, bus-barkers, and right there on the curb was the man with the giant telescope, ready to show you the craters of the moon for a dime."

A dollar went a long way in the 1930s, and nowhere in New York was the competition for it more clamorous than on 42nd Street. The brightly lit marquees of ten theaters still demanded attention, joined now by games arcades that opened at street level in a half-dozen storefront locations and in the subway passages at either end of the block. The arcades offered group games of chance like Pokerino and the electronic bingo game Fascination, as well as the solitary diversions of the shooting gallery and pinball machine. Hubert's, the self-styled "Annex and Congress of Strange People," was joined by Robert Ripley's Believe-It-Or-Not "Odditorium," which boasted "the world's largest torture collection," including a spiked whip, a flesh crusher, and a heretic catcher with spiked collar. Even many of 42nd Street's humblest attractions now proclaimed their presence in neon and employed barkers and spielers. "Every other door in the block between Eighth and Seventh Avenues on 42nd Street is a stay-put sideshow," observed the 1932 guidebook *The Real New York*. "Good old-fashioned country circus barkers line the sidewalks shouting, 'This way, Ladi-ees and Gentlemennnnn! The most wonderful show in town! See five dollars' worth for five cents!!' At the tag-end of the afternoon, the side-shows blink open their eyes like so many sleepy night owls."

The Minsky brothers, who turned Hammerstein's Republic into an eponymous burlesque house in 1931, upped the promotional ante on 42nd Street by paying Oscar Skyhook, "Tallest Stilt-Walker in History," to tramp up and down Broadway in a shirt whose buttons lit up with each step, along with the tip of his nose and his cigar. Next door to Minsky's was the Rialto movie theater, which promoted a film called *The Jungle Princess* by turning its lobby into a facsimile of a tropical kingdom, complete with genuine monkeys swinging from fake coconut trees and lion sound effects that could be heard two blocks away over heavy traffic. With Minsky's Republic and the Rialto going at it hammer and tongs at the corner of 42nd Street and Seventh Avenue, Hammerstein's old corner was probably the most stridently commercial intersection in Depression-era New York.

The theater on 42nd Street finally expired in the 1930s, but at least it went in style, offering some of Broadway's most noteworthy productions. *The Band Wagon*, starring Fred and Adele Astaire, was considered by many to be the greatest revue in musical comedy history. It had a lengthy run at the New Amsterdam, as did *Roberta*, which featured Bob Hope in his Broadway debut and a fine score by Jerome Kern and Otto Harbach. At the Times Square, the Gershwin musical *Strike Up the Band* was followed by Nöel Coward's *Private Lives*, starring Gertrude Lawrence, Laurence Olivier, and Coward himself. The show's producers solved the issue of top billing by putting Lawrence's name alone above the title on the marquee of the vacant Apollo Theater next door and giving Coward sole billing on the Times Square's marquee. The last few rounds of musicals that debuted on 42nd Street produced a treasure trove of standards, including "Dancing in the Dark," "Smoke Gets in Your Eyes," "Yesterdays," "Life Is Just a Bowl of Cherries," "What Is This Thing Called Love?" and "Body and Soul."

But the occasional masterpiece could not alter the calculus of doom. One by one, 42nd Street's playhouses were converted in the 1930s to movie or burlesque theaters. Burlesque was notoriously déclassé, but the growing predominance of motion pictures on the block also dimmed the theater block's glamour quotient. At a time when the studio-owned movie palaces along Broadway were luxuriating in opening-night pizzazz, 42nd Street was just too far removed from the spot-lit center of the action to compete with the likes of the Paramount, the Roxy, and the Capitol. As early as 1929, 42nd Street's lone movie palace, the Rialto, was forced to reinvent itself as a "grind" house. Selling cut-rate tickets to movies that had already opened elsewhere, the Rialto exhibited these second-run features on a round-the-clock schedule, charging twenty-five cents in the morning, forty cents at matinees, and sixty-five cents at night. Every movie house that opened subsequently on 42nd Street would follow the Rialto's lead and operate as a grinder.

You did not have to be a snob to believe that a Eugene O'Neill drama or a Gershwin musical was more culturally valuable than a Minsky show like *Fanny Fartsin From France* or the "Hidden Secrets of Sex" exhibit at Hubert's Museum. But the fact was that in the 1930s, no less than in the 1910s, the impresarios of 42nd Street were reacting to the imperatives of market demand. The street was not a pure product of capitalism, if only because of the government's habit of imposing moral sanctions with economic consequences—most notably the Volstead Act. On the other hand, its institutions had never supped from the flow of charitable donations and government subsidy that sustained symphonies, opera companies, and other high-culture bulwarks. They sold enough tickets to cover their costs, or they went out of business. The abundant cultural uplift this single block had provided in theater's heyday was a happy accident of its pursuit of profit.

In lamenting 42nd Street's decline, Broadway veterans like Brooks

Atkinson and Stanley Walker undoubtedly reflected the majority opinion. But to the performers and promoters of the grind era, the street continued to represent the pinnacle of glamour and achievement, just as it had to their "betters" in the "legitimate" stage. At Hubert's, the head barker (officially, the "Inside Lecturer") wore a dinner jacket, and even the Needle Swallower sported a tux. The shows that the brothers Minsky produced in Midtown were as down and dirty as those they had offered earlier in Harlem and on the Lower East Side, but the 1931 opening of Minsky's Republic, the first of 42nd Street's burlesque houses, was strictly black-tie. Gypsy Rose Lee, burlesque's superstar stripper, praised the Republic as "the most elegant burlesque theater" she ever played. "The doorman was garbed as a French gendarme, complete with mustache and red-lined cape. The girl ushers, wearing French-type maids' costumes with frilly skirts and long, black silk stockings, squirted perfume on customers as they came in. For the ladies there were gardenia corsages. Velvet draperies framed the combination hot dog–popcorn stand."

The first conversion of a 42nd Street playhouse into a grinder came in 1930 when an enterprising young movie theater operator from Brooklyn named Max A. Cohen leased Wallack's Theatre (originally the Lew M. Fields). A few months later, the Brandt brothers leased the Shubert's Lyric Theatre, which had been dark for almost a year. The Brandts, veteran film exhibitors new to Midtown, renamed the Lyric the Lyric Musical Hall and began presenting small-time vaudeville acts along with newsreels and short film subjects. That the large opening-night crowd was almost entirely male was "natural on 42nd Street, as the Brandts probably sense, since they are employing good-looking girls as ticket takers, candy sellers and usherettes," a *Variety* reviewer commented. When vaudeville failed to catch on at the Lyric, the Brandts successfully repositioned it as a straight picture house. The brothers then took over the Apollo in 1932 and the Times Square in 1934, and by the early 1940s would own seven of the eleven movie theaters on 42nd Street. For his part, Cohen would add the Sam H. Harris and the New Amsterdam to his portfolio by decade's end. With the ascendance of Cohen and the Brandts, the ownership of 42nd Street's theaters was transformed from musical chairs to Monopoly.

William, Harry, Louis, and Bernard Brandt had grown up on the Lower East Side, the sons of Jewish immigrant parents. William, the eldest brother, gave the family's first film showing in an empty lot behind a Coney Island hot dog stand in 1908, using a hand-cranked projector and a bedsheet for a screen. William and second-born Harry borrowed $1,200 to create a 299-seat nickelodeon in a former firehouse not far from their childhood home. The brothers acquired a second theater in 1915, and then it was off to the races. Bolstered by the addition of Louis and Bernard, better known as "Bingo," the brothers Brandt built a chain of movie theaters extending from the Lower East Side to encompass most of Brooklyn. In 1927, they sold their theaters to Fox Theaters, which later was folded into 20th Century-Fox. The brothers reinvested most of their profits in the stock market just in time to be wiped out by the crash of 1929. Led by the bumptious Harry, the brothers were ready by 1930 to give the movie business another go.

The Brandts built a second, larger theater chain in short order, mainly through shrewdly calculated buyouts of poorly run neighborhood houses unable to withstand the exigencies of the Depression. Harry and his brothers also pounced on the opportunity offered by the tribulations of Broadway's theaters to infiltrate Midtown Manhattan for the first time. In addition to the seven 42nd Street properties, the Brandts snapped up another half a dozen playhouses elsewhere in Times Square. The most prominent of these was the cavernous Globe Theater (now the Lunt-Fontanne), on Broadway at 46th Street. Despite its proximity to the Broadway movie palaces, the Brandts made the Globe into a grinder, like all their Times Square venues. Harry moved his office into the Globe, while his brothers set up shop in the Selwyn Theater on 42nd Street. The second Brandt empire extended far beyond its Gotham hub to encompass most of the Northeast. At its peak in the 1940s and 1950s, Brandt Theaters owned about 150 theaters, including 80 in the New York area.

Harry Brandt was a fiery, swaggering sort of leader whose intemperate criticisms of the Hollywood studio oligopoly were fodder for countless news articles. "As a self-appointed champion of the 'little man' he makes a big noise," the *New York Times* reported in 1940. "He sits in New York behind a large desk in a paneled office furnished with plushy, wine-red sofas. Flanked on either side by a pair of flambeau lamps, he cuts quite an impressive figure, resembling, as he does, a moon-faced double of Mussolini. His voice is smooth, high-pitched and emotional. He strides up and down behind the desk when his thoughts make him restless." This "veritable vortex of sound and fury" dominated the Independent Theater Owners Association of New York as thoroughly as he did Brandt Theaters, using the group as a bully pulpit for his anti-Hollywood fulminations. In 1938, the ITOA took out an ad blasting the studios for their reliance on over-the-hill stars. Among the actors designated "box-office poison" by Brandt were Fred Astaire, Mae West, Greta Garbo, Joan Crawford, Katharine Hepburn, and Marlene Dietrich. Threats of lawsuits only inflamed Brandt. "Let 'em sue," he said, though he later publicly apologized to Hepburn after she scored with *The Philadelphia Story.*

Harry and his brothers were masters of cost control, an essential component of the grind house business model, as Paramount belatedly discovered at the Rialto. Even as it led the way on 42nd Street in cutting ticket prices and adopting a continuous screening schedule, the Rialto had retained many of the trappings of its faded movie palace opulence. The result was big operating losses. By early 1933, Paramount was ready to default on its lease and abandon the Rialto. Instead, Paramount's ambitious young publicity chief, Arthur L. Mayer, persuaded his employer to transfer the lease to him and tear up his employment contract. Mayer, a literate and endearingly whimsical graduate of Harvard, put up no cash but did guarantee that he would split any future profits with the company. If the theater continued to post losses instead, Mayer promised to cover the entire deficit out of his own pocket.

Mayer took over the Rialto on March 4, 1933, the very day that Franklin Delano Roosevelt ordered a temporary shutdown of all the country's banks. Mayer put up a sign outside the Rialto saying that IOUs would be accepted in lieu of cash. The theater took in a few thousand IOUs, not one of which was ever redeemed. Even after it began insisting on cash payment of a quarter, the theater became a haven for unemployed men ostensibly out looking for work and needing a place to hide out for the day. Mayer turned the Rialto from a money loser to a profit producer by taking an axe to the theater's bloated overhead. He removed the marble stairway from the lobby, along with a truckload of marble Renaissance angels and busts of Beethoven, Grieg, and other cultural dignitaries favored by Roxy Rothapfel. He slashed the $5,000-a-week advertising budget to $500, canceled Paramount's 400-person free-pass list, and fired most of the staff. "The place was bristling with overpaid West Point–trained ushers instructing customers kindly to expectorate only into the sand-filled Grecian urns," Mayer observed in his self-serving but wryly hilarious memoir, *Merely Colossal.* "I replaced them with genial, slouchy, underpaid boys."

Mayer's partnership with Paramount ended in 1936 with the expiration of his lease and the reconstruction of the Rialto. A developer demolished the twenty-year-old movie palace and erected a handsome three-story Art Deco block containing offices, stores, restaurants, and a 600-seat movie theater: the new Rialto. Mayer's theater was the only one in the city that could be entered directly from the subway, through a basement arcade. The Rialto arcade soon became a notorious hangout for troublemakers of all sorts, less because of its amusements than for the fact that it afforded easy escape into the subway from truant officers, debt collectors, and cops.

The challenge of opening a new theater inspired Mayer to scale heights of promotional ingenuity beyond the ken of his main 42nd Street rivals, the Brandt brothers. Through his own admittedly unscientific survey, Mayer established that on any given day, five times more men than women passed by his corner of Broadway and 42nd Street. While the new building was still under construction, the *New York Times* obligingly published a tongue-in-cheek essay by Mayer in which he promised "a new deal for the forgotten man," by which he meant men in general. "The new Rialto will be the last refuge of the oppressed sex. Driven from presumably impregnable strongholds like the barbershop and the bar, here at least he will be catered to." Women will be allowed to enter, Mayer added, "but they will have to know their place. There will be no perfume machines, no candies on sale, and no pictures dealing with penthouses, English country life, adorable kiddies or mother love. We will make the theater as uncompromisingly masculine as a turbine and as offensively unfeminine as a sailor's pipe."

Mayer bolstered this clever attempt to turn the theater's cost-saving lack of adornment to advantage with a programming policy similarly calculated to turn the sow's ear of second-run films into the silk purse of genre appeal. The Rialto specialized in what Mayer called "the M Product—mystery, mayhem and murder." Instead of glorifying the American girl, Mayer's avowed goal was "to glorify the American ghoul." The old Rialto had been known as "The House of Hits." Mayer dubbed its replacement "The House of Horror" and inveigled the press into nicknaming him the "Merchant of Menace." He made the Rialto's lobby over into a virtual dime museum of horror, complete with fire-snorting, eye-rolling gargoyles, instruments of torture, a barrel labeled BEWARE, DYNAMITE, papier-mâché fists clutching bloodstained clubs, and a poster of a pinup girl writhing under a sadist's whip. A huge American flag rippled over the whole display, animated by a wind machine. For *The Mummy*, Mayer commissioned an electrified twelve-foot monster that won him a summons for blocking foot traffic on Broadway. The authorities also took exception to the script that Mayer wrote for the Rialto's telephone operator, who answered every call with variations of "Help, murder, police! This is the Rialto, now playing *The Werewolf of London*, best thriller of the year."

Mayer, who personally screened some six hundred B-rated pictures a year, "labored over the copy for his Broadway marquee as diligently as a haiku poet." He did not hesitate to change a movie's title to heighten its appeal. "Handicapped by weak casts, the titles of pictures played assumed even more importance than ordinarily," he explained. To *A Son Comes Home*, he tacked on *From Gangland*. He improved *Fit for a King* by inserting *Murder* ahead of it. *I'd Give My Life* was blithely transformed into *The Noose*. Mayer told a reporter that the Rialto's two least successful films were *Absolute Quiet* and *Revolt of the Zombies*. "I should have changed *Absolute Quiet* to *The Big Noise*," he said. "But what could you do with *Revolt of the Zombies*? The trouble with that picture was that the boys never found out what zombies were."

Like the cafeteria, the grind house was the rare business designed to prosper in hard times. Because second-run movies were cheaper to lease than first-run pictures the grinders could offer bargain-priced admissions and still turn a profit simply by attracting a crowd. And that they did, at all hours of the day and night. In 1936, the Rialto sold 1.4 million tickets, or about 4,000 a day—an astounding figure for a 600-seat theater. "Our seats are probably more used than any on Broadway," bragged Mayer, who now operated twenty-four hours a day. While the Broadway movie palaces drew mainly from the affluent classes, 42nd Street's audience was blue-collar. It also was disproportionately African-American, in part because blacks had never been welcome in the Broadway movie palaces. Some palaces barred blacks outright while in others "ushers were instructed to steer Negroes away from the center aisles and seat them instead next to the wall or in the balconies." The typical grind house patron probably was a bus driver or a Midtown secretary looking for a few hours of lively distraction at a bargain price before heading home to Brooklyn or the Bronx. However, the grinders' unusual hours of operation alone assured that they would attract outcasts and outliers of all sorts. Staying open all night "attracted many patrons who, for personal reasons, preferred to avoid the more populated hours," wrote Mayer, adding that his clientele included "practically every notorious gangster in New York."

Grinder film fare was predictable—comfortingly so to its fans—but there was no telling what might happen inside a theater once the lights went down and the Pinkerton guards dozed off in back. A homemade tear gas bomb detonated inside the Times Square Theater, a Brandt venue, in the middle of a movie one night in 1936. At most theaters, a loud explosion would have triggered a stampede for the exits, but the 42nd Street movie-goer had been conditioned to seek entertainment in mishap. "Word passed around that someone had attempted suicide, and most of the spectators, curious to learn what happened, kept their seats," the *Times* reported.

The Hollywood stars of the 1930s would steer well clear of 42nd Street's movie premieres, such as they were. But the street did figure prominently in one of the era's great movie musicals, Warner Bros.' *42nd Street*. This backstage tale of the trials and tribulations of producing a musical worthy of opening on 42nd Street was adapted from an about-to-be-published novel of the same name by Bradford Ropes, an obscure, twenty-eight-year-old vaudeville hoofer. Ropes's novel was notable only for its gritty cynicism and nasty, off-color wisecracks. At one point, a chorus girl describes a rival showgirl as "just one of Broadway's whoreified girls" (a play on Ziegfeld's Glorified Girls). Two other chorus girls are talking trash: "I hear old Lily Lowbottom, Andy Lee's girlfriend, ran around with Hughes for a while," says one. "Yeah? When was this?" "Oh, about five abortions ago." A *New York Times* reviewer dismissed Ropes's novel as "excessively vulgar, gossipy" and "definitely not a book to give to a maiden aunt."

Hollywood had an infinite supply of mediocre novels to adapt so why *42nd Street*? The film scholar Rocco Fumento surmised that it was Ropes's title above all else that Warner's found appealing. "Its title alone would bring in all those starry-eyed youngsters who dreamed of going to New York and to Forty-second Street, perhaps the most glamorous street in the world to starry-eyed youngsters back in 1933." The film did go to considerable lengths to build authentic backstage atmosphere, giving the rehearsal scenes a quasi-documentary feel. Enough of Ropes's sharp-tongued cynicism survived in *42nd Street*'s dialogue and characterizations to qualify it as the first "hardboiled musical." Even so, the movie's plot was pure melodrama. Peggy Sawyer (played by Ruby Keeler) is a virginal young actress who gets her shot at stardom when Dorothy Brock (Bebe Daniels), the nasty, sluttish star of *Pretty Lady*, breaks her ankle on the eve of opening night. Sawyer learns the part in five hours. As the curtain rises and the ingenue tremblingly prepares for her entrance, the musical's domineering director urges her on with the classic line, "You're going out a youngster. You've *got* to come back a star." She does, of course—and wins the offstage love of her leading man (Dick Powell) in the bargain. The movie's appeal was enhanced by a superior score by Tin Pan Alley veterans Harry Warren and Al Dubin that included "You're Gettin' to Be a Habit with Me," "Young and Healthy," "Shuffle Off to Buffalo," and the title song. The film also marked the Hollywood coming-of-age of choreographer Busby Berkeley, whose staging of the title tune was judged by the journal *American Cinematographer* to be "a production number so spectacular as to surpass anything of its kind seen before."

Filmed in late 1932, *42nd Street* was almost journalistic in its topicality. An embittered Julian March takes the job of directing *Pretty Lady* only because the stock market had wiped him out. "This time I'll sock my money away so hard they'll have to blast to find enough to buy a newspaper," he vows. The play's casting call ("Jones and Barry are doing a show!") is big news on Broadway, triggering a flurry of excited phone calls and a stampede of unemployed actors and chorus girls. *Pretty Lady* is at once a frivolous musical and a lifeline to which every member of its cast clings. "Two hundred people, two hundred jobs, two hundred thousand dollars, five weeks of grind, and blood and sweat, depend on you," Marsh tells Sawyer in his preshow pep talk. "It's the life of all these people who have worked with you."

During the final dress rehearsal, an "aged trouper" working as a cabdriver dies onstage after delivering *Pretty Lady*'s opening lines: "Forty-second Street! Sidewalks crowded with the ghosts of yesterday. Why—there's Eddie Foy stopping to shake hands with his old pal Raymond Hitchcock. Good old Sam Bernard. David Warfield—rest his soul. (Quoting) 'If you don't want her—I vant her.' And the grandest singer of them all—Nora Bayes. I can hear her singing now 'Shine on Harvest Moon'—and the master of them all—David Belasco. I remember them well and they're gone—all gone—except for me." The actor then collapses and dies, though director Marsh pretends otherwise. "Nothing to worry about!" he tells the cast. "He said before he fainted he hoped you'd all give a swell dress rehearsal!"

Forty-second Street was indeed on its last theatrical legs when the film was being made. But with the exception of this prophetic if rather clumsily staged scene, *42nd Street*'s portrayal of 42nd Street was decidedly postdated. The movie opened with a rapid-fire sequence of establishing shots—street signs, landmark buildings, crowd shots—that seemed to imply that not only the Broadway theater but all of New York City revolved around a 42nd Street that throbbed with activity. (Aside from these brief scenes, the movie was entirely shot on Los Angeles–area sound stages.) The film's happy ending cast a rosy glow over the entire theater district as it breathed new life into the hoary Broadway myth of overnight stardom. But above all it was Warren and Dubin's brilliantly evocative title song, that gave 42nd Street eternal life with its insistent use of the present tense to describe the block in its heyday:

> *Come and meet those dancing feet*
> *On the avenue I'm taking you to, 42nd Street*
> *Hear the beat of dancing feet*
> *It's the song I love the melody of, 42nd Street.*

Convinced of *42nd Street*'s hit potential, Warner's gave the film a boost by chartering a train for a whistle-stop promotional tour across the country. The "42nd Street Special" left Hollywood on February 2, 1933, loaded with Warner contract stars including Bette Davis, Joe E. Brown, and Tom Mix (none of whom appeared in the film) and other celebrities. The release of *42nd Street* was the first time a studio launched a film with screenings throughout the American heartland before gala openings in New York and Los Angeles. The movie's "world premiere" took place on February 23 in Denver, where the governor of Colorado greeted the tour. The train then stopped in Kansas City, Chicago, Toledo, and Memphis. In every city, the train's arrival touched off parades, radio broadcasts, and other promotional events, climaxing with a screening. The 42nd Street Special arrived in Washington, D.C., in time for FDR's inauguration on

March 4. Warner's, which unabashedly promoted 42nd Street as "Inaugurating a New Deal in Entertainment," even had its own float in the celebratory parade.

The 42nd Street Special pulled into Grand Central Terminal on March 9. A huge crowd waited. "If the gods had descended on Manhattan," *Photoplay* reported, "there couldn't have been more excitement." After a luncheon at the Commodore Hotel marking the 108th anniversary of the deeding of 42nd Street to the city of New York, the Hollywood party marched the length of the street, led by Tom Mix on horseback. However, the opening was held six blocks up Broadway at the Strand Theater, the original movie palace, which Warner Bros. owned. While the movie played, a fierce storm descended on the city, as winds of up to fifty miles an hour broke windows and uprooted trees. It only seemed a bad omen, as the film remained at the Strand until May. Nominated for two Academy Awards (for best picture and best sound recording), *42nd Street* ranked second in ticket sales among all films in 1933, trailing only the Mae West vehicle *I'm No Angel*.

When *42nd Street* began its run at the Strand in early 1933, five of the ten theaters on 42nd Street were still producing plays. But by the fall of 1934, only the New Amsterdam survived. The final edition of *George White's Scandals* opened Christmas Day in 1935 and ran for three months. The next year, the mortgage holder foreclosed on Abe Erlanger's heirs, who owed more than $1.65 million in back taxes and overdue interest. In January 1937, a dispirited version of Shakespeare's *Othello* closed after a brief run, ending a continuous forty-four-year run of theater on 42nd Street. Max Cohen outbid a burlesque operator to acquire the New Amsterdam for $1.5 million, with a hefty $500,000 down. Fittingly, Cohen reopened the New Amsterdam with a movie version of the first play ever produced at the theater: Shakespeare's *A Midsummer Night's Dream*.

With the creeping demise of the theater in the 1930s, live entertainment survived on 42nd Street mainly in the obstreperous form of burlesque, vaudeville's ne'er-do-well cousin. Burlesque was the raunchy residue left when variety was refined into vaudeville in the closing decades of the nineteenth century. As Irving Ziedman put it in *The American Burlesque Show*, "While variety became vaudeville and aligned itself with talent, burlesque became itself and aligned itself with dirt." In a word, burlesque was sex. "What has sustained burlesque more than any other feature . . . is none other than the old-fashioned hootchie-kootchie," also known as the bump and grind.

Like the theater and vaudeville, burlesque had given rise around the turn of the century to monopoly-minded promoters who gained control over numerous venues across the country and organized them into regional and national networks. Local promoters excluded from these burlesque circuits, or "wheels," found that the only way they could compete with the big combines was to offer a raunchier brand of entertainment—the local police department permitting, of course. In New York, defiant little clusters of independent, or "stock," burlesque houses formed around Union Square and on the Lower East Side. One of the most popular was the National Winter Garden on East Houston Street, run by the brothers Minsky—Abraham, M. William "Billy," Herbert, and Morton.

The Minsky boys were not underprivileged sorts driven into burlesque by the deprivations of the immigrant ghetto. Their father, Louis, was a New York City alderman and well-to-do property developer who put Herbert through Columbia University Law School and Morton through its New York University counterpart. Billy never had the patience for college but did serve an improbable stint as a newspaper society columnist. With the decline of the big burlesque wheels in the 1920s, stock houses sprang up around the country. Ignoring his father's advice—"Never go to work north of 14th Street"—Billy emerged from the obscurity of the Lower East Side to take burlesque to new heights of popularity—and notoriety—at Broadway and 42nd. What Hammerstein's Victoria had been to vaudeville, Billy Minsky's Republic was to burlesque: the ultimate, national showcase of a form of mass entertainment dying by degrees.

Billy Minsky traveled to 42nd Street by way of Columbus Circle, where he opened the Park Theatre in 1922, and Harlem, where the Apollo enlivened 125th Street beginning in 1924. The Apollo, an uptown clone of the National Winter Garden, thrived despite frequent police raids, but the Park's sanitized, G-rated brand of burlesque never found an audience. With the Park, a failure from beginning to end, Minsky succumbed to what Ziedman called the "occupational disease of burlesque operators": a yearning for respectability. He never made the same mistake again. Yes, he dressed burlesque in fancy clothes, both literally and figuratively, for 42nd Street's spotlight, but he also promoted his shows with defiant chutzpah. Willie Hammerstein was an aggressive pitchman, but he had not emblazoned the Victoria's marquee with titles like *The Sway of All Flesh, Panties Inferno,* or *Dress Takes a Holiday;* he never hired an airplane to buzz the city trailing a banner advertising his star attractions, and he never stationed a spieler on the sidewalk to bellow, "Watch her! Like a banana, watch her peel! Right down to the fruit!"

The Republic became available in 1931 because of the financial difficulties of Arthur Hammerstein, Oscar's son and heir. The Minskys leased the theater from Hammerstein's creditors in partnership with Joseph Weinstock, a wealthy building contractor who also was an investor in the Apollo. Minsky's Republic did not introduce burlesque to 42nd Street; the American Music Hall had experimented unsuccessfully with stripper-centric entertainment in 1929. But the American's programs, like all the pre-Minsky burlesque shows in Times Square, were little more than naughty miniature musical comedies, not unlike Billy's own failed shows at the Park. At the Republic, Minsky took a bolder, more frontal approach, as it were, that scandalized many opening-night reviewers. No one was more outraged than *Variety*'s burley-hating editor, who castigated the show as "just rotten, with parts of it lousy, comprising as it does the cheapest dirt, the dirtiest coochers ever forced upon a stage or platform and with no talent." The police department saw to it that Minsky toned down his act after the Republic's deliberately intemperate opening, but it hardly mattered. "The notoriety given the opening of the theater . . . served in reverse effect," Ziedman commented. "It became fashionable to attend burlesque on Broadway, instead of getting kicks in a moldy theater on a hidden side street."

Gyrating women in G-strings held center stage at the Republic, but around them Minsky created what, by burlesque standards anyway, was an elaborate variety show in a posh venue. Minsky featured all of the era's top strippers and paid top dollar for comics, rotating three or four through every show. The Republic also employed a first-rate "tit serenader" in the person of Robert Alda, the father of future actor Alan Alda, who sang straight numbers between strip routines and also filled the role of straight man in skits. Alda sometimes played eight or nine parts in a show while singing fifteen songs or more. Minsky's troupe also included comediennes, or "talking women," and a female singer, or "prima donna." The big production numbers that brother Billy dreamed up could be highly entertaining, even though—or often because—they lacked the panache and precision of such high-toned fare as the *Follies,* the *Scandals,* and the *Vanities,* all of which were still playing on the block when the Republic opened.

Gypsy Rose Lee never forgot the spectacle that unfolded onstage as she waited in the wings to perform for the first time at Minsky's Republic. "The chorus girls were dressed as cow girls and Indians with bows and paper arrows and pop guns that shot cotton balls out into the audience," Lee recalled.

> For the big finish, the curtains opened and two white horses raced madly on treadmills that revolved on the stage. Two of the showgirls, naked from their waists up, rode the horses. The treadmill made a loud grating noise and that, along with the clatter of horses' hoofs and the chorus girls letting out war whoops and firing the cotton bullets and paper arrows at the audience, made a spectacular production number. The audience, apathetic until then, applauded enthusiastically until one of the horses had an accident, then they began to laugh. They thought it was very funny while the treadmill faced the wings, but when it faced upstage and horses began kicking the manure all over the first five rows of the theater, they stopped laughing.

Lee, who was born Rose Louise Hovick, was a former child vaudevillian driven into burlesque by the deprivations of the Depression. Just seventeen years old when she first took the stage at the Republic in 1931, Gypsy already had perfected an ingeniously original style of stripping. "The remarkable thing about her . . . was that she had a very slim figure, and a flat bust, but she had mastered the art of the tease to such an extent that nobody minded," Mort Minsky recalled. "In a manner new to burlesque, she turned her essentially shy feelings about disrobing onstage into a mocking, spoofing jest." Gypsy's trick costume was held together by strategically placed pins that she removed one at a time and tossed into the audience. (Each pin could be redeemed at the box office for a free admission.) "While other strippers were scared to death at the thought of speaking words of more than two syllables," Minsky added, "Gypsy, in her expertise, let her erudite, insinuating chatter seduce the audience into a state of near-hypnosis."

Another young stripper who stepped up to stardom on the stage of the Republic was Georgia Sothern, born Hazel Anderson. Sothern and Lee were close friends but utterly dissimilar. Standing just five feet tall, Georgia was nearly a foot shorter than Gypsy and ferociously athletic. Ann Corio, another of 42nd Street's preeminent strippers, offered this admiring analysis of Sothern's distinctive act: "Her music, 'Hold That Tiger,' was wild, the orchestra played at full blast and full tempo, and Georgia came on stage in full flight. And she'd work up momentum. Faster and faster the music would roar, and Georgia would be at the front of the stage, one hand cascading her long red hair over her face, the other outstretched to keep her balance as her hips blurred back and forth at a fantastic tempo. . . . She was a cyclone of sex and she literally blew the walls down." Minsky put life-size blowups of Sothern in front of the theater to promote her opening, along with a huge sign that read THE HUMAN BOMBSHELL TO EXPLODE SUNDAY!

Minsky's Republic was a hit right from the start, selling out two shows a day at admission charges ranging from 75 cents to $1.50. Like many other burley joints, the Republic effectively lowered the cost of admission for diehard fans by selling season passes. The producers of 42nd Street's faltering theatrical productions did not take kindly to the cut-rate competition. George White, who was charging $5.50 a head for admission to the *Scandals*, popped Billy Minsky on the nose when he passed him on 42nd Street one day. The elfin, bespectacled Billy, who stood barely five feet tall, was too delighted to retaliate, according to brother Mort. "As far as he was concerned, this was just his initiation into the big time." When Earl Carroll opened *Murder at the Vanities* across the street at the New Amsterdam, Billy cheekily hung a two-story banner over his place that read *SLAUGHTER AT MINSKY'S*.

The Minskys did not have 42nd Street to themselves for long. Max Rudnick, a Brooklyn movie house operator and Broadway theatrical producer, leased the Eltinge Theater across the street at 236 West 42nd. In March 1931, just a month after the Republic opened, the Eltinge debuted with a grind policy of four burlesque bills interspersed with short films. The theater block's second burley house opened in such a hurry that its stagehands had to prop its runway on their shoulders because they hadn't had time to build proper supports. The Eltinge lacked the handpicked stars of the Minsky stable, but its shows were just as raw as the Republic's and much cheaper. Rudnick sent forth platoons of unemployed men in sandwich boards, advertising an early admission of just 15 cents. The Minskys never matched Rudnick's bargain price but did adopt a four-a-day grind policy themselves, with shows at noon, two, eight, and ten, plus a midnight show on Friday. The show changed every week, which meant that rehearsals had to be held every morning and auditions most every night. "When I say the theater contained elements of bedlam, I am not exaggerating," Mort Minsky said.

Star strippers like Lee, Sothern, Corio, Margie Hart, or Hinda Wassau could make $1,000 a week or more on 42nd Street, but the chorus girls earned just $20 for an eighty-hour week. The most ambitious of them made a bit extra by standing in the wings and catching items of clothing as they were discarded by the strippers. Most of the women who toiled at the Republic and the Eltinge roomed together in small hotels and rooming houses near the theaters, like the Dixie on 43rd and the Peerless Palace on 46th Street. Gypsy lived with her mother right on 42nd Street, paying $12.50 a week for a one-room kitchenette in the Cameo apartments, once part of Murray's Roman Gardens. "There were still traces of its past grandeur in the faded silk brocade on the walls and the water-stained mirrors in the dark, smelly halls," Lee recalled. "What had been known as the Garden Room now was filled with bed springs, mattresses, old awnings and boxes and trunks belonging to tenants past and present. Greasy aromas wafted up from the Nedick's hot dog joint down below, and the constant din of the traffic on 42nd Street made sleep difficult." But steady employment at a class joint like Minsky's made it all worthwhile. "The nicest part about it was that we could look out our window at my billing on the theater across the street," Gypsy continued. "When Mother and I worried about the future, and we worried a lot, we would look out the window and be reassured."

For the first time since Long Acre was made over into Times Square, an undertone of menace crept into 42nd Street's squalling street symphony in the 1930s. By 1934, Father Joseph A. McCaffrey, the outspoken new pastor of the Church of the Holy Cross at 329 West 42nd Street, was publicly complaining of "a hoodlum element that was frightening decent people off the street." The Broadway Association, which represented theater owners and other establishment interests, joined Father McCaffrey in calling for a crackdown. Meanwhile, the beleaguered owners of the Great White Way's surviving tourist hotels organized a new trade group called Hotels of Times Square to counter "the almost universal idea that Times Square is wicked . . . haunted by careless 'triggermen' and cutpurses." Crime rates rose throughout America during the Depression, but police statistics showed that 42nd Street and Times Square were no more dangerous than other parts of Midtown during the 1930s. The real problem was not crime, but fear of crime, and it would have taken a uniformed army to make pedestrians feel safe amid the scruffy panhandlers who now thronged the sidewalks.

In the early 1930s, some one million drifters and hobos roamed the land in the first occurrence of mass homelessness in U.S. history, and a good number of them passed through Times Square. Outcasts and hustlers seeking the sheltering anonymity of the crowd could do no better than 42nd Street and Broadway, especially now that it was "the Twenty-four-Hour Corner" as well as the Crossroads of the World. From the beginning, the Great White Way had been a late-night sort of place, geared as it was no less to a posttheater than to a pretheater scene. But with the advent of the movie grind house and the proliferation of the round-the-clock cafeteria and arcades in the 1930s, late night became all night, redefining 42nd Street as America's hangout street par excellence. Who needed to waste money on a room when ten cents bought you an overnight stay in a grind house and a nickel spent on a cup of coffee or a little pot of baked beans with a bacon strip entitled you to a table in Hector's or Bickford's for as long as you might require it? The Automat was particularly conducive to the loitering life because it employed no waiters or waitresses looking to turn over tables. (It did prohibit smoking, though.)

The economic recovery of the World War II years would diminish but not nearly eliminate the "hoodlum element" that so exorcised Father McCaffrey. A tenacious underclass of idlers, drunks, drug addicts, prostitutes (both heterosexual and homosexual), assorted misfits, and grifters had taken root on 42nd Street's teeming sidewalks and in its uniquely accommodating movie theaters, cafeterias, bars, and arcades. By the end of the 1930s, if not earlier, 42nd Street was known throughout the country as a paradise for losers. "I was stone broke and like every other young kid who hits the city broke I went directly to 42nd Street," recalled Herbert Huncke (rhymes with *junkie*), an itinerant addict, gay hustler, and petty thief who arrived in Manhattan in 1940 from points west.

From time to time in the 1930s, and over the decades to come, City Hall would order up a crackdown on the "undesirables" who had settled on 42nd Street like water collects in a hole. But there wasn't much the police department could do or, in truth, wanted to do. Loitering wasn't a crime (despite periodic attempts to make it one), nor, for that matter, was undesirability. The laws that were broken tended to be misdemeanors, punishable by small fines. Left to its own devices, the New York Police Department was content to prevent violent crime and keep traffic flowing on the streets and sidewalks. "By and large the man on the beat—there are two uniformed men on each side of the block twenty-four hours a day, in addition to the Transit Authority men below street level—handle (undesirables) simply by keeping them moving," the *Times* reported in an unusually lengthy front-page article—"Life on W. 42nd St.: A Study in Decay"—that singled out the theater block between Seventh and Eighth Avenues as "the worst block in town."

City Hall was much more aggressive—and effective—in going after the block's burlesque operators, who were equally offensive to the general public and, as businessmen, were much more susceptible to harassment than outcasts with nothing to lose and nowhere else to go. From its earliest days, burlesque had collided with obscenity laws virtually everywhere it played. But the judiciary's liberal interpretations of First Amendment protections of free speech had combined with the political influence wielded by well-to-do theater owners to keep burlesque alive, if not always thriving, in New York and many other big cities. In venturing out of the shadows onto Broadway, Billy Minsky and his brothers inflamed opposition of a less compromising sort. Or, as Morton put it, "Billy's new Broadway neighbors practically *plotzed* when they heard that a Minsky burlesque show was about to open on 42nd Street." The counterattack that the Broadway establishment launched against the 42nd Street burlesque houses in the mid-1930s was not the usual series of skirmishes but an all-out attempt to eliminate a rival form of entertainment. As such, it prefigured the antipornography crusades that would turn 42nd Street into a legal battleground from the late 1960s into the 1990s.

The Broadway interests prosecuted their campaign against the Minskys and their colleagues through two organizations never previously distinguished by reformist zeal: the 42nd Street Property Owners and Merchants Association and the Broadway Association. Their allies included most of the city's newspapers, with the *New York Daily Mirror* outdoing its fellow tabloids in the frequency of its exposés and vehemence of its criticisms. The Republic was raided so often that Billy Minsky installed a red "John Law Light" in among the stage footlights. If the ticket taker sniffed out an undercover cop, she set the light to flashing, a sign to the strippers onstage to tone it down. Even the hapless Oscar Skyhook, the Minsky's Stiltwalker, ran afoul of the law when he inadvertently destroyed a second-floor window on Seventh Avenue as he shooed away a pigeon that had mistaken him for a statue.

Burlesque's enemies were offended by more than its displays of female flesh on the hoof. Minsky's Republic, the Eltinge, and a third burley show that would take over the Apollo Theater in 1934 bridged the realms of risqué live entertainment for which 42nd Street long had been famous and the porno fare for which it would become infamous in the late 1960s. During intermission at the typical burlesque show, the "candy butcher" came onstage and retailed suggestive booklets and "French" postcards of seminude women, as well as candy. The postcards were their own best advertisement, but in her book *This Was Burlesque* Corio gave this sample of a butcher's sales pitch for his verbal wares: "This is the randiest story I personally ever have read . . . never will you see such descriptions . . . such detail . . . such words in a printed book unless you buy this little booklet in my hand. I promise you, it leaves nothing to the imagination." In reality, Corio scoffed, most of these booklets "wouldn't have shocked your grandmother." Lewder stuff was generally available outside the theater doors, where freelance peddlers of dirty pictures and other smut congregated before and after shows. During the 1930s, burlesque's "camp followers" offered increasingly explicit wares in response to the growing competitive threat of magazines like *The Nudist*.

After a series of the traditional police raids on 42nd Street ended in the traditional court acquittals, the opponents of burlesque pressured the administration of Mayor Jimmy Walker to reject the Republic's and the Eltinge's applications for renewal of their annual operating licenses, which came due May 1, 1932. At public hearings, a parade of witnesses not only inveighed against the immorality of the striptease, but also accused burlesque's curbside barkers, steerers, and dirty-picture vendors of despoiling 42nd Street—now "a cesspool of filth and obscenity," in the estimation of Holy Cross's McCaffrey. Billy Minsky, who had fallen terminally ill, was conspicuous by his absence, and Rudnick declined the opportunity to justify himself. It fell to the esteemed A. J. Liebling to defend the Republic and the Eltinge in the pages of *The New Yorker*, by heaping sarcasm on the proceedings. "Witnesses at the clean-up hearings . . . testified that idlers along 42nd Street have been eating peanuts and commenting on passing women. It is a short step between that and whittling," wrote Liebling, hailing Billy Minsky as "the workingman's Ziegfeld."

After the heavily publicized hearings ended, the city took no action against the theaters, which were allowed to continue operating without licenses. Billy Minksy, just forty-one years old, died of bone cancer in June, terminating the family's audacious plans to lease the Metropolitan Opera House on 39th Street and Broadway for a season of "super-burlesque." Herbert Minsky succeeded, though never fully replaced, Billy as manager of the Republic and the Central, assisted by fellow law school grad Morton. Over the next few years, the 42nd Street burley operators managed to keep the regulators at bay by agreeing to refrain from using the word *burlesque* in their advertising. In homage to the late Ziegfeld, the Republic renamed its show the "Frolic," and the Eltinge opted for the "Follies." What's in a name? In this case, not much. No one was likely to mistake Minsky's and Rudnick's latest strip-happy offerings for the second coming of Ziegfeld or even Earl Carroll.

The election of Fiorello La Guardia in 1934 as mayor was bad news for burley. The new mayor's "puritanical streak, that sense of moral outrage, was so highly developed that he could make no distinction between a truly original theatrical genre, and ordinary prostitution; or between a work of literature with some four-letter words, and magazines with flagrantly lewd cover illustrations publicly displayed; or between church bingo and the numbers racket," wrote La Guardia biographer Lawrence Elliott. "To him they were all the same, and he railed away at them with fine impartiality, sometimes making himself look silly." At the same time, though, the "Little Flower" brought a forcefulness to the mayoralty that expanded the possibilities of the office. La Guardia's crusade against burlesque was indeed silly in many respects but effective just the same.

La Guardia delighted the Broadway crowd by appointing one of its own as license commissioner. Paul Moss was the brother of producer B. S. Moss and a former theatrical producer himself. Moss began his campaign to clean up burlesque in mid-1934 by denying Max R. Wilner a license to open a third burlesque house on 42nd Street. Wilner, the former owner of the Irving Place Theater, where striptease supposedly was invented, leased the Apollo Theater at 223 West 42nd, just a few doors away from the Republic and opposite the Eltinge. Wilner promised that burlesque would be only a passing fancy at the Apollo. "I'll open up with burlesque to get my initial crowd and then try to get something else," he testified. "I'll gradually eliminate the word." When Moss asked him what word he would use instead, the burley man broke into a verbal soft-shoe. "That's just it, commissioner," Wilner said. "If someone could only think of a word, that would have saved all this trouble. But I'll get my data together to see if I can't solve this problem. You let me on 42nd Street and I'll set an example for you."

Moss rejected Wilner's application but was promptly overruled by a state judge. The victorious Wilner soon made a mockery of his testimony before Moss. The Apollo featured more strips per hour than any other burley theater in the country. The theater, which billed itself as "The Home of Glorified Burlesque," managed this feat without resorting to the sort of no-name teasers featured at the Eltinge. Wilner vied with the Minskys to book top strippers and comics alike. One of his coups was luring the comedians Bud Abbott and Lou Costello, the self-proclaimed "Bad Boys of Burlesque," away from the Republic, where they once had played a marathon game of pinochle, keeping score on the walls of their dressing room after they ran short of shirt cardboards. "By the time I joined the show the pinochle scores covered the walls and extended out into the hallway," recalled Gypsy Rose Lee, who played the Apollo herself once. It was during a thirty-week stint at the Apollo in 1936 that Abbott and Costello introduced their signature "Who's on First?" routine and positioned themselves at the threshold of crossover stardom in the movies.

Within days of the Apollo's opening in October 1934, Moss issued new rules for all burlesque shows in the city. His first commandment: "No female shall be permitted on the stage in any scene, sketch, or act with breasts or the lower part of the torso uncovered, or thinly covered or draped as to appear uncovered." He even tried to gag the comics: "No vulgar or obscene or indecent language offensive to decency or propriety shall be indulged in by performers in any scene, sketch, or act or play." Ann Corio appeared at the Apollo in a black chiffon gown with a huge lock on her back and sang along with the chorus, "I would if I could but I can't." Later in the show, Corio came out as a widow and sang "Mr. Striptease is dead" as comic Joey Faye was carried out on a board. But Mr. Striptease lived on at the Eltinge, where a pair of detectives went backstage at a matinee and arrested two managers and seven chorus girls at intermission, charging them with giving a performance that would "tend to corrupt the morals of youth and others." A judge threw out that case, but Moss continued to put the screws to the Apollo, the Eltinge, and the Republic. "I often thought we should have put revolving doors into the box office. We were open and closed so many times. Here a technicality, there a technicality," complained Mort Minsky.

Finally, in 1937, Moss refused to renew the licenses of all fourteen of the city's burlesque shows. "The lack of imagination and the lack of showmanship as well as the general caliber of the men running burlesque is such that they do not understand that clean entertainment pays and the vulgar, cheap performances do not," the license commissioner said. If by "pays" Moss meant turning a profit, he was utterly incorrect. That very January the resounding flop of an impeccably clean production of Shakespeare's *Othello* had doomed the New Amsterdam. The theater had died on 42nd Street for lack of profit even as its three burlesque houses were rolling in the dough. But money wasn't everything, and so Mayor La Guardia led the theater community in a standing ovation for Moss. "This is the beginning of the end of incorporated filth," the mayor declared. "God bless our license commissioner."

In August, Max Wilner decided there were easier ways to make a living and went off to direct a Yiddish playhouse in Brooklyn. However, the Republic and the Eltinge were granted provisional licenses after agreeing again to renounce the word *burlesque* and posting a $1,000 bond. (The Republic also had to forswear the use of *Minsky* in its advertising and promotion.) A citizens' censorship board was appointed to oversee the city's surviving burley houses, which had to make do with a smut-free brand of entertainment that played to half-empty houses. "If the audience couldn't have the old-fashioned strip, they were not coming back," lamented Morton Minsky. Old-time burlesque fans still went to 42nd Street but mostly to catch a special bus that transported them to the Hudson Theater in Newark or the Empire Theater in Union City, the twin hubs of the suddenly ascendant New Jersey burley scene.

By 1939, the Republic and the Eltinge were the last burlesque houses left in Manhattan, and they were but shadows of their former selves. From time to time, they would test the limits of censorship, antagonizing the ever-vigilant Moss, but for the most part they offered variety entertainment so devoid of smut as to inspire the newspapers to periodic mockery. "The Bishop—any Bishop—could take his sister—or anyone else's sister to the Eltinge on wicked 42nd Street and not a blush could possibly suffuse his, or her, countenance," the *Times* wrote of an "all-colored revue" featuring a twelve-man band, tap dancers, black-face comics, and chastely garbed chorus girls. "Not in the history of man has a cleaner or duller show been purveyed to the gullible sailors, soldiers, and bald-headed old men with nothing to do of an afternoon."

Birth of the Cool: Hipster 42nd Street

After the United States entered the war against Germany and Japan in December 1941, New York City authorities ordered the extinguishing of all lights above street level throughout the city, Times Square included. Despite the eerie "dim-out" that enveloped it nightly, West 42nd Street continued, as always, to draw a crowd. During World War II, an actual fighting force augmented the diminished army of drifters and vagrants who had haunted the street through the 1930s. Soldiers and sailors routed through New York City on their way to or from the battlefield passed through Times Square by the thousands in search of the cheap, round-the-clock carnival diversions that 42nd Street now epitomized. One Brooklyn-born soldier beginning his summer leave told the *New York Post* that after visiting his mother he planned "to go to Times Square and stand there practically all day smelling the frankfurters and breathing in the cold air from all those air-conditioned movie houses. And one of the things I want to do is yoohoo at every pretty girl who passes by."

Most of the GIs hit New York too late to visit the Republic or the Eltinge. During the summer of 1941, both reformed burlesque houses tempted fate by adding the occasional bump and grind to their variety bills. Instead of promptly taking action, License Commissioner Moss waited for the theaters' operating licenses to expire on January 31, 1942, to deliver the mortal blow. Renewal was simply out of the question, the commissioner proclaimed. "They had had repeated warnings," Moss said. "We have purposely not gone into court because we did not want to advertise the filthy shows. The Mayor has repeatedly stated that war conditions will not be permitted to lower the standards of morals and of decency in this city."

Burlesque's loss was the Brandt family's gain. Brandt Theaters acquired both the Republic and the Eltinge, turning them into movie grinders after renaming them to remove the lingering taint of burlesque; the Republic was now the Victory and the Eltinge the Empire. At the same time, the brothers purchased the land under two 42nd Street theaters they had operated since the 1930s: the Lyric and the Liberty. Billy Brandt told reporters that these investments were inspired by the family's belief that 42nd Street would be reborn as a legitimate theater hub after the war ended. With seven theaters, the Brandts now controlled more than half the frontage on the north side of the theater block. The brothers also paid top dollar for a small lunch counter wedged in between the Apollo and the Selwyn theaters, giving them continuous dominion over a swath of 42nd Street extending from the Victory at 207 all the way to the Selwyn at 229. Even before they closed this annoying little gap in their holdings, the Brandts began broadly hinting of a major development project—an office tower and a luxury hotel, perhaps, along with a Broadway house or two.

For two weeks in January 1943, the servicemen who thronged Times Square were themselves overwhelmed by tens of thousands of "bobby-soxers" attending Frank Sinatra's career-making performance at the Paramount on 43rd Street. Billed behind Bing Crosby and Benny Goodman and his band as an "extra added attraction," Sinatra stole the show, emerging overnight as the hottest musical act in the country. "Inside the theater, unruly crowds of teenagers screamed at the top of their lungs; outside an even bigger mob of girls launched an epidemic of mass truancy and motionless traffic that transformed Times Square into the world's largest parking lot." A few months after Sinatra had vaulted to stardom, a raw, moody young actor named Marlon Brando, newly arrived in New York from Omaha, Nebraska, established an observation post in a telephone booth at the Optima cigar store in the Rialto Building on the corner of 42nd and Seventh Avenue. "He loved observing people," wrote one Brando biographer, "listening to them cough and spit and yak: 'Hey, watcha doin'? Wanna hot dog?'" Occupying the booth for more than a few minutes at a time was an achievement in its own right, for it was part of a bank of telephones so heavily patronized that New York Bell Telephone had to replace the directories at least twice a week.

West 42nd Street now was a paradise lost for fans of burlesque, as it long had been for aficionados of the Broadway stage and of vaudeville. But for lovers of B movies and genre film, the street was nirvana, with all ten of its grind houses offering double and triple bills from morning to midnight. "In the early forties, my father would bring me from Brooklyn into Manhattan for a Sunday or something like that," filmmaker Woody Allen recalled.

> You'd ride the subway for a half-hour from Brooklyn, then walk up into Times Square and look in every direction, and there would be lit marquees from movie houses. I mean, where I grew up—and it was an abundant-movie neighborhood in Brooklyn, you know—there were a certain number of cinemas. But when you came up at 42nd Street and looked east and west on 42nd Street, and up Broadway, I never saw anything like it in my life. It was just one movie house after another, all lit up, a number of them with stage shows, and the streets were jammed with soldiers and sailors, 'cause it was during the war. And it was just what a choreographer would choose to exaggerate if he was choreographing a ballet about New York.

In the spring of 1944, the *New York Post*'s intrepid nightclub columnist, Earl Wilson, took a night off from posh places like the Stork Club and El Morocco to spend an evening on 42nd Street—"the so-called Flea Circus neighborhood"—with his wife. "We romped about till after 3 A.M.—on a total outlay of 82 cents," wrote Wilson, who characterized the theater block as "bubblingly alive."

The columnist considered buying a sporty cap at the Adam Hat Store at 218 West 42nd ("I should wear one, stick it in my hip pocket in nightclubs, and save hatcheck tips") and admired actor Cesar Romero's picture in the window of a photo shop. "Not long ago, one photo shop used girls in very tight sweaters, to beckon service men in," he commented. "Competitors complained of sweater girl decoys—now they wear slacks." Wilson bought a copy of *White Slave Confessions* (marked down to twenty-five cents from fifty cents) from a bookstore and then walked on to Hubert's Museum, where he let "Henry, the Juggling Flea" feed on his arm.

Wilson, not to mention the young Brando and the even younger Allen, found the chaotic vibrancy of wartime 42nd Street alluring. But the same Broadway theater producers and other businessmen who had strenuously objected to the presence of burlesque throughout the 1930s now complained that servicemen and their young female companions, or "V-girls," were turning Times Square into a "boomtown similar to those adjoining military posts." The arcades leading to the IRT and Eighth Avenue subway lines at opposite ends of the grinder block were particularly popular hangouts and magnets for trouble. A local military police commander bemoaned his inability to place the arcades off limits. "How could you stop a soldier from going to a subway?" he lamented. Although the full-fledged adult bookstore had yet to make an appearance on 42nd Street, risqué photos and magazines could be purchased under the counter at newsstands, bookstores, and even in some penny arcades. World War II gave a lift to America's nascent porn industry by creating a huge captive market of lonesome GIs. The era's principal innovation was the "girlie" magazine. Titles like *Laff* (founded 1939), *See* (1941), *Eyeful* (1943), *Titter* (1943), *Sir* (1944), and *Hit* (1945) greatly expanded the market for nude pictorials. By war's end, there were hundreds of girlie magazines in America, and many were discreetly available on 42nd Street.

The presence of all those men in uniform also was a boom to 42nd Street's homosexual underground. Homosexuals had cruised the street long before World War II, but it was not until the early 1940s that they began attracting the attention of the city's newspapers and the censure of its public officials. Most of the hard-core gay hustler bars were on Midtown's East Side, but 42nd Street between Seventh and Eighth Avenues now became the weekend Mecca for out-of-town kids, who loitered purposefully in open shirts and dungarees. Among them was the young playwright Tennessee Williams, only recently emerged from the closet. Williams recalled going up to groups of servicemen on Times Square street corners

to make very abrupt and candid overtures, phrased so bluntly that it's a wonder they didn't slaughter me on the spot. . . . Sometimes they mistook me for a pimp soliciting for female prostitutes and would respond, "Sure, where's the girls?"—and I would have to explain that they were

my cruising partner and myself. Then, for some reason, they would
stare at me for a moment in astonishment, burst into laughter, huddle
for a brief conference, and, as often as not, would accept the solicitation, going to my partner's Village pad or to my room at the "Y."

In 1944, the ever-vigilant Fiorello La Guardia, now in his third and
final term as mayor, tried to curb the burgeoning gay pickup scene on
42nd Street by ordering the nightly closing of Bryant Park, at Sixth Avenue and 42nd Street. Bryant Park's sudden inaccessibility merely had
the effect of pushing homosexual trysting off the streets and into the balconies and bathrooms of the 42nd Street grind houses. The Brandts were
not happy about it, but what could they do? Or, more to the point, the
family was not prepared to take any action that sliced into its profits;
those SWAT teams of uniformed ushers employed by the Broadway movie
palaces did not come cheap.

The news zipper that girded the Times Tower was darkened for most
of the war by blackout regulations, but it flashed back to life on June 6,
1944—"D-day." For eighteen hours straight, the zipper carried news of
the decisive Allied troop landings at Normandy. Times Square's role as
New York City's unofficial town square was transcendently affirmed on
August 14, 1945—V-J Day—as a crowd of about 750,000 gathered in
anticipation of an official announcement of the end of World War II. At
7:03 that evening the Motogram zipper on Times Tower went dark for a
few seconds and then flashed: ***OFFICIAL*** TRUMAN AN-
NOUNCES JAPANESE SURRENDER." (The stars in this headline were
a tribute to the three branches of the armed forces.)

The roar of the crowd could be heard all the way to First Avenue and
to the middle of Central Park. From all over the city, people poured into
Times Square by bus, subway, and auto. By ten o'clock, the blocks spanning 40th to 48th Streets were packed solid with two million celebrants
in the city's loudest party ever. "The victory roar beat upon the eardrums
until it numbed the senses," the *Times* reported. The celebration produced one of the twentieth century's most famous photographs: Alfred
Eisenstadt's shot of a sailor swooping a nurse into a bent-back embrace
in the middle of Times Square.

The return of millions of soldiers and sailors at war's end triggered the release of huge pent-up demand for public amusement all across America. On July 4, 1947, Coney Island registered record daily attendance, with 1.3 million visitors, equal to nearly one-fifth of the population of New York City. Times Square also was overrun with free-spending pleasure seekers from early afternoon late into the night, every night. The Depression had been vanquished along with the Axis, and almost anything seemed possible. As in the late 1920s, developers laid ambitious plans to line 42nd Street and Broadway with shiny new skyscrapers of the sort then springing up along Madison and Park Avenues. But a funny thing happened on the way to the postwar greening of 42nd Street that the Brandts and other property owners had envisioned: it stopped dead. For the first time, the fortunes of 42nd Street and of New York City began to sharply diverge. Even as a great burst of growth and development lifted the city and the entire country to new peaks of prosperous modernity in the late 1940s and 1950s, 42nd Street remained the same low-rise, low-rent entertainment quarter that it had become during the 1930s.

While 42nd Street stagnated, the Times Square stretch of Broadway suffered a sharp decline. One by one, its oversize movie palaces were partitioned, closed, or demolished. (The Paramount, the last of the palaces to close, fleetingly recaptured some of the old excitement by jumping on the rock-and-roll bandwagon in the late 1950s.) At the same time, there was a drastic thinning of the crowds that long had gathered in Times Square to follow elections, sporting contests, and other events via the news ticker on the Times Tower. Even the billboard salesmen had a rough time of it, as the number of "spectaculars" declined from forty-five in the 1940s to twenty by the early 1960s.

The main culprit was television, which began to come of age in the late 1940s, cutting into attendance at movies, plays, baseball games, amusement parks, and most every other form of popular entertainment. Both Broadway and Hollywood would survive television's rise to dominance in the 1950s, but the motion picture never again would reclaim its cultural primacy; television had replaced it as the nation's daily entertainment medium, just as the movies had supplanted vaudeville and the Broadway stage. More broadly, public amusement had been trumped by the solitary diversions of home entertainment. "What was formerly a man's castle is fast becoming his movie theatre," quipped Arthur Mayer, who made a well-timed exit from 42nd Street in 1948, selling the Rialto to the Laff Movie chain. (The Merchant of Menace wrote his own 42nd Street epitaph, displayed on the Rialto's marquee: "Goodbye to Ghouls, Farewell to Horror.")

At the same time, Times Square and other central-city entertainment districts around the country were devastated by a mighty demographic shift. After the war, white middle-class Americans began moving out of the metropolis in great numbers, hastened on their way to the suburbs by an expanding national highway system and the advent of federally subsidized mortgages. To some extent, suburbanization was rooted in the American pioneer tradition—homesteading in modern guise. But this latter-day yearning for a fresh start was as much a repudiation of the big city and its growing minority populations as it was an embrace of the blank slate of suburban living. According to the historian Kenneth L. Jackson, "After World War II, the racial and economic polarization of large American metropolitan areas became so pronounced that downtown areas lost their commercial hold on the middle class. Cities became identified with fear and danger rather than with glamour and pleasure."

Forty-second Street was hardly immune to the double whammy of "white flight" and television's emergence. In fact, the fledgling television networks competed more directly with the grinders than the Broadway palaces because the Hollywood studios would not supply them with first-run films. Meanwhile, Hubert's Museum suffered so grievously at the box office that it lost its place of pride within the arcade that housed it. In the mid-1950s, the arcade's owners forced the dime museum to move from street level into the basement. Heckler's Flea Circus remained Hubert's headline attraction, but the bejeweled, tuxedoed pretheater crowd of the good old days was long gone. "These days the audiences run to young toughs in long sideburns, black leather jackets with brass-studded shoulder straps; sinister, hard-faced irregulars with soft mouths, pale watery eyes," observed the author of *Wild Tigers & Tame Fleas,* published in 1958. "The banter is more raucous than in the more polite prewar days, the questions a little more uncouth."

Yet even as the film palaces on Broadway and hundreds of smaller neighborhood movie houses throughout the city closed their doors, Hubert's and all ten of 42nd Street's grinders survived. In fact, several new movie theaters opened on the street, most notably the Times Theater at

302 West 42nd. The movie theaters on 42nd Street survived for the same reason that a tumble out a first-floor window is rarely fatal: they already lived so close to the ground that they did not have far to fall. Considerably smaller than the movie palaces, the grinders were at once less costly to operate and not nearly as dependent on flighty white middle-class patronage. Max Cohen and the brothers Brandt were disciplined businessmen who were able to discount admissions to attract business and still turn a profit catering to working-class folks of all races.

During the Depression, the Brandts had broadened the appeal of their 42nd Street theaters by sweet-talking the Hollywood studios into a mutually beneficial arrangement. Paramount, MGM, 20th Century-Fox, and the rest were still not going to give Brandt Theaters access to first-run films at the expense of the theaters they owned themselves. But they were amenable to having a movie open simultaneously elsewhere in New York City and on 42nd Street, providing that the Brandts did no advertising. This way, the studios could broaden their distribution without running much of a risk that patrons of their upscale, full-price theaters would head to 42nd Street to see the same picture for less at a grinder. Eschewing advertising was no great sacrifice for the cost-conscious Brandts, who turned the Lyric and the Selwyn into outlets for the "finest first-run pictures direct from Broadway," as a company brochure put it.

The Brandt brothers shrewdly created a distinct genre identity for each of their five other grinders. The Liberty showed third-run films, and the Rialto, which the Brandts acquired from the Laff Movie chain in 1954, featured horror, just as it had in the Merchant of Menace's heyday. The Victory specialized in action and adventure, the Empire in crime and suspense, and the Times Square in westerns. As one of the first theaters in the country to specialize in international films, the Apollo was instrumental in winning U.S. acceptance for Ingmar Bergman, Federico Fellini, Jean-Luc Godard, and other postwar European directors. Its subtitled attractions also enlarged the 42nd Street film audience to include the deaf. During the daylight hours, 42nd Street's grinders collectively offered a haven for hooky-playing kids from all over the city. "I used to rush down there to West 42nd Street at eleven o'clock in the morning," recalled the writer Phillip Lopate. "I didn't know where to start to turn my head around and look. Heaven for a film-lover like me was ten marquees that changed bills every day. I used to cut classes to see *Rules of the Game* with my legs dangling over the Apollo balcony."

If there were a single movie star who defined the essence of 42nd Street's genre appeal in the postwar era, it was John Wayne. Classic Wayne "oaters" like *The Searchers* and *Fort Apache* ran in constant rotation at the Times Square along with such cult classics as the Randolph Scott westerns directed by Budd Boetticher, including *Seven Men from Now, The Tall T,* and *Ride Lonesome.* "Back when I was out of my head, I'd see seven movies a day on 42nd Street," recalled Hubert Selby, the author of *Last Exit to Brooklyn* and other gritty novels. "I loved shoot-'em-ups, Randolph Scott westerns, especially. That Randy was so cool." According to the eminent film writer Andrew Sarris, "Westerns were particularly popular with the 42nd Street crowd. The plots were prearranged, the good guy versus the bad guy, the tough babes, it was all there. Young black men would come into the theaters with toy six-shooters and talk out loud back to the screen, saying things like, 'All right, Hoppy, I'll take care of him for you' and 'shoot' at the screen."

The grinders remained the engine of 42nd Street's peculiar economy, drawing tens of thousands of people to the block every day. But the constant flow of movie house patrons was augmented by a huge influx of commuters and tourists after the Port Authority Bus Terminal opened in 1951. "Port Authority," as the terminal was known, was a massive four-story structure that occupied the entire block bordered by 40th and 41st Streets and Eighth and Ninth Avenues and connected directly to the Lincoln Tunnel by a labyrinth of ramps. For many of the 125,000 New Jersey residents who passed through the terminal every weekday morning and evening, the shortest route between it and their desks now lay down 42nd Street. Port Authority also served as the new gateway to New York City for all long-distance travelers arriving by bus, replacing eight private terminals owned and operated by bus carriers themselves. (One of the busiest of these privately owned facilities had been located inside the Dixie Hotel at 241 West 42nd Street.)

As intended, the huge new terminal reduced congestion on Midtown streets by rationalizing bus traffic, even as it inadvertently gave rise to new rip-off retailers. Fly-by-night stores selling overstock, seconds, and other dubious merchandise sprang up on 42nd Street and, to a lesser extent, on Broadway. They put up oversize signs advertising apocalyptic sales of a sort forbidden under the city's administrative code: CLOSE OUT STOCK AND ALL OUT SALE, LIQUIDATION SALE TODAY ONLY, RIOT SALE, ENTIRE STOCK MUST BE SOLD, WE DECLARE WAR. THIS IS IT! Many discount clothing and appliance stores employed "pullers-in," sidewalk barkers whose sales spiels added to the din on New York's loudest thoroughfare. As the competition for the pedestrian dollar intensified along 42nd Street, souvenir shops, penny arcades, record shops, and other establishments installed loudspeakers and pumped high-decibel music onto the street.

But for all its liveliness, 42nd Street also had become a kind of crypt. Most of its buildings—including the oldest of the theaters—were forty or fifty years old now and looked every year of it. The high-volume, low-margin businesses that defined the street generated profits large enough to keep the lights on but not to justify capital improvements. No property owner had made a significant investment on 42nd Street west of Sixth Avenue since the Rialto was reconstructed in 1936—and the new Rialto had been the first new building on the theater block in years. Even as Midtown's East Side boomed with new corporate headquarters construction throughout the 1950s, the Brandt family failed repeatedly to secure the financing it needed to construct either an office building or a new theater on 42nd Street. Big corporations, law and accounting firms, investment banks, and the like wanted no part of a street described by one writer who walked it in 1957 as "a neonized jungle, razzmatazz all the way; a notorious, gaudy midway leading to the topside of Hell's Kitchen. . . . Day and night the long block is thronged with riffraff, demimonde irregulars and sleazy down-at-heels transients."

During the 1950s, the writings of Allen Ginsberg, Jack Kerouac, William Burroughs, and lesser Beat Movement figures conferred a lasting aura of countercultural hipness on 42nd Street and Times Square. Ginsberg, who was studying history at Columbia University when he first began exploring Times Square in the late 1940s, recalled "hanging around Bickford's under the Apollo Theater marquee on Forty-second, when it was still there—an all-night population of hustlers and junkies, and just sort of wandering. . . . Street wanderers—intelligent Melvillean street wanderers of the night." In memory, Ginsberg exalted the Crossroads of the World as a "timeless room" with its "hyperbolic spookiness all taking place in an undersea light of Pokerino freak shows of Times Square. At the center of empire, the very square of time."

Ginsberg, Kerouac, and Burroughs each were introduced to 42nd

Street by Herbert Huncke, who was a decade older and far more worldly than the Beat Trinity, each of whom was still a bit wet behind the ears, existentially speaking. Huncke gave Burroughs his first fix of morphine and provided the Beat Movement with its name by remarking to Kerouac one day that he felt "beat," meaning exhausted. Kerouac, who struck Huncke upon first meeting as "a typical clean-cut American type," pounced on the offhanded comment and wrested symbolic meaning from it. "I knew right away what he meant somehow," Kerouac recalled. "Huncke appeared to us and said, 'I'm beat' with radiant light shining out of his despairing eyes . . . a word perhaps brought from some midwest carnival or drunk cafeteria." To Ginsberg, Huncke was nothing less than the first hipster. "As far as I know," Ginsberg recalled in 1968, "the ethos of what's charmingly Hip, & the first pronunciation of the word itself to my fellow ears, first came consciously from Huncke's lips; and the first information and ritual of the emergent hip subculture passed through Huncke's person."

Huncke had grown up in Chicago, middle-class and restless. He ran away from home for the first time at age twelve, making it as far as Geneva, New York, where the cops caught him and sent him home. In his teens, Huncke fell into gay hustling without quite realizing what it was and discovered heroin while working as a shill for a hermaphrodite with a midway act and a lucrative sideline in narcotics. In 1934, the nineteen-year-old left Chicago and hit the road, carrying the sum total of his worldly possessions in a cigar box as he rode the rails around the country. After six years of wandering, he hitched a ride into New York City and found a home of sorts on West 42nd. "I was always quick in picking up on the scenes, and I took to 42nd Street. I was a natural for it," he recalled. "It was exciting. . . . The Pokerino with its neon flashing, the little passageways from one street to another that were off the record, guys sitting around talking about the clip they'd made—all of this was completely new to me, and I was captivated by it."

Huncke was alive to minor money-making opportunities of all sorts, including breaking into cars and hotel rooms, but he supported his various drinking and drug habits mainly by servicing the older homosexuals who were cruising Times Square in increasing numbers. "I didn't mind being known as a 42nd Street hustler, but I sure did not want to be known as a 'faggot,'" recalled Huncke, a bisexual. "Faggots have a hard way to go—they're everyone's property."

Huncke was an unthreatening sort, small and dark with limpid eyes and sallow skin. Despite his low pursuits, he was an articulate man of refined manners and a resilient enthusiasm. His considerable powers of empathy made him an attentive listener, if not always a reliable friend. (Leave him unattended in your apartment and he'd steal you blind.) Above all, though, Huncke was a spellbinding teller of tales who often held court late into the night around a table at Chase's or Bickford's, where he was dubbed "the Mayor" by his fellow hustlers. "Talking is my stock in trade," Huncke said. "I think that led me to the road." Kerouac praised him as "the greatest storyteller I know; an actual genius at it, in my mind."

The New York Police Department had a nickname for Huncke, too—"the Creep." The first of his many arrests on robbery and drug charges came just a few months after he'd started working 42nd Street. More often than not, though, Huncke was so broke that he could not afford to scrape together a dollar or two to rent a flophouse bed. In his journal, he recalled in his impressionistic style of writing one cold snap that found him out on the street

huddled in coats—ear muffs—scarves—sweaters—gloves—shoulders hunched—from doorway to doorway—to restaurants—subway entrances—seeking shelter along sides of the great graystone buildings. At night the city streets became even more deserted with only a few to be seen on 42nd Street—probably one of the busiest streets of any city in the world—a few like myself living in cafeterias—sleeping in the all night movies—staying away from the cops on the beat—who were angry to be out—glad of any excuse to pick a man up—hurry him to the nearest station house in out of the cold—or—walking through the underground tunnels down toward the Penn Station—through the Station into the restrooms—sitting on the toilets sleeping—sometimes writing—looking to pick someone up who had money and wanted sex—willing to pay for it—anxious only for a place to sleep—take a bath—shave—obtain clean clothing—even food. Maybe steal a suitcase—roll a stray drunk—meet a friend—talk—make it till the morning and a cheap movie.

Huncke lived a bit better after Alfred C. Kinsey discovered 42nd Street. In the mid-1940s, Professor Kinsey began the research that would lead to the publication of *Sexual Behavior in the Human Male*. From his base at Indiana University, Kinsey traveled far and wide in search of enlightenment on male sexuality and inevitably fixated on 42nd Street. "He had walked up and down 42nd Street, and he realized there was action of some sort going on there," Huncke recalled. "Of course, he didn't know too much about the underworld aspect of it, but it was still pretty obvious. One walked by doorways and saw young men in tight pants with their whole profile on display. And there were the many flagrant queens that used to fly up and down the Street, not to mention the more sinister types that could be noticed if one paid attention."

Kinsey established contact with Huncke through one of his assistants, a beautiful Columbia University coed who approached the Mayor one afternoon in Chase's Cafeteria. Huncke was suspicious—"my immediate reaction was that there was some very shy strange character in the offing who was too shy to approach people himself"—but agreed to telephone Kinsey, who was staying at the respectable Lincoln Hotel on the East Side, and arranged to meet him in a Times Square bar. During several subsequent meetings, Kinsey recorded the details of Huncke's sexual history, a Herculean undertaking that the hustler found strangely liberating. The professor paid Huncke for his time and offered an additional $2.25 for every interviewee he sent up from 42nd Street. Soon, so many louche characters were sidling into the Lincoln that its manager asked Kinsey to leave. The professor moved to the Hotel Astor, which was closer to 42nd Street and housed a ground-floor bar that was itself a hub of New York's postwar gay scene. Gore Vidal, recently discharged from the army, recalled the Astor Bar as "easily the city's most exciting meeting place for soldiers, sailors, and marines on the prowl for one another. . . . At any time of day or night, hundreds of men would be packed six-deep around the long oval black bar within whose center bartenders presided."

Huncke took a shine to Kinsey, whose interest in homosexuality went beyond the professional, and introduced him to several Times Square hangouts that few denizens of the Astor Bar would have dared set foot in. These included the infamous Angle Bar, which was on Eighth Avenue between 42nd and 43rd Streets. The Angle, which took its name from its long, L-shaped bar, functioned as a kind of office for the more enterprising members of the 42nd Street underclass. "There were really people that lived right there and worked that street like it was a place of business," Huncke recalled. Besides the prostitutes, "there were burglars and thieves and muggers, people of that nature. They let you hang around the bar if you had enough to buy yourself a drink. You could stand at the bar, and before long, somebody would approach you." It was at the Angle that 42nd Street's *über*-hustler introduced Kinsey to Ginsberg, Burroughs, and Kerouac, all of whom obligingly allowed the professor to debrief them (as did Vidal, in the more congenial surrounds of the Hotel Astor mezzanine).

Huncke, never the most artful of outlaws, spent most of the 1950s in prison, even as the Beats made him and 42nd Street into icons of hipster cool with their first published works. Junkey, the protagonist of the first half of Kerouac's sprawling 1950 debut, *The Town and the City,* was based on Huncke, as was Elmo Hassel in Kerouac's 1957 breakthrough, *On the Road.* Huncke was Ancke in John Clellon Holmes's 1952 novel, *Go,* and served as the model for the title character of Burroughs's first book, *Junkie,* published in 1953. Huncke appeared under his own name in innumerable Ginsberg poems, and anonymously walked the "snowbank docks" with "shoes full of blood" in *Howl.* Huncke reappeared in Kerouac's later writing as the character Huck in *Visions of Cody* and in *Book of Dreams.*

The Beats defined hipster 42nd Street but did not have it all to themselves. The street figured at least anecdotally in the lives and work of numerous countercultural figures of the cold war era, burnishing its underground cachet. For a start, Huncke's direct influence extended beyond the Beat writers to encompass some of the leading figures of jazz's bebop era. Huncke not only frequented the jazz clubs clustered on 52nd Street but also socialized with Billie Holiday and the saxophonists Charlie Parker and Dexter Gordon. According to one account, Huncke was so close to Gordon that they used to break into cars together and sell stolen fur coats to prostitutes in Harlem.

Several generations of avant-garde film critics and first-rate filmmakers as diverse as Woody Allen, Martin Scorsese, and Stanley Kubrick took themselves to school at the grinders, which showed many movies that no other theaters in the city would screen. "Orson Welles's *Touch of Evil* was a genuine 42nd Street phenomenon," recalled Andrew Sarris, who edited the English version of *Cahiers du Cinema* from a tiny office at 303 West 43rd Street. "I think the John Ford movie *The Man Who Shot Liberty Valance* opened in Brooklyn for its first run, and the only other place you could see it in the city, certainly the only place in Manhattan, was on 42nd Street."

Kubrick included a scene filmed on 42nd Street in one of his early movies, *The Killing*. In this 1956 film noir, the actor Sterling Hayden goes into a chess club to secure the services of a hired killer played by a former Greco-Roman wrestling champion called Kola Kwariani, better known as "Nick the Wrestler." This was the Chess and Checker Club of New York, the best known of several late-night chess, backgammon, and bridge clubs operating on or near 42nd Street in the 1950s. Nicknamed the "Flea House" (in tribute to Heckler's Flea Circus down the block), the Chess and Checker Club occupied the third floor of 210 West 42nd Street. Kwariani really was a regular at the Flea House, which was known throughout the city for its eccentric, intense competitors. In fact, Nick the Wrestler was known to play chess for days on end without sleeping. "His opponents would change, but he kept playing," recalled Lonnie Kwartler, another club regular. "He would ask me, not for the time, but 'What day is it?'"

Meanwhile, Hubert's Museum's most devoted customers included the comic and satirist Lenny Bruce, who included a routine about the place in his earliest act, and the photographer Diane Arbus, who spent so much time at the dime museum that she risked being mistaken for one of the acts. She was introduced to 42nd by the avant-garde filmmaker Emile de Antonio. "Forty-second Street was dangerous. We'd pass a sea of empty beer cans, broken bottles, druggies, pimps, and then we'd go to Grant's [204 West 42nd] for clams and French fries," de Antonio recalled. At Hubert's, Professor Heckler welcomed Arbus to sit with him as his fleas fed from his forearm, but his colleagues were standoffish at first. "When she first approached the freaks offstage with her cameras, they stared at her blankly; they seemed haughty, taciturn," wrote one Arbus biographer. The photographer persisted, coming day after day to Hubert's to sit with various freaks, usually in silence, until they felt comfortable enough to pose for her.

Arbus took numerous photos of midgets, a three-legged man, and a pinhead, but took a special shine to Congo the Jungle Creep, who was not a freak but a histrionic "jungle" magician who performed in a fright wig and loincloth. He'd mix sand in a bucket of muddy water, shout "ugga mugga," and then scoop up a hidden wad of dry sand and flourish it at the audience. Congo also liked to light a cigarette, swallow it, drink a glass of water, and blow smoke out of his mouth and nose. He would grimace, let loose a bloodcurdling scream, and cough up the cigarette. According to the Amazing Randi, a magician whom Arbus befriended, Congo "believed so totally in his fakery that he was positively arrogant about it." Offstage, he carried himself with the same sort of excess self-regard that Broadway stars had displayed in making an entrance at Rector's and the other lobster palaces. Arbus and the Amazing Randi would occasionally run into the Jungle Creep, the last aristocrat of the 42nd Street stage, as he strolled Broadway during his work breaks. "He'd be wearing a natty suit, no fright wig, and lots of diamonds on his huge hands," the Amazing Randi recalled. "'Hi, Congo,' we'd say. But he'd studiously ignore us."

Naturally, 42nd Street was all the hipper for scandalizing ordinary folk and their elected representatives. But it wasn't until Democrat Robert F. Wagner Jr., the Yale-educated son of a U.S. senator, was elected mayor of New York in 1953 that the rising clamor of complaint about 42nd Street and Times Square really registered politically. Within months of Wagner's inauguration, the Board of Estimate approved draconian changes in the zoning code designed to "drive the honky-tonks from Times Square." The new rules prohibited the opening of freak shows, wax museums, shooting galleries, games arcades, open-front stores, sidewalk cafés, and ground-floor auction rooms in Times Square and all other "retail-1" districts in the city. Existing establishments were allowed to remain in business but could not remodel or expand. Edward T. McCaffrey, the new license commissioner, hauled the operators of all fourteen grind movie theaters on or near 42nd Street down to his office and informed them that they risked being closed down under the state's so-called decency statute unless they toned down their advertising displays.

In the public mind, the clamor and vulgarity of 42nd Street was linked with rising rates of assault, rape, and murder in the city. The violence was all the more disquieting to New Yorkers for being so unexpected. As one historian put it, "New York entered the postwar era believing that the era of major crime was behind it." The "crime problem" first surfaced as an outbreak of lethal turf clashes between youth gangs à la *West Side Story*, a sensation on Broadway in 1957. Gang members were the most malevolent species of a newly discovered genus—the juvenile delinquent, or JD, for short—that was befuddling adult America. Although the gang battles tended to take place in the outer boroughs, JDs from all over the city liked to come to Times Square in their dungarees with rolled-up cuffs and their dark "tee shirts" (the term was still so novel that reporters encased it in quote marks) to strut their stuff and make a nuisance of themselves.

At 9:30 P.M. on a sweltering night in the summer of 1954, a special task force of sixty police officers descended on Times Square in search of juvenile delinquents and what the *Times* described as other "undesirables"—prostitutes, "hoodlums," and "sex perverts." One of the highest-ranking officers involved, a deputy inspector, got into a fistfight with ten dungaree-wearing boys whom he had spotted walking in a phalanx down Broadway near 42nd Street, forcing other pedestrians off the sidewalk. The police crackdown continued for four weeks, expanding beyond Times Square all the way north to the gang redoubts of the Bronx. Some 1,500 arrests were made, mostly on charges of disorderly conduct, disturbing the peace, loitering, and vagrancy. The stiffest sentences handed out were $50 fines and thirty days in the workhouse, though many teenage offenders got off with suspended jail sentences and a lecture.

In the end, Wagner's flexing of NYPD muscle did nothing to pacify Times Square, much less reduce crime. Meanwhile, his administration's belated attempt to temper the Times Square carnival by amending the zoning code backfired badly. The ranks of midway attractions and rip-off retailers thinned out, as intended. But by restricting the demand side of the market for commercial space on 42nd Street, the new regulations gave a leg up to dirty-book dealers looking for storefronts. In the first few months after the zoning code was amended, five bookstores opened on the Sixth and Seventh Avenue blocks of 42nd Street. These were not the self-proclaimed "adult" bookstores of the 1970s but general-interest shops that kept the risqué stuff in the back room and also appealed to a hipster clientele by stocking avant-garde literary works that ran afoul of censors, including Ginsberg's *Howl* and other Beat manifestoes. Because they were not dependent on walk-in traffic—and lived under constant threat of police raid—the bookstores cultivated a much lower profile than the movie theaters, arcades, and open-front merchandisers with which they shared the street. The boldest of the bookstores was the Kingsley Book Store (220 West 42nd), Edward Mishkin's third bookstore on the block.

Mishkin, long one of the city's largest porn wholesalers, had opened his first two bookstores on 42nd Street in the late 1940s: the Times Square Book Bazaar at 225 and the Little Book Exchange at 228.

Mayor Wagner was appalled by the proliferation of dirty books and magazines on 42nd Street, in no small part because pornography was considered a root cause of juvenile delinquency and sexual deviancy. Although the movie grinders had emphasized sex and violence in their advertising displays for years, the films they showed rarely lived up to their billing. The 42nd Street bookstores took the opposite approach: their bland exteriors gave no hint of the lurid stuff within. For example, both Kingsley and Times Square Book Bazaar offered *Nights of Horror,* a series of fourteen booklets cataloguing sexual perversity at $1.98 to $3 a pop. In ruling that *Nights of Horror* was obscene, New York Supreme Court Judge Matthew M. Levy was particularly outraged by its many illustrations of men torturing women: "These gruesome acts included such horrors as cauterizing a woman's breast with a hot iron, placing hot coals against a woman's breasts, tearing breasts off, placing hot irons against a woman's armpits," and so on.

In the fall of 1954, the Wagner administration launched a drive to rid bookstores and newsstands of "all publications teaching lust, violence, perverted sex attitudes and disrespect for law and order." The crackdown encompassed the entire city but began, to no one's surprise, in Times Square. The city got a restraining order against four bookstores in Times Square that were selling *Nights of Horror* under the counter. Two of the stores quickly agreed to pull the title, but Kingsley and Times Square Book Bazaar refused to comply. The police raided Kingsley and seized 200,000 photos along with copies of *Nights of Horror*. Mishkin then sued the city, challenging a 1941 state law prohibiting the sale of obscene publications. Lawyers for the bookstores argued that the statute defined *obscene* so vaguely that it was not enforceable. Judge Levy's court ruled in the city's favor, finding *Nights of Horror* "indisputably pornographic, indisputably obscene and filthy."

The Kingsley/Times Square Book case ultimately ended up in the U.S. Supreme Court, which heard it in conjunction with a second case involving a far more notorious New York publisher and bookseller named Samuel Roth, who operated out of Greenwich Village. In June 1957, the U.S. Supreme Court upheld the convictions both of Roth and the 42nd

Street booksellers in what seemed at the time to be a severe setback not only for the defendants but also for the porn business as a whole. In the Kingsley/Times Square Book case, the high court affirmed New York's right to prosecute booksellers for violating antiobscenity laws and to seize materials deemed obscene before a trial was held. Moreover, in *Roth v. United States,* Justice William Brennan's majority opinion held that obscene expression was not entitled to protection under the First Amendment, which prohibits Congress from making any law "abridging freedom of speech, or the press."

Although Roth and Mishkin had suffered resounding personal defeats (Roth went to prison, but Mishkin only had to pay a fine), the rulings in these cases—especially *Roth v. United States*—were milestones that the pornography business could build on. The Supreme Court had upheld New York's right to bring obscenity prosecutions but had not ruled on the constitutionality of its antiobscenity statute. More important, the decision in *Roth v. United States* defined obscenity in a new way that made it far tougher for prosecutors at any level of government to obtain convictions. Previously, any work that tended to "deprave and corrupt those whose minds are open to such immoral influences" met the legal definition of obscenity. Justice Brennan's opinion gave defenses lawyers a lot more to work with. The new test of obscenity was "whether to the average person, applying contemporary local standards, the dominant theme of the material taken as a whole appeals to prurient interests." In addition, Brennan ruled, it must be "patently offensive"—that is, affronting community standards—and "utterly without redeeming social importance."

Prosecutors all over the country did what they could to counteract the permissive effect of high court decisions. In New York, the nation's pornography cocapital (with Los Angeles), the police routinely raided bookstores, wholesalers, and film processing laboratories and arrested their employees. The legal battles would rage on ad infinitum, but there would be no putting the porn genie back in the bottle after *Roth.* In New York City, obscenity acquittals outnumbered convictions by more than two to one in the 1950s, and jail terms were rare. Like 42nd Street's movie theaters, its adult bookstores now were a destination in their own right, pulling in customers from all over the city and beyond. In the estimation of New York Police Commissioner Michael J. Murphy, 42nd Street was not only the hub of the city's burgeoning porn scene but also "the greatest retail market for pornographic literature in America."

The adult bookstores led the way toward 42nd Street's X-rated future, with the movie theaters following cautiously a few steps behind. While maintaining the genre specialties of their theaters, the Brandts began working the occasional sex film—what now would be called softporn—into the mix at the Apollo, the Victory, and the Rialto in the late 1950s. Max Cohen did the same at his two 42nd Street movie theaters. The grinders experimented first with nudist colony films like *Garden of Eden,* which was released in 1957, and quickly followed by such pseudo-documentaries as *My Bare Lady* and *The Nude and the Prude.* By decade's end, and number of filmmakers had dispensed with the nudist-colony fig leaf and begun combining stag-film nudity with comic story lines and Hollywood production values to create the "nudie cutie." The box office success of 1959's *The Immoral Mr. Teas* and other pioneering nudie cuties launched the fast-growing adult film market in America and on West 42nd Street.

Milking an Ugly Cow:
Speculating on Redevelopment

The city would keep on fiddling with the zoning code and wielding the clumsy club of law enforcement against pornographers and other "undesirables" all through the 1960s. But the decade also saw a groundswell of interest in a seemingly more appealing solution to the problems of 42nd Street: redevelopment. The Broadway Association went so far as to commission an architect to design a rehabbed theater block. In a series of elaborate drawings, Richard Snibbe encased ten fully restored theaters within glass walls and a latticework of Victorian-inspired metal arcades that also included several new restaurants, cabarets, and a casino. He also extended a pair of two-story pedestrian overpasses across 42nd Street and ran a lush ribbon of foliage down its center. The effect was at once swanky and shopping-mall suburban—Fifth Avenue crossed with the Las Vegas strip.

Most of 42nd Street's denizens liked the place just fine the way it was and didn't want Snibbe or anyone else messing it up. Max Wilks feared that there would be no place on a gentrified street for the sort of sharp green trousers that he sold at his Dixie haberdashery. "People come from as far away as Connecticut to buy our merchandise, because we're more stylely," Wilks bragged. "We don't go in for ultra-conservative clothes." A few doors down at Hubert's Museum, Congo the Jungle Creep interrupted his performance one afternoon to counsel a *Newsweek* reporter gauging the winds of change. "Rube, they can't clean up 42nd Street," Congo said. "New York needs this drag. It draws the crooks and con men and queers from the decent neighborhoods." From a neighboring platform an elderly contortionist "burped ten-cent burgundy" and put in his two cents' worth: "The street's always been clean. It's the people on it need the wash job."

City Hall was all for redeveloping 42nd Street—as long as private business paid for it, that is. The Wagner administration, *Newsweek* chided, "looks down on Times Square as if from Mars." The Broadway Association paid for Snibbe's drawings, but that was as far as the group would go. Snibbe's design was not a plan, much less a project, as much as it was a shiny hook dangled before the real estate industry. No developer took the Broadway Association's bait, but there were two property men who boldly pursued their own personal visions of 42nd Street redevelopment at a time when their peers were inclined to sit back and wait for the Broadway establishment and City Hall to resolve their game of political chicken ("You go first. No, *you* go first"). From the late 1950s into the 1970s, Irving Maidman and Seymour Durst vied with each other to buy property along the entire length of West 42nd Street. But it was Maidman who first staked his claim and who made the first sustained attempt to return the legitimate theater to 42nd Street since the New Amsterdam had closed in 1937.

Born in 1897, Maidman grew up in a cold-water flat above his immigrant father's jewelry store on the Lower East Side. He was fourteen years old when he literally fell for 42nd Street at first sight. He had rented a bicycle to make his first trip "uptown." All went well until he reached 42nd Street and was bedazzled by its brightly lit theaters. "I was so busy looking at the buildings, I rode my bike into a subway pit," he recalled. "Took me two years to pay for the repairs." After World War I, he got his start in business selling insurance but soon switched to brokering real estate. In 1924, young Maidman sold an old stable on West 47th Street to Lee Shubert, the first of numerous transactions handled on behalf of the Shubert interests. During the Depression, he deepened his identification with the theater business by taking over the management of several Broadway houses on behalf of the banks that had foreclosed on them. In 1940, Maidman moved beyond real estate management by founding a company to buy property for his own account. In the early 1950s, the budding mogul began snapping up West 42nd Street real estate, including the twenty-story Remington Typewriter Building at number 113, the twenty-one-story Candler Building at 220–224, and the Samuel H. Harris Theatre next door at 226.

Unlike Maidman, a classically self-made man, Seymour Durst was a second-generation empire builder. Seymour was the eldest of three sons of Joseph Durst, who began buying and selling commercial real estate in Manhattan after selling his interest in a children's clothing manufacturer in 1915. Quick and impulsive by nature, Seymour nonetheless matured into the premier "site assembler" of the postwar era. That is, he excelled at the intricate and covert art of acquiring large development sites bit by bit, using decoy brokers, dummy corporations, and other masking techniques. Assembling a large site in Manhattan could require dozens of transactions and consume the better part of a decade, or longer. "I've walked 1,000 miles to assemble some sites," Durst recalled in 1969. "I go back and then back again to a prospective site, sometimes every day, for that's a way to get to know the area and to talk with people in it."

Seymour and his brothers started out as real estate investors, not builders. They added to the family fortune by selling the sites they assembled at big markups to developers. But in the late 1950s, the Dursts backed into building in a big way on East 42nd Street. The brothers had put together several choice assemblages along Third and East 42nd Street in anticipation of the dismantling of the Third Avenue El. Disappointed with the prices offered for their sites, the family decided to develop the properties itself. From 1959 through 1965, the Dursts laid the foundation for a much larger family fortune by constructing six top-quality office towers one after another: 200, 201, and 205 East 42nd Street and 733, 757, and 825 Third Avenue.

The Dursts were still in the early stages of their East 42nd Street building boom when Seymour began working on one of the biggest assemblages of his career at the far west end of the street. Maidman also was snapping up properties in this area, which was a few hundred yards west of the theater block but a world apart from the glitter of Times Square. This was the heart of Hell's Kitchen, a rough-and-ready working-class district that stretched from 30th Street to 59th Street and took its cues not from Broadway but from the rail yards and piers of the Hudson River waterfront. The block on which Durst concentrated his buying was almost entirely residential and yet had the highest commercial zoning allowed. In theory, a developer could transform it into a thicket of office towers with minimal finagling of the zoning code. Durst would invest several million dollars, yards of shoe leather, and the better part of a decade assembling the entire block from 42nd all the way to 43rd Street and from Ninth to Tenth Avenues. In the process, he bought seventy different properties, including several owned by Maidman. "This was one of my father's best assemblages," recalled Douglas Durst, Seymour's son and successor. "He was particularly proud of this one."

While Durst went to great lengths to disguise his purchases, Maidman purposely attracted attention with a host of developments throughout the middle section of Hell's Kitchen. On the southwest corner of 42nd Street and Eighth Avenues he bought five buildings in a row, including the Times movie theater and the Tivoli Hotel. He tore down the structures and put up a garage, contributing to Hell's Kitchen's one 1960s growth industry—parking. So many tenements were leveled to make way for parking lots and garages that Father Joseph McCaffrey of the Church of the Holy Cross ruefully proposed renaming his church the "Shrine of the Parking Lots." But these weren't just any parking lots; Hell's Kitchen had become a kind of research and development lab in the city's efforts to solve the worsening problem of automobile congestion. In 1961, the grocery chain heir Huntington Hartford opened the city's first completely "automatic" parking garage at 312 West 42nd Street, just west off Eighth Avenue. Operated by a single attendant, the Speed-Park garage was an eight-story, computerized machine that moved cars horizontally along rails and vertically by elevators, parking the average auto in a minute.

Maidman also owned a garage at 307–9 West 43rd and another at 306–18 West 44th, but for him parking was just a sideline. On 42nd Street's Ninth Avenue block he added to his Hell's Kitchen holdings by acquiring a host of small commercial buildings, including nos. 408, 416–18, 420, 422, and 440–44. On West 43rd, near Ninth Avenue, Maidman erected a twelve-story apartment building, the first new apartment house west of Times Square in three decades. But Maidman's signature Hell's Kitchen building was the West Side Airlines Terminal, which opened in 1955 at 460 West 42nd, just around the corner from the Port Authority Bus Terminal. American, Braniff, Delta, Eastern, and other airlines leased space in Maidman's terminal, through which air travelers were bused to and from the international airport in Newark.

Maidman also was instrumental in Hell's Kitchen's improbable emergence as a motel resort oasis. It began in 1958, with a developer's announcement of plans to build a 400-room motel—Motel City—on two and a half acres of converted rail yards at the foot of West 42nd Street. By this time, urban motels had sprung up in many cities, but not New York. Motel City was to be Manhattan's first motel and the largest motel in the world—a $4 million wager that many of the tourists putting in at motels on the Jersey side of the Lincoln Tunnel would rather stay in Manhattan if they didn't have to pay big city rates. The original design envisioned four separate buildings in the Dutch Colonial style enclosing a land-scaped courtyard connected by passageways to gardens, wading pools, and shuffleboard courts. According to the authors of *New York 1960*, Motel City was "a somewhat successful attempt to equip the moderately priced motel with resort amenities and, more important, to give it the distinct sense of being a series of cloistered retreats set apart from the turmoil of the surrounding city."

In the end, only two of the four buildings were actually constructed (at 510 and 515 West 42nd), and the Dutch Colonial architecture was scrapped in favor of a more conventional look. With 258 rooms, Motel City fell well short of world's-largest-motel status, and by the time it finally opened in 1962 it wasn't Manhattan's first motel either. That distinction was claimed by the Skyline Motor Inn, which opened at 49th Street and Tenth Avenue in 1959. Shortly after the Skyline opened, Maidman began work on a new 182-room motel on Tenth Avenue off 41st Street, facing the West Side Airlines Terminal. Maidman's Congress Riviera Motel featured Latin American styling, a lawn tennis court, a pitch-and-putt golf course, and other recreational amenities. The $2 million motel was hailed upon its opening in the fall of 1961 as a stellar addition to the "mushrooming vacation haven" of far West 42nd Street.

The Hell's Kitchen motel resort vogue would prove too short-lived to spark widespread redevelopment of the Hell's Kitchen section of 42nd Street. The Congress Riviera suffered a particularly ignominious fate. In 1967, it was purchased by the New York Department of Mental Hygiene to treat narcotics addicts convicted of felonies. The state ended up condemning the motel, after Maidman accused Mental Hygiene officials of reneging on a commitment to pay $2.5 million, instead of the $2 million the department finally did pay. But for a few halcyon years the Congress Riviera and its neighbors thrived, attracting not only tourists but also city residents looking for a weekend alternative to the Hamptons or Fire Is-

land and bringing what the *Times* characterized in 1963 as "a kind of Atlantic City-on-Hudson touch" to the West 42nd Street landing.

At the same time that Maidman was building motels on 42nd Street,
he hit upon the even more unlikely strategy of trying to improve the value
of some of his small commercial buildings on the street by turning them
into Off Broadway theaters. Off Broadway had emerged in the 1920s as a
circuit of 200- to 500-seat theaters offering a less expensive and more
adventurous brand of theater than Broadway itself. In many ways, the
1959–60 season was Off Broadway's finest ever. Daring new works by
Samuel Beckett, Harold Pinter, Jean Genet, and Bertolt Brecht were performed, a promising young American playwright named Edward Albee
made his debut, and such great actors as Colleen Dewhurst, Geraldine
Page, Jason Robards, and George C. Scott played to full houses. "While
Broadway turns every leaf and stone in a desperate search for a clue to its
survival," the *Times* observed, "Off Broadway blooms."

Maidman clambered onto the Off Broadway bandwagon in late 1959,
shelling out $100,000 to transform an old bank building that he owned at
416–18 West 42nd Street into a 199-seat theater called the Maidman
Playhouse. It opened in February 1960, with a musical revue inspired by
the illustrations of Russell Patterson. The versatile Patterson had designed costumes and sets for the *Ziegfeld Follies* and *George White's
Scandals,* which nearly excused a Maidman press release touting *Russell
Patterson's Sketchbook* as a bid to "return the beautiful American showgirl to her rightful position at the zenith of musical comedy." By all accounts, the Maidman Playhouse was a triumph, with its walls paneled in
emerald and ruby-hued velvet, its low-slung lantern lighting, and its excellent sight lines. The critics also were of one mind about the *Sketchbook,* the first legitimate theater opening on 42nd Street in twenty-three
years: it stunk. As one reviewer put it, "If the off-Broadway movement actually is intent on suicide . . . *Sketchbook* would make a dandy weapon."
Maidman, who had covered the entire $24,000 cost of the show out of his
own pocket, closed it after two performances. "At least they loved my
theater," Maidman said. "A 'jewel box' they called it. It is a gorgeous little house."

After the *Sketchbook* fiasco, Maidman locked his checkbook in his
desk and left the producing to the professionals. But despite favorable reviews, productions of Chekhov's *Uncle Vanya* and Anouilh's *Jeannette*
fared no better at the box office. In 1961, producer Dorothy Olim did

have a modest success with the Yiddish offering *A Worm in Horseradish,* her first and last play at the Maidman Playhouse. "It was what we call a 'good house,' but it was just too far off the beaten track," Olim recalled. "You went past Eighth Avenue and it was a no man's land. It wasn't dangerous particularly, just run-down and seedy." Maidman persisted in believing that there was nothing wrong with 42nd Street that couldn't be fixed by opening more theaters nearby. "We didn't get any business at the Maidman because no one knew a theater was there," he said.

In 1961, the developer opened two more small theaters on 42nd Street: the Mermaid at 420 and the Midway at 422. The next year he added yet another house on the same block, the Masque, at 442 West 42nd Street, next to the West Side Airlines Terminal. All three of these new theaters were 149-seat houses designed by Patterson. At the same time, Maidman opened a 299-seat theater, the Mayfair, in the heart of the theater district on 46th Street. In one of its first shows, the Mayfair presented a fully clothed Gypsy Rose Lee, now forty-seven years old, narrating a film-and-slide show about her career. The aptly named *A Curious Evening with Gypsy Rose Lee* closed after a mere twenty-five performances.

Maidman was right about one thing: five theaters attracted a lot more attention than one. The developer-cum-impresario now merited coverage not only in the city's newspapers but also in national publications like *Variety.* In 1962, Maidman personally approached Jean Cocteau and ended up buying the U.S. performance rights to five of the Frenchman's plays through his London agent at a bargain rate of $250 per play. And it was Maidman who came to the rescue when the Living Theatre, the avant-garde troupe headed by Julian Beck, was evicted from its Greenwich Village theater for nonpayment of rent and taxes. The Living Theatre moved its production of *The Brig* to the Masque, which Maidman provided free of charge. "It may be premature to say so," *Times* theater columnist Lewis Funke wrote, "but a twinkle in Mr. Maidman's eye indicates that he may in fact be on the way to being the Shubert of Off Broadway."

Premature indeed. From 1960 to 1965, Maidman's four theaters on 42nd Street presented thirty-five shows. While many of them had artistic merit, there was not a single box-office hit among them. By 1963, all of his theaters were dark almost all of the time. "The small theaters don't pay," the developer complained. "Off-Broadway already has too many theaters anyway." Maidman experimented with showing movies at a few of his houses before shutting them all down in the spring of 1965 and affixing FOR RENT signs on their doors. Many of the same theater columnists who initially had applauded the developer's quixotic venture to make avant-garde theater a business rather than a philanthropy now mocked him as "No Hit Maidman" as he exited the scene. "Like anyone else who goes from business to business, he didn't know all the jokes," recalled the Broadway producer Norman Twain. "He was trying to run a theater as a real estate business, and you can't do that."

Times Tower still lorded over Times Square, though the newspaper had relocated to much larger quarters on West 43rd Street in 1913. Adolph Ochs's descendants had held tight to their skinny skyscraper, preserving it as a monument to the founder as they leased out its twenty-four floors with increasing difficulty. The Ochs-Sulzberger family had occasionally updated the traditional annual New Year's Eve ceremony, but its efforts to exploit the building's promotional potential essentially ended with the addition of the news zipper in 1928. In 1959, the *Times* opened a new printing plant at 101 West End Avenue, near what is now Lincoln Center and safely removed from Midtown's traffic jams. On this three-block-long site publisher Arthur Hays Sulzberger eventually hoped to build a new headquarters for the *Times,* a colossal structure of steel and glass with a tower as much as twenty stories tall rising from its center. As it turned out, the newsroom would remain on West 43rd Street into the next century. But after an anguished debate within the Sulzberger family, Arthur's son and heir apparent, Arthur Ochs Sulzberger, persuaded his father to sell the Times Tower in 1961, "arguing that the coming West Side plant made it an extravagant heirloom." The buyer was Douglas Leigh, a wealthy advertising man who long had yearned to possess the building.

Leigh, who had gotten his start in the midst of the Depression, had created many of Times Square's greatest "spectaculars," including the steaming A&P coffee cup, the Bond Store's waterfall, and the Camel sign that puffed smoke rings. His three-story box of Super Suds detergent blew real soap bubbles. A transplanted southerner who owned sixty bow ties and always sported a fresh boutonniere of cornflowers in his tweed jacket, Leigh promptly announced plans to modernize Times Tower from top to bottom. An observation deck and restaurant would be installed up

above while the cavernous underground space that once housed the
Times presses would be made into an exhibition hall and amusement center. The zipper would be enlarged, and its diet of news bulletins enlivened with pictures and other feature material. Oh, and Times Square's
namesake building would be renamed. "We will eventually reidentify the
building," Leigh said, "and name it after a leading American company
that becomes a prime tenant."

Leigh's search for such a tenant was hampered by a fire that ignited
in the tower's subbasement in late 1961. Two firefighters and a building
employee were killed and twenty-four firefighters injured in the five-
alarm blaze, which enveloped most of Times Square in a sooty cloud of
smoke. The tower was structurally intact but heavily damaged. The heat
created a vacuum that blew out most of the tower's windows, and the interior sustained heavy water and smoke damage. Not only did the repairs
prove costly, but Leigh's rental income vanished as almost all of the
building's 110 tenants vacated. As the ad man realized that he was in
over his head financially, his search for an anchor tenant turned into a
desperate search for a buyer. It took him a year and a half, but Leigh finally found the Allied Chemical Corporation, which acquired Times
Tower in 1963.

Persuading Allied Chemical to take a chance on Times Square was
one of the great sales jobs of Leigh's career. Allied was a conservative
pillar of the American corporate establishment that had established itself
as the world's largest chemical manufacturer by selling bulk commodi-
ties like ammonia and sulfuric acid. In the 1950s, the company awakened to the growth potential of the consumer market and began trying to
raise its profile. Luckily for Leigh, an open-minded new chief executive
named Chester M. Brown took charge of Allied in 1962. "Let's face it,"
Brown said. "Allied . . . is in need of an improved public image. We need
recognition in all communities on all levels." Brown maintained Allied's
headquarters at 61 Broadway in the Wall Street district but decided that
the money that previously had been earmarked to create an exhibit at the
1964 World's Fair in Flushing, Queens, would be better spent transforming Times Tower into a more lasting symbol of the company. "We will be
the showcase of chemistry in Times Square," Brown declared.

Allied Chemical's CEO would come to regret this decision, but he
made it knowing full well that he was binding his company's image to a
place where the established interest in chemistry was notoriously of the

sexual sort. All Brown had to do was take a peek at the marquees of the two Brandt grinders that flanked Times Tower, the Globe and the Rialto. On the day that Brown announced Allied's purchase of the building, these two theaters were featuring four films between them: *Wild Is My Love*, *Strip for Action*, *Nude Camera*, and *Pagan Island*.

Allied stripped the Times Tower down to its steel girders and clad it in white marble and dark glass. Four forty-foot neon signs saying ALLIED CHEMICAL were affixed to the top of the tower, one on each face. These were the highest electric signs in Times Square, visible for a great distance in every direction. The news zipper was re-created in fancier form, operated now by the Associated Press and *Life* magazine. A restaurant was installed on the fifteenth and sixteenth floors, and Allied sales personnel occupied all of the office floors. The bottom three floors were made into an exhibition hall featuring Allied products as well as nonproprietary science and technology displays, including a demonstration of an Apollo space shuttle landing on the moon and an imaginary lunar city circa 2000.

The *Times'* feisty architecture critic, Ada Louise Huxtable, managed to trash both the Allied Chemical Building and the old Times Tower in a single piece entitled "How to Kill a City." "The Times Tower was never a masterpiece; it was ambitious, pedestrian and dull. But it was legitimately conceived for its day, and such buildings, as they embody and preserve historical attitudes and styles, actually improve with age," Huxtable opined. "The new design is also ambitious, pedestrian and dull, but without the virtue of singularity that marks its predecessor."

Meanwhile, Maidman and Leigh joined forces to buy an eighteen-story building directly across 42nd Street from the remodeled tower. Completed in 1910, the Crossroads Building was an oddity even by Times Square standards. Originally known as the Heidelberg Tower, it consisted of two distinctly different parts: a seven-story Gothic-style office block at its base and an eleven-story tower that sat atop the base. The upper portion was a simulacrum of an office building, a hollow shell of rough terra-cotta blocks designed to do nothing more than hold big advertising signs. Over the decades, various developers had floated schemes to topple the Heidelberg's architectural prosthesis and turn it into a genuine office tower, but none of them got off the drawing board. Like every other commercial structure on 42nd Street, the Crossroads had suffered the cumulative effects of decades of neglect as the street deteriorated. By the time that Maidman and Leigh bought it in 1964, the building was, in a word, a wreck.

Maidman and Leigh clad the Crossroads in white marble identical to the Allied Chemical building, creating a matched set of remodeled towers on either side of 42nd Street. At first, they had planned to cover the seven-story base of the building in glass and turn it into a new kind of automobile showroom. The latest model cars were to be loaded onto an oval conveyor belt in the IRT subway arcade and then cycled up, around, and down in continuous display. In the end, Leigh was unable to persuade either General Motors or Ford Motor to follow Allied Chemical's lead onto 42nd, and the Crossroads Building remained an office building. The lower seven floors were extensively remodeled, but the 11-story ghost tower remained, a trompe l'oeil monument to its own uselessness and the high cost of demolition. Maidman was so pleased with the results that he moved his own offices from the penthouse floor of the Paramount Building to the seventh floor of the Crossroads Building.

The refurbished Crossroads and Allied Chemical towers aside, West 42nd Street was literally crumbling in places for lack of investment, and yet its renegade entertainment economy was flourishing in the ruins. "It's an ugly cow," one real estate broker observed, "but it gives a lot of milk." The ten grind houses on the theater block sold nine million tickets in 1965, one of the best years ever. Bingo Brandt, the theater family's X-rated specialist, converted the Rialto back into a first-run theater again, albeit a "class sex" venue offering the subtitled, steamily arty likes of *I, a Woman* and *Thérèse et Isabelle*. The cheap "sexploiters" that formerly played the Rialto now were featured directly across Seventh Avenue at another of Bingo's theaters, the Globe. This attempt at market segmentation proved so remunerative that Bingo soon converted the subway arcade under the Rialto into a second sex cinema, the 300-seat Rialto II.

Six more sex-oriented bookstores opened on the block between Sixth and Seventh Avenues in 1966 alone, boosting rents to as much as $2,000 a square foot at the Crossroads of the World. "It's probably the highest rent area in New York for stores of this size," said Maidman, who had settled for less than top dollar in leasing out the ground floor of the Crossroads Building to a restaurant and other nonporn tenants. Maidman was still looking to add to his holdings at this end of West 42nd Street but could not find any bargains. "It's hard to assemble lots," he complained to a reporter. "Businesses are doing well as the street is now."

Hard but not impossible, as Seymour Durst proved in spectacular fashion while Maidman was sitting on his hands in the mid-1960s. Beginning in 1964, Durst methodically acquired virtually the entire five-block area from 42nd Street north all the way to 47th Street between Sixth and Seventh Avenues. Usually, Durst began assembling a site without knowing what use he ultimately would make of it. This time, though, he was in stealthy pursuit of the grandest vision of his career. Durst envisioned a billion-dollar complex of as many as ten office towers interconnected by plazas providing midblock access to a host of beautifully restored Broadway playhouses—a project that rival Rockefeller Center in its scale and its architectural unity.

To look at John Vliet Lindsay, it seemed entirely possible that he had been sworn in as Gotham's new mayor on New Year's Day, 1966, without ever having set foot on West 42nd Street. It wasn't that he was a prig. But this Ivy League–educated son of a Wall Street investment banker epitomized the Upper East Side WASP to such a degree that it was impossible to imagine him deigning to partake of the Deuce's tawdry pleasures. A photo taken during the 1965 campaign shows a lean and tautly muscled Lindsay in madras trunks suspended in midair high above a public swimming pool in Queens. His six-foot-four frame is perfectly horizontal in a posture of such equipoise—head up, arms flared, legs clamped together, toes pointed—that he looks less like someone in mid-dive than a god descended from above to demonstrate proper flying technique to outer-borough mortals. Energetic and devastatingly handsome, Lindsay infused the mayor's office with charisma, a quality in short supply since Fiorello La Guardia retired, and with a glamour that it had never known. He was the John F. Kennedy of a City Hall previously occupied by a succession of Bowery Boys.

Lindsay, a liberal Republican running on a "fusion" ticket, managed to defeat his Democrat opponent without repudiating Robert Wagner's tax-and-spend philosophy. If anything, he would outdo Wagner in the fervency of his Great Society liberalism. His ambition was nothing less than "to raise the quality of life for everyone," concluded the historian Roger Starr. "Everyone in this case tended to mean the poor, especially the minority group poor, and the rich." The poor were to be given heaping second helpings of the social services that Wagner had promised and, to some extent, delivered. But it was at the opposite end of the social spectrum that Lindsayism took its most distinctive form. "The rich," Starr added, "were to get a more interesting city, culturally and architecturally, a city with soul, an intellect, and style." For better or worse, Lindsay put greater emphasis on the look and feel of the city—on the aesthetics of the urban experience—than any mayor before or since.

Lindsay came to office not knowing what to do about 42nd Street but aware that he had to do something, if only out of self-defense. The news and entertainment media had combined to make Times Square into a politically potent symbol of America's urban crisis. Lindsay could work miracles in the ghettoes of Harlem and Bedford-Stuyvesant, but his claims to national leadership—and to higher office—would ring hollow unless he could make Times Square a visibly improved place. Political calculation aside, the place affronted Lindsay's patrician aesthetic. Lindsay was a pretty even-tempered man, but he was known to fly into a profanity-spewing rage at the sight of a public building defaced by graffiti. To a man of Lindsay's sensibilities, 42nd Street was just plain ugly. How could he hope to beautify the city and to elevate its cultural life with this honky-tonk strip running right through its midsection?

Lindsay came to office having formed a deep, personal attachment to the Broadway stage. His mother, the former Florence Eleanor Vliet, had been a professional actress before she married, acting in Broadway touring companies at a time—the 1910s—when 42nd Street was the pinnacle of the American stage. Vliet won excellent notices for her performance as "Jo" in a *Little Women,* and as a scrubwoman in *The Governor's Lady,* which had made its debut at the Belasco Theater on 42nd Street. Despite its brevity, Vliet's acting career was a deeply felt act of self-assertion by a young woman born into the straitjacket of high social position. As her admiring son put it, "In her time, after all, 'good girls' didn't go on stage, but that's what she wanted to do, and she did it." John began attending Broadway plays at an early age with his mother and delighted her by taking music lessons and acting in plays throughout his school years. Although he never seriously considered a stage career, Lindsay remained an avid theatergoer his entire life and, for a politician anyway, was an accomplished song and dance man. He was, in short, the first mayor that Broadway could truly call its own, and the first since La Guardia to make a determined effort to improve 42nd Street and Times Square. In this undertaking, as in so many of his initiatives, Lindsay promised far more than he delivered. But his election was a godsend nonetheless for a Broadway theater industry that needed all the help it could get.

In Lindsay's City Hall, the indispensable agent of progress was not the cop on the beat nor even the social worker, but the "urban designer"—a new reformist breed of city planner/architect that had sallied forth from the halls of academe to slay the urban crisis with fresh thinking. Jonathan Barnett, Lindsay's designer-in-chief, defined urban design as "designing cities without designing buildings." Barnett's official title was director of the Urban Design Group (UDG), a kind of SWAT team that Lindsay attached to the stodgy, developer-dominated City Planning Commission to serve as "the design conscience and design brain of the city government." The UDG began with a professional staff of five, all of whom were Ivy League–educated architects in their late twenties or early thirties. Reflecting Lindsay's own priorities, Barnett and his colleagues made Times Square their first battleground in the UDG's assault on convention.

By the time Lindsay was elected, the consensus within government and business alike was that the Broadway theater district's days were numbered. Architecture critics might have objected to Allied Chemical's renovation of the Times Tower, but the project had convinced the city's developers that it was only a matter of time until the tsunami of Midtown office tower development crashed through the Sixth Avenue corridor and flooded the antiquated, low-rise precincts of Times Square with lucrative new skyscrapers. "That was a breakthrough," said Robert W. Dowling, chairman of City Investing Company, a major theater district property owner. "That put the stamp of approval of a great American company on the whole area." After the Times Tower changed hands, speculators began driving up land prices all along Broadway in anticipation of the theater district's impending annexation into the Midtown corporate headquarters complex.

In January 1966, Lindsay's first month in office, the Minskoff family, one of Manhattan's oldest and richest developer dynasties, sounded what was presumed to be Times Square's death knell by buying the Hotel Astor for $10.5 million. The Astor had opened in 1904 and was no less a landmark than the Times Tower, though it occupied vastly more real estate—the entire block between 43rd and 44th Streets on the west side of Broadway. With scarcely a bow to the Astor's storied history, Sam Minskoff & Sons announced plans to tear down the hotel and replace it with One Astor Plaza, a fifty-four-story tower sheathed in granite and glass and containing 1.4 million square feet of office space. One Astor Plaza would be the first big new office building in Times Square since the thirty-three-story Paramount Building opened nearby in 1927.

The prospect of an office boom was hailed as a deliverance, not only by most of Times Square's long-suffering property owners but also by advocates of morality in entertainment. Profitable though they were, grind movie houses and adult bookstores could not begin to compete with major corporations and law and accounting firms for space in the shiny new office towers that would arise in place of their old haunts. They would vanish, along with the fleabag hotels, freak shows, arcades, lunch counters, cut-rate merchandisers, and miscellaneous tourist traps that gave 42nd Street and Times Square its distinctively raffish, time-warped flavor. To the city's corporate elite, this was progress. But the theater community feared that it would be eliminated along with the sleaze that its leading lights had complained about for so long. To an office tower builder, the playhouses in the area were no less ripe for demolition than Times Square's many rickety prewar tenements. Since the late 1920s, no fewer than forty-five Broadway theaters had been demolished or converted to other uses. Of the thirty-four that remained, 40 percent had been built before 1920, and the rest were predominantly of 1920s vintage. In real estate terms anyway, Broadway was obsolete.

Broadway did not need to shout to get the ear of Mayor Lindsay, who believed that the theater was vital not only to the city's image but also to its economy. As the UDG's Barnett put it, "The theaters in the Broadway area had become part of a series of interconnected land uses. Restaurants, hotels, film theaters and shops all benefited from each other's presence. Pull out the theaters and you damage them all." However, it did not follow that all or even most of Broadway's old theaters were worth saving. They were inefficient and, in the opinion of Richard Weinstein, the UDG's resident theater expert, not distinctive enough architecturally to deserve protection as landmarks. Lindsay and his designers concluded that what Broadway needed to assure its survival was *new* theaters, and lots of them. Left to his own devices, no office builder would erect a theater in lieu of a skyscraper on a prime Times Square site. But perhaps developers could be persuaded to construct office towers that included new theaters.

The Wagner administration had attempted something along these lines, amending the zoning code in 1961 to allow developers to build an office tower with 20 percent more floor space than otherwise permitted if a public plaza was incorporated into the design. The Minskoffs had counted on taking full advantage of this allowance in building One Astor Plaza, but Lindsay's urban designers insisted that the developers put in a theater instead. After months of butting heads with the UDG, the Minskoffs appealed to the mayor, who refused to second-guess his design squad. Minskoff & Sons handed the UDG a major victory by agreeing to incorporate two theaters into One Astor Plaza: a 1,621-seat playhouse and a 1,500-seat movie theater.

The Lindsay administration tried to build on this triumph by floating a proposal to create a "special theater district" extending from 40th Street north to 57th Street and from Sixth Avenue west all the way to Ninth Avenue—all of greater Times Square, in other words. After the city council voted it unanimous approval, Lindsay said that he hoped that the measure would reinvigorate the theater to the point that even "those run-down movie houses on 42nd Street" would again be used as legitimate theaters.

In the end, Lindsay's special theater district was much ado about not very much, resulting in the building of only three more playhouses. Demand for new office space was so robust by the late 1960s that developers could make the economics of skyscraper construction work without availing themselves of the 20 percent bonus. By decade's end, six office towers were under construction on Broadway from 39th Street up to 54th Street. None of these new skyscrapers included a playhouse, but neither had any existing theaters been demolished to make way for them. On balance, the Lindsay administration welcomed these projects as a stimulus to the theater district's flagging economy.

But even as Broadway boomed with new construction, no developer was prepared to venture onto 42nd Street, theater bonus or no. This was not only disappointing but also embarrassing to the mayor, who had told the *Times* at the end of 1968 that redeveloping 42nd Street was his top priority for the coming year, outranking even a ten-cent transit fee for the elderly. "You'll be seeing new buildings all along that street," including six office towers, *each* with a new theater on its ground floor, Lindsay predicted.

In the spring of 1969, Lindsay underscored the urgency of 42nd

Street redevelopment by shifting responsibility for it away from the City Planning Commission to a new agency, the Mayor's Office of Midtown Planning and Development, which reported directly to him. The mayor appointed Jacquelin Taylor Robertson, a founding member of the Urban Design Group, to serve as director. Just thirty-six years old, Jacque (pronounced "Jack") Robertson was cut from the same patrician cloth as was Lindsay. His father, Walter S. Robertson, was a Foggy Bottom legend, having served as ambassador to China and as assistant secretary for far eastern affairs. The younger Robertson was dapper, nearly as handsome as Lindsay, and paradoxically oozed both Ivy League sangfroid and southern planter charm. William Bardel, a lawyer who was Robertson's second in command at Midtown Planning, nicknamed him "Silver Tongue."

Robertson assembled a staff of two dozen architects and planners—most of whom were even younger than he was—and set up shop in a beautifully restored suite on the penthouse floor of the 42nd Street theater block's only skyscraper, the Candler Building, which Irving Maidman had sold to an insurance company. The space came cheap, reflecting the increasing difficulty in attracting prime corporate tenants to 42nd Street. It is unlikely that the staff of any municipal agency in history ever boasted more impressive academic credentials than did the Mayor's Office for Midtown Planning and Development. Like Robertson, Deputy Director Bardel was both a Yalie and a Rhodes scholar—and had a Harvard Law School degree, to boot. Five of his colleagues held Ph.D.s, and master's degrees were too common to warrant mention. Robertson filled out the group with a half dozen young actors and actresses, on the theory that aspiring thespians tend to make more intrepid workers than do civil service lifers.

In the end, the Mayor's Office of Midtown Planning and Development could claim some accomplishments during Lindsay's two terms as mayor, chief among them a huge new hotel on Broadway at 45th Street and an imaginative zoning amendment that revitalized the market for Times Square's signature electric signs and billboards by mandating their use on new office buildings. But Midtown Planning never did much of anything to improve 42nd Street in the Lindsay era, and neither did any other city agency. "Lindsay was unhappy that more wasn't done on 42nd Street. We all were," conceded Donald Elliott, a lawyer who served as chairman of city planning during nearly all of Lindsay's tenure. "The essence of the problem as we perceived it was that the block from Seventh to Eighth Avenues was so far gone that you really had to do the whole block at once. We had hoped in due course that 42nd Street would get redeveloped, but no one came to us with a good proposal, and we never could figure one out ourselves."

Midtown Planning was typical of the Lindsay administration in that its lofty aspirations were undermined by managerial ineptitude and intellectual self-absorption. Preoccupied with big, ambitious ideas, Robertson had little interest in or aptitude for the minutiae of administration. Nor did anyone else in the office. As a result, even the junior planners and designers were given considerable latitude to develop their own ideas at their own pace. Robertson presided over innumerable skull sessions wreathed in pipe smoke and high concept. "John Lindsay was a man of vision and guts—he had to be to put all these eggheads in the middle of the problem and say, 'fix it,'" said Richard Basini, a former Marriott Corp. manager and the only Midtown Planning staffer who had ever worked for a big company.

Basini took a particularly intense dislike to a smug young architect who spent month after month designing a waterfront promenade that would have replaced the pier operated by the Circle Line tour boat company at 42nd Street's west end. "One day I said to this guy, 'What about the Circle Line?' He said, 'They'll just have to move.' The intellectual arrogance was just rampant," recalled Basini, who vented his disdain by spilling a cup of coffee over the architect's drawings. When the man complained, Basini fetched the office coffeepot and dumped the whole thing over his desk. "There was such a waste of public money going on in that office, but this guy was having a great time," said Basini, who reddened at the memory. "I wanted him to go to Jacque and complain and have Jacque look over his plans and say, 'Why are you doing this, anyway?'"

West 42nd Street remained an airy abstraction to many of Midtown Planning's professionals, even though they set foot on it every day. To Robertson, who commuted to the Candler by taxicab, working out of an office on "the seedy side of the city," as he put it, was a mildly amusing form of slumming. He liked to tell the story of how Kingman Brewster, the president of Yale, stopped by the Candler one day for a visit. "He had the correct address, but his chauffeur took him to East 42nd Street by force of habit," Robertson recalled. "He finally found me, and the head of the vice squad happened to be in the office along with Red Ryan, who was a headbanger for the Longshoremen." Brewster purred with mock concern, "My, my, Jacquelin."

Midtown Planning employed a couple of young black men from Project Return, a drug rehabilitation program, to make deliveries and run errands. One afternoon Basini was walking down 42nd Street when he bumped into one of the Project Return runners. "He started laughing at me," recalled Basini, who had asked the runner to take him on a tour of the block. "I wanted to see 42nd Street through his eyes," Basini said.

So we go to Orange Julius and he explains that it's a drink that mixes especially well with methadone. You could also buy any kind of drug you wanted there. Then we go to a movie theater and he says that when you need money to buy more drugs you just sit behind some dude and cut out his wallet with a razor blade. He took me to a place where you could buy a knife or a gun. He showed me a whole self-contained world on the street that I hadn't even noticed in which all these people had their own turf, a place where they went to work every day. He said, "You guys are urban planners, right? You can plan all you want and you're never going to come up with something that works better than this."

Marty Hodas and the Rise of XXX

The growth of the "adult entertainment" business in America is often explained as the inevitable result of high court decisions that progressively narrowed the legal grounds for obscenity prosecution. This is true as far as it goes, but it underplays the entrepreneurial impulse as a motive force in pornography's transformation from the covert cottage industry of the mid-1960s to the brazen multibillion-dollar enterprise of the mid-1970s. The Bill Gates of 42nd Street porn was Martin J. Hodas. Like Gates, Hodas would become an object of intense suspicion and determined, if not very adept, prosecution. But unlike Gates, whose Microsoft Corporation crushed legions of rivals, Hodas lacked the business skills and ruthlessness required to parlay his pioneering into enduring dominance of the business he created. The federal government eventually would take Hodas down—on a rather skimpy tax evasion conviction—but in the jackpot years of 1967 to 1970 the combined might of the mayor's office and the New York Police Department was no match for the "King of the Peeps."

A barrel-chested fireplug of a man at five feet seven and two hundred pounds, Hodas was hardworking, unpretentious, loud, emotional, profane, and a lot shrewder than he let on. He might not have been strictly faithful to his marriage vows, but at least he was no bachelor hedonist padding about a bunny-filled mansion in silk dressing gown and slippers. For Hodas, the girls and the parties were a minor distraction from what was first and foremost a moneymaking proposition. By nature and habit a family man, he lived with his wife and four kids in a $175,000 four-bedroom home on the water in Lawrence, Long Island, directly across from a yacht club that refused to admit him or his forty-foot cabin cruiser. Hodas equipped his dream house with a swimming pool, a pagoda-shaped steam room, and a basement filled with jukeboxes and pinball machines. "I'm not a religious man. That is, I don't go to the synagogue," he helpfully informed a reporter. "But I do play paddleball religiously, at least twice a week to keep in shape."

Born in 1931, Hodas was the second child of European-born Jews who settled in the East New York section of Brooklyn. His father, Louis Hodas, sold eggs door-to-door. Louis was in business with his brother, who owned a farm near Tom's River, New Jersey. Money was always tight around the Hodas household. Marty and his sister never went hungry, but the boy had no spending money unless he made it himself. At eight he started lugging a shoeshine box around. Later, he sold magazines and newspapers outside the Fulton Street El station in Brooklyn at rush hour, netting a couple of dollars a week. Marty spent his summers working on his uncle's New Jersey chicken farm, where he muscled up on hundred-pound feed sacks and developed a precocious interest in entomology. "It's the most fascinating thing there is," Hodas recalled decades later. "You can't know about the world or the universe without knowing about insects. Every insect out there has been put here for a purpose, even if you don't know what it is."

Hodas drove himself and his neighborhood buddies to Franklin K. Lane High School in Queens in a rattletrap of a car he bought for sixty dollars. "I was never arrested as a juvenile delinquent or nothing, but we did have our own little gang—Jews, Irish, Italian," he said. "You had to be in a little bit of a gang then in East New York, though we didn't use the word *gang*." At school, this self-proclaimed "muscle kid" liked to show off his strength by picking up his classmates and carrying them around the hallways like furniture. Yet Hodas also joined the science club, won a math prize, and set his sights on attending Cornell University. His inscription in the senior yearbook was downright cuddly: "No living creature can come to harm/If Hodas is down on the farm."

Hodas graduated in 1949 but was unable to persuade his father or his uncle to help foot the bill for Cornell University. He enlisted in the army and was relieved to avoid combat in Korea, serving out his two-year tour of duty at bases in France and Germany. Honorably discharged in 1954, he returned to New York and enrolled in a community college on the GI Bill. Hodas majored in petroleum engineering while working a part-time job servicing gumball machines in stores and restaurants in Brooklyn. After marrying in 1956, he quit college and bought a seat on the Chicago Mercantile Exchange. From a tiny office in the Wall Street district, he traded futures contracts in eggs, the one commodity he knew from personal experience. He also kept plugging away at his gumball route even as the two brothers who employed him fell behind on their payments to him. In lieu of cash, they finally gave him ten jukeboxes, which served as Hodas's entrée to one of the most famously mobbed-up businesses of the 1950s.

Hodas entered the jukebox trade at a time when Mafia families were making a concerted effort to expand their stakes in coin-operated machine rackets in New York City and elsewhere. This led to an epidemic of coercion and violence that attracted the scrutiny of the federal government and put the jukes front and center in nationally televised hearings in 1959 orchestrated by Robert F. Kennedy, counsel to a U.S. Senate committee investigating labor racketeering. By this time, Hodas had long since discovered the darker realities of his accidental calling, for he had survived a perilously close encounter with Kennedy's star witness, Brooklyn's own "Crazy Joe" Gallo, the most feared jukebox hoodlum of all.

By the time that Hodas got into the business, most every tavern, diner, pool hall, and bowling alley in America already had a jukebox. It was almost impossible for a newcomer to gain a toehold without replacing someone else's machines with his own—a tactic known as "jumping a spot." Hodas jumped so many that he placed all ten of his jukes around East New York within a few months and began buying more machines as his finances permitted. One day in 1957, Hodas jumped the wrong spot—Sal's Luncheonette on Church Street and McDonald Avenue in Brooklyn. Sal's was a few doors down from the Okay Restaurant, which was one of the hubs of Joey Gallo's fledgling criminal enterprise. When Hodas returned to Sal's a few weeks later to change the records, he found that his Seaburg B had been unplugged and shoved into a corner. In its place was another machine with a sticker that read GALLO VENDING. Infuriated, Hodas shoved the replacement machine aside and plugged his jukebox back in. The next time Hodas's route brought him to Sal's he found his $300 jukebox lying in pieces at the bottom of the basement stairs. "I was making about $100 a week, trying to bring up my little family. I was devastated," Hodas recalled. "Then I made a mistake." He took Crazy Joe's juke and shoved it down the stairs, too.

Important people in jukebox distribution urged Hodas to sit down with Gallo under their supervision and work out a truce. Hodas had better things to do. He was driving on the Belt Parkway one afternoon when three bullets came flying at him from a passing car. He escaped with a flesh wound but decided a meeting wasn't such a bad idea after all. The "sit-down" took place at the offices of a large jukebox distributor at Tenth Avenue and 44th Street, in the middle of Hell's Kitchen. "They didn't give a shit about me dying. But they figured if Joey killed me, they would have in the headlines 'Jukebox War,'" Hodas recalled. The arbiters awarded Sal's to Gallo, who also got to salvage the two broken jukes for parts. Hodas got a measly $50. "It was a compromise only because Joey didn't want to give me anything at all," Hodas said. "After it was all over Joey came over to me and said, 'Nobody fucks with me like you did.' I said, 'Joey, to tell you the truth, I didn't know who you are. What the fuck did I know? I'm just a hardworking guy with a wife and kids.' And he laughed and put his arm around me and said, 'Hey, you're one tough son of a bitch'. We became friends. He liked me. I sorta liked him, too. If you're on the right side even of a killer, you can like them."

Hodas curbed his suicidal spot-jumping and built a route of fifty jukeboxes and thirty coin-operated games in Brooklyn and Queens. To this day, he insists that neither Gallo nor any other mobster pressed him to join the Automatic Amusement Machine Operators of New York, the front group through which the Mafia dominated the jukebox business during most of the twelve years Hodas spent in it. This sounds implausible, but his name never surfaced in the numerous prosecutions of Crazy Joe and other jukebox gangsters. "I came across a lot of people that were connected," Hodas said, "but I was never big enough for them to care about."

From the start, Hodas had made regular trips into Hell's Kitchen to transact business with the jukebox suppliers clustered along Tenth Avenue. He liked to stop on the way and check out the latest adult bookstore on 42nd Street, but it wasn't until 1966 that the million-dollar idea popped into Hodas's brain. En route to visit his uncle in Tom's River, he stopped at a roadside game arcade in New Jersey. Hodas was well acquainted with the peep show equipment common to arcades from Times Square to Coney Island. He'd played them in his youth and now owned a few himself—rickety little contraptions that he threaded with Mickey Mouse cartoons or Tom Mix clips. But this Jersey arcade featured a dozen of the biggest coin-operated movie machines Hodas had ever seen. The 16-millimeter device was the approximate size and shape of a coffin or a refrigerator. Hodas slipped in a quarter and watched a woman of average endowment lackadaisically strip to her underwear. This was pretty tame stuff even then, but it excited Hodas just the same. "I thought, 'Wow! What these machines would do on 42nd Street, busy place like that.'"

This was not exactly a new thought. The sex peep show was as old as Times Square—considerably older, actually. Thomas Edison had first made pictures move by inventing the kinetoscope, the original peep show, in 1891. Early penny arcades featured rows of kinetoscopes and Mutoscopes offering a variety of moving pictures. The kinetoscope had debuted with a thirteen-second film clip of Annie Oakley and Buffalo Bill, but it did not take long for arcade operators to figure out that sex sold best, or that posting a sign reading FOR MEN ONLY above a machine rendered even such mildly risqué fare like *How Girls Undress* or *French High Kickers* irresistible to inquisitive youth. "Because so many of the boys who gathered around the Mutoscopes were not tall enough to reach the eyehole, arcade managers had to supply them with stools to stand on." More stools than ever were needed as machines making use of new film projection systems supplanted the kinetoscope and its offshoots.

The peep show proved a durable form of arcade amusement, surviving the advent of Broadway theater, feature films, radio, television, and countless lesser diversions. When Hodas had his roadside Eureka moment, the peep show patron still could choose from among nine or ten arcades in Times Square, the longtime hub of the New York arcade scene. The persistence of the peep show's appeal was all the more remarkable considering how little it evolved, either in the technology employed or in the content featured. The celluloid strip routine that Hodas watched in New Jersey (and could have watched in any of the Times Square arcades) was more overtly sexual than a faux instructional like *How Girls Undress*, but it contained the same amount of actual nudity: none. Over the years, there had been sporadic attempts in some cities to thread arcade movie machines with explicit stag film loops, but these experiments all foundered on society's basic refusal to allow an amusement hall for kids to become an instrument of sexual revolution.

The Wagner administration had tolerated the traditional presence of peep machines in Times Square arcades but exerted heavy pressure to keep them out of sex bookstores as they proliferated on 42nd Street. The few shops that had experimented with peep show exhibition in the 1950s got extra unloving attention from the police department and received threatening notices informing them a city license was required to show movies. This was a legally dubious assertion, but the bookstores meekly accepted the city's rejection of their applications for film exhibition licenses. They were equally unwilling to take the Lindsay administration to court over the issue, as Hodas discovered when he cold-called every bookstore manager on 42nd Street after his revelatory trip across the river. "They all said the same thing, 'You gotta have a license,'" Hodas recalled. "So I said, 'What if I can get the license?' 'Yeah, sure. No one can get a license. We tried.'"

Hodas turned to Charles Carreras, a Queens lawyer who specialized in dealing with the Liquor Control Commission, New York State's liquor licensing authority. In the early 1960s, Hodas had made a brief, ill-fated foray into tavern ownership in Brooklyn and Queens and had hired Carreras to represent him. Charlie Carreras failed to get Hodas his peep machine license. But after many inconclusive phone calls and meetings, the lawyer emerged from the bureaucratic thickets in mid-1967 with the next best thing: a letter from the chief of the license issuance division of the Department of Licenses stating that no city license was required to "install in the New York City area a coin-operated machine that shows movies." Hodas was ecstatic. "Holy shit! I did it! I did it!" he shouted when Carreras read him the letter over the phone.

Hodas waved his letter all over 42nd Street, but the bookshop owners remained leery with one exception: Hyman Cohen of Carpel Books, which had been operating at 259 West 42nd Street since 1954. Under the terms offered by Hodas, Cohen would not be required to shell out any money at all—no lease payments, no security deposit, no maintenance fees. Hodas would cover all the operating costs and split the incoming revenues with Cohen fifty-fifty. The only drawback that Cohen could see was that the police department might find some pretext for shutting him down, letter or no letter. He decided that this was a risk worth taking. Hodas drove to New Jersey and bought the arcade owner's entire inventory of strip loops and all twelve of his 16-millimeter machines, known in the trade as "Panasonics." He took immediate delivery of four of the machines, all of which he installed in Carpel Books.

A few days later, Cohen called to complain that two of the machines had broken down. Hodas rushed down to 42nd Street and pushed his way through the crowd gathered around the machines. He unlocked one of the broken-down contraptions and found that dozens of quarters had overflowed from the coin box, bollixing up the works. "I was as amazed as anybody," Hodas recalled. The news of the long lines at Cohen's place traveled fast along the block. "Every single guy who had a bookstore was calling me up, saying, 'Hey, Marty, wanna put some machines in my store?'"

Hodas placed his remaining Panasonics in bookstores at 113 and 210 West 42nd Street and 1498 Broadway and began making the rounds of the big coin-operated vending distributors in New York, trying to interest them in going into the peep show supply business with him. "They all told me the same thing," he said. "'Who are you to do this? Who's Marty Hodas? If this thing could make money, don't you think someone big would already be in it?'" Hodas also scoured the New York metropolitan area for more Panasonics but found none for sale. Finally, he got a line on a little Kentucky manufacturer called Urban Industries and flew down to Louisville, where he placed an order for thirty machines, paying $10,000 cash in advance. Hodas found that a Panasonic paid for itself in about a month. By the time that he returned to Louisville to pick up more machines, he was well on his way to becoming a rich man.

In late 1967, Hodas rented a small office on the third floor of 233 West 42nd Street and put a help-wanted ad in the newspaper. It was answered by Herbert J. Levin, a hulking, six-foot-three former factory foreman and airplane mechanic. Levin earned Hodas's trust—but not until he'd passed two lie detector tests. When Hodas finally incorporated his peep show business as East Coast Cinerama Theater in March 1968, he had some fifty machines in stores and had a hundred more on order. Two or three times a week, Levin trudged from bookstore to bookstore, pulling a wheeled steamer trunk behind him. He weighed the quarters on a balance scale, dumped Hodas's half share into the trunk, and hauled the coins to the Chemical Bank on 42nd Street at Eighth Avenue. Soon, Levin and a half dozen helpers were making daily deposits of as much as

$15,000—60,000 quarters. Fully 85 percent of the quarters that this Chemical branch shipped to bank headquarters had been extracted from Hodas's peeps.

Hodas used his peep show profits to build a diversified little empire of smut, beginning with the 42nd Street Photo Studio. He turned most of the space that he rented for his office at 233 West 42nd into a little rabbit warren of rooms, each outfitted with a simple prop or two—a stage, a built-in table, a couple of chairs. He stuck a GIRLS WANTED sign on the building's front door and took his pick of the many nubile young women who climbed the stairs to inquire. "In those days, you weren't allowed to show nude girls in a film," Hodas explained. "But I found out that it was legal for a man to take a private photo of a nude girl as long as it was his personally. You couldn't distribute it." For ten dollars a half hour, Hodas supplied a Polaroid camera, a willing girl, and a private room. The models got a cut of the ten-dollar camera fee, plus tips.

In concept, the photo studio was a clever finessing of the law, complete with posted signs asking "members" not to touch the models during photo sessions and advising the models not to assume "lewd or suggestive" poses. But Hodas set up 42nd Street Photo Studio knowing full well that his customers were not going to be satisfied with picture taking. "I didn't really want it to happen because I was trying to stay legit," he said. "But you get a guy alone in the room with a girl. He gets himself a nice big boner and he propositions the girl. She figures, 'Hey, for an extra twenty dollars why not?'"

Hodas also started making twenty-minute sex movies through a start-up company he called Dynamite Films, which operated out of a basement apartment on West 14th Street. In a 1969 press interview, Hodas came across like the Orson Welles of 42nd Street, boasting that his "short films are the finest in the business." Although Hodas awarded himself a director credit at every opportunity, the footage was actually shot by Robert Wolf, a longhaired, Village bohemian photographer who was a partner in Dynamite Films. While the move into filmmaking certainly gratified Hodas's ego, it also made solid business sense. The peep show patron had a voracious appetite for novelty, and Hodas found that he was unable to satisfy it relying wholly on outside film suppliers. He paid his actresses $125 a movie (the actors got $75 tops) and rented all the equipment he and Wolf needed. Films like *Elevator Orgy* and *Flesh Party* took three hours to make and could be cranked out at the rate of two or three a week.

Hodas's bookstore clients were delighted to be able to sell copies of the same films featured in their peep machines. He also built a sizable mail-order trade.

This budding porn-film auteur also began using his peep show profits to acquire real estate, usually under long-term lease but occasionally through outright purchase. Most of his properties were on 42nd—including nos. 210, 233, 247, and 414—and most of them already were providing space to adult bookstores. By becoming a landlord, Hodas bolstered his cash flow with a steady stream of rental income. But he also was trying to safeguard his bookstore clients from eviction by landlords less committed to the porn business and more susceptible to political pressure than he was. Hodas also needed more space for his own growing business. He soon moved his own offices to the eleventh floor of a Maidman-owned building at 113 West 42nd while East Coast Cinematics took over the basement of 210 West 42nd for use as a peep machine repair shop.

New York's newspaper readers were introduced to Hodas after *Times* reporter Richard F. Shepard dropped by his 42nd Street office for an interview in mid-1969. The Peep King gloried in the attention. "Book store proprietors do not like to discuss their peep shows, but Martin Hodas . . . is happy to let the world know about the career he has forged for himself," wrote Shepard, who described his subject as "stocky, mustachioed and a familiar figure on West 42nd Street, where many of the street's motley regulars chat with him as he walks by." Hodas asked Shepard, "Do you know what luck is? Luck is careful planning, taking advantage of opportunity. Show me any man who has achieved success and it's not luck." Hodas would rue the day that he stepped out front to strut his stuff for Shepard. The *Times* profile marked the beginning of a snowballing notoriety that would establish Hodas as public porn enemy number one during John Lindsay's second term as mayor.

Low-level mobsters had owned bookstores on 42nd Street at least since 1959, when Joseph Charles Pucciarelli, a Lucchese family soldier better known as "Charlie Bull," opened the Bee See Book Shop at 117 West 42nd. Soon, Charlie Bull was joined by various relatives, including one nephew who was a Genovese family soldier and another nephew who worked as a butcher in an A&P store in Brooklyn until the siren song of smut lured him to Midtown. The Pucciarelli clan prospered in its new calling, eventually adding three more stores on 42nd—VIP Novelties at 136, the L & R Book Shop at 147, and Whiteway Books at 224—as well as two outlets elsewhere in the Square.

For a time, Marty Hodas supplied peep machines to all six of Pucciarelli's stores. Another of his best customers was Joseph "Joe Bikini" Brocchini, an up-and-coming soldier in the Lucchese family. Brocchini owned three stores on 42nd Street, including Black Jack Books, which occupied the ground floor at 210 West 42nd. Hodas owned this building, making him both landlord and supplier to Joe Bikini. Hodas didn't care much for the Pucciarelli boys, but he and Brocchini were friendly. "Joe was not only connected, Joe was the type of guy that would blow you away. But me and Joe got along fine because when you're making money together everyone gets along fine," Hodas recalled. "We went on vacation together, his family and my family. We talked, had fun, barbecued. If Joey liked you, you couldn't ask for a nicer guy."

But what goes around comes around. On the day that Joe Bikini's corpse was found in the back room of a car dealership that he owned in Queens, he was due at Hodas's 42nd Street office at ten in the morning. The two were buying an adult bookstore together, and Brocchini was going to deliver the cash needed to close the deal. "So I'm waiting—ten o'clock, eleven o'clock, twelve o'clock," Hodas recalled. "Then my cousin that works for me comes up and says, 'You hear the news? Joey Bikini's dead!' I said, 'He's dead! He's supposed to come up here with $76,000. How did he die?' My cousin said, 'Natural causes.' Natural causes? 'Yeah, two bullets in the head.' I'll never forget that. 'Natural causes, two bullets in the head.' We all laughed at that one."

Knowing that he would not have the peep machine supply business on 42nd Street to himself for long, Hodas required all of his bookstore customers to sign contracts obligating them to use his machines exclusively for three years. Hodas expected competition, he just did not expect it to come from the Colombo family, which in the late 1960s was second in clout only to the Gambinos among New York's five families. Joe Colombo and his gang essentially had ignored Times Square until the glint of peep show coin caught their eye. In 1968, the NYPD's mob squad noticed that three Colombo bosses had begun visiting bookstores on 42nd Street with suspicious regularity. They included John "Sonny" Franzese, who was second in command to Colombo himself. Franzese was a disciplined, self-effacing mobster who had incongruously made a specialty out of nightclub and recording industry racketeering. After Frank Sinatra Jr. opened to disappointing crowds at the San Su San nightclub on Long Island in 1963, Franzese worked the phones. "The next night," *Newsday* reported, "the nightclub was jammed wall-to-wall with wildly applauding gunmen, extortionists and bookmakers."

Hodas unwittingly crossed paths with Franzese in late 1967 when he installed his machines in a new bookstore at 1498 Broadway and another at 1111 Sixth Avenue. Both stores were run by Robert Genova, a photographer turned salesman of "girlie" photos. But just a few months after Genova had signed Hodas's standard three-year contract, he bought his own equipment and put East Coast's peep machines out on the sidewalk. Hodas stormed over to 1498 Broadway and angrily confronted Genova, who just laughed in his face. It turned out that Genova had organized a new company called Motion Picture Vending to compete with East Coast Cinematics in the peep supply business. Hodas was stunned by Genova's audacity until he discovered that Motion Picture Vending was controlled by Sonny Franzese.

Hodas went to see his uncle Carl, a retired bookie who lived in Brooklyn. Uncle Carl had never talked much about how he made his living, but Hodas had always considered him shrewd and well connected. "Now began, you could say, my whole new life," Hodas recalled. "My uncle said to me, 'Marty, I'm gonna introduce you to some people, and we'll see what we can do.'" These people included a leader of the Westies, an ultraviolent Hell's Kitchen gang, and a Jewish mobster whom Hodas will refer to only by the pseudonym "Benny." According to Hodas, Benny and the Westies took him under their joint protection, enabling him to compete against Motion Picture Vending without suffering violent reprisals. (Soon, East Coast also had to cope with a second rival, Mini-Cine Enterprises Inc., which was backed by the Genovese family.)

The only previously published account of how Hodas got married to the mob can be found in the writing of William Sherman, a reporter for the *Daily News*. Sherman quoted unnamed police sources who said that "Hodas has for years been paying off John (Sonny) Franzese." When the cops raided Hodas's office in early 1972, they supposedly found a note, handwritten by Hodas, in a desk drawer, Sherman reported. "John gets $4,000 each week until $100,000 is received. Thereafter he receives

$1,000 each week for the rest of the year. All new stores, Marty puts up 50 percent cash with John and we are partners. Marty assumes all responsibility for running the stores." The police told Sherman that this referred to Franzese, though the assistant district attorney conceded that prosecutors had no evidence directly tying Hodas to the Mafia. For his part, Hodas told Sherman that he did know Franzese but refused to identify the John in question and dismissed the arrangement outlined in the memo as a "business deal" that fell through.

Sherman offered a much different account in *Times Square,* a nonfiction book that he published in 1980. ("Behind the glitter and the lights: the true story of an undercover cop on the toughest beat in America.") Sherman quoted an unnamed informant "who knew Hodas well during those days" and asserted that this man's account of how Hodas made peace with the Mafia "was more widely accepted on the street" than Hodas's claim that he affiliated only after he was muscled by Colombo goons. "Don't believe Marty's bullshit," the informant said. "Oh, maybe the wise guys were nibbling around, but it was Marty who made the arrangement. He had competition, he needed the okay to expand more into other cities, so he was looking to get connected." This same source told Sherman that "a well-known loan shark named Whitey Leibowitz" set Hodas up with the boss of a major Mafia family. The tab was $1,000 a week. "Whitey promised to spread the word that Marty was okay, that he could use some names. See, Whitey had two guys on the street, collectors named Rusty and Mike. Mike was a little Irish guy. You could never tell it by looking at him, but he was a killer."

Hodas became enraged when this passage was read to him some thirty years after Sherman had written it. He said that he would gladly have paid protection money, but that his uncle's friend asked nothing of him, except to provide employment to a few people. "He told me, 'Me and Carl ran together years and years ago. We owe each other a lot,'" Hodas said. "'You're the same as Carl to me. I'm glad to help.'"

By mid-1970, about 1,000 peep show machines were installed in bookstores and X-rated venues throughout Manhattan, according to information compiled by the State of New York Commission of Investigation. Hodas, with 350 machines on the street, still held the largest share of the market, having managed to hold his own against the Colombo-controlled Motion Picture Vending, which had 180 machines in circulation. But Mini-Cine Enterprises Inc., controlled by the Genovese family, was gaining fast, with 320 machines in circulation. The two Mafia challengers were offering bookstores the same basic terms that East Coast did, notably a straight fifty-fifty revenue split.

For bookstore owners, who bore none of the cost of equipment or film-loop purchase, peep show revenue was almost pure profit. The machines also pulled in scads of new customers, broadening the retail sex market in Times Square to an extent that startled even Hodas. "Don't ask me where they came from, but they came: doctors, lawyers, tourists, kids, fags," he told a reporter with characteristic rough aplomb. "Everybody. And they were fighting to get to those peep machines." Peep show profits financed an explosion of the Times Square smut business in the late 1960s, as the number of adult bookstores more than doubled to sixty-eight in 1970, from about thirty in 1967. West 42nd Street remained the center of the city's X-rated action, with eighteen bookstores and five sex cinemas between Sixth Avenue and Eighth Avenue alone.

For years, the feminist writer Susan Brownmiller walked the theater block of 42nd Street when making her way from the Port Authority Bus Terminal on Eighth Avenue to the New York Public Library on Fifth Avenue. About 1970, Brownmiller was horrified to see her route transmogrify "from a familiar landscape of tacky souvenir shops, fast-food joints, and kung fu movie houses into a hostile gauntlet of Girls! Live Girls!, XXX, Hot Nude Combos, and illegal massage parlors one flight above the twenty-five-cent peeps. It wasn't just the visual assault that was inimical to my dignity and peace of mind," she recalled. "The new grunge seemed to embolden a surly army of thugs, pimps, handbag snatchers, pickpockets, drug sellers, and brazen loiterers whose murmured propositions could not be construed as friendly."

As Brownmiller implied, 42nd Street's sex establishments were proliferating not only in number but also in kind. The live sex show re-emerged on a scale not seen since the heyday of burlesque, but with a vulgar artlessness that made Billy Minsky seem like Flo Ziegfeld by comparison. By late 1970, the New York Police Department identified six strip joints and five "live-sex exhibition halls" in the city, all but one of which was located in Times Square; the number of sex clubs would double within a year. Garrett Williams, who owned a couple of bookstores with Marty Hodas–supplied peeps, pioneered the latter innovation. A six-foot-two, 350-pound behemoth of a pornographer, Williams rented a storefront on Eighth Avenue near 45th Street, installed a stage and a mattress, scattered a dozen chairs, and stationed a barker outside. *Voilà*, the live sex club. "It was all authentic," recalled Hodas, who took in the occasional Williams show in the interests of customer relations and his own libido. "It would be a guy and a girl that would do everything on the stage for a half hour. No one could complain for five dollars."

In hopes of warding off police raids, Times Square's live sex clubs cloaked their shows in trappings of art and sociology. Club Orgy posted a notice declaring that "the lectures and demonstrations are intended to help audiences lead healthier and happier lives." The pretext devised by the Mini Cinerama, which occupied the second floor of the old Wurlitzer Building at 120 West 42nd, was that of providing tours of a working film studio. You paid five dollars and were ushered into a small room equipped with wooden benches and a double bed. As a nude couple demonstrated their mastery of the *Kama Sutra*, a fully clothed man circled them with an 8-millimeter movie camera, murmuring encouragement. Farther west along 42nd Street were two more live sex halls: the Club Za-Za at number 410 and the 42 Playhouse at 416, formerly the Maidman Playhouse.

Then there was the live peep show, the first of which—Peepalive—opened in 1970 on the second floor of 109 West 42nd Street. Built into a wall were a bank of what appeared to be peep show movie machines but in reality were empty, curtained boxes equipped with viewing slots. You put in a quarter, a screen dropped inside, and a Live Nude Girl! materialized behind a window. She worked through various poses while rotating on a revolving drum. After five or six minutes, the woman left and another would take her place. The live peep was also a Garrett Williams innovation, though Hodas made a few halfhearted stabs at appropriating credit. Hodas put his own live peep into his building at 113 West 42nd, two doors down from Williams's joint.

While the live sex show was bringing pornography to three-dimensional life, the advent of the massage-parlor brothel elevated prostitution to a prominence and a prevalence unequalled in Midtown since 42nd Street's emergence as the city's new theater district in the early 1900s. During the 1960s, prostitution had remained hidden in Times Square's shadows, confined to a relative handful of run-down old hotels and eclipsed in the public consciousness by pornography's fresher and higher profile offenses against decency. During the "free love" era, paid sex seemed passé, "its style an anachronistic hangover from earlier times: street hookers and their pimps, call girls and their furs, Cadillacs and heroin, Iceberg Slim and Butterfield Eight."

New York City had been home to brothels masquerading as massage parlors since the turn of the century. On balance, though, the ancient healing art of massage was practiced so benignly that in 1967 the city council discontinued the longstanding requirement that operators obtain an operating license. In early 1971, the New York State Assembly unwittingly did its part to spur an incipient massage parlor boom, enacting legislation that reduced the criminal penalties for prostitution. These two deregulatory measures combined to open the sex-for-hire floodgates. By the time Mayor Lindsay and the council finally got around to passing a new license law in early 1973, there were 199 massage parlors in the Yellow Pages, only a dozen of which were legit.

Like the speakeasies of an earlier age, the illicit massage parlors sprouted all throughout Midtown, east and west. They ranged from filthy, two-hooker stands that dispensed with the niceties of talcum powder and rubbing oil, to large and luxuriously appointed theme clubs done up like Roman baths or Tahitian hideaways. The classiest establishments were found on the East Side; Times Square parlors tended to feature only the rude basics, recruiting girls off the streets or renting them from pimps. Owners generally kept the fifteen-dollar rubdown fee and gave the talent a share of the "tips," as the extra charges for sex were called. Within the theater district, the parlors were concentrated in parallel strips that bookended Broadway's playhouses: one ran along Eighth Avenue from 42nd Street to 50th Street and the other was east of Times Square proper, between Sixth and Seventh Avenues. The differences between these two prostitution belts were largely a matter of real estate. While the Eighth Avenue parlors operated out of dingy tenements, their counterparts to the east occupied decrepit hotels.

The theater block of 42nd Street per se was relatively free of massage parlors and even of streetwalkers. "There was just too much action for prostitutes to work effectively, and also they may have got in the way of the pickpockets and hustlers who worked 42nd Street in great numbers," recalled Milton "Mickey" Schwartz, who was commander of the NYPD's Midtown South precinct in the early 1970s. "There were times that I used to put sixteen officers on the shift from 4 P.M. to midnight and it was so crowded you could not even see them. They were lost. It was a mass of people." However, Schwartz added, the much less populated block between Ninth and Tenth Avenues—Irving Maidman's block—"had the seediest, dingiest massage parlors I'd ever seen in my life."

Most of the whorehouse hotels near Times Square were owned by Seymour Durst, whose attempt to build the 42nd Street equivalent of Rockefeller Center had backfired horribly. By Durst's own count, the five blocks he had assembled contained twenty-six small hotels of ancient vintage. For years, these hotels had housed dozens of poor families on the dole. But in the mid-1960s the city began relocating most of these welfare cases, leaving a void that was filled by brothel operators. "Things got really bad," recalled Douglas Durst, who had joined his father at the Durst Organization in 1967. "Every other place was a massage parlor and they all had these barkers out in front, saying 'Check it out, check it out.'" Of course, Seymour had acquired these buildings intending to demolish them but had badly misjudged the demand for new office space. The Dursts did manage to erect one new tower within their Times Square assemblage, but they were unable to line up tenants to fill a second skyscraper—much less the nine that Seymour had envisioned—in the moribund real estate markets of the early 1970s.

Most of the Dursts' flesh-peddling tenants had come with the buildings they had acquired, but father and especially son only had themselves to blame for the "Italian American Social Club." When its "president" had come calling, Douglas had naively taken the man's claims at face value and leased out the entire ground floor of 156 West 44th Street to what was a brothel, pure and simple. The prostitutes who worked the place sat together on a bench outside the building, glumly soliciting customers. The Dursts' repeated threats to evict the "club" served only to inflame the thugs who managed the place. "These guys who had seen too many gangster films gave us a hard time," Douglas recalled. "They'd stand in front of the building and heckle us whenever we walked by."

In mid-1971, Mayor Lindsay announced an all-out crackdown on Midtown smut. Under the direction of a new task force headed by Police Commissioner Patrick V. Murphy, two new NYPD "macro-precincts" were created on the West Side—Midtown South and Midtown North, with 45th Street acting as a boundary between the two. Some six hundred police officers of various ranks were drafted from the outer boroughs and divided equally between North and South. New patrol cars, vans, and walkie-talkies were purchased. Deputy Inspector Charles F. Peterson, the brainy, gung ho commander of Midtown North, personally designed a handsome collar insignia for his men, a brass pin stenciled with MIDTOWN NORTH.

Massage parlors presented a particularly thorny enforcement challenge. Prostitution was patently illegal, but evicting a brothel holding a valid lease meant proving in court that its operators were knowingly using the premises illegally. No doubt the cops could have brought more pressure to bear had they been able to enter massage parlors at will, instead of having to get a warrant every time they had reason to believe a crime was occurring. By contrast, inspectors from city regulatory agencies were free to enter sex shops of all sorts and order them closed for any number of minor infractions. Lindsay created a bigger enforcement club than the NYPD could wield on its own by establishing the Times Square Inspectional Task Force under the auspices of the city's Commission of Investigation. It paired cops with inspectors from fire, health, buildings, and other municipal departments to form a unified antismut strike force.

Midtown North and South also experimented with new smut-busting techniques of dubious legality. Big, flashy cars were presumed to be "pimpmobiles" and often towed even when properly parked. The horizontal wooden barriers that the police erected along both sides of Eighth Avenue from 45th to 50th Streets served a dual purpose: they obstructed access to massage parlors while denying streetwalkers a place to solicit trade. In addition, uniformed officers sometimes stood out in front of parlors with cameras. There was no film in the cameras, but plenty of johns were scared off by the mere thought of a cop taking their picture entering a brothel. Some beat cops even imposed their own curfews, arbitrarily ordering massage parlors to close at 5:00 P.M. or 8:00 P.M. on some days and letting them run into the wee hours on others. Midtown North in particular came on like gangbusters. "You'd better get down here before massage parlors become extinct," Charlie Peterson bragged to a reporter.

At the same time, the Lindsay administration cracked down hard on the adult bookstores and live sex shows, raiding them frequently and hauling their employees off to jail under various obscenity charges. In the spring of 1972, the Department of Consumer Affairs gave the NYPD a new legal basis for raiding bookstores by requiring them all to obtain a city amusement license for their peep shows. To qualify, a bookstore with even one machine had to meet the same stringent building code strictures imposed on a legitimate Broadway theater. In practice, licenses for peep shows proved even harder to obtain than those for massage parlors, some of which were medically accredited, after all. By the end of 1972, Consumer Affairs had not granted a single license.

As his peep show business dwindled under the pressure of the city's clampdown, Marty Hodas railed against the city's "Gestapo tactics" on television talk shows, in letters to the editor, and in press interviews. John Corry of the *Times* called on the King of the Peeps in his office one afternoon and found him angrily waving a sheaf of summonses.

"Every day I walk in I don't know if I'm in business or not," he shouted. "There's no law prohibiting a peep show, and so the cops charge me with anything. We're becoming a scapegoat for all the ills in the city."

Just because Hodas was paranoid did not mean that they weren't out to get him. Things first started to go seriously wrong for Hodas in the fall of 1970, when the state's Commission of Investigation subpoenaed East Coast Cinematics' books as part of a probe into organized crime's influence over the pornography business. In 1969, the company had reported revenue of $310,000. Albert Sohn, the commission's chief accountant, devised an ingenious method of checking this figure. He was able to establish that Hodas's peeps had burned through 831 of a certain lightbulb manufactured by General Electric and that these bulbs had an average life of three hundred hours. On this basis, Sohn calculated East Coast's actual 1969 revenues as $1,860,000—six times the reported figure. Faced with this "astronomical" discrepancy, Sohn did other sleuthing, including an examination of East Coast's bank transactions. After making several adjustments, Sohn concluded that Hodas had failed to report nearly $600,000 in revenue in 1969 alone.

The Commission of Investigation took no action against Hodas or anybody else but did turn over the information it had gathered to city, state, and federal tax agencies in hopes of "dislodging the racketeers and other undesirable elements that have infiltrated in this seamy business." The Internal Revenue Service warned Hodas that it would immediately indict him for tax evasion unless he signed a waiver. Under the existing statute of limitations, the IRS had to bring an action no more than five years after the alleged offense had been committed. The waiver that

Hodas signed, on the advice of his lawyer, effectively froze the statute of limitations clock for a year.

The IRS backed off after Hodas signed the waiver, but the Lindsay administration sure didn't. From 1970 to 1973, Hodas was arrested twelve times on misdemeanor charges of promoting obscenity and indicted three times for felonies. All of the charges were dismissed in court except the most serious of them: arson in the second degree, which carried a maximum prison term of twenty years. The arson rap stemmed from a massage parlor price war that broke out on far West 42nd Street shortly after Hodas leased the ground floor of a building he owned at 414 West 42nd Street to a couple of Times Square hustlers he'd become friendly with named Jerome Gomberg and George Kaplan. In late 1971, the duo opened a no-frills massage parlor called the Geisha House, whose initial success excited Hodas's envy. "I couldn't for the life of me believe that these guys were making the money that they were making," recalled Hodas, who was only Gomberg and Kaplan's landlord, not their business partner.

The bonanza ended abruptly after a few months when competing massage parlors opened on either side of the Geisha: the Palace at 410 West 42nd and the French Model Studio at 436. A three-way price war erupted that drove the going rate for a basic fifteen-minute session down from $15 to $7.50. Early one morning in May 1972 the Palace burned to the ground. Several tenants living on the floors above the massage parlor were injured in the blaze, which had been ignited by a crude but powerful bomb made of soap, ball bearings, alcohol, lighter fluid, and adhesive. In July, the French Model Studio was heavily damaged in an equally suspicious fire. The Manhattan District Attorney indicted Hodas, Gomberg, and Kaplan and tried the three men together in late 1973. The trial lasted seven days, ending in convictions for Kaplan and Gomberg, each of whom was sentenced to eight years in prison. Hodas was acquitted.

The not-guilty verdict was a great relief to Hodas. "It was the first night I started living again," he recalled. He took his wife and kids to the Dutch Antilles for a week but returned home in a dark mood. East Coast Cinematics was down to about 75 peep machines, from a peak of 350, and almost every dollar of Hodas's diminished cash flow was going to legal fees. He had beaten the city at every turn in court but was convinced that his legal victories would serve only to inflame the authorities' desire to nail him for something. Paula, his wife, no longer even got out of bed most days. His kids were being taunted and bullied in school. "Would I do it over again?" Hodas said in 1974. "No way. A man would have to be sick."

When the IRS proffered the usual waiver in 1975, Hodas refused to sign it, for no good reason. "I just decided that's enough, I'm not signing the waiver anymore," he recalled. Hodas and Herb Levin were promptly indicted in federal court in Manhattan on charges of tax evasion. The case against them was narrowly drawn, covering only 1968, East Coast's first year of operation. The company had reported net income of about $4,500 on revenues of $86,000 in 1968 and paid just $172 in income taxes. But prosecutors alleged that the company actually had earned $140,000 on revenues of $360,000 and thus had underpaid its taxes by $65,000. Prosecutors charged Hodas and Levin with conspiring to defraud the IRS by keeping two sets of books: a fake set that was provided to East Coast's outside auditors and a second, secret set containing the real numbers.

After four days of testimony, the jury exonerated Levin but found Hodas guilty. Hodas "seemed somber but not surprised," according to the *Times*. Judge Charles M. Metzner fined Hodas $130,000 and sentenced him to a year in jail. Before Hodas was packed off to Eglin Air Force Base prison camp in Florida he sent Metzner a long handwritten letter that was more an existential lament than a plea for mercy. "Your Honor," he wrote, "I have no complaint with your one year sentence. For what prejudice I have seen in my life I honestly expected more because of my reputation. But how much suffering should one person endure? And just how much more is in store for us?"

Other than Hodas, very few of the kingpins of Times Square's sex trade ever went to jail, at least not for more than a night or two. The city—under Lindsay and his successor, Abe Beame—tried to criminalize activities that, in the considered opinion of judges and juries—especially federal ones—were not illegal and should not be made illegal. And even with the financial damage done by police harassment and forced closures, not to mention lawyer's bills, supply and demand remained profitably aligned in the Midtown sex trade. In short, the powers that be again had demonstrated the futility of using the blunt instrument of law enforcement as a tool of urban renewal. "We were the Band-Aid applied to a financial-political failure," contended Chief Schwartz, who succeeded Charlie Peterson as commander of Midtown North.

As part of the city's desperate attempts to stave off municipal bankruptcy, the NYPD fired three thousand officers in July 1975, paring its specialty antivice units to the bone. "We have . . . very little street enforcement of prostitution, massage parlors and the porn stores," admitted a top police official. The NYPD continued its round-the-clock foot patrols of 42nd Street, but with the limited objective of keeping all hell from breaking loose. "We did not want a riot breaking out there over a prostitution arrest," Commander Schwartz recalled.

The sex trade's offenses against conventional morality fast became a sideshow to crime and mayhem on the streets. In 1975, more rapes and robberies were reported within Midtown South than any other precinct in the city, by a margin of two to one. Times Square's prostitution hotels and massage parlors were particularly dangerous. During a single month, the police counted two murders, three shootings, five stabbings, six drug overdoses, and fourteen robberies at a single hooker hotel—the infamous "123," located in the heart of Durst country at 123 West 44th Street. Forty-second Street—better known now as the "Deuce" or "Forty Deuce" to its denizens—had become an open-air black market. Sidewalk merchants of dubious provenance hawked illicit wares of all sorts, from stolen typewriters and televisions to handguns and underage sex. But drugs were the staple of the Deuce's economy. Every narcotic imaginable was available, including heroin, but the heaviest traffic was in marijuana, mainly "loose joints" going for a dollar apiece. "I stood on that corner last year [42nd and Seventh Avenue] and sold 240 joints in one day," one dealer boasted to a researcher. "Most of these dudes sell 100 joints a day easy. I got a bunch of regular people who be coming to me every day. Even when it rains I make money—sometimes more money because people be buying a whole bunch of joints at one time before they go to the movie. I never make less than $50 a day."

The intersection of 42nd and Eighth Avenue was particularly rife with miscreants and vagrants of all sorts—both aboveground *and* below, in the IND subway and adjoining arcade, where the Time Square Boys, the Sabbath Skulls, and other youth gangs liked to hang out. "These were big heavy gangs that used to stab and rob each other and they'd stab and rob the public," recalled Joe McGarry, a transit cop who was just two years out of the academy when he began patrolling "the four two and eight" in 1974. In his twelve years on the 42nd Street beat, Officer Mc-Garry would sustain multiple injuries. He was pushed into a moving train and suffered a skull fracture in one incident. He also would have taken an ice pick in the back if not for "Cadillac," a huge wino who lived in the bowels of the Eighth Avenue station. "One day I was down in the arcade in an altercation with a couple of Savage Skulls and a young man tried to ice-pick me from behind. I didn't see him, but Cadillac just happened to be walking by," McGarry recalled. "He gave the guy one punch and knocked him through a window. After that, I made sure that Cadillac did very well. And occasionally drank very well, too."

The same hustlers, pickpockets, and thugs who crowded the subway station and the sidewalks also worked the Port Authority Bus Terminal. The Port Authority did maintain its own sizable police force, augmented by Military Police patrols and a special antitruancy squad that the board of education stationed in the terminal. With the FBI, and assorted other federal agents often lending a hand, the bus station was "perhaps the most heavily policed square block in the United States," according to Port Authority chairman Alan Sagner. But that did not stop packs of mug-gers from brazenly roaming the place. "Every day I'd see some business-man on his way home, passing through the terminal, and he'd get 'wolf-packed,' attacked by a group of young toughs like hyenas in a jun-gle," recalled John F. Ryan, a Port Authority police lieutenant who spent two decades working the terminal. "By the time we could get to him they'd have ripped off his pants so that along with being robbed he'd have to suffer the humiliation of standing in the middle of the terminal in his underwear."

The street life of the Deuce might have seemed chaotic but in fact was highly organized. In 1978, a twenty-person research team headed by City University of New York sociologist William Kornblum spent four months on the street at all hours of the day and night. Kornblum's report, "West 42nd Street: The Bright Light Zone," included detailed maps showing the day and nighttime routes or "strolls" staked out by the most prevalent types of 42nd Street habitués: prostitutes, drug peddlers, and alcoholics. "The strolls cover regularly traveled routes which usually be-come longer and more heavily traveled at night," the report observed. While female prostitutes tended to be flamboyant and obvious, the sub-tler modus operandi of the male hustler "permits the activity to be lost in the great bustle of activity taking place on 42nd Street." Like the homosexual prostitutes, the three-card monte men, the chess hustlers, and the merchandise peddlers generally were found in one place but worked "only when conditions are propitious"—that is, when the cops were nowhere in sight, "Bright Light" observed. "Stepped-up police work, like the weather, is viewed as another obstacle to overcome with cunning and luck."

All the various types of street hustlers competed for the same customers and also would "run games" on one another, Professor Kornblum observed. The following excerpt from a CUNY researcher's notes convey the texture of street life on the Deuce in the 1970s, with its overlapping hustles and afflictions:

> Weather was terrible; raining. A small crowd was milling about Senor Taco's. Several "regulars" were on the street taking refuge under the marquees. Took up position. A slender Puerto Rican man asked me if I had any Valium. Saw G. today. He seemed to be simultaneously under the influence of alcohol and drugs. He asked me if I wanted to "get down on a half bottle of wine." I gave him fifty cents and said I had to run. . . .
>
> Finally hit the players' bar. B———, the owner, called me a "stranger" and asked me where I'd been. Told him I'd had no money and he laughed. I watched four prostitutes (three white and one Black Puerto Rican) come in and sit far away from several "player types" (Black) who were trying to crack on them. It's interesting that white and Black prostitutes come here unaccompanied but never to the Playpen. The white prostitutes, whom I've seen on several occasions, spend a lot of money which leads me to surmise that they are "independents" in charge of their own bread. In contrast to the ones at the Playpen these women are younger, "fresher" looking, seemingly non-addicts, and often white, whereas the opposite is true for the Playpen—although the same players frequent both places. White prostitutes automatically consider any black male to be a pimp.
>
> While I was there I saw a Black dude trying to peddle a minicomputer and a poorly dressed Puerto Rican trying to peddle some joints. A well-dressed Puerto Rican asked me where he could find a lady to do a live act with him onstage. He had a "connection" and they could make good money. I put "ice into my game" and said I didn't know. He asked me if a girl could make $835 a week on the street—his rationalization for a girl doing a live show. I laughed and said it would take ten of these hookers to make that kind of money on the stroll.

The maelstrom of mid-1970s 42nd Street spawned one of the most celebrated vigilantes in the history of American film: Travis Bickle, the cabbie protagonist of Martin Scorsese's searing *Taxi Driver*. A former marine in his midtwenties who has drifted into the big city from the Midwest, Travis is a misfit desperate to forge human connection but clueless about how to do it. "I go all over," Bickle, played by Robert De Niro, confides to his diary. "I take people to the Bronx, Brooklyn. I take people to Harlem. I don't care." But when the taxi driver is alone in his cab at night, he obsessively cruises Times Square's main thoroughfares—42nd Street, Broadway, Eighth Avenue. Studying the sidewalk orgy in mute fascination, Bickle occasionally stops to make a note in his journal, simultaneously drawn to and repulsed by what he sees through the windows of his cab. In his screenplay, Paul Schrader described Travis as having "the smell of sex about him: Sick sex, repressed sex, lonely sex, but sex nonetheless."

Few films have meshed theme and location as powerfully as did *Taxi Driver*, the ultimate urban nightmare movie. Scorsese's timing was exquisite. He shot his film on location over a period of forty days and forty nights in the summer of 1975, an unbearably hot season that marked the steepest angle of New York's descent into financial crisis. *Taxi Driver* is no documentary, but Scorsese made his fever dream of a film all the more evocative by grounding it in recognizable places. The taxi garage where Travis punches a clock is just down 57th Street from the Swedish American line pier on the Hudson. On his breaks, he hangs out with other cabbies at the Belmore Cafeteria, a legendary all-night spot in the Murray Hill neighborhood at 28th Street on Park Avenue South. But the axis of Bickle's automotive orbit—and the touchstone of *Taxi Driver*'s visual style—is 42nd Street. The first time we see him behind the wheel of his cab he is cruising the Deuce's Seventh Avenue block, creeping past the Empire Theater, Hy Cohen's bookstore, and the Fascination arcade. "All the animals come out at night—whores, skunk pussies, buggers, queers, fairies, dopers, junkies. Sick. Venal," Travis writes in his diary. "Someday a *real* rain will come and wash all the scum off the streets."

Bob Moss and Fred Papert:
Urban Moonwalkers

The renaissance of 42nd Street was the product of a complex layering of action and reaction, of cause and effect, heaped up over decades. But if there was a turning point—the beginning of the beginning of the new 42nd Street—it was the cold day in December 1974 that Robert Moss called on Irving Maidman in his office in the Crossroads Building and leased the moldering two-story pile of lumber and concrete that was 422 West 42nd Street. "When I go to 42nd Street now, past the multiplexes and the gorgeously restored theaters, I remember Bob Moss," the playwright Wendy Wasserstein recalled in 2000. "He was Neil Armstrong planting his not-for-profit flag on the moon."

There was, to be sure, nothing Armstrongesque about Moss's landing on 42nd Street. The first time that he set foot on its 400 block he was so scared that he walked down its centerline in traffic rather than risk human contact on the sidewalk. Moss, the forty-two-year-old founder of an exceptionally prolific Off Off Broadway theater company called Playwrights Horizons, would come to believe in 42nd Street's potential for cultural rebirth far more passionately than Maidman ever had. But at the start, his vision of its future extended no further than the six-month term of his initial lease of 422. "I had no intention of staying there a minute longer than I had to," Moss recalled. Moss was not a politician looking to score with crime-fearing voters, nor a police captain bucking for a promotion, nor an urban planner looking to leave his imprint on the city. Unlike Maidman, he wasn't even looking to make a buck. This not-for-profit impresario was compelled to breathe life back into Maidman's theater by a desperately simple desire: he needed a place to put on a show, and he needed it fast.

Over the next twenty-seven years Playwrights Horizons would put on dozens of shows on 42nd Street, including such staples of the contemporary American theater as Albert Innaurato's *Gemini,* Alfred Uhry's *Driving Miss Daisy,* Christopher Durang's *Sister Mary Ignatius Explains It All for You,* and Wasserstein's *The Heidi Chronicles.* Playwrights Horizons' success was noteworthy in its own right, but what elevated Moss's achievement into the realm of the extraordinary was his use of his troupe to seed a whole new community of Off Off Broadway playhouses known as Theater Row. Its improbable birth on one of the city's most debauched blocks inspired hope all along the Deuce. "They should rename 42nd Street 'Bob Moss Avenue,'" said Marshall Mason, the longtime creative director of Circle Repertory Theater. "It all started with him."

Moss was born in 1934 in Newark, right across the Hudson River from the bright lights of Broadway. His father was a union organizer who moonlighted at two jobs to make ends meet. Bob was eleven when his parents took him to his first Broadway play, Cole Porter's *Around the World in Eighty Days,* starring Orson Welles. Fifty-five years later Moss still could recall the exact moment that bound him to the theater for life. "In the second act there is a scene in a railroad car, which is racing across a bridge," Moss said. "There is a blackout. The lights come up on two papier-mâché mountains and then the train blows up. The audience gasped, and I remember thinking, 'This is what I'm going to do'—I mean work in theater, not blow up trains." A few years later Moss won a bit part in a community theater play. When the production shifted in the summer to a theater in Cherry Grove, Moss convinced his parents to let him tag along. The fourteen-year-old swept floors, carried props, and acted, taking the stage name "Robert Harris." (Harris was his middle name.) In the fall, Moss enrolled at Arts High School in Newark. In his four years there, he appeared in every school play. Each summer he returned to the Meadowbrook. By the time Moss graduated from high school in 1952, he had acted in sixty plays.

Moss enrolled at Queens College, where he excelled only as a mem-

ber of the campus theater group, and soon shifted from acting to directing. "The second I did it, the second I stood in front of a group of actors,
I thought, 'This is the place for me,'" recalled Moss, who dropped out in
his junior year and poured every dollar he could save or borrow into
putting on plays in rented rooms throughout Manhattan. He got a job as
shop manager of a summer stock company in Nantucket, Massachu-
setts, which led to a stage-managing job at an Off Broadway house in
Greenwich Village. Surrendering to his accidental calling, Moss worked
his way to Broadway. In 1963, he became production stage manager for
the Phoenix Theater, home to one of the great repertory companies of
the day, the Association of Producing Artists. With the APA, Moss practiced stage managing as a form of voluntary servitude. He not only
fetched coffee for Helen Hayes and other actors but also literally insisted on stirring in the sugar himself. "It sounds hokey, but I never
thought when I was stage managing that these were jobs," Moss said. "I
thought I was helping these actors do their work. It was a gift I gave the
actors."

This could be construed as arrogance of a sort, but if Moss was slow
to grasp his entrepreneurial destiny, it was because he lacked the imperial ego of an Oscar Hammerstein or a Flo Ziegfeld—volatile men compelled to impose an idiosyncratic personal vision on all they touched.
During his first two decades in the theater, Moss gladly adapted himself
to circumstances fixed by others as long as he felt he was serving the
higher calling of putting on a good show. Moss was so friendly, so enthusiastic, so utterly enthralled with the theater that people tended not to
take him seriously at first. His appearance only reinforced the notion that
he was thirty-two going on eighteen. He was short—a shade under five
feet six—and slight, with thick black bangs and an elfin grin. With Moss,
what you saw was not entirely what you got; he kept his private life private, for one thing. But if Moss's relentless avidity, his unshakable posi-
tivism, was an act, it had become so deeply engrained by the mid-1970s
as to amount to an aspect of character. "All of Bob's friends are more pes-
simistic than Bob," said Kenneth Pressman, a playwright and close
friend of Moss's. "I'm not saying that he never felt despair, but I never
saw it."

Moss founded Playwrights Horizons in 1971, sharing space in the
YWCA branch at 51st Street and Eighth Avenue with the Clark Center
for the Performing Arts, a not-for-profit dance company. Right from the

start, Playwrights was prolific beyond all of its predecessors and its peers. Yet Moss also said "No" more than any other producer. He had to, for he was deluged with manuscripts; the 30 works that PH staged in 1974 were winnowed from 800 submissions. To support himself and his troupe, Moss staged fashion shows and collected intermittent unemployment checks. Before every performance, he got up and asked the audience to fill a battered gray plastic bag with cash in an appeal that mixed communal idealism with comedy. "It was very corny, very wonderfully Bob," recalled Barry Keating, a director who also acted at the Clark Center. "You'd sort of roll your eyes, but that's what kept it all going."

In mid-1974, Moss finally began to put his troupe on firmer footing, winning commitments from the New York Council on the Arts and the Edward J. Noble Foundation to provide a total of $32,960 in grants for the following year. But then the YWCA suffered a sharp financial reversal that forced it to close six of its branches, 51st Street included, in August 1974. Moss, who thought he had secured a professional home for life, was devastated. He felt as if he had scaled a mountain peak only to find himself hanging by his fingernails over a chasm.

Moss bicycled all over the city in search of new quarters, even crossing the bridges into Brooklyn. He could not afford a telephone but maintained contact with playwrights and actors by keeping regular office hours of a sort in the lobby of the Plaza Hotel. A number of experimental theater companies had taken refuge in churches, an arrangement that Moss found appealing. But none of the churches Moss approached wanted to risk being overshadowed by a resident theater, and commercial landlords wanted no part of a not-for-profit tenant. In early December, he got a call from Ellen Rudolph, his contact at the New York Council. For the fourth time in as many months, he had to admit that he was still looking for space. "Then we're going to have to give the money to someone else and put you on the rolls for the following year," Rudolph said.

Moss felt an adrenaline rush of panic. "Can you wait five minutes?" he said.

"Don't do anything foolish, Bob," Rudolph cautioned.

Moss left his apartment on Christopher Street in Greenwich Village and headed uptown with his friend Ken Pressman to take a look at a locale he had been avoiding—the 400 block of 42nd Street. Moss had not set foot on the Deuce since attending a show at the Maidman Playhouse in 1964, but he knew it by reputation to be "wildly dangerous."

Maidman had won a series of court battles to evict deadbeat porn tenants from the tenements that he owned at 420, 422, 424, and 440 West 42nd Street, and then made his erstwhile Off Broadway playhouses available to "legit theater groups for dramatic and/or musical comedy presentations." Prospective tenants were not exactly beating down his door, so Maidman decided to publicize the availability of his properties by inviting the *Times*' Ralph Blumenthal to join him on a walking tour in late 1972. But when the landlord and the reporter came to 424, they discovered that the male strip joint that Maidman thought he'd evicted was still very much in business. Maidman walked up to the ticket window and demanded to see the manager of the Tom Kat Club. The cashier told him to talk to the man down the block at 416. "I've spent so much money on the courts here, and they laugh at you," the landlord snarled. "It's sickening." Luckily for Maidman, the *Times* failed to point out that the man at 416 was Maidman's own employee, Moishe Baruch, who had leased the building and put in the block's biggest X-rated attraction, a seedy strip joint called the 42nd Street Playhouse.

By the time desperation drove Moss to inspect the 400 block two years later, it looked like Berlin circa 1946. The sidewalks were strewn with rubble, and many of its buildings were vacant. Clustered together near the Dyer Avenue cut were four sex venues: the Geisha House had been reincarnated as a massage parlor called the Studio at 414; the tassels were still twirling in Baruch's 42nd Street Playhouse at 416–18; a new massage parlor with a magnificently silly name, the International Body Rub Institute, occupied 420; and the Tom Cat was still embarrassing Maidman at 424. These businesses formed a phalanx of sleaze broken only by 422, which was vacant. The 400 block was a commercial wasteland, and yet its sidewalks teemed with activity, just like the theater block to the east. Winos, derelicts, and even the occasional Gypsy family coexisted here with prostitutes, drug dealers, and their customers.

From the middle of the street, Moss spied a FOR RENT sign on 422. He was appalled by his first look inside the building, which basically was a garbage dump enclosed by walls. But beneath the mounds of refuse Moss could make out the ghostly outlines of the 150-seat Midway Theater. Maidman sweetened the deal by packaging 422 with an office floor at 440 West 42nd Street for a total rent of $1,400 a month. Pressman was incredulous. "My view was that 42nd Street was just not a place where an audience would come to see a play," he said. Moss feared that his friend was right. But there was a chance he was wrong, and it was the only chance Playwrights Horizons had.

Moss telephoned everyone he knew to ask for help in transforming his trash bin of a building into a functioning theater. About noon on New Year's Day, 1975, some twenty volunteers—including several members of PH's board—followed Moss into the breach. The stench was like a punch in the gut. Gene Nye, a cofounder of the Lion Theater, a sister company to PH, wrote a self-published novel in which he described the awfulness of this moment. Woody, the protagonist of *Behind the Port Authority*, pulls his scarf over his face as "the sickening stench of urine, saliva, semen, vomit, and feces joined forces for a direct assault on his olfactory nerves. . . . The come-stained, soggy carpets squished under his feet." Nye neglected to mention the forest of mushrooms that had sprouted in what remained of the Midway's aisles. There was nothing like a few hours of swabbing filth to take the fun out of Moss's 42nd Street adventure. Every other day he had to work the telephone to find replacements for workers suddenly summoned to out-of-town auditions and family emergencies.

As soon as the cleanup began, Moss set an intentionally unrealistic date—January 30, 1975—for the theater's opening. None of Playwrights Horizons' established authors had a new work ready to go, so Moss called Dennis Hackin, a playwright recently arrived in New York from Arizona, explaining that what he had in mind was not a full-scale production but a six-day workshop with a single performance daily. Hackin accepted. He had heard good things about Moss and Playwrights Horizons. He'd never set eyes on 42nd Street, but how bad could it be? Hackin had not been in town long, but he already had learned a hard lesson: bona fide theaters were in far shorter supply in Manhattan than unproduced plays by unknowns from the hinterlands.

Hackin had just finished writing a dark, absurdist comedy entitled *Carcass Chrome*. He assembled a cast and crew, drawing mainly from the ranks of the Tucson theater buddies who had joined him in New York. The Arizonans not only supplied their own costumes but also had to clear a rehearsal space within the delapidated confines of 422. "It was like the aftermath of a bombing raid," Hackin recalled. "You were pushing aside a lot of timber." Getting to the theater was no less an adventure. "I can't say that I was afraid of 42nd Street after fighting in Vietnam, but I did carry my knife in my pocket at all times," the playwright said. "Every day you'd get propositioned on the street, or get offered drugs, or see someone getting head in an alley."

The dangers of the street paled next to those inside 422. Moss decided that he could make a better theater by reducing the seat capacity to 70, from 150, and by ripping out the first-floor ceiling and turning two floors into one. He didn't bother seeking Maidman's permission to remodel—"It was utterly audacious of me, but I knew that the building would probably never have another tenant after we left"—but did ask an architect friend to come by and take a look before he and his amateur demolition crew started hacking away at the floorboards. The architect was right: the building did not collapse. But rehearsals of *Carcass Chrome* were interrupted one afternoon by a thunderous noise and a choking cloud of dust just the same. In trying to dress up the remaining ceiling by creating an exposed-beam look, Moss and crew had brought it crashing down on their heads. They crafted a new ceiling from Sheetrock, only to have it fall again. No one was seriously injured, but these and other screwups inflated the remodeling budget from the $500 that Moss had hoped to spend to the $5,000 the project actually cost. Of course, a professional job would have been far beyond Playwright Horizons' means.

On January 30, *Carcass Chrome* opened in a partially remodeled space. Shovels and other equipment ringed the performance area. Worse, Moss had not been able to fire up the heater. "There are some funny parts in the play, but it was hard to draw laughs because the audience was freezing," recalled actor Peter Alzado. "I remember looking out and seeing everyone sitting there with their arms folded, shivering." Alzado, who played the part of a boy who had been shut away in a closet for ten years, turned the setting to his advantage by going down into the basement and rolling in the thick layer of dust that covered the floor. When he made his entrance, billowing dust, he looked the part of someone who had been locked away for a decade. *Macbeth* it was not, though a rat did dart portentously across the stage during one performance.

Carcass Chrome was a trial run; Playwrights Horizons' new theater officially opened two weeks later with *Last Week in Bogotá* by Robert Cessna, another young playwright new to Moss. By the time that the curtain rose on *Bogotá*, the heat was on at last and 422 had been scrubbed from top to bottom. Moss pulled out all the promotional stops to ensure a full house, making the theater's debut the occasion of a PH fund-raiser to pay off that $5,000 remodeling bill. PH's board members all attended, as did many officers of the YWCA, invited as special guests. These were proper ladies of a certain age, in hats and gloves. Moss's precurtain speech was even more high-spirited than usual. The evening was off to a fine start. But then the play began.

The set consisted of an open living room, a kitchen, and a stairway to a closed second-floor room. *Bogotá* began with the sound of a doorbell. A man sitting in the living room shouted, "Can you get that?" A voice from upstairs replied, "You get it!" And so on. Finally, a man wearing nothing but a pair of gold high heels descended the staircase. "You know I always masturbate at this time of day," he complained. It was an homage of sorts to the theater's 42nd Street location, but the scene unnerved the Y ladies, many of whom were sitting together in a row of folding chairs only loosely fastened together. Playwrights' board member Gene C. Gill, who was sitting directly behind the Y ladies, could feel their row start to tremble as soon as Gold Shoes made his entrance. "One lady got so upset that she broke her chair, and I had this vision of the whole row of them going down like dominoes," recalled Gill, who steadied the broken chair before it could set off a chain reaction. For her part, Gill wasn't offended by the nudity but considered *Last Week in Bogotá* the single worst play she had ever seen.

Although much of his audience did not stick around for *Bogotá*'s closing curtain, Moss left the theater that night utterly elated. Playwrights Horizons not only had survived its ordeal of dislocation but also now had a theater of its own. Despite the X-rated surroundings, he had filled the new house. The next day this cockeyed optimist was standing on the sidewalk outside the theater when an epiphany arrived. "I thought, 'Wait a minute, we're on 42nd Street! This is the middle of the world! This is a good place to be. We're going to stay,'" recalled Moss, who immediately went to Maidman's office and opened negotiations on a five-year lease extension.

Moss was confident that he could maintain the core of his old subscriber group while exploiting the risqué novelty of the 42nd Street location to entice a new element to Playwrights Horizons. But other than an increased emphasis on publicity, Moss did not change his approach one whit on 42nd Street. PH was as prolific as ever, staging sixteen different productions in its first five months. These ranged from *Rhinegold,* a rock-and-roll version of the Wagner opera *Das Rheingold,* to the wistful parlor drama *I Remember the House Where I Was Born.* The future film star

Kathy Bates made her New York debut in a play—*Casserole*—directed by Garland Wright, a young Texan also destined for greatness as the creative director of Minneapolis's Guthrie Theater. When Playwrights took its usual summer hiatus in 1975, Moss turned his new theater over to Wright and his Lion Theater Company. Gene Nye, an actor who had co-founded Lion, recalled that the troupe found inspiration in the enveloping squalor. "We were all very young and gorgeous, and all taking some sort of drug," Nye said. "It was an adventure."

Not everyone found the setting appealing. "I guess I wasn't bright enough to use fear to benefit my acting," said Kathleen Chalfant, a young actress who doubled as Moss's assistant. None of the cast or crew of Playwrights Horizons or Lion Theater were assaulted on the street, though there were a number of close calls. Once, about twenty-five feet from Playwrights theater, Chalfant was menaced by a man who lifted a big chunk of concrete above his head and aimed it at her. She froze. The man promptly lost interest and walked away, still holding the concrete.

Nye had an equally unexpected but benign interaction with another of the squatters who lived in the block's vacant buildings. In a kind of basement cavern next to Tony's, a scruffy old saloon that catered to workers from the Port Authority, lived a middle-aged woman with an extensive wardrobe of fine clothes hanging from subterranean pipes. Although she was always well dressed, her mood swung unpredictably from profanity-spouting fury to the poised graciousness of the woman she might once have been. One Sunday afternoon, she swept into the theater as if it were a Park Avenue salon. "She was this grand lady come to call," Nye recalled. "I got coffee for her and we sat and talked. She kept insisting that she was related to Richard Nixon and was very disappointed in him."

The intersection of Ninth Avenue and 42nd Street was home to one of the city's largest colonies of transvestite prostitutes. In his novel, Nye described them as looking like "Victoria's Secret let out of Pandora's box . . . linebacker legs were squeezed into fishnet stockings with feet crammed into men's size twelve spiked heels." In winter, the "she-hims," or "shims" as they were known, wore loose-fitting coats over hot pants and push-up bras. Most shims carried a weapon or two: shivs, box cutters, blackjacks, razors, even the occasional derringer hidden in a bouffant do. A dozen or more "squeegee boys" of the sort that later would so famously drive Mayor Giuliani to distraction also worked the Ninth Avenue intersection in the mid-1970s. Like the shims, all of the squeegee kids were black. Most were in their teens, though some were as young as nine or ten. If a motorist made a scene, the squeegee boys could get nasty fast. As Nye put it, "They seemed not to have a conscience."

One afternoon, Moss asked the playwright Barry Keating to go over and check out the 42nd Street Playhouse, Playwrights' next-door neighbor. "I think Bob was embarrassed to go in himself," Keating recalled. "I walked in and there were three people in the audience with trench coats on their laps. A fat woman came out onstage. She didn't strip because she was already naked. She walked around for twenty minutes to a record. It was awful beyond description. But I could see that you could make it into a good theater. In fact, Bob started thinking that all the buildings there could be theaters. I know it was Bob's idea because it was crazy."

Moss had first viewed 42nd Street through the narrow lens of self-interest but had quickly awakened to its larger possibilities. "We came here because it was the only theater we could find, and we desperately needed a theater," he wrote in a letter to the editor of the *Times* just six weeks after he'd leased 422. "Now we are excited about the cultural possibilities. We think that our block . . . could be a cultural catalyst for the whole area." By the fall of 1975 the impresario was urging the NYPD to butt out, in so many words. "The way to clean up this area is not to harass the prostitutes, but to open up the theaters," Moss declared. "The rest will follow."

With Moishe Baruch serving as tour guide, Moss inspected all of Maidman's former playhouses and glimpsed in each the remnants of a serviceable theater beneath the ruins. A consultant helped Moss put together a capital improvement plan for all four buildings. He estimated that it would cost at least $106,150 to get all four up to code, with the two most decrepit buildings—420 and 424—accounting for $79,000 of the total. Practicality demanded raising another $32,500 to cover first-year operating costs. The total tab of $138,650 was a king's ransom in the penurious realm of Off Off Broadway.

In late 1975, Moss registered a new not-for-profit corporation with the aim of leasing 416–18, 420, 422, and 424 from Maidman. His plan was to consolidate them into a single performing arts center called the West 42nd Street Theater, and to sublease auditoriums and office space within it to ten not-for-profit theater and dance companies. The new corporation's name, the 42nd Street Gang, was a stroke of promotional genius. It stirred memories of 42nd Street's heyday in quoting from the theatrical equivalent of "The Star-Spangled Banner," George M. Cohan's "Give My Regards to Broadway," an anthem first sung in 1904 in the Liberty Theater on 42nd Street: "Tell all the gang at 42nd Street/That I will soon be there." At the same time, it evoked the shadowy presence of organized crime along the Deuce. In fact, Playwrights Horizons' incredulous lawyer had to file an affidavit asserting that the Gang was not in fact a criminal enterprise before the secretary of state's office in Albany would approve its incorporation. Ira Weitzman, a member of Playwrights Horizons' production staff, cut the words *Mob Boss,* a delightfully inapt spoonerism for *Bob Moss,* out of a newspaper headline and pasted the clipping on Moss's office door one day. Moss had *Mob Boss* stenciled on the back of his Playwrights Horizons jacket, attracting puzzled glances on the subway.

As Moss had hoped, the 42nd Street Gang name was a real door opener on the fund-raising circuit. "Everybody wanted to hear the story of what we were up to on 42nd Street," Moss recalled. "But no one would give me any money after they'd heard it." Despite Moss's persistent fund-raising efforts, the Gang never raised a penny. It wasn't just the improbability of a large-scale theater revival on 42nd Street that put off donors. It was Moss. He had proven he could manage a not-for-profit theater group, but what did he know about real estate development? The capital improvement budgets he'd drawn up were amateur's work and plainly inadequate to the requirements of persuading a bank or foundation to put up money. Moss realized that he was out of his depth when he visited the Rockefeller Brothers Foundation and gave Marilyn Levy, its program officer for the arts, one of his most inspirational the-show-must-go-on speeches. Had he delivered it to an audience from the stage of 422 his plastic bag would have bulged with cash. But Levy just stared and said, "I don't want to be rude, but are you for real?"

Moss realized that he needed an ally, a partner who could wrap a not-for-profit real estate project in an aura of financial credibility. One afternoon in early 1976 he was in his office when the solution to his problem materialized on the sidewalk. Through his office window he saw two men in suits pointing at the building like they owned it—or soon would. Moss dashed downstairs to confront them. He recognized one of the men as Richard Basini from the Mayor's Office of Midtown Planning and Development. The other turned out to be a repentant advertising millionaire named Frederick Papert, who informed Moss that he was going to revive 42nd Street from river to river and begin by razing this very block. Moss was flabbergasted. *Who the hell was Fred Papert?*

Moss invited Papert and Basini up to his office and as calmly as possible outlined his plans for making Playwrights Horizons the nucleus of a community of not-for-profit theaters on the block. Basini had heard Moss's pitch before. In fact, he had brought Papert to meet Moss, hoping that these two self-styled 42nd Street visionaries might find common ground. Soon, Moss and Papert were so deeply engrossed in conversation that Basini departed without bothering to say good-bye. "They got along right away," Basini recalled. "I doubt if they even noticed that I was gone."

Born in New York in 1927, Papert habitually described himself as a child of the Depression, but this generic label did not do justice to the drama of his particular form of deprivation. His father, Emile Papert, was a Lithuanian Jew who settled first in Wisconsin and moved to New York after establishing himself as a manufacturer of raccoon coats. Fred had not yet turned three when his father died of a heart attack. The "Raccoon Coat King" left a large estate, but his son and daughter never saw a penny of it. Fred grew up hearing his mother complain about how Emile's trustees had cheated her out of her inheritance. The widow Papert rebounded to make a good living as a saleswoman of women's apparel at Saks Fifth Avenue, Bonwit Teller, and other carriage trade outlets. Fred and his sister never went hungry, but Emile's vanished fortune hung over their youth like a shimmering fog of foregone possibility. The family lived in a genteel section of the Upper East Side but regularly moved from one apartment to another to exploit the rent concessions and free paint jobs offered by landlords. Fred received a quality education, but at P.S. 6 and the Bronx High School of Science rather than at the more prestigious private academies that he had come to know so well from the outside, longing all the while to be inside.

The patrician veneer that Papert cultivated masked an intense drive to succeed. He wanted to get rich, at least as rich as he would have been had his father's fortune been preserved for his benefit. He earned a degree in journalism at the University of Missouri and returned to New York to go to work for an advertising agency. After pinwheeling through six different agencies in ten years, he finally began to hit his stride when he founded his own firm in 1957. Papert was a first-rate copywriter but a better salesman, and proved it by persuading the rambunctiously talented team of Julian Koenig and George Lois to leave their big-agency home at Doyle Dane Bernbach and cast their lot with him. Known as "the wild men" of Madison Avenue, Koenig, a copywriter, and Lois, an art director, practiced advertising as a form of creative outrage.

Papert did not do much copywriting at Papert, Koenig, Lois Inc., in part because he recognized Koenig's superior talent with the pen. In his autobiography, Lois mockingly described Papert at the time he first met him as "an extremely likable smoothie. . . . He had Park Avenyoo class—sweetly fawncy, with a graceful set to his clothes and a perfectly dog-eared jacket." As PKL's front man, Papert applied his virtuoso patter to the pursuit of new business and the courting of the press. "Fred's selling quality, other than his intelligence, is that he doesn't sell with adjectival exuberance," Koenig recalled. "He sells with diffidence. It's unexpected, and effective. The attitude was, 'If you don't want to take what I'm saying at face value, it's perfectly all right.' He'd leave the impression that he was doing you a favor by offering to take your business."

At times, this approach worked for Papert even when he screwed up. In the climactic stage of his pursuit of National Airlines, Papert flew to Miami to screen a reel of television commercials for Bud Maytag, the company's president. "I'm racking this thing up and having a hard time of it. The film is backward," Papert recalled. "I turn it around and it breaks. I gather it up and throw it in the wastebasket. I said, 'Let's forget the whole thing.' Maytag comes running out to the car as I'm leaving. He says, 'All right, we'll do it.' I said, 'Do what?'"

PKL peaked in 1967, with billings of $40 million, and then imploded. There were many larger ad agencies, but even at its modest size the firm had exceeded its founders' capacity for administration. Papert alone stayed until the end, trying to salvage what he could of the Roman candle that was Papert, Koenig, Lois. "In the end, we pissed everybody off," said Papert, who amassed a fortune of $5 million to $10 million through well-timed sales of PKL stock. Papert emerged from PKL a deeply conflicted man. A parsimonious sort, he took comfort in knowing that he was set for life at fifty but felt guilty about how he had made his pile. Paradoxically, it also irritated him that PKL's achievements were not accorded more respect within the profession even as he came to look upon advertising as an ephemeral, mercenary occupation. Said Papert: "I think the life I made for myself after leaving advertising was a way of redeeming myself from that life of shadow, which was all ether, all nothing, as opposed to substance."

Papert made his debut as a civic activist in 1970, when he took the lead in founding Carnegie Hill Neighbors to fight the construction of a forty-story luxury apartment building on East 89th Street, just south of his home on 90th Street. It was a losing battle, but it moved Papert into the orbit of the Municipal Arts Society, which appointed him to its board in 1973. Founded in 1893, the MAS was an important if erratic force for historic preservation and progressive urban planning in New York. It was an elite private organization, supported by the thin stratum of upper-class society that was both artistic in outlook and activist by temperament. To its critics, the society was little more than a club for Upper East Side "limousine liberals." But in 1975, the Municipal Arts Society boldly stepped to the fore and led a valiant effort to save Grand Central Station from the wrecking ball. Papert played so commanding a role in the Grand Central campaign that he was named president of the society in 1976, virtually by acclamation.

In the Grand Central campaign, Papert made shrewd use of Jacqueline Kennedy Onassis, who had called the Municipal Arts Society out of the blue to volunteer her services. "While she had a good working relationship with many people in the society, she developed a special relationship with Fred," recalled Kent Barwick, the Muncipal Arts Society's director. "She really liked him a lot and trusted his judgment." The Grand Central struggle would drag on until 1978, when the U.S. Supreme Court handed Papert and the MAS an historic victory, upholding the station's landmark status and denying a construction permit to its owner, the Penn Central Railroad.

The Grand Central crusade was a long way from over when Papert began casting about for his next cause and found 42nd Street. Every native New Yorker has a connection to 42nd Street, but Papert's ties were more personal than most. In the 1920s, two of his maternal aunts had appeared in the *Ziegfeld Follies* at the New Amsterdam while his mother and yet another aunt worked as chorus girls in *The Greenwich Village Follies*. Papert's father also had been a show business figure of sorts. Emile

Papert not only sold fashionable raccoon coats by the dozens to theatrical producers but also invested in plays and dated starlets. His marriage was a classic union of a wealthy, middle-aged stage-door Johnny and a pretty young chorine. But unlike Mayor Lindsay's mother, Mrs. Papert made no effort to inculcate a love of the Broadway theater in her children and warned them to stay away from 42nd Street. "My sister remembers my mother telling her not to go anywhere near 42nd or she'd be drugged and abducted and end up in Brazil or some other South American country," Fred recalled. "I had never been there, but I knew the legend of it. Everybody did. It was the fabled 42nd Street."

On April 15, 1975, the Committee to Save Grand Central held a noon concert outside the terminal's south entrance. East 42nd Street was blocked off for two hours to accommodate the throng that turned out to hear Benny Goodman, Henny Youngman, Tony Randall, and a half dozen other performers. When the concert ended at about 2:00 P.M., Papert asked Kennedy Onassis to join him on a westward walk across 42nd Street. "Jackie was game," he recalled. "Jackie was always game." Jackie O attracted plenty of unwanted attention as usual, but she and Papert toured the Deuce without harm. At Eighth Avenue, they hailed a cab and beat a hasty retreat uptown.

To save Grand Central, Papert had dipped into the same bag of tricks he had used to help PKL's clients move their merchandise. He had transcended the profit motive, to be sure, but still there was something self-defeating about using advertising and promotion to redeem himself from his career in advertising and promotion. Aesthetic concerns were a factor on 42nd Street, but the essential issue was not preservation but *reclamation*—in exactly the way that Webster had defined the word: "A restoration, as to productivity, usefulness, or morality." This could not be accomplished by massaging public opinion—or by legal argument, for that matter. In terms of the redemption potential offered self-loathing advertising men, saving Grand Central from architectural impairment paled in comparison to saving 42nd Street from itself. Papert held discussions with many of his fellow MAS members but made no attempt to put the issue on the society's agenda. The Grand Central crusade was the public affairs equivalent of a Cecil B. DeMille epic; the MAS's committee had eighty-eight members. But at the outset of his 42nd Street campaign Papert stood, quite happily, alone. "I think Fred began with huge aspirations," recalled Jane Stanicki, a loan officer at the Bowery Savings Bank, which eventually backed Papert. "He really did want to be the King of 42nd Street."

Confident to a fault of his ability to improvise, headlong in his enthusiasm, Papert began soliciting grants from private foundations before he had a clue as to what he would do with the money. Despite his superior business credentials, Papert did no better with Marilyn Levy than Moss had. Levy later became friends with Papert, but this was their first meeting and it scarcely could have gone worse. Papert was directed to Levy because she had developed something of a specialty at Rockefeller Brothers in real estate development. "It was obvious that he was very committed, but the problem was he had no particular plan, no program," Levy recalled. "We took a very systematic approach to funding requests, a real take-it-apart-and-look-at-it approach. I explained to Fred at some length what I needed to put a proposal before the board."

Papert replied, "But why won't you help me?"

Levy repeated herself at a bit less length.

Papert repeated himself, too. "Why won't you help me?" he demanded.

With fraying patience, Levy again explained to her uncomprehending visitor that the fund needed a concrete proposal. "I went through it four or five times, and each time was at least five minutes," she recalled. "Saying no to people was a big part of my job, but this was more than exasperating. I really did think I'd have to call security to get rid of him. But finally he left and I thought to myself, or perhaps said to one of my colleagues, 'I am never going to voluntarily speak to that man again in my life.'"

Like Moss before him, Papert found that donors were fascinated by the notion of fixing 42nd Street but loath to kick in money toward its improvement. In his first year and a half of soliciting, Papert collected a mere $60,000 in grants. The largest contribution was $25,000 from the J. M. Kaplan Fund, the city's most generous backer of historic preservation. The Kaplan fund was run by Joan Davidson, a strong-willed and feisty heiress who recognized Papert as a kindred spirit. "We didn't have all that much confidence in the [42nd] project, but we had a lot of confidence in him and his ability to pull it off," Davidson recalled. "We loved Fred. Always had. He has big ideas, and I'm not afraid of going along with them."

Papert's enthusiasm for 42nd Street lacked definition until he met Bob Moss. By the time that Papert incorporated the Forty-Second Street Development Corporation on February 1, 1976, he had toned down his ad man's rhetoric and sharpened his focus. "The Corporation would take on four decades of accumulated, renewal-resistant blight, but we knew it could be done only one small step at a time," he recalled. "The idea was to concentrate first on those blocks of West 42nd Street in which there was the greatest chance of success, Ninth to Tenth Avenues." Papert applied to the city for a charter as an urban redevelopment corporation, or URC, which could condemn property and defer payment of real estate taxes. The city did not confer these formidable powers casually. To qualify as a URC, Forty-Second Street Development would have to devise a scheme that would have to win City Council approval.

Although Papert struggled to find donors, he infused clout into his corporation at its founding by forming an alliance with the Port Authority of N.Y. and N.J. "Fred did have some credibility, if not an actual plan, but I'd have to say that the Authority would have welcomed association with anyone who was going to clean up the area," said Gene Gill, who was a manager in Port Authority's community outreach department as well as a Playwrights Horizons board member. "Fred was it. No one else cared." Port Authority was not allowed to donate cash to private groups, but it backed Papert in other ways, assigning four of its employees to work full-time for Forty-Second Street Development. The agency was a famously progressive employer that believed so strongly in encouraging the development of its managers that it even allowed them to work temporarily for other organizations—going on "mobility assignment," it was called. "Port Authority paid all our staff salaries for ten years or so—a couple million dollars—on the reasonable belief that we were doing their dirty work for them," Papert said. In addition, William Ronan, the recently retired chairman of Port Authority, agreed to become the first chairman of the high-powered board of directors that Papert assembled.

Papert was a persuasive man, but Port Authority had a direct stake in the cause of 42nd Street redevelopment as one of the street's largest property owners. In 1970, the agency had decided to expand its now badly overcrowded bus terminal between 40th and 41st Streets by extending it through the adjoining block all the way to 42nd Street. Over the next few years, the authority assembled the site, paying $10 million to buy and demolish a phalanx of decrepit smaller buildings that wrapped around the corner of Eighth Avenue all the way to the McGraw-Hill Building at 330 West 42nd Street. By the time that construction finally began in 1976, sixty million passengers a year were passing through the old terminal, compared with thirty-nine million during its opening year of 1951. Plagued by delays and cost overruns that pushed its cost to $160 million, from $79 million, the new terminal would not be completely finished until 1981.

The Port Authority's expansion filled a void left by McGraw-Hill Book Company, which in 1972 had ended four decades of residence on 42nd Street by relocating its headquarters to a brand-new fifty-story skyscraper on 49th Street and Sixth Avenue. McGraw-Hill had outgrown the Green Building, it was true, but the building—or rather its location—also had become an embarrassment to the publishing giant. As a real estate appraisal done for the company noted, "The building's immediate environment, particularly West 42nd Street and radiating a block or two west and north of the property is one of the most tawdry, degraded neighborhoods in the city. Day and nighttime street crime is rampant here. This area alone contains the greatest concentration of vulgar entertainment establishments in the country."

While Papert was still getting organized, Bob Moss pounced on the chance to acquire the 400 block's most promising theater site, 416–18 West 42nd. Consolidated Edison had cut off the power to the building five years earlier, not long after Maidman had stopped paying the electric bills. Baruch had kept the lights on at the 42nd Street Playhouse and the International Body Rub Institute by illegally patching into the Con Ed lines supplying neighboring buildings. The utility was slow to discover the ruse but took decisive action once it did. One morning in June 1976, a workman climbed down a manhole in the street and cut the wires to 416.

Originally the headquarters of the United States Bank, 416 was twice the size of 422 and as solid as a vault. The bank had been designed to act as the base of a twenty-two-story office tower, but the Crash of 1929 scared the developer away, never to return. The moment Moss learned of Con Ed's cutoff, he was on the phone to Maidman with an offer to buy 416. The property mogul would have been delighted to accept, but it turned out that he did not own the building; he held it under long-term lease and was a couple of years in arrears in his payment to the Frank family, the owner-proprietors of the big butcher shop around the corner, the Washington Beef Company. Lee Frank, the president of the family business, wanted to hold on to 416, but he was willing to formally terminate Maidman's lease if Playwrights Horizons would agreed to rent the building. Frank wanted nearly $3,000 a month, double what Playwrights Horizons paid at 422. It seemed like a bargain to Moss, but his directors again required serious persuading. "I had a huge fight with the board. I told them, 'We must take this building,'" recalled Moss.

As soon as Moss signed the lease he issued a press release inviting reporters to come by the next day to witness "a major event in the rebirth of West 42nd Street": the toppling of the building's garish LIVE BURLESK marquee. Unaware of the ceremony, which was to start at noon, Charlie Tyndall, Playwrights Horizons' technical manager, organized a wrecking crew that went to work on the big sign not long after sunrise. Joan Egan, the company's publicity director, freaked when she arrived at 10 A.M. and found the sign lying on the sidewalk. Tyndall and crew finished reerecting the marquee a few minutes before its demolition was scheduled to begin. Reporters from many newspapers and television stations showed up, as did a smattering of politicians and Broadway celebrities. Before Tyndall attacked the sign a second time, a group of actors got up on a makeshift stage and performed the song "42nd Street," altered for the occasion: "Hear the beat of dancing feet/It's time for change, we're rearranging 42nd Street."

After a Playwrights Horizons banner was hoisted into place on the facade, Moss stepped before the cameras and exuded his trademark optimism. "Pretty soon, we'll have six important theaters on this block. Sparks will be flying," he said. "We'll be a center of Off Off Broadway. We'll have glamour, accomplishment." He glanced at an abandoned lot buried in debris. "Oh, and we'll have fine restaurants here, too. Maybe a little park."

How long will it take, a reporter asked. Five years?

Moss shook his head. "Sooner," he said.

Two years?

Moss smiled and replied, "Sooner."

Turning the Corner in Hell's Kitchen

All seven deadly sins have their Manhattan constituencies, but the quintessential vice of the most densely populated borough might well be apartment envy. Start with the fact of shortage; the supply of quality shelter chronically lags demand, and so landlords put a window in a closet and call it a "studio." Factor in New York City's status as the national capital of rent control and other forms of subsidized living. Manhattan apartment dwellers, like airline passengers, pay wildly divergent prices to temporarily occupy nearly identical spaces. A flight ends in a few hours and the deck of special fare deals is reshuffled. But what if you discover that the guy across the hall or the old lady on the seventh floor pays a fraction of what you are laying out for the identical one-bedroom? Or that so-and-so at the office lucked into a great deal on a loft in Tribeca or a carriage house in the Village or a luxury high-rise on West 42nd Street?

Yes, 42nd Street. While Theater Row was beginning to take shape on the south side of the 400 block, a new apartment complex across the street—Manhattan Plaza—became the object of envy of a scale and intensity rare even for Manhattan. The battle over its 1,688 apartments convulsed all of Hell's Kitchen (or Clinton, as the neighborhood's champions now preferred to call it) and the entire Broadway theater community, pitting neighbor against neighbor, union against union, and Seymour Durst against almost everyone. After a compromise was hammered out at the highest level of city government, Manhattan Plaza emerged as a towering monument to the peculiarity of the borough's housing market: America's first—and undoubtedly the last—federally subsidized apartment complex for actors, dancers, pit musicians, and other performing artists. And by enabling an underemployed stand-up comedian named Kenny Kramer to befriend the aspiring television writer Larry David, Manhattan Plaza inspired *Seinfeld,* the definitive portrait of that segment of the city's population—the affluent, self-involved singles set—in which apartment envy approached mania.

Manhattan Plaza arose on the block that Durst had assembled in Hell's Kitchen in the mid-1960s. Reverting to his traditional modus operandi, Durst had decided against building on the property himself, selling it for $13 million—a good $10 million more than he had paid—to Richard Ravitch, one of New York's most ambitious young housing developers. A third-generation builder, Ravitch headed a family company, HRH Construction, that was one of the city's biggest general contractors. Ravitch had cut his teeth as a developer in the mid-1960s on Waterside Plaza, an East Side apartment complex supported by the city's Mitchell-Lama housing subsidy program for middle-income residents. He envisioned Manhattan Plaza as a West Side equivalent to Waterside: a multitower, heavily subsidized housing complex designed to lure relatively prosperous tenants to a dubious neighborhood.

Long before his tortuous negotiations with Durst were completed, Ravitch hired Ballard Todd Associates to design a block-square apartment complex. The Todd firm packed 1,688 apartments into two huge towers—one forty-five and the other forty-six stories tall—that spanned the site like giant bookends. Unlike Waterside Plaza, Manhattan Plaza was not designed with families in mind. Who would want to raise kids on 42nd Street? For that matter, HRH was convinced that it would take something more than below-market rents to attract upwardly mobile office workers to Manhattan Plaza. Ravitch had Ballard Todd set the towers on a low-rise podium that was to contain posh shops and a first-rate health and fitness club, including tennis courts and a regulation Olympic swimming pool complete with a hundred-meter diving tower.

The Mayor's Office of Midtown Planning and Development had nothing but praise for Ravitch's bold 42nd Street scheme. By the early 1970s, years of profligate spending on social services had pushed New York City to the brink of financial collapse. Even so, Mayor Lindsay pushed for and won Board of Estimate approval of a generous $90 million Mitchell-Lama loan to HRH, which estimated the project's total cost at $95 million. In its eagerness to get Manhattan Plaza under way, the city invoked its right of eminent domain to buy out a couple of recalcitrant lot holders even before Ravitch had closed on his purchase of the Durst properties in late 1973. Launched in haste and ill conceived in many ways, Manhattan Plaza was the single largest real estate gamble in a city facing an increasingly dire fiscal outlook.

Forty-second Street's twin towers had nearly been completed when construction was halted in the spring of 1975. The problem wasn't merely that HRH had run out of cash, but also that the economic foundation of Ravitch's project had turned to mush. Many observers feared that Manhattan Plaza's financial structure could never be set right, that it was a "red brick elephant," as the *Times* put it. Manhattan Plaza is "one of the more frighteningly spectacular failures of the city's current economic paroxysm," the newspaper's Francis X. Clines wrote in early 1977, nearly two years after work had stopped. "From a distance, through the Times Square foreground of mongrel leisure and merchandized desire, the sight of two new forty-five-story apartment towers standing empty can seem as eerie as Stonehenge. What are they doing there? Did they break loose from the East Side during some midnight convulsion of the financial crisis?"

HRH Construction originally had hoped to lure yuppies to West 42nd Street with rents of $55 a room or about $400 for a one-bedroom apartment. This was triple the going rate in Hell's Kitchen but well under what a comparable unit cost in a more fashionable section of town. However, a pair of overlapping catastrophes wreaked havoc on HRH's projections. The first was the OPEC-induced explosion in energy prices, which sent electricity tolls soaring. The other was New York City's financial crisis. Recklessly, the city had taken on huge loan commitments but had not actually raised most of the money it was obligated to provide. By 1975, bond investors no longer considered New York creditworthy, forcing the city to pay usurious rates of interest to obtain the relatively small sums it could borrow. For Manhattan Plaza, this meant a mortgage rate of 8.5 percent to 9 percent instead of the 5.5 percent to 6 percent that HRH had planned on. To cover the added costs, Ravitch had to boost rents to $150 a room, rendering the complex all but unmarketable to the emerging yuppie hordes.

The die was cast in the sense that the city was obligated to loan Ravitch the full $90 million and that the developer was responsible for at least $8 million a year in interest payments. The city could have waited for HRH to default on its mortgage and then seized Manhattan Plaza and resold it to the highest bidder. But since the complex was worth no more than $45 million, the city then would have taken a $45 million hit that it could ill afford. Or the Beame administration could have carried HRH, letting it make partial payments in the hope that rents eventually would rise to the break-even point. This scenario also would have forced the city to take a loss, which would be small initially but could vastly exceed $45 million in the long run. In mid-1975, Mayor Beame and his minions came up with a third option that had the virtue of sticking Uncle Sam with the bill for Manhattan Plaza. That is, the U.S. Department of Housing and Urban Development was persuaded to provide $11.5 million a year in so-called Section 8 rent subsidies for forty years, more than enough to cover the required mortgage payments. The catch was that Section 8 was a program for the poor, not the middle-class. The unhappy history of subsidized housing for the urban poor suggested that Manhattan Plaza was fated to become a slum that would do nothing to lift 42nd Street out of the gutter and might even make it worse, if such a thing were possible.

The moment that the Beame administration floated the Section 8 idea, "such a hullabaloo broke loose as you cannot possibly imagine," recalled Roger Starr, a senior city housing official who happened to be a friend of Ravitch's. Starr had expected an outcry from the Clinton neighborhood groups, from Broadway theater owners, and from Durst, who still owned a lot of property on adjoining blocks. What surprised him was that Ravitch also protested—loudly. "My number one hullabaloo was raised by Dick Ravitch and particularly by his limited partners," Starr said. (Ravitch had sold much of his equity to a group of tax-shelter investors that included the cosmetics mogul Estée Lauder.) Lawyers representing the owners argued that Section 8 would erode the value of their investment by "demeaning" Manhattan Plaza's value and, furthermore, would breach the city's contract with HRH. "We had a very bitter argument," Starr recalled. "I said, 'I will foreclose your mortgage if you don't [go along with Section 8].'"

To the rescue came Daniel Rose. Like Ravitch, Rose was a third-generation scion of a leading Manhattan real estate dynasty. He also was a bona fide lover of the arts, steeped in classical learning and popular culture alike. HRH had hired Rose Associates to act as the managing agent for Manhattan Plaza, but it was starting to look to Rose like there would be nothing for his family firm to manage. It occurred to him that the way forward was to identify a category of low-income tenant that would qualify for Section 8 subsidy yet "would not be perceived as a group of the dysfunctional poor." In other words, Rose said, "It seemed to me that what you required here were middle-class psyches without money." He considered medical students, divinity students, and the elderly before deciding that young actors and other up-and-coming performing artists best fit the bill, given Manhattan Plaza's proximity to the theater district. But were there enough deserving theater folk in the city to fill so large a complex? And how many of them would hazard living on 42nd Street?

HRH liked Rose's idea, as did Starr and his colleagues at City Hall. But to Rose's surprise, none of the eight principal labor unions that represented Broadway performers would even talk to him at first. "When they heard the story, they didn't believe it," he recalled. "There was such a feeling of hostility, suspicion, and lack of credibility." Rose persisted, and in time the unions not only overcame their mistrust of developers bearing rent-subsidized gifts but eventually lurched to the opposite extreme, maneuvering to maximize their potential share of Manhattan Plaza apartments. Support for the Rose solution grew markedly after the Settlement Housing Fund, an influential independent agency, documented the existence of 65,000 performing artists who qualified for Section 8 assistance—enough to fill Manhattan Plaza many times over.

However, neighborhood groups in Clinton did not like the idea of actors getting preference over local residents who couldn't sing, dance, or soliloquize. And politicians representing the Bronx and Brooklyn did not see why such a large portion of the Section 8 funding available to the city should go to Manhattan. But the biggest obstacle to the rebooting of Manhattan Plaza as performing artists' housing was Seymour Durst, who castigated the notion as a "forty-year, $400-million mistake." The essence of Durst's complaint was that a Section 8 project would be a drag on the surrounding area by definition—that a welfare tenant was a welfare tenant, no matter how middle-class his psyche might be. Durst convinced his fellow board members at the Broadway Association to sue HRH and the city to block the project. Ravitch was incensed at Durst and told him so in an angry phone call.

As the battle raged, HRH hired a soft-spoken, gracious southerner named Richard Rodney Kirk as Manhattan Plaza's first managing director. Kirk had no previous experience in real estate management, but he brought to his job a moral authority lacking in most landlords. Kirk was an Episcopal priest who had spent a decade as Director of Ministry with the Arts at the Cathedral of St. John the Divine.

During a job interview with Clara Fox, the Settlement Housing Fund's executive, Reverend Kirk asked a shrewd and cheeky question of his own. "Miss Fox," he said, "can you tell me, am I being used?"

"Well, yes, dear," Fox replied. "All of us are being used."

"Should I wear my collar?" Kirk said.

"Yes, when you're being used for that reason you should wear your collar."

Kirk helped negotiate a compromise that reserved 70 percent of Manhattan Plaza's apartments for performing artists and 30 percent for Clinton residents, with half of this latter quota reserved for the elderly. The project had to renegotiate the gauntlet of public review, and did not finally win Board of Estimate approval until March 1977. Along the way, Gerald Schoenfeld, president of the Shubert Organization, Broadway's largest theater owner, switched from con to pro. Schoenfeld later encouraged the misperception that he had favored the housing-for-artists plan from the outset—a deception also attempted by various union leaders. "You have all sorts of people taking credit for it who wouldn't even take the trouble to listen to it or who opposed or even fought it down to the last day. . . . Voltaire would have understood," complained Rose, referring to Voltaire's famous dictum: "History is lies agreed upon."

The task of sifting through 5,000 applications to fill 1,688 apartments fell to Kirk, who was besieged by personal calls from public officials. The favor game was standard procedure in a Manhattan "rent-up," but Kirk was determined to allocate the apartments only to qualified tenants in order of application received. So many well-to-do actors wanted in on this experiment in communal living—Estelle Parsons, Angela Lansbury, and Jack Warden among them—that a decision was made to rent 10 percent of the apartments to unsubsidized tenants. But to qualify for Section 8 assistance, you could not make more than $18,000 a year. To enter under the performing artists' quota, you had to prove that you had "actively pursued" a career in the performing arts over the last three years, or that more than half your earnings came from the entertainment business, or that you belonged to a "professional performing arts organization." You didn't actually have to be a performer; stagehands, ushers, electricians, broadcast engineers, and sound effects technicians all were deemed Plaza-worthy. College students and models, legitimate or otherwise, were not. Manhattan Plaza received its first tenants in June 1977 and was fully occupied by the end of the year, with a waiting list of 1,000 prescreened applicants.

Each Section 8 tenant paid rent equal to 25 percent of his or her projected income for the coming year. If you earned less than expected, you got a refund. But it was much more common for income to exceed projections, in which case you got a retroactive rent bill and two years to pay it. In 1978, the federal government paid $7 million in subsidies to Manhattan Plaza residents, well under the $11.5 million Section 8 allowance. During the complex's first decade, the annual subsidy never topped $8.5 million. Even so, Roger Starr admitted in 1986 that if he had to do it over again, he probably would not have put Manhattan Plaza into Section 8. "It was so damned expensive that nobody, at least in the foreseeable future, is going to be in a position to build a project like that with federal subsidies that are as deep," Starr correctly predicted. "If you add up all the subsidies that [went] into the project, they are monstrous."

But unlike most bounteously subsidized New York City housing projects, Manhattan Plaza was, by all accounts, a place capable of inspiring the greenest apartment envy—"like a country club in the middle of Manhattan," as Kenny Kramer put it. The complex was not only luxuriously endowed with recreational facilities but also well managed, beautifully maintained, and so secure that it was dubbed the "Actor's House of Detention" by visitors. Durst was wrong: up-and-coming actors, dancers, and musicians did indeed make superior welfare tenants. Manhattan Plaza was afflicted by none of the usual pathologies of housing projects—crime, vandalism, financial delinquency. Manhattan Plaza even became the first Section 8 project in the country to generate an annual operating surplus, thanks to the fees brought in by its thousand-car parking garage and its health club, which sold memberships to nonresidents. "All of us like to think that we're a better place because Seymour said we would fail," said Reverend Kirk.

Founded in 1976 by Sidney J. Baumgarten, a special assistant to Mayor Abe Beame, the Mayor's Office of Midtown Enforcement brought a ferocity to Midtown smut-busting not seen since the heyday of Fiorello La Guardia. On paper, Sid Baumgarten was a liberal of the sort that Richard Nixon loved to hate: a Jewish, Ivy League–educated lawyer and club-house Democrat. But Baumgarten also happened to be an army combat veteran and National Rifle Association member who believed viscerally in the social primacy of law and order. Erudite and outwardly calm, he seethed with frustration over Times Square's transformation into Sodom and Gomorrah. "I am not a moralist, though no one would ever believe it," Baumgarten recalled years later. "I was passionate about doing my job and fulfilling my charge as a public official."

As conceived by Baumgarten, Midtown Enforcement was the old Times Square Inspectional Task Force on steroids. The Lindsay task force had been a first attempt at increasing the enforcement clout the city wielded against the sex industry by pairing police officers with teams of civilian inspectors drawn from health, fire, buildings, and other regulatory agencies. Lindsay's SWAT teams had made life miserable for porn operators for a time but suffered from disunity and erratic judgment. The Inspectional Task Force had no institutional life of its own, consisting of a constantly revolving cast of characters seconded from other agencies. By contrast, Midtown Enforcement employed its own full-time staff of a dozen inspectors and lawyers answerable only to Baumgarten, who, in turn, reported directly to the mayor.

Baumgarten greatly strengthened Midtown Enforcement's hand by shepherding the Nuisance Abatement Law through the City Council in mid-1977. Drafted by a Fordham law professor on retainer, the law gave civil libertarians conniptions but survived all legal challenges. Now, if a sex-related business logged two convictions for prostitution or five for drugs or gambling, Midtown Enforcement could go to a judge and get an *ex parte* order to close an establishment—that is, without notifying its owners in advance. "Under the law, there had to be a public hearing within three days," explained William Daly, Midtown Enforcement's senior investigator. "But the ability to shut a place down first and have them raise questions later was a very powerful weapon. To set aside a closing, a brothel operator had to show that prostitution had ceased. Shifting the burden of proof gave us a real psychological edge."

Baumgarten left office with Beame at the end of 1977, but Midtown Enforcement soldiered on under Koch appointee Carl Weisbrod, methodically using the Nuisance Abatement Law to gain the upper hand over Midtown's sex industry. By 1985, the number of sex-related businesses in Times Square had plummeted to 53, from 132 in 1976. No genre of smut was immune, as adult movie theaters decreased to 18 from 27, bookstores/peep show parlors to 16, from 31, live sex shows to 6 from 13, topless bars to 5 from 20, and massage parlors to 2 from 42. These figures were net reductions; the absolute number of establishments the city closed was much greater. In 1982, Midtown Enforcement published "What Are They Now?" which listed 347 porn outlets closed from 1976 through 1982 alone. Of the 30 XXX shops that had shut down on West 42nd Street, 11 had been replaced by tenants of Theater Row or other Papert-sponsored projects and 8 by fast-food restaurants or budget clothing stores.

A convicted murderer named Robert Brown was an improbable but vital contributor to Midtown Enforcement's success in turning back the porno tide. As the agency's "conditions investigator," the soft-spoken, street-smart Brown was its eyes and ears on 42nd Street and the rest of Times Square from 1978 to 1989. Working a 9 P.M. to 2 A.M. shift through the weekends and holidays—prime time for crime—Brown walked the streets looking for evidence of brothels, drug hangouts, gambling dens, youth gangs, and even illegal construction work. From the typewritten reports that he filed nightly, his police colleagues culled incriminating information used to make dozens of arrests and shut down scores of establishments on public nuisance charges. "Bob was one of the few cons who was truly rehabilitated," recalled Daly, who succeeded Weisbrod as director in 1984. "He gave us a great picture of the streets."

Brown knew Times Square inside and out, for it had figured as prominently in his criminal career as it did in his rehabilitation. Born in 1928 in the charity ward of an East Side hospital, Brown began stealing at age five, lifting nickels from the candy counter at Catholic school. He had lived in five foster homes by age thirteen, when he was placed in an orphanage at St. Agnes' Convent, twenty-five miles north of the city. Brown soon began running away and hitchhiking down to Times Square, where he broke into hotel rooms and stole cameras, jewelry, and anything else of value that he could unload to the pawnshops on Eighth Avenue. When the cops caught the boy, they sent him back to the orphanage, where the nuns shaved his head in punishment. He was booted from the orphanage not long after his sixteenth birthday. "I gravitated right back to the excitement of Times Square," Brown recalled. "For a couple of years, I literally lived out here."

In 1945, Brown enlisted in the Marines, but went AWOL after six months. He began sticking up bars and delis in Times Square with a .32-caliber pistol that he had stolen from a fellow Marine. In 1948, the twenty-year-old shot and killed a clerk while robbing a hotel at 91st Street and Broadway. Brown claimed that his gun had accidentally discharged, but he escaped the electric chair only by pleading guilty to murder in the second degree. In 1948, Brown was sentenced to forty-five years in prison. He was released on good behavior in 1971, after New York's sentencing laws were liberalized. He had undergone intensive psychotherapy in prison and emerged from his cell a truly changed man, though the nightmares persisted. "There's always some character wearing a white-on-white short-sleeve shirt with a red blotch on it," Brown recalled in 1989. "I don't even remember what I saw that night—my psyche won't allow me to—but it must have been the impression I got."

Brown worked a series of mundane jobs—nurse's aide, sporting goods salesman, shoe shiner at Grand Central. While working as a lecturer for the Fortune Society, a prison reform group that employed ex-cons, Brown befriended a number of police officers. In 1978, some of his cop buddies recommended him to Midtown Enforcement, which was looking for an investigator. "We needed a better understanding of street conditions, not during the day, which was easy to determine, but at night and on the weekends," Weisbrod recalled. "I needed someone who was mature enough not to get into trouble but savvy enough to understand what he was seeing and explain it." Weisbrod decided to take a chance on Brown, and Mayor Koch signed off on the appointment, which, luckily for all concerned, went unnoticed by the City Hall press corps.

Brown was not a young man and had a lot of ground to cover every night, so the city gave him a car during his second year. He got a driver's license—his first—but soon gave up the car because the necessity of double-parking made him conspicuous. Brown returned to pavement pounding, even though running the obstacle course of pimps, drug dealers, addicts, and lunatics on 42nd Street made him particularly uncomfortable. Brown adhered to a few simple survival rules on the Deuce: walk fast, stay close to the curb, do not make eye contact, and never, *ever* stop. "My senses alert me to the problems," said Brown, who, as a convicted felon, could not carry a gun. "I'll feel tension in my shoulders, my neck, all over. Then I'll become wary."

Bob Moss was a born dreamer, but no dream could touch the reality of May 13, 1978, a sunny spring day on 42nd Street. Some fifteen thousand people roamed the 400 block as rock bands played from stages set up in the street and clowns and jugglers performed. On the south side of the street five shiny new Off Off Broadway theaters and a fancy French restaurant stood where once there had been only filth and decay. On the north side were two enormous apartment towers filled with actors, playwrights, and other theater folk paying below-market rents courtesy of Uncle Sam. To the open-air podium set up in the courtyard of Manhattan Plaza stepped Walter Mondale, vice president of the United States, to praise Theater Row as a triumph of farsighted vision and, paraphrasing E. B. White, to declare that "New York City is to the country" what the church spire "is to the village—the visible symbol of faith and aspiration."

Fred Papert and Moss also made speeches, after Mayor Edward Koch fulsomely, and Governor Hugh Carey briefly, heaped praise on Theater Row. After the ceremonies, Moss strolled the block, basking in the warmth of the sun and the improbability of all that had been accomplished in the three and a half years since he had first set foot on 42nd Street. He bumped into Marilyn Levy, the Rockefeller Brothers Foundation official who had so curtly rebuffed his fund-raising appeal two years earlier.

"Marilyn," Moss said sweetly. "I'm real."

"I know you are," Levy replied.

Later, Moss was standing outside Playwrights Horizons' theater at 416, the former Maidman Playhouse, when up walked Helen Hayes on the arm of Irving Maidman, of all people. Moss had known and loved the great actress ever since their years together at the Phoenix Theater but had not realized that she was friendly with his former landlord. It turned out that Hayes and Maidman both lived in the Hudson River town of Nyack, where the developer was a leading benefactor of the arts.

Oscar Hammerstein I dressed, as usual, as if for opening night. (CULVER PICTURES)

The Paradise Roof Gardens atop Hammerstein's Victoria, 1901–1902. (PHOTOFEST)

Hammerstein's Victoria (far left) oversees the construction of Times Tower, 1903. (BROWN BROTHERS)

The New Amsterdam Theater, the crown jewel of 42nd Street's theaters and national headquarters of the Theatrical Syndicate, 1905. (CULVER PICTURES)

Rector's, the quintessential Broadway lobster palace.
(FREDERIC LEWIS / GETTY IMAGES)

The Lyric Theatre, built by the Shubert brothers, and the Belasco Theater, 1905.
(GETTY IMAGES)

Florenz Ziegfeld Jr., 42nd Street's master showman, with a 77 ½–pound sailfish trophy. **(CULVER PICTURES)**

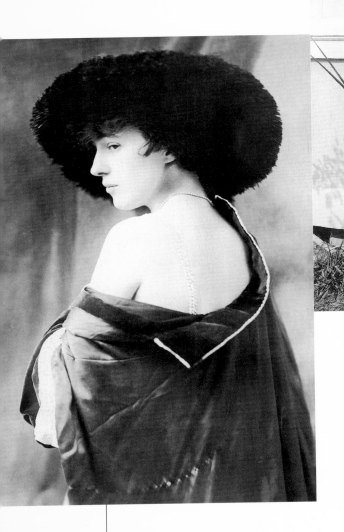

Minsky's Republic, 42nd Street's classiest burlesque joint, 1933. **(PHOTOFEST)**

Evelyn Nesbit, the Girl on the Red Velvet Swing, *starred in a misbegotten 42nd Street love story for the ages.* **(CULVER PICTURES)**

Balloon girl Helen Barnes appeared in the Ziegfeld Midnight Frolic at the New Amsterdam Roof.

Gypsy Rose Lee lived with her famously domineering mother in an apartment on 42nd Street across from Minsky's Republic.
(THE SHUBERT ARCHIVE)

Unidentified stripper in action at the Republic, circa 1937. Cameras were strictly forbidden at the Minsky's. These photos were taken covertly by a patron "just to see if he could get away with it." (CULVER PICTURES)

Hubert's Museum, 1939.
After it opened in 1929,
John Barrymore, Fred
Astaire, and Gertrude
Lawrence shared 42nd
Street's spotlight with the
likes of Andy Potato Chips,
Sealo the Sealboy, and
Olga, the Bearded Lady.
(COLLECTION OF THE AUTHOR)

Arthur Mayer (right) presides at the
unveiling of a Three Stooges mural
in the lobby of his Rialto Theater,
1939. Mayer, of the Merchant of
Menace, introduced the grind-film
format to 42nd Street. (PHOTOFEST)

Professor Roy Heckler (right) inspecting talent, 1951. Heckler's Marvelous Trained Flea Circus was Hubert's headline attraction for years.
(JOSEPH SCHUPPE/BETTMANN/CORBIS)

Looking west down 42nd Street from Seventh Avenue, 1939. The McGraw-Hill Building looms in the background. (COLLECTION OF THE AUTHOR)

Herbert Huncke, street hustler and Beat icon, in his later years. In the 1940s and 1950s, Huncke often held court late into the night at Chase's and other 42nd Street cafeterias.
(CHRISTOPHER FELVER / CORBIS)

The theater block in the early 1950s in the height of the grinder era. Forty-second Street was New York's great movie street longer than it was its great theater street. (GETTY IMAGES)

Marty Hodas, the King of the Peeps.
(J. MICHAEL DOMBROSKI. COPYRIGHT, 1974,
NEWSDAY. REPRINTED WITH PERMISSION.)

*Inside The Studio, a massage parlor
at 414 West 42nd Street, early
1970s.* (COURTESY OF PETER HOWARD)

*Show World Center, the superstore
hub of Richard Basciano's porn
empire, 1986.* (TED THAI/GETTY IMAGES)

Seymour Durst, 42nd Street property speculator, with his collection of Times Square memorabilia, 1989. (CHERYL KLAUSS)

Fred Papert, Jackie Onassis, and Bob Moss (left to right) in front of Playwrights Horizons 42nd Street theater, late 1970s. (COURTESY OF BOB MOSS)

Antiporn demonstration, 1983. (SYLVIA PLACHY)

Fred Papert, the diehard champion of 42nd Street redevelopment, 1984.
(JACK MANNING/*NEW YORK TIMES*)

Hustlers on 42nd Street, 1983. (**VINCENT CIANNI, 1999**)

The Deuce in all its déclassé 1980s glory. (**ANDREW GARN**)

Rebecca Robertson and Cora Cahan, 1993. Mass evictions turned 42nd Street into a ghost block in the heart of the city. (**MARILYN K. YEE**/*NEW YORK TIMES*)

The main auditorium of
the New Amsterdam as
the Nederlanders left it
(left) and as restored by
Walt Disney Co. (right).
(WHITNEY COX)

Neon burns bright on the
new 42nd Street, 2002.
(RACHEL ROYSE/CORBIS)

"Be a good boy and put my name back on the building," Maidman said to Moss.

"You can do that, can't you, Robert?" Hayes cooed.

Moss beamed and shook his head. He'd spent the early 1960s happily fetching coffee for Hayes, but this was one favor he was not about to do even for her.

Maidman and the block's other property owners had been so eager to rid themselves of their buildings that they signed them over free of charge to Forty-Second Street Development Corporation on the condition that Papert also take over their mortgages. By 1978, Papert had taken title to fourteen buildings between Ninth and Tenth Avenues, all on the south side of 42nd Street, facing Manhattan Plaza. "We paid no cash, but it was not hard to do," Papert recalled. "The owners had nothing to lose. It's not like they took great satisfaction in renting to porn establishments."

Papert's not-for-profit company did have to shell out $1 million to gut the six buildings in phase one of Theater Row and remodel them into a complex containing five 99-seat theaters and ten floors of rehearsal and office space. Papert covered half the tab with grants and charitable contributions, including $250,000 from the Port Authority. The rest was supplied in the form of a $485,000 long-term mortgage by a group of banks lead by Bowery Savings. The mortgage was secured by the $120,000 in annual rental payments the theaters were obligated to make to Forty-Second Street Development, but in its own way it was a gift, too. Because the ability of Papert's tenants to actually pay $120,000 a year was highly questionable, Theater Row was not "bankable" in any conventional sense. However, Papert had made an ally of Morris "Rusty" Crawford, chairman of the Bowery Savings Bank, then one of the city's biggest real estate lenders. In fact, Crawford, a civic booster par excellence, had agreed to chair Forty-Second Street Development.

Even so, the Bowery would not have made the loan had not Papert persuaded the city and state to free Theater Row of the burden of property taxes. At first, the foot soldiers of City Hall were not favorably inclined toward Theater Row, to put it mildly. "When I was first assigned to it, my boss said, 'We want you to work on this, but don't worry, it will never happen,'" recalled Paul Travis, a Public Development Corporation project manager. "People like the idea of Theater Row. It was hard *not* to like. But everyone was nervous about the economics of 99-seat theaters supporting all these buildings." Before long, though, Travis noticed that his superiors were sitting up a little straighter when he delivered his progress reports. "Fred's success really came in persuading the big-picture guys—Koch, Carey, [U.S. Senator Daniel] Moynihan," Travis added. "They really got it in a way that the people in the agencies had a much harder time with." The alliances that Papert had formed with the Port Authority, Bowery Savings, and other powerful institutions helped open doors, as did Jackie Onassis, who joined Forty-Second Street Development's board in 1977 and sprinkled her potent brand of fairy dust all over Theater Row.

Forty-Second Street Development donated all of the buildings it had acquired to the Urban Development Corporation, the state's principal redevelopment agency, which then leased the properties back to Papert's company for thirty years. Government sponsorship came at a cost, for it spooled Theater Row in red tape. The UDC inserted itself into every aspect of the project, including Papert's lease negotiations with his tenants. On opening night at one of the theaters, a UDC representative showed up just before the curtain rose and demanded that the lighting system be changed to conform to the precise specifications in the lease. A crew member punched the UDC man in the face, knocking him to the ground and allowing the show to go on, as Broadway legend required.

The development agency leaned particularly hard on Theater Row's single for-profit component, the restaurant La Rousse, initially demanding a percentage of its revenues. After months of negotiation, La Rousse co-owner Peter Howard, a former actor, refused to cut the UDC in on his cash flow but did submit to censorship. La Rousse occupied the ground floor of 414 West 42nd Street, formerly the Studio massage parlor. Howard preserved one element of the massage parlor's lurid decor: a much-larger-than-life mural of a reclining nude woman nicknamed Lola. She had been painted by an Israeli counterman at a nearby deli who had graced several Maidman buildings on the block with murals. At the UDC's insistence, the lease that Papert offered Howard stipulated that Lola could stay only if she covered up: "Nothing less than completely and opaquely covered human genitals, pubic region, buttocks, female breasts below a point immediately above the aureole." Howard signed the lease but ignored its modesty clause, leaving Lola's fleshy charms on full display in La Rousse's front room.

Moss made his chief contribution to the organizing of Theater Row in recruiting theater companies to 42nd Street. Under Papert's letterhead,

Moss sent solicitation letters to three hundred troupes, one-third of which responded. But as 1977 wore on, the ranks of the interested dwindled alarmingly. Many companies, including Charles Ludlum's Ridiculous Theater Company, grew tired of waiting. Others had second thoughts about the viability of 42nd Street and Papert's role as *über*-landlord. In the end, Theater Row had exactly the number of applicants that it had spaces to lease. This was fortuitous in a way, but Moss was so dismayed that he wasn't sure he wanted to proceed. He had a long talk with one of his mentors, Hugh Southern, the head of the Theater Development Fund, then an omnipresent force in New York theater. "We were all disappointed," Southern recalled. "But I couldn't imagine passing up the opportunity to get a ship out of the harbor and on the high seas just because the quality of the crew was not up to expectations."

Besides Playwrights Horizons, the opening-day cast of Theater Row included: the Black Theater Alliance, a service organization for sixty-one black theater and dance companies; the Actors and Directors Lab, a Los Angeles theater school just beginning to establish a New York presence; Ticket Central, which opened in space donated by La Rousse, and sold tickets to all Theater Row venues and to many other Off Off Broadway theaters, as well; Harlem Children's Theater, a black touring company hankering for a Midtown base; INTAR Hispanic American Theater, which hoped to attract a larger audience on 42nd Street than it could on 53rd Street; Lion Theater Company, the actors troupe that replaced Playwrights Horizons at 422 West 42nd Street; South Street Theatre Company, which used the piers at South Street Seaport as a stage; and the Nat Horne Musical Theater, a black dance group founded by a former hoofer in the Alvin Ailey company.

The utopian all-for-one-and-one-for-all philosophy on which Theater Row was founded soon crumbled under the weight of financial reality. Forty-Second Street Development had provided raw space, leaving it to each theater company to install a stage, seats, lighting, and so forth. The tenants, all not-for-profit groups, also had to pay for electricity and heating. Theater Row was costly beyond the expectations—and the means— of all of its original occupants, with the exception of Playwrights Horizons. By the end of 1980, all seven of Papert's theater tenants (Playwrights leased its space from the Frank family) were in arrears on their rent—defiantly so, in some cases. "A number of people thought Theater Row was going to be a free ride," Moss recalled. "The feeling was, 'I shouldn't have to pay any rent. I'm an artist.'" This attitude of entitlement infuriated Papert, who freely vented the contempt he felt for his deadbeat tenants. A diplomat he was not. "I have exactly the wrong mentality for the work I got into," Papert said later. "One of my granddaughters has a teddy bear and if you pull the paw it says, 'That's a wonderful idea!' I never learned how to do that. My reflex reaction when someone says something I think is stupid is, 'What the fuck are you talking about?'"

In the end, the fractious union that was Theater Row was preserved when Papert, Moss, and others joined forces to raise nearly $200,000 from the Theater Development Fund, the Ford Foundation, and other charitable sources. Most of the money went to reimburse the strapped theater groups for their capital expenditures. At the same time, Forty-Second Street Development amended the tenants' leases to allow them to rent out their theaters between performances for commercial uses— something many of them had begun doing covertly anyway. Theater Row lived on, and so did the bad blood between Papert and his tenants. "I don't think I ever trusted Papert from the moment I met him," said Gene Nye of the Lion Theater. "We were told that he came from advertising and was doing this out of the kindness of his heart. I never bought it."

Even as Papert was restructuring Theater Row's finances, he pushed ahead with the second development phase of the project. At a cost of $9.5 million, Theater Row II proved far more expensive than I, mainly because it included the West Side Airlines Terminal, once Maidman's flagship Hell's Kitchen property. One by one, the airlines had pulled out of the terminal, forcing it to close in 1972 after a seventeen-year run as the starting point for New York City travelers flying out of Newark. The Port Authority had taken over the terminal after Maidman defaulted on his mortgage, and signed it over to Forty-Second Street Development free of charge. Papert's group lavished $4 million on a botched effort to turn the terminal into what would have been Theater Row's largest performing arts center, but managed to avoid disaster by leasing much of the building to a television production company for use as a studio. Theater Row's second phase extended Forty-Second Street Development's zone of reclamation west all the way to Tenth Avenue, adding two more restaurants and three small not-for-profit theaters.

Papert also went to work on the neighboring blocks. It would take him nearly five years, but he succeeded in turning a former Mack Truck garage at 621 West 42nd Street (between Eleventh and Twelfth Avenues) into a stable for Troop B, the NYPD's mounted police unit. In 1976, city budget cutters had forced Troop C to abandon its stable at 55th Street and Tenth Avenue and disperse to distant locations. Mounted police still patrolled Times Square, moving their horses back and forth from distant stables by truck, but much less intensively than before. Putting thirty horses on 42nd Street enabled Troop B to increase by half the number of officers on mounted patrol in the theater district. Forty-Second Street Development scored an equally hard-won triumph in transforming part of an enormous building once used as an Army Reserve Training Center into loft housing that sopped up some of the waiting-list overflow from Manhattan Plaza.

Papert's energy and imagination did not always carry the day on 42nd Street. He was particularly disappointed at the failure of an attempt to develop a year-round farmers' market on a vacant four-acre plot between Eleventh and Twelfth Avenues owned by the Chrysler Corporation. Papert hired the architects who had designed Boston's Faneuil Hall/ Quincy Market. Their design was impressive, but in the end Chrysler wanted more for its land than Forty-Second Street Development could afford to pay. Papert also failed in his persistent efforts to buy the Holland Hotel at 351 West 42nd Street in partnership with American Youth Hostels, which eventually decided against moving its headquarters into the building. Papert's hopes of upgrading this notorious welfare dumping ground and drug den into midpriced tourist hostelry called the Theater Row Hotel finally were dashed when he was outbid by an expansion-minded slumlord.

Thanks largely to Papert—and Midtown Enforcement—far West 42nd Street now was hurtling toward respectability, even though the transvestite prostitutes who worked the area refused to take the hint and leave. "They're like locusts," Reverend Kirk complained. "They light around a car even if it's moving—four, five, six at a time." The transvestites infiltrated the Manhattan Plaza parking garage, preferring it to the open Port Authority parking lots nearby for turning car tricks. Often when Bob Nahas, owner of the Curtains Up! restaurant across the street from Theater Row, came to work at two-thirty in the morning, a couple of shims would jump up and down on the hood of his car in greeting. "You don't see transvestites that are five foot two, OK? They're six foot four and they're really rather menacing," complained Richard Hunnings, Manhattan Plaza's director of operations. "And they don't have the best taste in clothes and makeup and all. I figured if we were stuck with them . . . we should bring them into the Ellington Room, and I was going to bring people from Stagelight cosmetics and we were going to teach them to do their hair and makeup properly and get them dressed right."

Feared and condescended to in roughly equal measure, the shims would continue to work the intersection of 42nd Street and Ninth Avenue well in the 1980s, but their presence no longer defined the area. By 1979, if not earlier, all of the usual signs of rampant gentrification were plainly evident throughout Papert country. Brownstones were being fixed up, abandoned commercial buildings sported new FOR RENT signs, and upscale shops and restaurants were proliferating. Amazingly, Shopwell opened a deluxe 18,000-square-foot supermarket, the largest grocery store in all of Manhattan, within Manhattan Plaza. Seymour Durst was not about to admit that he had been wrong about Manhattan Plaza's socioeconomic impact, but at least he had the good grace to acknowledge the obvious when a reporter asked for his assessment of the neighborhood. "Real estate values are improving in the immediate vicinity," said Durst, who was pouring millions into the renovation of apartments along 43rd and 44th Streets. In 1975, no one—not even that pie-eyed optimist Bob Moss—would have predicted that the gentle balm of not-for-profit theater could cure what ailed far West 42nd Street. But the fact was that by decade's end Theater Row had combined with Manhattan Plaza to permanently alter the chemistry of one of the city's most despoiled neighborhoods.

The Theater Preservation Follies

By 1980, the number of people alive who had walked 42nd Street in the 1920s was minuscule. Yet the collective memory of the street's theatrical golden age lived robustly on, its history having been alchemized into twenty-four-karat legend by anecdotes, stories, and song lyrics, and by scores of Broadway-inspired movies from the 1930s, especially *42nd Street* itself. In the 1950s and early 1960s, the movie had been seen as a campy artifact of the early Depression years. But then came a Busby Berkeley revival that elevated the critical reputation of *42nd Street* along with that of its choreographer. By the time Berkeley died in 1976, the 1933 film was revered as the archetypal backstage musical—the one that "gave life to the clichés that have kept parodists happy," as Pauline Kael put it—and had gained a place on many best-movies-of-all-time lists. In other words, the 42nd Street of myth gained force even as the street itself deteriorated into a slum. Planted deep in the minds of millions of people was an image that bore no visible connection to the diminished reality of the place. In legend only, 42nd Street was still the thrill of opening night, the sound of the brasses, the euphonious thunder of dozens of tap-dancing feet.

In August 1980, the mythological 42nd Street was gilded anew by the spectacular debut of a stage musical, David Merrick's *42nd Street,*

which would play on until January 1989. This string of 3,486 performances established *42nd Street* as the second-longest-running musical
ever, behind *A Chorus Line*. (In time, it would slip to third, when *Cats* surpassed *A Chorus Line*.) But *42nd Street* assumed an even larger position
in the popular psyche than its commercial success alone warranted, for
the story of its making was a backstage drama more compelling than its
movie namesake.

The idea of turning *42nd Street* into a big-budget musical first occurred to *Hello, Dolly!* librettist Michael Stewart in 1976 while he
watched the film at a West Side revival house. The movie contained only
five songs, so Stewart and his collaborator, Mark Bramble, riffled through
the entire twenty-two-film oeuvre of songwriters Harry Warren and Al
Dubin and acquired the rights to another eleven tunes, including "We're
in the Money" and "I Only Have Eyes for You." They brought their project to Merrick, who had triumphed in the 1950s and 1960s as Broadway's
greatest hit-maker but had sidetracked himself producing mediocre
movies in Hollywood. Merrick was in his late sixties but he grabbed hold
of *42nd Street* with his old ferocity, seeing it as a potential monster hit
that would silence the drama critics who dismissed him as a relic of a by-
gone era. Merrick, a perfectionist bully who gloried in his nickname, the
"Abominable Showman," was hardly a sentimentalist, but 42nd Street
did hold special meaning for him. It was where he had gotten his start in
the mid-1940s, working as a lowly assistant to producer Herman Shumlin
in the Selwyn Building at 229 West 42nd Street.

Forty-Second Street was the eighth collaboration between Merrick
and Gower Champion, the great choreographer-director. Champion recently had been diagnosed with Waldenstrom's disease, a rare blood disorder that often progresses slowly but is almost always terminal.
Champion's doctors advised him against work, but he decided "to muster
all his reserves for one glorious production—even if it proved to be his
last," as journalist Cliff Jahr put it. It was futile for Champion to pretend
he was healthy—his temperature spiked to 104 one day during rehearsals—but he disclosed the nature of his illness only to Wanda
Richert, a twenty-two-year-old unknown cast in the ingenue role of Peggy
Sawyer. Throughout his career, Champion had habitually taken a mistress or two from his casts. This time it was Richert, who so bewitched the
fifty-nine-year-old director that he neglected to take the routine precaution of hiring an understudy for her—an oversight that Merrick corrected,

much to his director's annoyance. On the last day of previews in Washington, D.C., Champion finally told Merrick that he had Waldenstrom's, but neither man grasped the severity of the director's condition. "Gower had no notion he had a short time to live. Nor did his doctor," Merrick recalled. "He just described some blood ailment he had."

Merrick poured $3 million into *42nd Street,* more than anyone had ever spent on a play. With fifty-four actors, four hundred costumes, and twelve lavish sets-—including a full-length Pullman car—this was a colossus of a musical. Most shows fit comfortably into six trailer trucks; this one needed twelve. Merrick, a diabolical genius of a publicist, outdid himself with *42nd Street.* The Abominable Showman built a wall of secrecy around his megamusical, refusing to commit to an opening date while issuing cryptic written warnings to reviewers. A sneak preview of the play was canceled minutes before the curtain was to rise when a roving five-man squad of black-suited bouncers discovered an uninvited reviewer on the premises. "A snake was loose in the audience," said Merrick in explaining his decision to cancel. On August 15, the producer took out a full-page newspaper ad announcing that *42nd Street*—"The All Singing All Dancing Extravaganza with a Cast of 54 (Some Younger)"—would open August 25 at the Winter Garden, the big Shubert-owned theater on Broadway at 50th Street.

On August 20, Richert found Champion unconscious in his apartment and rushed him to Sloan-Kettering. Four days later, his kidneys failed. Champion died early in the morning of August 25, opening day for *42nd Street.* Merrick pleaded with hospital officials and Champion's relatives to refrain from announcing his death until the curtain rose that night. He also summoned his actors to the Winter Garden early, effectively sequestering his cast from the rumor mill by ordering them to rehearse right through to the curtain. Merrick was seeing to it not only that his show would go on, but also that coverage of its opening would move from the arts page to the front page. For all the producer's ruthlessness, though, he was not without feeling. He arrived at the Winter Garden at four o'clock in the afternoon "bursting to tell someone the news. He fell onto Bramble sobbing, genuinely shattered by the loss. But he swore Bramble to secrecy. . . . Amazingly, when the curtain rose, the secret was still a secret."

The musical played beautifully, punctuated by roars of approval from the audience. In translating *42nd Street* to the stage, Champion and Merrick had excised its dark, sardonic undercurrents and piled on the jubilant song and dance numbers. Only at the very end, with Jerry Orbach's melancholic final turn as director Julian Marsh, did the tone turn bittersweet. "As he sings a reprise of the title song," wrote one admiring critic, "chanting of 'naughty, bawdy, gawdy, sporty 42nd Street,' he seems really to be evoking its successor—the crummy, scummy, bummy, slummy 42nd Street of today, the reality that lurks inside the showbiz fantasy we can't surrender."

Orbach exited to deafening applause. The cast took ten curtain calls. After the curtain rose the eleventh time, a haggard-looking Merrick walked out onstage to a huge ovation. "I'm sorry to have to report . . . ," he began, but was drowned out by laughter and clapping. "No, no," the producer continued, looking a bit angry now. "This is tragic. You don't understand. Gower Champion died this morning." A moment of stunned silence was shattered by shouts and shrieks. As members of the cast began to sob, Orbach shouted to the curtain pullers, "Bring it in! Bring it in!"

The play won raves from virtually every reviewer, with Champion's choreography singled out for special praise. As Champion's "final display of blazing theatrical fireworks," *42nd Street* was "a perfect monument to his glorious career," Frank Rich wrote in the *Times*. Life imitated art when Richert became an overnight sensation. Merrick's histrionics would leave a bad aftertaste, but for better or worse he had engineered what might have been the most memorable opening night in Broadway history. "In thirteen hours," biographer Howard Kissel wrote, Merrick "had left the realm of showmanship and entered that of myth."

The producer would continue to live up to his nickname, minimizing Champion's posthumous billing and scheming to minimize the royalties paid to his estate and to the show's other authors. The abominable one would live on until 2001, but *42nd Street* was his last big hit, his swan song. At the final performance of its original Broadway run, Merrick sat alone on the aisle in the last row of the St. James Theater, weeping inconsolably.

As a lavish musical constructed on a foundation of Tin Pan Alley tunes and "the most thrillingly atavistic of noises, the sound of mass unison tap dancing," *42nd Street's* appeal was essentially nostalgic. Yet its evocation of the Great White Way in its heyday was right on the news in a sense, for the beginning of its lucrative run coincided with the demolition of three historic Broadway theaters to make way for a city-subsidized Marriott hotel. The Bijou, Morosco, and Helen Hayes theaters were just a couple of blocks north of 42nd Street—in the heart of Times Square—and their demise would significantly influence the drive to redevelop 42nd Street.

It seems astounding today that as of 1980 the New York City Landmarks Commission had conferred landmark status on only one Broadway house—the Lyceum, on 45th Street. Of the ninety legitimate theaters that had been built in the greater Times Square area between 1895 and 1932, nearly half had been torn down or converted to movie theaters by this time. For years, theater owners had staunchly opposed any government plan that impinged on their prerogatives to do with their properties as they saw fit, including selling them to a developer if they wanted. Even so, a strong case could have been made for landmarking the Helen Hayes in particular. Specialists employed by the Landmarks Commission thought so, describing it as "architecturally . . . one of the finest theaters in the Times Square area" in an internal report. However, the commission ignored its own staff and rebuffed calls for public hearings. Any other outcome would have been heroic, for the commission's members served at the pleasure of the mayor, and Edward Koch was bound and determined to ram a $300 million hotel project through to completion. "Implicit in the beginning was our willingness to accept demolition of the Helen Hayes," recalled Ken Halpern, whom Koch appointed director of the Mayor's Office of Midtown Planning and Development. "We were looking to do whatever was necessary to get the hotel built."

A series of lawsuits delayed the inevitable until 1982. The Bijou was the first to fall, toppling in January. On March 5, a large group of actors began a nineteen-day "Save the Morosco and Helen Hayes Theater Vigil" with seventy-two straight hours of speeches and readings from a makeshift stage on Broadway. On March 22, a few days after the U.S. Supreme Court had rejected a final petition to halt demolition, hundreds of demonstrators gathered in the empty lot where "Godzilla," a forty-ton Traxcavator, waited to begin demolition. Chanting "Shame on Koch," 170 people submitted to arrest in a televised act of civil disobedience. They were taken to the local precinct in paddy wagons, booked on charges of criminal trespass, and released. Meanwhile, back on 45th Street the remaining protesters sang "Give My Regards to Broadway" and "America the Beautiful" from behind police barricades as Godzilla began to roll.

The Morosco and the Helen Hayes came crashing down, but the two-year battle to save them combined with the enormous success of *42nd Street,* the musical, to create a groundswell of popular support for saving historic Broadway theaters. Over the next six years, the Landmarks Commission would landmark twenty-eight Broadway theaters, including the Little Theater, which was renamed the Helen Hayes, and the New Amsterdam, 42nd Street's great slime-encrusted jewel. To the consternation of theater owners, the commission extended its protection to interiors as well as exteriors, thereby requiring that fleurs-de-lis, sconces, lunettes, rosettes, and a profusion of other decorative details be restored to their original state after every production run.

The Landmarks Commission no doubt would have protected other 42nd Street playhouses besides the New Amsterdam had not the Koch administration had bigger plans for them under the 42nd Street Development Plan (42DP) that the city and state put together in the early 1980s. Nine of the ten historic playhouses between Seventh and Eighth Avenues were to be restored to entertainment uses. Even with the loss of the Morosco and the Hayes, it was not clear that Broadway *needed* nine more theaters, or that playhouses of such ancient vintage could be made competitive in the city's crowded entertainment market. But after the PR pounding that Koch had taken in the Marriott hotel battle, he would not allow his planners to even consider tearing down a single theater on 42nd Street. "We had to preserve *everything,*" said Paul Travis, now director of the Public Development Corp., the city's urban development agency. PDC ran the 42nd Street urban renewal effort for the city in collaboration with its state counterpart, the Urban Development Corp.

Koch's plan was derived from a stillborn Papert-inspired project called the City at 42nd Street. This $600 million venture failed despite the backing of some of New York's most prestigious private institutions, including the Ford Foundation, the Rockefeller Foundation, Chase Manhattan Bank, Equitable Life Assurance, and Salomon Brothers. "Anybody who knew anything about it thought that the City at 42nd Street would be a phenomenal thing," recalled Jane Stanicki of Bowery Savings, another of the project's backers. "What we have now on 42nd Street is almost retro, where the City at 42nd was farsighted, a brilliant idea ahead of its time."

Papert was deeply involved in the City at 42nd Street, particularly at first. However, the project's prime movers were Roger G. Kennedy, the Ford Foundation's vice president for the arts; Donald Elliott, a lawyer who had chaired city planning through most of Lindsay's tenure; and Richard Weinstein, an architect who had brashly filled the role of Broadway expert at the Urban Design Group.

The basic idea was to convert the Deuce's historic theaters to upscale entertainment uses, creating a kind of high-tech urban theme park for adults covering two and a half square blocks. Only the New Amsterdam would be revived as a legitimate theater. "The problem was that the theaters with two balconies just didn't work economically," Weinstein recalled. The Victory would become a miniature opera house while the Selwyn, the Apollo, and the Harris would be rehabbed, renamed, and used for concerts and other live performances. The facades of the Times Square, the Empire, the Lyric, and the Liberty would be preserved while their interiors were gutted and used for exhibits and rides. The lower floors of the Candler Building would be made into a center for small performing arts groups. Meanwhile, all of the other buildings between 41st and 43rd Streets from Seventh to Eighth Avenues would be leveled and replaced with new exhibit halls, restaurants, and stores. To ensure that the $600 million complex would be a paying proposition, three office towers would be erected at 42nd Street's intersection with Seventh Avenue and a huge merchandise mart constructed along Eighth Avenue.

The flavor of the City at 42nd Street was best evoked by "Slice of the Apple," which was Weinstein's favorite of all the proposed attractions. "[Imagine] one long, continuous peel, a concept not unlike the Guggenheim, where, as you walked along starting from one hundred feet below New York's streets, you viewed one long progressive, life-size cutaway of the infrastructure of the city—the water, the electricity, gas, and cable systems—until you reached the top of the World Trade Center," Weinstein said. "At each one-hundred-foot-high level the view of the actual city would change, so that as you'd pass by you could, for instance, see through the rose window of St. Patrick's Cathedral. . . . When you got to the top, you were ready to go on a four-hundred-foot Ferris wheel at one end of the development that curved out over Seventh Avenue as it went around. If you were on it facing north, you could see straight up to Central Park, and south down to the lower tip of Manhattan."

The City at 42nd Street was rooted in the belief that the old theater block of 42nd Street, like parts of the South Bronx and central Brooklyn, had deteriorated beyond all hope of self-redemption and could be "saved" only if it was first destroyed. Over the decades the crime rate on 42nd Street had fluctuated with the police department's enforcement zeal, but the Deuce's economic decline had been inexorable and extreme. By 1979, the assessed valuation of the entire area targeted by the City at 42nd Street—land and buildings—was a mere $34 million, less than many a single Midtown office tower; for example, Citicorp's new headquarters at 53rd Street and Lexington Avenue was assessed at $70 million. The area contained 2.1 million square feet of commercial space, one-third of the 6.1 million square feet allowed under the zoning regulations already in place. Only about 915,000 square feet was occupied, with many buildings wholly vacant above the ground floor.

In commercial terms, West 42nd Street was Midtown's Dead Zone. Even so, demolition on as massive a scale as proposed by the sponsors of the City at 42nd Street flew in the face of the new orthodoxy that had come to dominate American city planning after the failure of the federal urban renewal programs of the 1950s and 1960s. Thousands of inner-city acres had been razed and rebuilt across the country, accomplishing little in the end but to replace "bad" neighborhoods with worse housing projects at great cost to the public purse. Such books as Jane Jacobs's *The Death and Life of Great American Cities* had persuasively argued that run-down urban districts were far more complex socially than could be appreciated from the outside and were best improved incrementally, one careful step at a time.

The work that Forty-Second Street Development Corp. had done in the far reaches of the Deuce fit the new urbanist prescription exactly, but even Papert despaired of applying the theory of incremental redevelopment to the old 42nd Street theater block. The sex establishments that had blighted Theater Row's future home had existed at the margins of the Times Square XXX scene and were so financially enfeebled that Papert had easily dislodged them. But at its core, a few blocks to the east, the 42nd Street sex trade was still powerfully entrenched. Within the bounds of the City at 42nd Street project area, there were twenty-four sex-related businesses, nineteen of them on the theater block alone. In the view of

Roger Kennedy, Papert, and their colleagues, this concentration of smut rendered useless the baby-step-at-a-time approach to urban renewal. "There was general agreement that the only way to reduce or eliminate fear from the 42nd Street area is for a total physical catharsis to occur," read the notes from an early organizing meeting for the project. "Piece-meal changes will not work."

Despite two years of intensive efforts by its sponsors, the City at 42nd Street died on the drawing board, a victim of its own grandiosity and of Mayor Koch's animus. At first Koch had supported the project, go-ing along with the recommendation of his city planning chairman, Robert Wagner Jr. (the son of the former mayor). The City at 42nd Street is "an ambitious, expensive, and potentially risky undertaking, but just as cer-tainly it is an extraordinarily exciting idea, which, if successful, could transform the heart of the Times Square area," Wagner wrote in a confi-dential memo to Koch in 1978. "I believe the concept deserves City sup-port." The city had promised that it would convene public hearings when developers had committed to the project. Yet when Elliott and Weinstein presented Koch with signed letters of intent from three big-time develop-ers in the spring of 1980, the mayor turned on the City at 42nd Street with a vengeance, variously denouncing it as "junk," a "monstrosity," and "Disneyland on 42nd Street."

What happened? In a word, politics. It appears that Koch's strongest objection to the City at 42nd Street was that he could not claim it as his own. In outline, the 42nd Street Development Plan was so similar to the City at 42nd Street as to verge on planning plagiarism. It laid out a virtu-ally identical urban renewal zone covering about 2½ blocks, or 13 acres, but piled much more square footage of new commercial space atop it. The city-state plan added a fourth office tower to the City's three-skyscraper cluster at the Crossroads of the World and paired a new 550-room luxury hotel with the previously proposed wholesale merchandise mart. The plan aped its predeccesor in calling for the restoration of nine theaters under contracts that the city and state would award to private developers. To hear Mayor Koch tell it, the project would take 42nd Street back to a glorious future. "Forty-second Street was once famous for its theaters and night life," the mayor declared. "When this project is completed, night life and theaters will make it famous once again."

Other than the old theaters, only three buildings within the project area were to be spared from the wrecking ball: the Times Tower, the Candler Building, and the Carter Hotel. The original cost estimate was $1.6 billion but soon would swell to $2.5 billion, ranking 42DP as the costliest commercial development project in New York State history. "Our plan was Neronian in scale," declared William J. Stern, chairman of the Urban Development Corp. "Everything had to go forward at the same time, we felt, since the sheer momentum of the development would push out the sleaze for good."

The City at 42nd Street had been no sure thing commercially, but at least Weinstein and company had devised detailed and often imaginative new uses for each of the theaters. By contrast, the government scheme that replaced it advocated the restoration of eight theaters as legitimate playhouses but was suspiciously vague on the details. Tellingly, neither the Actors' Equity Association nor Save the Theaters, the city's leading theater preservation group, endorsed 42DP. "It is unclear whether funding for the theaters will be sufficient; it is unclear how they will be operated," said Jack Goldstein, Save the Theaters' director. "Instead of a cohesive plan for the sensible management of the 42nd Street corridor as an entertainment complex of mixed performing arts uses, the plan simply proposes that some of the theaters be thrown into the competitive commercial market of Broadway."

By the time that the city and state announced 42DP in early 1981, the Brandt family, 42nd Street's own theater dynasty, already was doggedly pursuing its own modest plan to redevelop the Deuce, one converted grind house at a time.

In mid-1978, the Brandts decided to switch off the movie projectors at the Apollo and rehab the historic theater for legitimate use as the New Apollo. The new theater was the spitting image of the original, except that its front entrance now was on 43rd Street, which was just as sleazy as 42nd Street but not as crowded with the sort of street folk that theatergoers presumably found scary. On March 1, 1979, the New Apollo presented *On Golden Pond,* the first full-fledged legitimate production on 42nd Street since *Othello* closed at the New Amsterdam in 1937. The play was well received but was overshadowed by the praise heaped on the theater itself. In the *Times,* Paul Goldberger pronounced the New Apollo "one of the best medium-sized theaters in town (the Apollo has

1,163 seats) with a tight compact auditorium that nonetheless has a graceful, flowing air to it. . . . It is a far cry from the shabby, decaying auditoriums of so many of Broadway's legitimate theaters." The Brandts also had restored the facade of the Lyric, next door to the Apollo, in anticipation of its eventual return to the legitimate fold, spending a total of $500,000 to fix up both theaters.

The New Apollo, the Lyric, the Victory, the Selwyn, the Times Square, the Empire, and the Liberty theaters were all controlled by the descendants of Harry and William Brandt and by Martin Levine, the Brandt in-law who had been running Brandt Enterprises' 42nd Street subsidiary since the late 1940s. Bernard (Bingo) and Louis, the youngest member of the founding quartet of Brandt brothers, were still alive and coming into the office every day but had sold most of their New York movie theaters, with the prominent exception of the Rialto I and II. In the spring of 1979, with the City at 42nd Street then commanding center stage in the debate over 42nd Street's future, the Bingo and Louis Brandt families announced plans to spend $250,000 to convert the Rialto I into a 499-seat playhouse. When the new and improved Rialto I opened in early 1980 with a revival of the musical *Canterbury Tales,* the Rialto II was still showing adult films. Robert Brandt, the eldest of Bingo's four sons, said that he hoped it, too, soon would be made over into a playhouse. "The principal impetus for reclaiming the Rialto was economic," Brandt said at the time. "There is now a strong demand for legitimate theater in New York City, and we felt we could compete in the marketplace."

At the same time, the family hedged its bets by angling for a starring role in 42DP. No business owner within the urban renewal zone had more to lose than did the Brandts. There were the seven historic playhouses it owned plus the two Rialto theaters, which were housed in a mid-rise building owned by Bingo and Louis. The Rialto Building was one of the more strategic pieces on the redevelopment chessboard, sitting smack in the middle of the site earmarked by 42DP for a complex of four giant office towers. The Bingo/Louis interests also owned three other buildings marked for demolition under the city-state plan: 210 West 43rd Street, 1481 Broadway, and 1485 Broadway, home of the infamous Playland Arcade. Acting on the theory that the best defense is a good offense, the two branches of the family joined together to bid for the 42DP development rights for the midblock. As outlined in a two-inch-thick prospectus prepared by some of the best consultants money could buy, the Brandts de-

vised an ambitious scheme that encompassed not only their seven theaters but also the three houses on the block controlled by Mark Finkelstein: the New Amsterdam, the Harris, and the Anco (originally the Lew
M. Fields).

Robert and his cousin Richard Brandt, the late Harry's son, represented the family in lengthy negotiations with city and state officials beginning in 1980. Actually, there were two sets of simultaneous
negotiations that were separate in theory but linked in practice. Each
party held something the other desired: the Brandts wanted the development rights to the midblock theaters, and the government wanted to acquire the Rialto Building and the Bingo/Louis interests' three other
commercial properties without having to resort to the time-consuming
trouble of condemning them. The situation argued for compromise but
produced rancor instead. By mid-1981, the two sides were sniping at
each other in the newspapers. An unnamed Koch aide complained to a
reporter that the Brandts were acting like they were indispensable to the
redevelopment of 42nd Street. "They're not," he sniffed. "We can go on
without them." Retorted Robert Brandt: "We do not intend to voluntarily
transfer property that has been in our family fifty years to someone else to
do something we could do better."

The Brandt plan had its flaws, but it was a credible, professional effort based on a much more authoritative analysis of the theaters than anything the city's own planners had attempted. But to include the Brandts
would imply that there were aspects of 42nd Street worth saving. A great
many New Yorkers in fact did feel this way, but the scope and scale of
42DP could only be justified by the need to wipe the street clean of the
smut and decay of the last half-century. The Brandts, in short, were a serious PR liability. Vincent Tese, who succeeded Stern as chairman of the
UDC, castigated the family as "the people who brought 42nd Street to its
knees." A few friends in high places might have saved the day for the
family, even so. But they were not big contributors to Mayor Koch—or to
any other politician—and had no intention of trying to curry favor with
City Hall by cutting their asking price for the Rialto Building.

The clan's latest foray into the legitimate theater also ended disappointingly, exposing Robert's belief in the family's ability to compete
with the Shuberts and the Nederlanders as wishful thinking. In the theater business, size definitely did matter. At the same time, the Brandts
demonstrated that they were movie people who appreciated and liked the

theater but had no talent for picking hit plays. Of the seven productions that Levine booked into the New Apollo and the Rialto from 1979 to 1982, only one had a good, long run. *Fifth of July,* the Lanford Wilson masterwork about the Vietnam era, played for 511 performances at the New Apollo.

Harry's and William's descendants also suffered from an architectural disadvantage, in that the Apollo and the Lyric—like all of the old 42nd Street theaters—were cursed with second balconies. "No producer wants a theater with a second balcony," Levine lamented. "We didn't know the second balcony would be such a serious problem." Levine had forgotten his history, for it was the second balcony, with its poor sightlines and great distance from the stage, that was largely to blame for dooming the 42nd Street playhouses to obsolescence in the first place.

In Levine's defense, the second-balcony problem did limit his choice of plays. In the end, he was unable to arrange even a single booking at the Lyric. At the Rialto, on the other hand, the Bingo and Louis interests were undone by choice, careening from flop to flop. Robert and his relatives received bids from twenty producers before deciding on *Canterbury Tales* as "an appropriately upbeat" opening show for the Rialto. The musical closed in two weeks. A revival of the Yiddish theater classic, *The World of Sholem Aleichem,* lasted just twenty-two performances. These at least were respectable failures, decent plays that earned mixed reviews. *Marlowe,* on the other hand, was savaged by *Times* reviewer Frank Rich as "a wholly ridiculous show" that was so bad it was unintentionally entertaining. This rock musical about the life and times of Christopher "Kit" Marlowe, the Elizabethan playwright, featured a song and dance number in which Marlowe and "Willie" Shakespeare smoke marijuana given them by Sir Walter Raleigh, who'd scored it off Pocahontas. "The scraggly chorus of Elizabethan 'chroniclers,' wearing Day-Glo tights, performs dance routines that might be ragged run-throughs for a Jordache jeans commercial," Rich wrote. "They inhabit a balconied set that suggests how sixteenth-century England might have looked had cellophane, aluminum foil, and Con-Tac paper only been invented back then."

The Brandts might have been able to hang on longer had not the Broadway boom of 1973–1981 turned so abruptly to bust in 1982. It turned out that the "New Broadway" of the 1970s was no more an engine of permanent prosperity than the illusory "New Economy" of the 1990s. Attendance went into free fall as a barrage of truly awful plays finally triggered an audience revolt against years of relentless ticket price hikes. People stayed away in droves. The Brandts gave up on the Rialto first, reverting to film in the winter of 1982. The last play at the New Apollo, *The Guys in the Truck,* closed the day after it opened in June 1983. Soon, the Brandts quietly announced the return of motion pictures to the Apollo. "We can change the theater again overnight if a good play comes along," the ever-optimistic Levine said. But there would be no encore for the Brandt family, whose long 42nd Street run was drawing to an end.

West 42nd Street had been America's great movie street for longer than it had been America's great theater street. Yet 42DP had no use for movies whatsoever. The omission prompted many complaints at public hearings, but officials made only a minor concession, amending the redevelopment plan to provide that one or two of the restored theaters could be used for "first-run movies," but only "on an interim basis while being renovated or until theater use becomes feasible." The sociologist Herbert Gans, whom the Brandts hired as a consultant, argued that 42DP's aversion to film was revealing of its underlying agenda of "class-displacement . . . to move out lower-income citizens and taxpayers and to replace them with more affluent ones. This bias is so extensive that it even pervades the architectural jargon. For example, the bright lights that are now condemned as 'garish,' will after redevelopment supply 'glitter and excitement.'"

B movie fans from all around the country rallied to the suddenly urgent cause of 42nd Street grind house preservation. John Bloom, better known as "Joe Bob Briggs," author of the nationally syndicated column "Joe Bob Goes to the Drive-In," was particularly jazzed. Joe Bob urged his many readers to use "postcard fu" to pressure officials into saving the "one place in New York City you could see a decent drive-in movie." The 42nd Street movies houses rightfully belonged to all Americans, "or at least to all of us who have ever had to take grandma to see *Fiddler on the Roof,*" and should be preserved as places where "Charles Bronson can be seen thirty feet high, as God intended," he wrote. Briggs, a transplanted New Yorker, published a list of favorite memories of the Deuce: the sign on an all-night theater reading ADMISSIONS GOOD FOR 24 HOURS ONLY; a cannibalism movie called *Make Them Die Slowly* that ran for three years straight; and countless Italian horror films that "all starred Tony Franciosa and had a level of gore undreamed of by the makers of *Friday the 13th*."

The grind houses had no greater fan than Mark Jacobson, who had grown up in Queens but come of age on 42nd in the 1960s. "Ever since I could cut junior high school, I've been drawn to this place as if it were an electromagnet and I had a steel plate in my head," recalled Jacobson, who matured into a writer with a gift for Gonzo-style journalism. At age thirteen, he was accosted in the washroom of the Lyric Theater. "A huge guy with a fedora and a red nose came on my sweater while I was taking a piss during the intermission between two westerns," he wrote. "He was about to bear hug me when I zipped up and ran for the subway." A few days later, the boy tried to buy a switchblade on the Deuce but left the store empty-handed. The salesman kept "flicking gravity knives in my face," he recalled. "'How 'bout *this* one or *this* one?' the sadist asked over and over." A few years later, Jacobson witnessed a murder at the corner of 42nd and Eighth Avenue after a "wacko bum" stomped a blanketful of eyeglasses a female street peddler had laid out on the sidewalk. "The woman tried to stop him, and he knocked her to the ground," Jacobson wrote. "Then, quick, another man came out of the crowd and stuck a shiv in the bum's stomach. He bled and bled."

Ah, sweet memories. Long after his hooky-playing days ended, Jacobson kept returning to 42nd Street hunting fun with a rebel edge. One night in the 1970s, he found it on the back of a Triumph 650 motorcycle driven by a Vietnam vet, Jay from Avenue J. "Jay was up to speed before the Broadway intersection," Jacobson recalled.

We were airborne by the New Amsterdam. Passing the Lyric we began to swerve. At the Selwyn, I was halfway off the back end of the motorcycle. The next eternity was a nightmare of blurred black sky, streaking neon and swirling marquees all saying *Shaft*. Fisheye-faced dealers and chickenhawks with mossy mouths a mile wide yelled, "Jump!" But all of a sudden, the panic melted. I was floating, sailing unattached, spread-eagled like a trapeze flyer who doesn't care if the catcher's a lush as long as he gets the spotlight at the zenith. I was Icarus of sleaze street! Finally, after years of failed attempts, I knew I was about to put the critical inch between me and the middle class. . . . The exhilaration of that split second lasted long after Jay's arm pulled me back from the abyss and onto the vinyl seat.

But mostly Jacobson kept returning to the Deuce for the movies. "Forty-second Street was a genre freak's paradise, a sleazoid cinematheque," he rhapsodized.

> Who could care that eight-year-old boys were selling themselves in Grant's, or that pimps were beating their whores raw around the corner? Grunge paled in the presence of the Muse. . . . For every vicious little private eye-meller and shopworn western that turned up on the Street I loved the place more. I didn't care that the theatres smelled like the inside of a Lyon's House mattress. Or that people would jump on the stage and demand to know who threw a shoe and a saltshaker out of the balcony. I sat in the orchestra with the newspaper men and nobody ever bothered me but the snorers. The projection was better than in the $4 theatres on the East Side, and the price was right. But best of all, there were quirky planets inside those smelly theatres. The Street was a creep's Greyline tour though the Grade A and B obsessions that the movie mind had consolidated into genres. All you had to do was call out WAR! And the Harris had it.

The diminishing of B movie choice along the Deuce no longer seemed so dire a threat to Jacobson when first the City at 42nd Street and then 42DP came along to threaten his beloved "sleazoid cinematheque" with oblivion. In 1981, Jacobson interviewed Midtown Enforcement's Carl Weisbrod for a *Rolling Stone* feature entitled "Times Square: The Meanest Street in America." After delivering a long monologue on the indispensability of the grind houses, Jacobson offered Weisbrod some free advice. "If the city is really interested in the occult vibe in this country," the writer said, "they ought to nationalize Forty-second Street as a center for sleazological cinema studies." (Weisbrod, an affable former 1960s activist, played along. "That's funny," he said. "Remind me to mention that to the City Planning Commission.")

There was no doubting Mark Jacobson's passion for 42nd Street; his experience of it seems to have been incorporated into his very identity. But unlike his spiritual forebear, Herbert Huncke, he did not live on the Deuce, nor work there, nor own anything there. He was not even particularly welcome there, it would pain him to discover. For Jacobson and other members of what might be termed the hipster resistance to 42nd Street redevelopment, the grim actualities of the Deuce in the 1980s seemed to matter less than the *idea* of it as the ultimate antistreet. For them, the Deuce was an irredeemably, dangerously funky chunk of urban authenticity in a city led by a mayor in thrall to Big Real Estate. Jacobson was unusual among the 42nd Street preservationist intelligentsia in continuing to hang out on the Deuce throughout the 1980s and into his forties. But you did not have to actually roll in the gutter to take comfort in knowing it was there, affronting bourgeois pieties by its very existence.

To his credit, Jacobson recognized the inadequacy of his own advocacy, turning his *Rolling Stone* piece into a surprisingly self-critical quest to come up with a real answer to the parting question that Weisbrod had put to him: "Well, then, what would you do about 42nd Street?" The more time that the writer spent prowling the Deuce, the more he felt that he did not belong there, that he was slumming in what had turned into a black and Puerto Rican neighborhood. The article ended with Jacobson allowing himself to be mocked by a pimp of his acquaintance named Willie as they drank coffee out of styrofoam cups at a Blimpie's on 42nd Street.

"What the fuck is wrong with you? You on a sociology binge again? Don't you fucking ever give up?" Willie demanded. "Why don't you just go back down to St. Mark's Place and drink *cappuccino*?"

Jacobson persisted, asking Willie what he thought of the city's plans to replace people like him with office workers. "If I were a member of the landlord class, a Rockefeller, I wouldn't want me around either," Willie said. "Makes perfect logic."

But is it fair? Jacobson demanded.

"Fair? What's fair when you're a person like me?" Willie replied. "I'll go wherever it is. That's my life. If they move it to Lincoln, Nebraska, I'll be there. If they move it to China, I'll be there."

Unlike the Brandts, Mark Finkelstein never wanted in on the redevelopment of 42nd Street. Finkelstein, the late Max Cohen's accountant and business partner, had argued for years that there wasn't anything wrong with the Deuce that a police crackdown could not fix. "The city is not giving us law enforcement," he complained in late 1981. "It should be cleaning up the area so there's no dope peddling." A few months later, Finkelstein began negotiating to sell the New Amsterdam to the Nederlander Organization, Broadway's self-proclaimed "Avis" to the Shubert Organization's Hertz.

By the time that 42DP began offering up the old theaters for redevelopment, the Nederlanders owned ten Broadway houses and were keen to add more. James Nederlander and his four brothers were not unaware of the New Amsterdam's glorious past, but there was no romance in their ardor for "the House Beautiful" or in their attachment to the theater generally. The Nederlander definition of an excellent play was one that filled the seats. "Being a theater owner means you're in the moving business," Jimmy once explained. "You move 'em in, you move 'em out." The Nederlanders owned apartments on Park Avenue and had standing reservations at the 21 Club, but when it came to business, the brothers were famously frugal—not the Avis but the Rent-a-Wreck of Broadway. The trademarks of a Nederlander theater, one critic noted, were "worn-out seats and carpeting, unkempt ushers, crumbling drywall in the lobbies, and visible electrical tape."

The deal that Jimmy and his brother Robert cut in the early 1980s to acquire the New Amsterdam was shrewdly calculated to capitalize on the city's eagerness to revive 42nd Street. The Nederlanders did not have to shell out any cash because the New York City Industrial Development Agency, an arm of city government, stepped in and bought the theater from Finkelstein for $5.3 million. The agency then conveyed the New Amsterdam to the Nederlander Organization under a long-term lease. The family had to pay the interest on the bond issue that the Industrial Development Agency floated to finance its purchase—this amounted to $250,000 a year—and also had to cover the cost of restoring the theater out of its own pocket. In essence, though, the city had made a gift of the New Amsterdam to the Nederlanders in the hope that they would restore it to productive use. The Koch administration officially approved this arrangement in April 1982 by awarding the Nederlander Organization the 42DP redevelopment rights to both the New Amsterdam and the Harris, which Finkelstein still owned.

As the Brandts' attempt at reestablishing the legitimate theater on 42nd Street was sputtering to an end, the Nederlander clan, Broadway's pretenders, swaggered onto the Deuce in the spring of 1982 with ambitious plans of its own. Instead of waiting until 42DP had safely cleared its final political hurdle—Board of Estimate approval—Jimmy declared that renovation of the New Amsterdam would begin at once so that the main auditorium could be ready to reopen in the fall. "This is a structurally sound theater," echoed his brother, Robert Nederlander, a lawyer who was second in command to Jimmy. "We want to reopen it as soon as possible."

Robert had no good reason to be so confident about the theater's condition. Perhaps because they were essentially getting the New Amsterdam for free, the Nederlanders did not have the theater checked out until long after they had bought it. The structural engineer they finally brought in, Robert Silman, was top-notch. Jimmy also hired Roger Morgan, a leading theater designer, and the architecture firm of Ehrenkrantz Eckstut & Kuhn, theater experts. The Nederlanders hired the best, but they kept them tightly leashed to a chintzy budget. "Jimmy kept saying it's a $1.5 million deal, a $1.5 million deal," recalled Theo Prudon, the Ehrenkrantz Eckstut architect assigned to the project.

Morgan, who had renovated historic theaters all over the country, marveled at the magnificence of the New Amsterdam. "The construction of that building is unbelievably elegant; it is one of the most beautifully put together theaters I have ever seen," Morgan recalled. But the New Amsterdam now was seventy-six years old and looked it. As Silman began drilling exploratory probes in the base of the theater's supporting columns, Morgan and Prudon planned the restoration of the 1,700-seat main auditorium. They worked under a tight deadline, for Jimmy not only wanted the theater to begin generating income in short order, but also kept titillating the press with the particulars of his plans for shows. Jimmy's original prediction—that the New Amsterdam would reopen in the fall of 1982—was quickly exposed as impractical. At year-end, the Nederlanders amended their plans: the theater would reopen in the fall of 1983 with a Ziegfeld-like revue called *The New Amsterdam Follies*. A month later, Jimmy's credibility began fraying in earnest. Forget the *Follies,* he said, the first booking will be a revival of *Mame.*

Jimmy's focus shifted abruptly from the New Amsterdam's downstairs auditorium to its roof garden theater when director Peter Brook took a shine to Flo Ziegfeld's old haunt. Brook, who was famous for staging productions in dilapidated settings, wanted to use the roof garden for the American debut of *La Tragédie de Carmen,* his reworking of Georges Bizet's opera *Carmen.* Brook wanted a space that felt like an arena and sent over an architect from Paris, his base, to assist Morgan and Prudon. The team designed a 499-seat theater with tightly cupped seating that required the demolition of the remnants of the old balcony and construction of a new one. Crews began pouring cement before the methodical Silman had examined the roof of the building and before a budget for the project could be hashed out in tense meetings at the Palace between Nederlander executives and their advisers. Arthur Rubin, the theater company's general manager, ran the sessions, with the nattily attired Jimmy making cameo appearances, entering the dimly lit conference room stage left and exiting stage right. Jimmy rarely sat down, staying only long enough to remind one and all that he was prepared to spend $1.5 million and no more.

In May 1983, Jimmy hosted a celebrity-packed champagne reception on the roof theater's new stage and announced that *La Tragédie de Carmen* would open October 24. The roof "is exactly what we were looking for," Brook said. "It is a rough, undefined space that leaves the imagination free. . . . It is a rough story and this is a rough place and a rough location."

A few weeks after the reception, Silman finally worked his way up to large boxlike trusses on the roof of the New Amsterdam. The new balcony under construction was not supported by the floor but hung from these trusses. Silman had uncovered a lot of water damage to various steel structural supports in the lower floors, but nothing as extensive as the corrosion he found in the trusses. The bottom core of most of these ten-foot girders had rusted clean through, weakening them dangerously. Repairing the trusses was essential but would delay the completing of the new roof theater by several months and add at least $1 million in cost. However, Peter Brook could not wait and the Nederlanders would not pay. Jimmy ordered a halt to the remodeling job. "The Nederlanders produce shows," Prudon said. "I don't think they were prepared to produce a building."

Down and Dirty on the Deuce

Sony Corporation had introduced the first videocassette recorder in 1975, the year that Marty Hodas was convicted of tax evasion. Like most truly revolutionary new consumer technology, the VCR was slow to catch on. It had not put an appreciable dent in the 42nd Street porn trade by the time Hodas returned to New York in early 1977 after serving his prison sentence for tax evasion. But, in the 1980s, it would be all downhill for Hodas and most of his customers, as the number of American homes with VCRs soared to forty million by 1987, from three million in 1979. The popularity of home viewing—of cable television as well as videocassettes—brought huge overall growth to the porn business even as it undermined its established storefront distribution network. Why risk a trip to Times Square when you could rent X-rated videos and watch them at home?

The Darwinian dynamic of the Times Square sex business in the 1980s was plainly evident in the diverging fortunes of Marty Hodas and Richard Basciano, his successor as the Kingpin of 42nd Street smut. With the dwindling of his peep show supply business in Times Square, Hodas went in search of new markets to conquer and discovered a large one to the north called Canada. He negotiated a deal to transport 1,700 XXX videocassettes to Toronto via Buffalo, but he was arrested when his customer turned out to be not an aspiring porn entrepreneur but a Royal Canadian Mounted Police corporal working undercover. The authorities dubbed the five-month sting "Operation Blizzard" in reference to Hodas's supposed desire to "blanket Canada with pornography," as the U.S. attorney in Buffalo put it. In 1984, Hodas pleaded guilty to a charge of conspiring to ship obscene material across state lines and was sentenced to a year in the federal penitentiary in Lewisburg, Pennsylvania. In anger and frustration, Hodas sold his seven remaining Times Square properties to Basciano for one-third of their market value. "I don't want to have anything to do ever again with the porn business," Hodas told a reporter. "It's shown me nothing but misery."

The Times Square porn trade was not unlike a game of musical chairs, with dozens of owner-operators rotating through the same bookstore/peep show/movie theater locations one after the other. Many contenders simply could not cut it as businessmen, while others ran afoul of Midtown Enforcement or their own gangster partners. When the music finally stopped—that is, when the government condemned a vast swath of 42nd Street in the early 1990s for 42DP—it was Richard Carmello Basciano who sat atop the golden throne of Times Square smut. Eight of the seventeen buildings that Basciano owned in the Times Square area were located within the 42nd Street urban renewal zone. In the end, New York State would pay Basciano about $20 million in cash for these properties—three or four times more than he had paid for them. Yet this was the smaller part of the $100 million fortune he amassed over the years by using his porn profits to buy commercial properties in Philadelphia, Baltimore, and Boca Raton, as well as New York.

From the mid-1970s into the 1990s, city, state, and federal law enforcement would probe the surfaces of Basciano's lucrative franchise in Times Square, looking for a structural defect that could be exploited to put him out of business or, better yet, behind bars. Basciano's education had stopped at high school, but the Baltimore native was a disciplined, meticulous operator who created a fortress of a XXX business, impregnable to the assaults of prosecutors and competitors alike. "We did sometimes cite him for fire code or health violations, but by the next day he'd ask for a reinspection because the violation would have been cured," said Midtown Enforcement's Bill Daly. "If anyone working at one of his places were arrested for prostitution, he would fire them. At one time, there was a rumor that one of his most trusted lieutenants was dealing coke to his girls. He fired him, too. Whether it was Basciano's doing or his lawyer's, they knew exactly what they could and could not get away with."

Basciano kept an apartment above his largest establishment, Show World Center, complete with gym and regulation-size boxing ring. But unlike many of his porno peers, Basciano was all-business. "The difference between Richie and the others is that he was not interested in me physically," recalled Amy, a dancer/prostitute who worked many of Times Square's live sex theaters. "He didn't even 'hey, sweetheart' me or try to cop a feel." To get a job at Show World, Amy had to produce her passport, fill out a W-2 withholding form, and promise to report all of her income to the IRS. "I think some of the girls were dating his friends, but Richie was always pure business. He was not a double-talker, and he didn't mince words. If you did right by him, he'd do right by you."

Basciano had two main business partners: Sam Rappaport, who for many years was the ranking commercial slum lord of Philadelphia; and Robert "DB" Di Bernardo, a Gambino family member who was considered the most powerful Mafia porn boss in America when he suddenly vanished in 1986. In the end, Basciano would outlast or outmaneuver everyone: his Times Square competitors, city and state redevelopment officials, the NYPD, the FBI, and organized crime. No wonder Hodas was jealous. "Basciano was a very, very nice guy when I first met him—humble, not much money," Hodas recalled. "But as the years went by and he got both rich and powerful his attitude changed, and naturally not towards the better."

Actually, there is no indication whatsoever that success corrupted Basciano's disciplined approach to the smut trade, but he was quick to take offense when not accorded the respect he believed was his due as a "man of honor." Rebecca Robertson, who would run the 42nd Street redevelopment project for the state, experienced "a spasm of moral outrage" the first time she met Basciano and could not bring herself to shake the hand the pornographer extended in greeting. Basciano stomped off and sent a formal letter of complaint to Robertson's boss, Vincent Tese, head of the state's Urban Development Corporation. A chastened Robertson had to telephone Basciano and apologize. They got on famously thereafter. "If you were receptive to Richie, he'd treat you with extreme courtesy, almost friendship," Roberston said.

Biographical information about Basciano is scant. Born Carmello Richard Basciano in Baltimore in 1925, he came from a family that had distinguished itself only in the boxing ring. His father, Nicholas J. Basciano, was a hard-punching middleweight who compiled a 35–5 record as a professional and was famous in his day for knocking out two opponents in a single night. One of Richie's maternal uncles, Salvatore Ranzino, had contended for the national featherweight title. The boy strapped on the gloves at an early age, starting out as a middleweight but moving up in class as he grew to five feet eleven and 190 pounds. "He was one hell of a fighter," recalled Lou Levy, a Baltimore boxing coach who knew him well. Basciano enlisted in the army as soon as he turned eighteen in 1943 and, according to one of his lawyers, saw combat in both the European and Asian theaters. Returning to Baltimore, he married in 1949. He went to work at the *Baltimore Sun*, rising to the position of street sales supervisor. At some point, Basciano left the *Sun* to start his own newsstand, his portal into porn. By 1964, he was doing well enough to move out of Baltimore and buy a house in the affluent suburb of Glen Burnie.

In 1967, Basciano was convicted of a crime for the first and only time. A federal grand jury in Baltimore indicted him on thirty-eight counts of mail fraud, a misdemeanor. He pleaded nolo contendere on four counts and got off with a fine of $750 and three years' probation. According to the government's complaint, from 1961 to 1966 Basciano conspired to defraud General Foods, Johnson & Johnson, Campbell Soup, and other consumer products giants that used coupons to promote sales. Basciano collected coupons in bulk and sold them at a discount to grocers who then redeemed them at face value. By all indications, this was a penny-ante scheme involving five dollars here or twenty dollars there, suggesting either that Basciano was extraordinarily greedy or that he was not yet getting rich selling XXX books and magazines. In any event, he behaved himself during his probation and was discharged on schedule in 1969.

It appears that Basciano first met Sam Rappaport in the mid-1960s. Basciano had opened an adult bookstore in downtown Philadelphia in a building that Rappaport later bought, according to Morris P. Hershman, a lawyer for Rappaport, who was a few years younger than Basciano. "They got to know each other first as landlord and tenant and over time became friends and business partners," Hershman said. Rappaport, who had started as a shoe shine boy in Brooklyn, was a nasty piece of work. In 1960, he and two other men were convicted of mail fraud in what a U.S. district court judge called "the worst criminal case to come before this court in all my years of service." Rappaport was sentenced to a year in prison for his part in swindling 371 companies out of $100,000 through a series of dummy companies. In 1963, Rappaport attacked his wife in a courthouse during divorce proceedings, breaking her jaw with a punch.

From his hotheaded friend, Basciano learned the art of speculating in distressed real estate. Rappaport, who sported a diamond-studded belt buckle in the shape of the Rolls-Royce logo, amassed a fortune of more than $100 million by buying decrepit buildings in depressed areas of Philadelphia that seemed ripest for eventual redevelopment. Rappaport squeezed maximum rents out of his properties while making minimal improvements—an approach that inevitably made him a landlord to many adult bookstores and XXX theaters. He labored to keep his name out of the newspapers but made himself a target of civic outrage by allowing landmark buildings to deteriorate. Rappaport was nothing if not audacious. As the *Philadelphia Inquirer* put it, "Complaints of neighbors, historians and city officials fell on deaf ears while Mr. Rappaport appealed to the city to lower his property taxes."

Basciano invested alongside Rappaport in several commercial properties in Philadelphia, including Jerry's Corner, an indoor market near the airport. But on 42nd Street, the partners used a different strategy. Typically, Rappaport would buy a property and then transfer, or "flip," it to Basciano and Di Bernardo. It's not clear why this approach was taken, since Rappaport hardly afforded a respectable front. But the flipping stopped in the late 1970s, and Basciano began buying Times Square real estate directly.

The origin of Basciano's association with the Mafia is murky, but law enforcement officials believe that he already was connected when he landed in New York in the late 1960s, perhaps through Rappaport, who had ties to the Philadelphia Mafia family headed by Angelo Bruno. "What I'd heard was that the five families in New York made a deal with the Philly mob to share the porn trade here, and that's how Basciano came up from Baltimore," Daly said. "Nobody from the police ever said that Basciano was a member of the Bruno family. But he was always said to be involved, and I'm sure he was."

Hodas recalled that when he first met Basciano in the late 1960s, he was working a sales job at Star Distributing, the hub of Di Bernardo's pornography empire. The Star firm occupied a huge warehouse on

Broome Street on the fringes of the SoHo district and, by most accounts, was the largest and most profitable wholesaler of pornography in the country. Basciano left Star's employ in 1969 to open the first of a string of bookstores that included 101 Book Center (at 101 West 42nd Street), Civic Paper Back (103 West 42nd), 1111 Book Center (on Avenue of the Americas, near 42nd), and 1605 Book Center (on Broadway and 49th). In 1972, the Dursts evicted 101 Book Center and locked Basciano out of the premises. Hodas, who had peep machines in all of Basciano's stores, joined with his customer in suing the Durst Organization for $4 million in damages. In a sworn affidavit, Basciano sounded a lot like Hodas in accusing his landlords of using "discriminatory tactics totally unjustified in law and befitting only a Gestapo State." But because Basciano wisely shunned the media spotlight, he did not provoke the wrath of law enforcement the way that Hodas did until well after he opened Show World Center in 1975. "When Show World opened, they were still going after me, not Basciano," Hodas complained. "They didn't know from Basciano."

Occupying 22,000 square feet on the bottom four floors of a narrow twelve-story building on Eighth Avenue between 42nd and 43rd Streets, Show World was the largest sex venue in New York City, if not America. It was the XXX equivalent of a Sears or a Wal-Mart, a superstore offering one-stop shopping for the bargain-hunting consumer. Show World had it all: twenty-four film and twelve live peep show booths the size of telephone booths; live sex shows of both heterosexual and homosexual bent; every hard-core magazine and film loop on the market; and every sexual aid imaginable. But it wasn't size alone that separated Show World from the typical Times Square "scumatorium." Show World's wide, well-lit aisles, its gleaming surfaces of steel and Formica, and its spotless tile floors would have made any customer of Safeway or 7-Eleven feel at home. It took a year and a half and $400,000 to transform an ancient hardware store into Show World, and it showed. Here was the prototype of a new breed of sex emporium designed to entice middle-class customers while confounding city inspectors.

Show World was an instant success, attracting four thousand customers a day. Over the next two decades, Show World would be the first establishment to adapt to most every innovation in the dwindling Times Square XXX market, if it did not pioneer it itself. Show World even created its own currency, an octagonal, twenty-five-cent token inscribed with

"World's Greatest Showplace." All over Midtown, these tokens were left in taxicab ashtrays and telephone booth change slots and strewn across parking lots and subway platforms—telltale evidence ditched by Show World customers heading home to their women. Nothing would have burnished Mayor Koch's porn-busting credentials like putting Show World out of business, but the mayor wisely resisted the temptation to gerrymander 42DP's boundaries to include it. Buying out Show World would have boosted the project's cost, for Times Square's largest pornotorium remained highly profitable, the emergence of the VCR notwithstanding. In fact, the advent of video worked to Show Center's benefit by winnowing the ranks of its competitors. The average Joe might now prefer his own living room to the average porn store, but Show World was a labyrinthine funhouse not replicable at home, and its superstore format easily accommodated one of the city's largest selections of X-rated videocassettes.

In mid-1986, Basciano's partner and protector, Robert Di Bernardo, vanished without a trace. Basciano was said to be fond of DB, who was an unconventional mobster in many ways. He'd finished high school, for one thing, graduating in 1955, and would have gone on to college had he not succumbed to the siren call of the Brooklyn rackets. DB was the anti-Gotti in the sense that business acumen rather than brute force powered his rise. He made money in restaurants and in auto repair but first made a name for himself as a "big earner" in pornography, building New York–based Star Distributing into the largest wholesale supplier in the country. Di Bernardo also owned minority interests in dozens of retail XXX outlets, including most of Basciano's places. DB's porn business was his own, not part of the Gambino portfolio. His essential role within the family was as Godfather Paul Castellano's emissary to the International Brotherhood of Teamsters' Local 282, which represented the drivers of concrete-mixing trucks. Through its control of Local 282, the Gambino family extorted kickbacks from every big construction job in New York City. Di Bernardo shared responsibility for this exceptionally lucrative racket with hit man Sammy "the Bull" Gravano, who would laud DB posthumously as "a brilliant, wealthy guy."

Di Bernardo commuted daily to Star Distributing's offices in SoHo from his million-dollar estate on the water in Hewlett Harbor, one of Long Island's Five Towns. The typical Mafioso rarely rolled out of bed before noon, but DB was behind the wheel of his white Mercedes sedan every morning by 9:00 at the latest and usually made it home in time for dinner with his wife and kids. On Saturdays, he coached Little League baseball; his youngest, Robert II, was an excellent pitcher. Tall and slender, Di Bernardo cut a slick figure in his pinstripe suits and calfskin loafers, and had the manners to match. "DB was always a real gentleman, very polite, even in his dealings with the FBI," recalled former agent J. Bruce Mouw, who spent many years investigating the Gambino family.

DB might not have looked the part, but he was a gangster, and he proved it by conspiring with John Gotti, Gravano, and a handful of others to plot the assassination of Castellano in late 1985. "DB is our messenger back and forth, the in-between guy," Gravano recalled. "He's giving us information about Paul. . . . He's involved in some of these conversations in the beginning stages. Then we exclude him because he's not a hit guy. He's an earner, but he's got no crew, no strength and power." Gotti, the new godfather, showed his gratitude to DB by ordering Sammy the Bull to kill him. Gotti "worried about DB taking his position," Mouw said. "DB was one sharp guy and the other families liked and respected him."

On June 5, 1986, DB left Star Distributing's office in SoHo in mid-afternoon and drove to Brooklyn for a 5:30 P.M. meeting at Sammy the Bull's place. "I sent the girl in my office home at five," Gravano recalled. "Me, my brother-in-law, Eddie, and Old Man Paruta were there. DB came in and said hello. I told Paruta to get him a cup of coffee. In the cabinet, there was a .380 with a silencer. Paruta took it out, walked over to DB, and shot him twice in the back of the head. We picked up DB and put him in a body bag we got from the Scarpaci funeral parlor. We locked it in the back room." When Gravano turned state's evidence and testified against Gotti in 1991, the Bull would admit to seventeen murders, including DB's.

With Di Bernardo out of the way, Gravano assumed sole responsibility for Local 282 and was named underboss of the Gambino family. But neither Gotti nor Gravano knew the smut trade or took an interest in DB's pornography business. A few midlevel Gambino soldiers did try to muscle Basciano but found that he was not easily intimidated. "They made some inquiries but didn't get very far and gave up," Mouw said.

Di Bernardo's interests in Star Distributing and in Basciano's operation passed to his six children, though the disposition of his estate was delayed by the absence of a corpse. (DB was officially an "absentee" until he was declared legally dead in 1993; his remains still have not been found.) Basciano offered to buy out DB's heirs for $600,000 cash, payable over five years. An independent accountant named Robert D. Baron testified that $600,000 was a fair price given the difficulties of valuing a XXX business. "These businesses may not be saleable in the normal sense," Baron declared. "It may not be reasonable therefore to assign any good will value. The only real value may be the tangible salvage value of the fixed assets if liquidated." Basciano agreed to make additional payments to DB's kids if 210-212 and 259 West 42nd Street were condemned by the government for 42DP. In valuing DB's interest in 210-212 at a mere $1,800, Baron properly assigned no value to Basciano's negotiating skills. But the porn dealer would get $10 million for the buildings, enriching DB's heirs by $1.6 million.

Even as the Midtown massage parlor neared extinction in the mid-1980s, Bob Brown's reports began documenting a sharp increase in juvenile prostitution on 42nd Street. Homeless minors had been turning tricks along the Deuce for decades, but there were more of them now and they were younger than before and more brazenly pimped on street corners and in the arcades and fast-food restaurants. "Street kids start their day in the afternoon," wrote Trudee Able-Peterson, a former prostitute who founded the not-for-profit Streetwork Project in 1984 to tend to the street kids in Times Square.

> Some of their friends might be lucky enough to have had the $2.99 required to get into the all-night theater down the block and are still sleeping on the sticky floors. When the noises of the daytime life most of us lead finally penetrates their drug/alcohol/street life consciousness, they shiver, stretch and head for the commuter bathrooms to relieve themselves. If they have spent all the money they made from prostituting or begging or stealing to buy crack, or speed, or pot, or downs, or crystal, they are broke and need another pipe, or needle, or pill, or joint. They go back to the stroll.

Streetwork Project operated on a much smaller scale than did Covenant House, which was the largest and best-known private agency for runaways in the entire country. Father Bruce Ritter, a Franciscan priest, had founded Covenant House in a skid row apartment on the

Lower East Side in 1969. Ritter shifted his base of operations to Times Square in the late 1970s, but not before a walk on 42nd Street nearly caused him to flee the country. "I found myself in Times Square—Eighth Avenue and Forty-second Street—one sultry July night in 1975, about 1:00 in the morning. I became very afraid," Ritter recalled.

> I don't remember now why I was there. Perhaps I had gone to the theater with a friend. The streets were awash with people: drifters, nomads, hustlers, pimps, street people, gawkers from the suburbs. The violence, the foreboding—the air of malevolence—was actually palpable. Standing on the corner of Eighth Avenue and Forty-second Street I became aware of this very powerful, gut-wrenching conviction that if I remained in child care, I was going to wind up in Times Square with these people. I felt as though I had been kicked. I decided on the spot to resign from Covenant House. India was the answer. I would go to India!

After his 42nd Street revelation, the charismatic, melancholic Ritter chose a successor and began taking flying lessons, intending to buy a used plane and fly himself to India. But before he could put this crackpot scheme into motion, the Times Square Community Planning Board asked Covenant House to open a shelter for runaway girls. The request revived Ritter's flagging ambition. "I said to the local community board that what you really need in Times Square is a crisis center for kids," he recalled. "Someplace they can come and get the no-questions-asked help they need twenty-four hours a day."

In search of a building for such a center, Ritter walked every block from 34th Street to 59th Street and from Sixth Avenue to Eleventh Avenue. At 692 Eighth Avenue, a bit north of 43rd Street, the priest found a pair of large, empty buildings connected by a catwalk. For years, this had been the headquarters of the Christian and Missionary Alliance, a Protestant evangelical group that sent missionaries all over the world. But by the mid-1970s the area had gotten so depraved that the Alliance had moved out to a sylvan locale in Westchester County and put its Times Square property on the market. Offers from porn operators poured in as the missionaries prayed with increasing fervency for a respectable buyer, never imagining that a Roman Catholic priest would deliver them from evil. Ritter paid about $1 million for the buildings, borrowing the funds needed from his superiors in the Catholic Church and from a private foundation. Ritter renovated the beautiful old chapel and remodeled the rest of the space into office quarters and a storefront youth crisis center he called Under 21. "My staff is forbidden to turn anyone under the age of twenty-one away," Father Ritter declared. "If they do, I fire them."

Under 21 was not intended to be a dormitory, but many of the kids who dropped in were homeless and did not want to leave until morning. Soon, forty or fifty kids a night were sleeping on cots and large cushions on the floor of the center, and another twenty or so were curled up on the chapel floor or in the pews. Some five hundred kids cycled through Under 21 in its first month alone, five thousand during its first year. Most had become cogs in the wheel of what Ritter called "the billion-dollar Times Square sex industry," an industry centered, in Father Bruce's view, on "Forty Deuce."

A bundle of nervous energy, Ritter rarely slept and walked the Deuce into the wee hours. "I went out again about two in the morning to get a bite to eat, and stepped over the drunk in my doorway," he recalled in one diary installment. "There were seventeen (I counted them) prostitutes across the street, moving slowly back and forth. It was a warm night, and the streets were crowded with hundreds of the night people, washing up and down the littered sidewalk. There was an indescribable sense of violence and electric tension, a fascination, the anticipation of something about to happen." Outside a porn store on 42nd Street, Ritter came across a group of seven boys. He recalled that the eldest, a sixteen-year-old working as a runner for a pimp, "touched me on the arm. 'Which one do you want?' he asked. 'You can have any one you want for twenty dollars.' I said I wasn't into that, but he didn't believe me. He called over one of the kids. 'Take this one,' he said. 'You'll like this one. His name is Nandy. He's eleven.'"

This runner knew a hard case when he saw one, even if he was wearing a clerical collar. Rumors of Ritter's sexual misconduct with boys in Covenant House's care began circulating within the child care community in the early 1970s but would not burgeon into public scandal until 1989. The priest would resign in disgrace from Covenant House without ever admitting to any of his well-documented transgressions or, for that matter, acknowledging his homosexuality, but it had not required much reading between the lines of his newsletters to realize that this was a deeply conflicted man attracted to and repulsed by the debauchery of 42nd Street in roughly equal measure. Succumbing to sin even as he compulsively did the Lord's work, Father Bruce ignored the advice that his aged mother persisted in giving him: "He who touches pitch will be defiled by it."

Father Bruce did not hesitate to use hard-knuckled and conniving tactics to advance Covenant House's agenda of charity and kindness. In 1979, Ritter decided to expand Under 21 and began negotiating to buy or lease a building on 44th Street, just down the block from one of Broadway's great theaters, the St. James. The League of New York Theaters and Producers and various community groups strenuously objected to Ritter's plan and asked the city to stop Covenant House's expansion. A formidable political street fighter from way back, Father Bruce countered with a threat to open a soup kitchen for the homeless of all ages on the corner of 44th Street and Eighth Avenue. "My heart rejoiced," he acidly observed in one of his columns, "at the thought of a couple hundred Times Square derelicts lined up in the lobby of the St. James Theatre."

Mayor Koch intervened, offering to find Covenant House new quarters safely removed from the Shubert blocks. Ritter refused to close Under 21's storefront on Eighth Avenue but did agree to house the kids who slept in Covenant House at another, more suitable location. Koch had engineered a compromise, but he did not carry through on his promise to help Ritter find an expansion site. Father Bruce started looking himself and soon discovered that a state agency was about to vacate a complex of three 8-story buildings that occupied the entire block front between 40th and 41st Streets on Tenth Avenue—the heart of Fred Papert country. This was the former Congress Riviera Motel built by Irving Maidman in 1961 and later condemned by the state for use as a jail for narcotics offenders. The center was shutting down, and the New York City Department of Corrections wanted to use the building as a jail. Ritter appealed to Governor Hugh Carey, a devout Catholic, who decided that providing a safe haven for Times Square runaways was a higher use than relieving overcrowding in the city's jails. The state leased the complex to Covenant House for $1 for five years.

By the mid-1980s Covenant House's twin outposts in Times Square were the hubs of an international organization with crisis centers in fifteen cities, including Fort Lauderdale, New Orleans, Anchorage, Toronto, and Guatemala City, Guatemala. Father Bruce's empire building rubbed a lot of other youth-care professionals the wrong way. Covenant House's centers were considered too big and haphazardly administered to be safe, much less effective in rehabilitating street kids, especially since Father Bruce typically insisted on locating them in the worst part of town. Ritter's newsletters were filled with touching anecdotes about the very young kids who sought shelter at Covenant House. But most of his "clients"—as many as 80 percent, by some estimates—were legally emancipated eighteen-, nineteen-, and twenty-year-olds. For many of them, Covenant House was little more than a free bed conveniently located to the crime center that was 42nd Street. According to Charles Sennott, Ritter's biographer, the police department developed "a simmering antagonism with Ritter in part because of a perception that the charity harbored young criminals who operated in the Times Square area."

Despite the backlash building on the street, Ritter's prodigious talents for direct-mail fund-raising and self-serving publicity burnished Covenant House's reputation to a high gloss. President Ronald Reagan praised Father Bruce as an "unsung hero" in his 1984 State of the Union Address, and Mother Teresa was among the many luminaries who toured Covenant House's Times Square facilities. By decade's end, the charity had amassed a list of 800,000 donors and an annual budget of $85 million—three times the sum that the federal government was spending on runaways.

The Times Square runaways were products not only of neglect and abuse but also of the rampant homelessness among New York's poor. As late as the 1960s, the city's vagrants were predominantly down-and-out older white men who congregated along the Bowery, with its mile-long skid row of flophouses, missions, and rough taverns. But in the 1970s, visible homelessness began spreading in every sense as many marginal neighborhoods throughout the city were gentrified, eliminating 100,000 rooms in single-room-occupancy hotels and driving up rental rates. Reagan's election in 1980 brought a series of sharp cuts in federal support for low- and moderate-income families around the country. By 1988, 100,000 families were illegally doubled up in apartments in New York City and another 5,200 families had no place to live at all. A random survey of Times Square street kids in 1987 found that 70 percent of them were from one of the five boroughs, usually Brooklyn or the Bronx.

The city's homeless shelters were unable to handle the deluge, prompting the Koch administration to put up hundreds of families—most of which consisted of single mothers with kids—in fifty-five decrepit "welfare" hotels. Three of them were on the Deuce: the Holland Hotel at

352 West 42nd, the Hotel Carter at 250 West 43rd, and the Times Square Motor Hotel at 255 West 43rd. In the name of political and financial expediency, the city funneled hundreds of impressionable young children and rebellious teens into the cauldron of vice and degradation that was 42nd Street in the 1980s. "It's got to be one of the rottenest places in the world to grow up. It's a street right out of hell," Ritter warned. "It's the largest classroom in the world for the teaching of depravity." Father Bruce had a point, though he seemed oblivious to the fact that his kids were taking instruction in the same school. Whether they slept in the Hotel Carter or at Under 21 a block away, a growing percentage of the underage prostitutes and drug dealers on the Deuce were not runaways but residents, as it were.

In the summer of 1984, the *Times'* Maureen Dowd spent an afternoon at the Hotel Carter, which, with 640 rooms, was the city's largest welfare hotel. In front of the hotel, "there were children everywhere, hanging off the door of the Rose Saigon restaurant, swinging on fire hydrants, wrestling in piles of beer cans in paper bags," Dowd wrote.

> Angel, 4 years old, played with an empty Bacardi rum bottle. Ann, 6, mimicked a common sight on the street, pursing her lips and sucking in, as though dragging on a marijuana cigarette. Michael, 9, held on to his baby sister's carriage and watched wide-eyed as police officers led away a handcuffed woman, in a purple jumpsuit, screaming obscenities. . . . It is jarring to listen to the children's conversations, so peppered with the imagery of violence. "I call it the murdering area," said Jennifer Riccardi, 10. "A man tried to touch me," said her friend, Tara Smith, a small 9-year-old in a pink ruffled dress. "Two days ago on the corner they stabbed a man," said Eddie Baker, 14. "At night, the big teen-age dudes have bum rushes, ripping off old people, snatching pocketbooks and stuff," said Clarence Simpson, 11. "It gets me nuts— the pushing, pulling, scratching, raping, kicking fighting," says Luis Carion, 8. "To death it scares me."

The Carter was owned by a hard-bitten Vietnamese refugee named Tran Dinh Truong, who had arrived in the United States shortly after the fall of Saigon, carrying two suitcases full of gold. This much about the mysterious Truong was agreed upon: during the war he had run the Vishipco Line, a big South Vietnamese shipping company in Saigon. But was he a war profiteer, as alleged by one of his own captains and a top officer in the South Vietnamese Navy, or a war hero, as he himself maintained? The *Times* did not attempt to answer this question until 1994, when it shredded Truong's claim that he had used Vishipco's cargo fleet to evacuate thousands of his countrymen along with American soldiers and civilians as South Vietnam finally fell to the North Vietnamese forces in the spring of 1975. "First of all, there weren't any soldiers left in 1975," Richard Armitrage, the American official who ran the U.S. Navy evacuation, told the *Times*. "Second, we didn't use merchant ships to carry American civilians."

In New York, Truong added a new line to his résumé: welfare hotel slumlord. He parlayed his gold bars into ownership of three foundering hotels in New York City—the Carter, the Kenmore, and the Long Acre—and one in Buffalo. He made the Hotel Carter his headquarters, living there with his wife in a three-room suite. Truong's basic business strategy was to squeeze profit out of his hotels by cutting to the bone expenditures on security, maintenance, and repairs. "He just bleeds these places dry," said Daly of Midtown Enforcement, which clashed repeatedly with the notoriously uncooperative Truong. No building within the 42DP renewal zone was more deserving of condemnation than the Carter, but emergency shelter for the homeless was in such short supply that the Koch administration excluded the hotel from the project. Truong drove a hard bargain, requiring the city to pay luxury-apartment rental rates of $1,700 to $1,800 per room even as he amassed hundreds of health, safety, and building code violations and fell hundreds of thousands of dollars behind on his property taxes.

Thanks to the prospect of government-sponsored redevelopment, the land under the Hotel Carter soared in value in the 1980s even as the hotel itself fell apart. By some estimates, the market value of the land just outside 42DP's boundaries tripled in value from 1980 to 1984. This delighted Father Ritter no less than it did Tran Dinh Truong. Covenant House could have reaped many millions in profits had it chosen to sell Under 21's buildings and adjoining properties on 44th Street. Instead, Father Bruce decided to double down on the Deuce, paying $17 million in late 1984 to buy the Times Square Motor Hotel on the corner of 43rd and Eighth Avenue, across the street from the Hotel Carter. There were not many charities that aspired to fattening their endowments by speculating in real estate, but Father Bruce was not called "the Donald Trump of Catholicism" for nothing.

Like the Carter, the vast, yellow-brick Times Square was a relic from the Roaring Twenties that had seen better days, as evidenced by the spiral staircase and 1820 grandfather clock that still graced its lobby. By the time Covenant House bought the Times Square, it was New York City's largest surviving single-room-occupancy hotel. Elderly longtime tenants and former mental patients paying as little as $85 a month under rent control occupied 400 of its 740 rooms. The rest of the rooms were made available to budget-minded travelers, but the Times Square averaged 200 to 300 vacancies a night after the warm-weather tourist season ended. The investment bank Salomon Brothers advised Ritter that the land under the hotel soon might be worth as much as $40 million, if sold to a single developer. While awaiting an opportune moment to "flip" the Times Square, Ritter laid plans to remodel three of its fourteen floors into office space for Covenant House and turn two more floors into yet another shelter for homeless young adults.

In mid-1985, a few months after Ritter closed on the purchase of the Times Square Motor Hotel, the City Council imposed a five-year moratorium on SRO conversions. Covenant House suddenly found itself walled into the SRO business, losing money at the rate of $3 million a year, with no exit in sight. "I'm trapped," Father Bruce lamented. Covenant House tried to cut its losses by reducing operating expenses and booting welfare tenants at the slightest provocation. Dennis Katz, a disabled veteran, was served with an eviction notice when his government check was late. Katz was so disgusted that he finally decided to move out rather than fight. "Don't let that collar fool you," he said. "Father Ritter should be in a gray suit."

In November 1987, the Koch administration announced that the city was going to buy the Times Square Motor Hotel and convert it into a combination homeless residence and work-release jail. If Covenant House would not sell at a reasonable price, the mayor's minions warned, the city would use its powers of eminent domain to seize the hotel. The city offered $20 million, a bit more than what Covenant House had paid, but never received a definitive response. Instead, Ritter sold the Times Square for $21 million to International Hostel Corp., which earlier had leased part of the hotel. International Hostel put down a mere $500,000 and obtained a mortgage from Covenant House. Koch was furious but wisely chose not to follow through on his condemnation threat.

Within six months, the new owners had defaulted and put the Times Square Motor Hotel into Chapter 11 bankruptcy, leaving Covenant House holding the bag as its largest creditor. Although the hotel now was available for much less than $20 million, the city had no interest in bailing out Ritter. The bankruptcy court received just one bid to operate the hotel, from none other than Tran Dinh Truong. Over the vehement objections of Times Square's tenants and of city officials who cited Truong's "misconduct, gross mismanagement and/or incompetence" in running the Hotel Carter, a federal bankruptcy judge approved Truong's managerial takeover of the Times Square in 1988.

The Times Square's new operator made Father Bruce seem munificent by comparison, cutting the number of housekeepers to six, from twenty; janitors to three, from sixteen; and security guards to three, from ten. The reports filed by the examiner that the bankruptcy judge had appointed to keep an eye on the Times Square were a catalogue of horrors. Hookers and crack dealers paid bribes at the front desk and then broke down doors to find a place to do business. Garbage was piled everywhere, and leaking water cascaded from floor to floor. The sound of fire alarms and the occasional gunshot echoed through dim hallways. Under Truong, the hotel's roster of pending safety and building code violations, rose to about 1,500, from 1,000, when he took control. The Koch administration did not just stand by and do nothing: it rewarded Truong, paying him as much as $2,640 a month per room to house the homeless in squalor, claiming that the continued loss of SRO capacity elsewhere left it no choice but to patronize the Times Square. By late 1989, 278 homeless families were living in the 43rd Street hotel, which, in addition to its many other deficiencies, recently had been found to contain illegal levels of lead paint.

In November 1989, Ed Koch's twelve-year run came to an end with the election of David Dinkins, New York's first African-American mayor. The city promptly derailed Truong's gravy train, informing him that it would no longer issue rent checks to homeless families living in the Times Square Motor Hotel. In January 1990, Truong withdrew as the hotel's operator and was replaced by the city, which never before had assumed direct control of a welfare hotel. On the first day of city management, workers in masks removed two hundred bags of garbage. "The only difference between the street and the Times Square was that the street didn't have a roof," said Susan Urban, the city official now in charge. Despite overwhelming evidence to the contrary, Truong stuck to his story, which was that he was a conscientious businessman victimized by circumstance. "Those big hotels, Helmsley and Trump, they send the bad people to Truong," he declared. "The city should thank me for taking care of so many poor and homeless."

Midtown's Dead Zone

To general astonishment, in the spring of 1982 Park Tower Realty was awarded development rights to the 42nd Street Development Project's largest and potentially most lucrative piece: its four-tower office complex. George Klein, an heir to the Barton's kosher candy fortune, controlled Park Tower. Klein, who had gotten his start building government-subsidized housing in Brooklyn, had recently completed two smallish office buildings in Midtown and had a third one under construction in the Wall Street district. So far so good, but Klein's accomplishments—and his family's net worth—did not measure up to those of the Dursts, Milsteins, Tishmans, Minskoffs, and other Manhattan skyscraper dynasties. Even so, in his eagerness to grasp the rare opportunity that 42DP offered to "shape a city," as Klein put it, the upstart committed to paying $25 million more to buy the site for the office towers than the next highest bidder, a consortium headed by Milstein Properties. Like most New Yorkers, Fred Papert had never heard of Klein but was delighted that the developer was willing to roll the dice on 42nd Street. "It was a miracle," Papert exclaimed after Klein emerged from nowhere (or Brooklyn, anyway) to stake his claim to the Crossroads of the World in partnership with the Prudential Insurance Co. of America. "Klein should be rocked in our arms."

Klein had more going for him than guts and the ambition to make it big in Manhattan real estate. Like his father before him, George was a devoted supporter of Orthodox Jewish causes and was well connected politically because of it. Nicknamed "the Candy Man," the younger Klein "became a valued liaison with politically conservative Jews of New York." Although Klein was a hard-right Republican, he had earned Democrat Koch's gratitude in the late 1970s by using his contacts to help the Democratic mayor lobby Congress for various aid programs to New York City. Koch was even more thankful when Klein made large donations to the mayor's winning reelection campaign in 1981, the year that the 42nd Street redevelopment contracts were put out to bid. The developer wrote another big check for Koch when he ran for governor against Mario Cuomo in 1982, the year Park Tower Realty was officially designated 42DP's office tower builder. Koch's gratitude to Klein was no secret. In *Mayor*, the first of his autobiographies, Koch ranked Klein "at the very top of my campaign contributors when I ran for reelection in 1981 . . . and at the top of my list of contributors in 1982 when I was running for governor."

In fairness, Klein also had helped his cause by cultivating a well-deserved image as a quality builder. He accomplished this mainly by hiring big-name architects—I. M. Pei & Partners, Edward Larrabee Barnes & Associates, Philip Johnson & John Burgee Architects—to custom design towers for such blue-chip tenants as IBM, Dillon Read, and Chase Manhattan Bank. "The mere act of hiring these three architects alone would set Mr. Klein apart from most New York real estate developers, who seem to operate on the principle that any architect good enough to be famous is too good to design a building for them," the *Times* observed.

The architecture firm that Klein hired to design the 42nd Street office complex, Johnson & Burgee, was constrained in their work by 150 pages of exceptionally detailed design guidelines that had been incorporated into 42DP to preserve Times Square's "special ambience and visual character" as Manhattan's unofficial town square. To this end, the guidelines not only limited the height and bulk of the office towers but also required the use of bright lights and electric signs on their facades. However, Klein disdained Times Square as a sinkhole of decay and immorality unworthy of preservation. Guidelines or no guidelines, he intended to make the Crossroads of the World safe for Manhattan's corporate elite by encasing it within a group of buildings of such size and class that his complex would be acclaimed as the second coming of Rockefeller Center. "A total feeling has to be engendered," Klein said in unveiling Johnson & Burgee's design for Times Square Center in 1984. "What Rockefeller Center did for New York in the 1930s, this has the potential for doing in the 1980s and 1990s. You cannot build these buildings one at a time because you cannot displace the garbage that way." Added architect John Burgee: "We're giving Times Square an identity it doesn't have now."

Times Square Center trashed 42DP's official guidelines in numerous ways large and small. Olympia & York, the Canadian developers who had been part of the City at 42nd Street, had bowed out of the bidding for 42DP because project officials refused to even consider letting the company demolish the historic Times Tower. But Klein's architects obliterated the landmark anyway, unveiling plans that showed their towers fronting an open plaza where the Times Tower had stood since 1904. If the landmark building were demolished, one architecture critic sneered, "one would have to rename the square and revise the way we think about it: we could acknowledge its privatization and rename it Klein Square." Johnson & Burgee gave their polished red-granite towers a staid, neoclassical look, with immense formal archways on their ground floors and glass mansard roofs on top. At twenty-seven, thirty-nine, forty-seven, and fifty-four stories, the buildings were not terribly tall by Midtown standards, but they were hugely bulky, employing none of the setbacks that had been mandated by the guidelines to reduce mass and let light into the street. The basic measure of a building's density relative to the parcel of land it occupies is its floor-area ratio, or FAR. The city's new zoning regime had increased the maximum allowable FAR on the West Side to 18. Yet the FARs of the Johnson & Burgee towers ranged from 24.3 to a staggering 46.3.

After a few months of renegotiations with Klein, the city and state junked its own design guidelines and approved Times Square Center with only slight modifications. When Koch had summarily killed the City at 42nd Street on the grounds that the city would be better off relying on public bidding to produce a scheme that was authentically, organically Big Apple, most people had given the mayor the benefit of the doubt. But now architects, preservationists, planners, and civic activists of all sorts turned on 42DP with a vengeance. Brendan Gill, a longtime architecture critic for *The New Yorker* as well as a stalwart of the Municipal Arts Society, lambasted the office towers as "exceptionally repellent, great gray ghosts of buildings, shutting out the sun and turning Times Square into the bottom of a well." Gill's objections went far beyond issues of scale and design to the underlying rationale of 42DP. "The idea that you can solve profound sociological problems by building skyscrapers is transparently false," he argued.

Mayor Koch and Governor Cuomo had been advised to expect lawsuits against 42DP, but forty-seven of them, including seven federal cases? This surfeit of suits brought against the 42nd Street project went beyond the usual environmental impact challenges to allege abridgment of First Amendment rights, equal protection rights under the Fourteenth Amendment, violation of antitrust prohibitions, and so on. The first group of twenty-seven cases was settled by 1986, but two subsequent rounds of litigation blocked the project's advance until mid-1989. Ultimately, every suit was dismissed by the courts, but because many of them were skillfully crafted and raised legitimate legal issues, they could not quickly be resolved. Virtually all of the suits were brought by plaintiffs who had no real hope of winning on the legal merits but hoped to prevail just the same by forcing delays on 42DP. Real estate is a boom-and-bust business, making large development projects in particular vulnerable to litigation-driven obstructionism.

The anti-42DP lawsuits were prolific by any standard but measured only the moneyed opposition. For every plaintiff, there were a dozen other businessmen who could not afford to bring a suit that had little chance of winning but who dug in their heels and refused to leave the demolition zone, forcing the state to play out the time-consuming and legally fraught process of condemnation to the bitter end. In mid-1988, 42DP officials mailed buyout offers totaling $121 million to dozens of businesses and property owners. Not one was accepted. To outsiders, it no doubt was surprising that the residents of what appeared to be a sleaze-ridden commercial slum would want to stay put. But most of these people were making a decent living and did not want to go through the trauma of moving in any event. Be it ever so humble . . .

With the notable exception of Richard Basciano, the Deuce's pornographers did not offer much resistance. Most smut merchants rented on

month-to-month leases and were barely hanging on as it was. Although
the notoriety of West 42nd Street's XXX shops and movie theaters long
had defined its public image, fully two-thirds of the 400 businesses facing eviction had no involvement in the porn trade. The Deuce was stud-
ded with long-established little businesses that had waited out the
block's decline in storefronts sandwiched in between the X-rated emporiums. Forty-second Street was an odd location for a dive shop, but
Richards Sporting Goods had been selling aqualungs, spear guns, and
other scuba gear out of 233 West 42nd Street since 1946, remaining open
until eleven o'clock most nights to serve a clientele that included
Jacques Cousteau and Prince Alexander of Yugoslavia. Seymour Post,
the shop's owner, thought there was nothing wrong with his location that
improved lighting could not fix. "Light up the street!" exclaimed Post,
who would be one of the last merchants forced off the Deuce. "The people will come." Another diehard holdout was Harry Kakoulides, the
Greek immigrant owner of Bill's Deli, a fixture at 206 West 42nd Street
since it opened in 1970. "City, I don't have nothing to say just, '*Molon
lave*,'" Kakoulides told a reporter, quoting the taunt that King Leonidas
of Sparta had shouted at the invading Persian army in 480 B.C.—"Come
and take it."

Gough's Chop House at 212 West 43rd Street had been the bar of
choice for *New York Times* workers—linotype operators no less than reporters and editors—ever since it opened in 1947. A.J. Liebling set an
early section of *The Honest Rainmaker* in Gough's, replete with a detailed
description of the large painting of a formally attired John L. Sullivan that
hung on the wall. A plaque identifying Sullivan was affixed to the painting after a squint-eyed patron reported to Naval Intelligence that the bar
had a life-size portrait of Joseph Stalin with a votive light over it. Before
the *Times'* composing room was rebuilt for computers, the wall above the
page-one makeup stone bore Gough's three phone numbers. Despite a
mid-1980s remodeling, noted one of the tavern's admirers, "time has not
made invalid the classic question of the legendary *Times* correspondent
Homer Bigart, who once gazed into the greenish haze of the bar and en-
quired of his companion, 'Which day of the week do they change the air
in here?'" Like a number of other business owners on the Deuce, James
"Buddy" Coen, Gough's proprietor (and the stepson of its founder), was
able to forestall condemnation by agreeing to vacate on thirty days' notice. But Coen's cooperation was grudging at best. "It all stinks, there

ain't nothing sweet about it," he complained. "They got the ball, bat and field with that eminent domain."

Unlike Gough's, most of the Deuce's surviving G-rated businesses were safely removed from the hurly-burly of the sidewalk, occupying space in one of two 12-story buildings that flanked the Times Tower at the Crossroads of the World. These buildings—the Long Acre and the Ninth Precinct Building—were concrete and steel time capsules containing dozens of garment industry firms as well as bit players in the business drama of Broadway: talent agents, managers, publicists, musical instrument makers, sheet music publishers, song pluggers, wig makers, tailors, hairdressers, and so on. There were two screaming exceptions to the anonymity of this 42nd Street urban village: Joe Franklin, the king of Broadway nostalgia and *Guinness Book* record holder for hosting the longest-running talk show; and Richard R. Falk, an old-fashioned theatrical publicist with a handlebar mustache and a badge that proclaimed him the "Mayor of 42nd Street."

Franklin had first discovered 42nd as a boy, taking the subway down from the Yorkville neighborhood to go to Laff Movie and have a hot dog at Grant's. A few years after he began hosting his first radio show in 1948, he set up Joe Franklin Productions in a tiny room in 220 West 42nd Street that he sublet from a dental technician for thirty dollars a month. The amiable young hustler outgrew the space not long after he had made his television debut in 1951, and then moved to 152 West 42nd Street, the former Knickerbocker Hotel, where he indulged his aversion to waste disposal to the fullest. By the time that *The New Yorker* profiled him in 1971, Franklin's ratty one-room office had become an urban legend. "It has a quality that goes beyond mere grime and disorder," wrote William Whitworth. "If it were a person, it would be a bum." Retorted Franklin: "I love that description, but I think it's unfair to bums."

In 1981, Franklin moved across Broadway, to 1476 Broadway, otherwise known as the Long Acre Building. On its fourth floor, Franklin recreated his masterpiece of mess, erecting piles of old newspapers, unopened press releases, vaudeville-era sheet music, record albums, film canisters, and used coffee cups, along with such treasured mementos as a pistol owned by Edward G. Robinson, a violin played by Jack Benny, and a dress worn by Marilyn Monroe. Franklin's tottering towers of miscellanea soon collapsed, burying his desk and flowing out the open doorway into the hallway. For the better part of a decade, Franklin worked in a clearing by the door, sitting in a chair that he and his secretary took turns using. Franklin had his pocket picked a few times on 42nd Street. "They would cut your pants with a scissors and take your wallet," he recalled. "They're like butter; you don't even feel it. There was a lot of aggression on that block." Even so, he did not want to move. What pack rat does?

Franklin knew Dick Falk well, for the publicist worked out of an office one floor down in the Long Acre, which was to be replaced by the fifty-eight-story centerpiece of George Klein's Times Square Center. Falk had got his start working as office boy for the Shubert brothers during the Depression and then hung out his shingle as a press agent, developing a specialty in bizarre publicity stunts. He hauled a cross up Broadway to promote a show about Jesus, dressed a model in a bikini made of frank-furters, and tried to check a trained flea—"the Great Herman"—into the Waldorf-Astoria. By his own estimate, he generated five tons of press clippings during his career and supplied gossip columnists with made-up quotes from ten thousand clients, including Sonja Henie, Jayne Mans-field, and Salvador Dalí. "I am a liar for hire," Falk boomed. "Of course, 50 percent of what I say is true, so I'm not really a liar. I'm an embel-lisher." The publicist carried with him at all times a bronze badge im-printed with the words MAYOR OF 42nd STREET. Former mayor Robert Wagner had awarded him the badge, which had proven sporadically use-ful over the years for fending off parking citations.

Falk despised 42DP from the start and cranked out a series of in-flammatory "press releases" with headlines like "WORLD'S BIGGEST SWINDLE!!" "The public likes to come here and spend money and see life, and it's crowded all the time," Falk argued. "The do-gooders who want to get rid of it don't come here—they all live on Park Avenue. When is Park Avenue ever crowded? To me, 42nd Street is the most beautiful street in the world. It's the center of Earth, and I'm it. I'm actually 42nd Street." Falk figured that the fixtures in his narrow, paper-strewn office were worth at least $30,000, or $28,877 more than 42DP had initially of-fered him.

The most resourceful opponent of 42DP in every sense was the Durst family, which by the mid-1980s had amassed a net worth estimated at $500 million to $1 billion and reserves of guile and obstinacy nearly as deep as its pockets. Carl Weisbrod had gotten along famously with the Dursts—especially Seymour, the family's curmudgeonly patriarch—dur-ing his six-year stint as director of Midtown Enforcement. But soon after

Weisbrod was named president of 42DP in mid-1987, his relations with the real estate clan turned venomous. The Durst Organization hired a remorselessly creative lawyer named Gary Rosenberg, who brought five strategically spaced lawsuits against 42DP on its behalf. Despite the Dursts' repeated denials, project officials believed that the family helped finance numerous other suits brought by other plaintiffs.

The bad blood spilled across the pages of the city's newspapers as the Dursts and Weisbrod traded blows in a series of nasty op-ed pieces and letters to the editor. Seymour Durst started it with "Times Square: The Big Con," in *Newsday*. "Oblivious to the natural cycles of redevelopment and government's limited ability to shape them, a plethora of competing government agencies are sponsoring the construction of four oversized buildings for Times Square," Durst wrote. "Construction of this arc of skyscrapers will entomb this world-famous crossroads and entertainment center while failing in its promise to control the crime problem." Durst had refrained from naming Weisbrod or any other public official, but that did not stop 42DP's chief from getting personal in two stinging rebuttals, "He's Got No Street Smarts" and "42nd Street Landlords: Greed Inc.," which blasted both the Dursts and the Brandts. "Despite having soaked up taxpayer dollars for decades and having given next to nothing in return, the property owners now say, 'Trust us, we'll clean up 42nd St. ourselves,'" Weisbrod wrote in the latter piece. "They pay lip service to the public's desire to see the block cleaned up. But, in truth, they are committed to defeating the only serious effort to reclaim 42nd Street, all in an apparent attempt to maintain business as usual on this tragic and dangerous block." The rhetorical slugfest between Weisbrod and the Dursts was best judged a draw, with both combatants left bloodied but unbowed.

The *Times* once called Durst the "Champion of Midtown Laissez-Faire," but in truth he turned his rhetorical cannons on government "intrusion" in the real estate markets wherever he countered it, steadfastly opposing the construction of the World Trade Center in lower Manhattan, for instance. When the *Times* and other city dailies tired of publishing his op-ed screeds and letters to the editor, Durst began taking out small but strategically placed classified ads. "Karl Marx government doesn't work in Moscow—Marx Brothers government doesn't work in New York," declared a typical Durst squib that appeared on the bottom of the *Times'* front page.

But for all his vociferousness, Seymour Durst had never been one to put ideology ahead of his financial self-interest. The 42nd Street Development Plan was government intervention writ large, but the Dursts' initial response was tempered by their desire to benefit from it. The family owned sixteen of the thirty-one parcels composing the block between 42nd and 43rd Streets and Sixth and Seventh Avenues and hoped eventually to build at least two office towers here. When the Koch administration put out its initial request for proposals in 1980, the Dursts decided to play along, submitting a detailed plan for sprucing up their block that involved rehabbing some blighted buildings and replacing others with new commercial structures. "The idea was not so much developing office buildings, but cleaning up the area to open development west of Sixth Avenue," Douglas Durst recalled. Cleaning up 42nd Street was what 42DP was supposed to be all about, but Koch and his minions dismissed the Durst proposal out of hand, infuriating Seymour and his son.

The redevelopment project also faced opposition of a sort from within. Rebecca Robertson, a career urban planner who was Weisbrod's deputy and eventual successor, loathed the sleek, overpowering bulk of Klein's Times Square Center. Above all, though, she feared for 42nd Street's historic theaters, which had been given short shrift ever since Mayor Koch had disingenuously proclaimed in 1981 that fixing them was 42DP's essential and defining purpose. "Rebecca was very up-front with her criticism. She didn't keep much to herself," Weisbrod recalled. "There are people who find her abrasive because she is so forthright, yet she does not have the fatal flaw of being impolitic."

Born and raised in Canada, Robertson was the daughter of one of Toronto's preeminent real estate lawyers. She graduated from the University of Toronto in 1974 with a degree in urban planning. Eight years later, Robertson moved to New York and landed a job with the City Planning Commission. In her five years in the planning office, she was primarily responsible for rezoning wide swaths of Manhattan, and for getting the East River Esplanade built. Robertson's effectiveness was a product of enormous energy, feisty charm, and studied pragmatism. "I'm a technocrat, not a politician," she said. "I think I understand how to make things happen. If you get too political, you can't do that. I believe in vision as a practical matter." Weisbrod, who had come to admire Robertson while working with her at city planning, persuaded her to join 42DP in 1987.

As a woman operating in the macho world of big-time real estate development, Robertson faced long odds in every sense. She was not without allies but probably was better connected politically in her native Toronto than in New York. She wasn't even a U.S. citizen when she joined 42DP. Yet perhaps because she was an outsider, her vision of what 42nd Street could become was rooted not in Gotham realpolitik but in a passionate if secondhand appreciation of what the street had been in its Golden Age. Robertson would make no attempt to re-create the good old days; she knew that clocks did not run backward. But as she pushed the project forward she took her inspiration not from the skyscraper dreams of George Klein, but from the ghosts of Oscar Hammerstein, Flo Ziegfeld, Billy Minsky, and Arthur Mayer. Ed Koch had cynically exploited the mythic appeal of old 42nd Street to forge political support for an office scheme masquerading as theater rehabilitation. Robertson would turn Koch's rhetoric into reality by reversing 42DP's priorities. Her approach was: fix the theaters and the rest will follow. "No one cared about the theaters," Robertson recalled. "I felt lonely almost."

The New Amsterdam, Empire, Anco, and Apollo theaters now sat shuttered, their marquees bare. But the Deuce still commanded the loyalty of enough diehard grind movie fans to support five of the old theaters on abbreviated schedules: the Liberty, Harris, Selwyn, Times Square, and Lyric, as well as the Cine 42, a 300-seat theater that opened in the mid-1980s and offered four kung fu pictures for $4. The Victory, too, was still offering discount films, but of the X-rated sort. With screen space at a premium throughout the city, 42nd Street continued to serve the thankless role of exclusive showcase for many horror and action new releases.

Robertson was confident that sooner or later 42DP would win court approval to seize all of the historic 42nd Street theaters, with the possible exception of the New Amsterdam. But what then? Park Tower and Prudential's contract obligated them to finance 42DP's purchase of the theaters at an estimated cost of $11 million and to kick in another $9 million for renovating them. But the project provided no funding at all for operating and maintaining the theaters, not even for the two—the Victory and the Liberty—that had been designated for nonprofit uses. From the outset, the Koch administration had assumed that 42DP would induce private developers to step in and restore the 42nd Street playhouses to their original glory. But this hope had been exposed as a pipe dream by the time that Robertson joined up in mid-1987. Broadway attendance had plummeted from 11 million during 1980–81 to a low of 6.6 million in the dismal 1985–86 season. With half of its houses dark at any given time, Broadway could no more sustain a half dozen new theaters on 42nd Street than the office market could support four colossal new towers at the Crossroads of the World.

In Robertson's view, the demise of what might have been termed the Broadway bailout wasn't all bad. The notion of lining the Deuce with refurbished sixty-five-dollar orchestra seats from one end to the other struck her not only as economically impractical but elitist—and thus at odds with the street's historical identity. In its heyday, 42nd Street had been a place where high and middlebrow culture coexisted at excitingly close proximity, where Lionel Barrymore might deliver Hamlet's soliloquy at the Lyric even as Fred Astaire performed a Gershwin tune in the theater next door and Professor Heckler was putting his fleas through their paces down the block at Hubert's Museum.

To begin to give shape and form to her populist vision of a revived 42nd Street true to its roots, Robertson commissioned the architect Robert A. M. Stern to do a planning study of six theaters: the Apollo, Lyric, Selwyn, Times Square, Victory, and Liberty. Stern's 42nd Street study, released in the fall of 1988, concluded that although all of the theaters were "in relatively good structural condition with few signs of distress or structural deterioration," many distinctive architectural elements had been sacrificed to piecemeal remodeling over the decades. Stern recommended that such lost features as facades, outdoor canopies, box seats, and murals be restored even as the theaters were adapted to modern entertainment uses. He floated three alternative development scenarios, ranging in cost from $50 million to $75 million—or three to four times the $20 million contribution that Klein and the Pru were to make.

To Robertson's delight, the Stern study broadened public discussion of the future of 42nd Street far beyond the Broadway theater while shifting press attention from the office towers to the theaters. Robertson followed up by issuing a formal call for redevelopment proposals for the theaters. The proposals submitted excited perfervid press coverage. "From Tap Dance to Redford, Everyone Wants 42nd Street," read one *Newsday* headline. Robert Redford's Sundance Institute proposed a children's theater. Imax's $13 million plan envisioned a 500-seat theater with a screen seven stories high and eighty feet wide. Dance Theater of Harlem wanted to make its home on 42nd Street, as did the American Tap Dance Orchestra. Other ideas included Off Broadway repertory theaters, comedy clubs and cabaret, jazz and rock venues. But Robertson's public enthusiasm masked private discouragement. "The line was that we interviewed eight hundred entertainment companies, collected forty-four proposals, thirteen of which were 'commercially viable.' Actually, I don't know how viable they really were," she admitted later.

Robertson might not have been political with a capital "*P*," but she was well versed in the art of bureaucratic maneuvering. Perhaps the most important—and certainly the most audacious—element of her theaters-first strategy was a scheme to transfer control of the historic theaters from the public sector to a newly created not-for-profit company. In effect, Robertson liberated 42nd Street's derelict showpieces from government control and gave them a life—or at least the hope of a life—separate from the project that she directed but privately suspected was doomed to fail. As a state employee herself, Robertson effectively conspired to diminish her direct influence over the theaters. But in her view, the theaters were the unloved stepchildren of 42DP and would languish unless removed to the care of private-sector foster parents, in the person of a board of prominent, influential New Yorkers who truly cared about the theaters and their fate.

To this end, Robertson thought up the idea of the Forty-Second Street Entertainment Corporation (42EC), patterning it after the entity that ran the Lincoln Center for the Performing Arts. She credited her boss and ally, Weisbrod, with persuading city and state officials to sign off on its formation. "Carl was brilliant at playing it down," Robertson said. A series of low-key memos and phone calls carried the day. The city agreed to cede legal control of six of the 42nd Street theaters to 42EC under a ninety-nine-year lease. The governor of New York had the right to appoint its directors, but the board itself would fill vacancies as they occurred. In other words, the nonprofit corporation would be self-perpetuating and thus truly independent, insulating the theaters from the vagaries of electoral politics and municipal budgeting.

By persuading Marian Heiskell (née Sulzberger) to serve as chairman of 42EC, Weisbrod and Robertson surmounted another serious impediment to 42nd Street's rebirth: the chronic indifference of the Sulzbergers, the *New York Times* dynasty. Marian was a granddaughter of Adolph S. Ochs, builder of Times Tower, and elder sister to Arthur Ochs "Punch" Sulzberger, publisher of the *Times* from 1964 until 1992. Over the decades, generations of *Times* reporters had covered the paper's namesake neighborhood with a thoroughness and intensity that no other publication in the city came close to matching. The paper also had published dozens of editorials in support of various plans to remake 42nd Street—and an equal volume of architectural and planning criticism that took many of those very same plans severely to task. But throughout it all, the Sulzbergers as business owners had held themselves aloof from the cause of 42nd Street redevelopment. In the late 1970s, Donald Kennedy of the Ford Foundation had made a determined effort to enlist Sulzberger support for the City at 42nd Street project but failed utterly. "Marian Heiskell, who is a good soul, is really proud of what her family did fifteen years later on 42nd Street, but . . . ," said Kennedy, his voice trailing away. After a lengthy pause, he added, "That's all I am going to say about the Sulzbergers."

The *Times'* owners certainly did not lack for incentive to lend a hand in cleaning up the Deuce. Directly across from the entryway to the newspaper's offices on 43rd Street were some of the roughest sex bars and crack dens in all of Manhattan. By any reasonable standard, the Sulzbergers had to be counted among the most civic-minded of New York City's business dynasties. Beginning in the late 1970s, Mrs. Heiskell and brother Punch both had played leading roles in organizing a successful citizens' campaign to liberate Bryant Park from the drug dealers and homeless men that had colonized it. Bryant Park was on 42nd Street just east of Sixth Avenue, but it was defined by its proximity to the New York Public Library, one of the preferred institutions of the city's moneyed elite. The Deuce, though just one block removed from Bryant Park, represented the opposite pole of philanthropic fashionability in the city. The general view among the ruling classes was that 42nd Street was not only unspeakably filthy in every sense but also beyond hope of improvement, and therefore doubly unworthy.

The beauty of the 42EC, which was soon renamed the New 42nd Street Inc., was that it redefined the problem of 42nd Street as a not-for-profit theater development project—a familiar staple of upper-class philanthropy. After much importuning, Mrs. Heiskell agreed to take on the job, but only if the full-time, salaried position of president of the New 42 was filled by Cora Cahan, a cofounder of the Joyce Theater, the city's only theater designed exclusively for dance, and director of the Feld Ballet. Petite, high-strung, and fiercely efficient, Cahan was a professional dancer turned arts administrator. She accepted the New 42 job despite deep misgivings. "I didn't know anything beyond the world of dance," she recalled. "I hadn't dealt with the city or state or with famous people. The first year was terrifying."

The New 42 assembled an exceptionally diverse and high-powered twenty-four-person board of directors that included playwright Terence McNally, the performers Chita Rivera and Bill Irwin, and executives from Viacom International, HBO Video, the American Red Cross, Chemical Bank, and major league baseball. The board was largely Heiskell's creation, and its birth was labored. "Marian twisted arms to get the board together," Robertson recalled. "You can imagine how important people must have felt about spending their time on a project that had gone nowhere on a grotty street in Midtown."

In the spring of 1989, 42DP made a deliberately stingy offer to the Brandt family to purchase all seven of its 42nd Street theaters. "We thought we could buy them out for less than the condemnation awards we would eventually have to pay them," explained Robertson. The Brandts were embittered, but the fight had gone out of them after the last of their lawsuits had been dismissed. Robertson had nearly wrapped up the purchase when a city official leaked word of the impending $2 million transaction to a newspaper reporter, who put it in print. Not long after the article appeared, Douglas Durst was in Robert Brandt's office with a $2.5 million check that Brandt was only too pleased to accept without giving project officials a chance to raise their bid. "Durst made a better offer," Brandt recalled. "Financial considerations are the primary reason for any deal, but the city and state had been difficult to deal with."

Durst immediately sent in teams of riggers to remove the clutter of signs and cladding that obscured the theaters' historic facades, which were cleaned and pointed. With the help of the Landmarks Conservancy, the Durst Organization restored and lit the marquees of all seven theaters. For the first time in forty years, the 42nd Street houses looked pretty much as their makers had intended—from the outside anyway. Durst's plan was to remodel their interiors one by one, beginning with the Apollo, which he renamed the Academy and made available to HBO, which filmed a Carly Simon special there. The developer secured a cabaret license in order to pursue plans to turn both the Academy and the

Lyric into nightclubs. In the meantime, Ron Delsener produced a series of rock concerts at the Lyric. Durst planned to operate the Victory, Times Square, and Harris as first-run movie houses during the week and as rock concert halls on the weekends. The Selwyn was to become the home of a not-for-profit performing arts group, possibly the Roundabout Theater. Durst's progress slowed to a crawl when the plans he had submitted to the Department of Buildings mysteriously vanished for several months, but in January 1990, he announced a $25 million redevelopment plan for the theaters.

Durst allowed a troupe of topflight actors organized by the director Andre Gregory to begin rehearsing *Uncle Vanya* at the Victory, the former home of Minsky's. Aside from a few by-invitation-only previews, this *Vanya* never was publicly performed at the Victory or anywhere else, though the rehearsals, which continued sporadically for five years, did form the basis of a critically lauded 1994 Louis Malle film, *Vanya on 42nd Street*. Even so, in early 1990 Durst succeeded in bringing the legitimate theater back to the Victory, the oldest theater in Times Square. Mac Wellman wrote *Crowbar* specifically for the Victory. The play was a countercultural sensation, praised by all the New York papers and favorably reviewed in such national publications as the *Nation,* the *New Republic,* and *Variety.* "As an evocation of ghostliness I can't recall anything in live theater to equal it, and as an evocation of the ill-fated Victory Theater it is genuinely poignant," wrote the *Nation*'s drama critic.

En Garde Arts, which produced *Crowbar,* was an experimental theater troupe that specialized in performing in unusual locations—warehouses, abandoned storefronts, parks, and the like. Anita Durst, Douglas's twenty-one-year-old daughter, was an aspiring actress who had coproduced a Samuel Beckett play for the group. In late 1989, Anita took Anne Hamburger, En Garde's founder, on a tour of all of the Dursts' 42nd Street theaters. "It was the most amazing thing to walk in and out of them and think what they once were, to think what this block once was—ladies in fine evening gowns, tremendous cultural activity," said Hamburger, who took such a shine to the Victory in particular that she later decided to hold her wedding ceremony there. Doug Durst not only agreed to let Hamburger use the Victory for her next production, but also covered much of the $80,000 cost of producing *Crowbar.*

Wellman intended his play as a ghost story, basing his wraiths on real New Yorkers who had died the week that the Theatre Republic opened in

1900, plus the spirits of Oscar Hammerstein and David Belasco. Durst had the auditorium vacuumed and brought up to fire code, but otherwise it remained frayed and a little smelly. Most of the audience sat onstage, looking down at the threadbare red orchestra seats and up at the two dimly lit balconies and the theater's cherub-encircled dome, grimy but intact. The play made reference to the secret apartment that Belasco kept for his mistress above the dome, Hammerstein's famous roof garden with its working Dutch village, and the artificial lake beneath the stage where Harry Houdini hid the elephants that he magically disappeared. An accompanying slide show displayed the theater in its heyday. "The early pictures are almost painfully nostalgic," one reviewer commented. "How beautiful it was, this wreck we're sitting in." The actors flitted through the entire auditorium—even appearing aloft in the dome—as spotlights illuminated the theater's every cobwebbed nook and cranny, transforming the Victory into a spook house for sophisticates.

Crowbar, which opened in early February 1990, was scheduled for a limited two-week run but played to full houses into the spring. Robertson was so bewitched by the play that she accepted Hamburger's invitation to join her nemesis, Durst, on En Garde Arts' board of directors. With the success of *Crowbar*, Durst did more than prove that quality theater could again draw a crowd to 42nd Street. "I have a very strong feeling that this one production really woke people up to the potential of the theaters on 42nd Street," Roger Morgan said. "Until *Crowbar*, the only people who were going into the old theaters were people like me—designers, architects, theater administrators. But now, for the first time, regular people were let inside. It was still a dirty old theater, but you looked up at cherubs on the ceiling and you know what? They were looking back at you."

To Durst's great annoyance, he was not allowed to reap the benefits of this surge in appreciation for the theaters. On April 18, 1990, the New York State Supreme Court awarded 42DP title to two-thirds of the thirteen-acre project site, including Durst's theaters. "We're in the get-it-moving phase. It's a relief after all the years of litigation," crowed Robertson, who happened to succeed Weisbrod as president of 42DP on the very day that the condemnation order was handed down.

Durst, who estimated his total investment in the theaters at $10 million, turned over to 42DP all of the consultants' reports and architects' plans he had commissioned during his year as the theater boss of 42nd

Street. But the role of gracious loser did not suit Durst. "They *stole* those theaters from us," he complained. When a reporter asked him for reaction to Robertson's promotion, he said, "Good luck to her. She's going to need it." It was a churlish comment but not intended as a threat. "All I meant," Durst explained later, "was that there was no market for office space in Midtown and here they were still planning to add four million square feet."

Jeffrey Gural, the president of Newmark & Company, took it upon himself to try to make peace between Durst and Robertson. Like Durst, Gural was a third-generation Times Square property owner and had known Douglas his whole life. Gural did not know Robertson as well but liked and respected her. The three of them met for lunch at Charlotte, a posh restaurant in the new Macklowe Hotel on 46th Street just off Broadway. Durst was his polite but taciturn self. "We got through it all right," Robertson recalled. "It wasn't torture."

As the meal was ending, Durst produced a big box and carefully laid it on the table. "I've got a present for you," he told Robertson. Pleasantly surprised, Robertson unsealed the package and for once in her life was struck utterly dumb: Durst had given her a stinking pile of horse manure. While Durst looked on poker-faced, a horrified Gural hastened to explain that this was not just any old manure; it was top-grade stuff from Durst's three-hundred-acre farm in Westchester County, the largest organic farm in New York. "I took the box with me," Robertson said, "but I still wish it had been maple syrup."

It was not until the state of New York finally took title to nine acres of the 42DP site in the spring of 1990 that most businesses within the redevelopment zone had to begin leaving. Robertson's instructions were to empty each condemned building one by one, starting at the Seventh Avenue intersection and moving methodically westward along the Deuce, squeezing the block like a tube of toothpaste. Just five tenants remained in the Long Acre Building on the summer day in 1991 that a man with a wheelbarrow transported Joe Franklin's mounds of memorabilia to 303 West 43rd Street, an office building owned by Richard Basciano standing just outside the project's boundaries. "He made about five hundred trips," Franklin recalled wistfully. Much as he liked Franklin, the publicist Dick Falk was happy to see his upstairs neighbor depart. Falk "was absolutely determined to be the last tenant in the Long Acre and was constantly checking to see who was left," Robertson said. The Mayor of 42nd Street got his consolation prize, finally moving in early 1992 into a little office on Broadway at 48th Street where he closed out his days in "exile," as he put it.

State officials had condemned thirty-four buildings and evicted 236 of the 267 tenants occupying the eastern half of the project zone by the time that Governor Mario Cuomo made a humiliating announcement on August 3, 1992. Acknowledging the impossibility of filling four new office towers anytime soon, Cuomo said that 42DP was putting Times Square Center on hold. "It doesn't make sense to go forward immediately with the building of the office towers," the governor acknowledged. "There's no market for them. To hold these people to the contract is to ask them to commit an act of economic self-mutilation." In other words, George Klein and his government sponsors had tacitly conceded that 42DP had failed, at least as originally conceived. Seymour Durst celebrated with "Times Square: We Told You So," a cheeky op-ed piece. "Are office buildings economically viable on 42nd Street? Certainly, if they're grounded in reasoned judgment. But not if government simply declares a sudden need for four huge office towers," Durst chided.

The developer was turning verbal cartwheels, but Times Square Center's collapse only exacerbated the sore feelings of the folks who had been forced from their offices and stores to make way for the towers. Franklin, Falk, and their fellow evictees had no legal recourse against the government or anyone else, and scant hope of ever returning home. Having already shelled out $170 million to cover condemnation awards made by the state, Park Tower and the Pru intended to hold tight to their right to develop the Crossroads of the World. The state was still planning to demolish the Deuce's condemned buildings but could no longer say when or exactly what would replace them.

Eviction had transformed 42nd Street into an eerie ghost block in the vibrant heart of Manhattan. The Selwyn, the Lyric, and the Harris were still showing movies, albeit on an abbreviated schedule to mostly empty houses. But three-fourths of the Deuce's stores and fast-food joints had been shuttered. Hundreds of desks still sat in the empty Long Acre and Ninth Precinct buildings, the chairs pushed back as though their occupants had just wandered off momentarily. The grill still waited behind the grimy windows of Tad's Steaks, and Pizza by Fiorentino's sign still proudly proclaimed its presence as THE PIZZA KING. The Art Deco clock above the marquee of the New Amsterdam was frozen at 1:50. The crime rate on the theater block had plummeted, it was true, but only because the crowds that had thronged it round-the-clock ever since the turn of the century had vanished. Some twenty porn stores were still operating, huddled together near Eighth Avenue in the last stand of buildings that the state had yet to condemn, but most of the pimps, hookers, drug dealers, drunks, and vagrants had packed it in, leaving the theater block of 42nd Street as still as a tomb.

Rebecca's Magic Wand

In the fall of 1992, Rebecca Robertson scored a critical victory—for 42DP and the city in general—by finally prizing the New Amsterdam Theater from the grasp of the Nederlander Organization. After the Nederlanders had abruptly abandoned their attempt to return theater to the New Amsterdam a decade earlier, Jimmy and his minions had made a few short-lived attempts to finish what they had started and then sat on their hands. In the mid-1980s, the producers of the famed Moulin Rouge revue in Paris had taken a keen interest in putting a dinner theater into the New Amsterdam, sending over an architect to work with Theo Prudon, the Nederlanders' architect. The French pulled out after it became apparent that city and state officials did not see a place on the new 42nd Street for even mildly risqué entertainment. A subsequent scheme to turn the roof garden theater into a conference center got off to a promising start but had to be shelved when the Klein office tower to which it was to be attached failed to materialize. "We're not going to do anything until we're assured that the project is going to go forward," Nederlander general manager Arthur Rubin declared in 1989, "because otherwise, if I fix those theaters up and spend a couple of million dollars, who's going to book them?"

Rubin had a point; the Nederlanders could not have been fairly expected to sacrifice their financial interests on the altar of 42nd Street improvement. On the other hand, they could have sealed the New Amsterdam's roof instead of just tossing a few tarps over the open trusses. "The fallacy in their thinking was that the construction halt was just temporary," Prudon said. "In architecture, it's a rule that everything temporary becomes permanent." Left open to the elements, the interior of the only surviving large Art Nouveau theater in America suffered grievous damage from top to bottom. Douglas Durst toured the theater in 1989 and was shocked at its decrepitude. "I remember having my breath taken away," recalled Durst, who promptly lost all interest in adding the New Amsterdam to his collection of 42nd Street theaters. "We would have had to put at least $20 million into it to make it usable. They had just destroyed it."

In May 1990, Robert Silman, the structural engineer whom the Nederlanders had belatedly hired to inspect the New Amsterdam in 1983, returned to the theater for the first time in years. Silman was appalled to find that the domed ceiling of the main auditorium now was marred by a gaping hole created when waterlogged plaster had crashed to the floor. In what had been the roof theater, whole sections of wall had fallen away, exposing the steel beams. Most of the balcony and large portions of the ceiling had collapsed as well. In the basement-level men's smoking lounge, the murals had peeled from the walls and were moldering on the floor in pools of stagnant water. However, a Nederlander spokesman claimed that Silman had concluded that the water damage had not caused any structural damage. "I said nothing of the kind," an angry Silman snapped. "It's a travesty to say they fixed the roofs. The water is still pouring in."

The Nederlanders were famously cheap, but how could the city and state have allowed the theater centerpiece of its biggest redevelopment project ever—a landmarked building, no less—to be trashed like this? Although the contract that 42DP had signed with the Nederlander Organization required it to renovate the New Amsterdam, it was poorly drafted in that it set no deadline and did not require the family to maintain the theater in the interim. But in September 1990, shortly after the *Village Voice* story appeared, the city's Department of Buildings cited Nederlander Productions for failing to properly maintain the theater's brick exterior and gave it ten days to correct the "hazardous defects." A few months later, the very same citation was issued again—and was again ignored. Robertson urged the Landmarks Preservation Commission, which had not been a party to the contract, to sue under the landmarks preservation law.

The commission had always shied away from such battles for fear that the statute on which its authority to impose penalties might be invalidated in court, depriving it of even the threat of legal retaliation. But by early 1991, Laurie Beckelman, its chairwoman, was growing exasperated with the Nederlander Organization. "The deterioration must be stopped," she declared in a letter to Robert Nederlander. This demand apparently did not deprive Jimmy and his brothers of any sleep, for in May, Beckelman lodged a second, no-less-ineffectual complaint. "Despite repeated requests that you make repairs," she wrote, "parapets remain partially demolished, probe holes from earlier studies are open, coping is failing, debris stands all over the roofs, windows and doors are open or missing." The Nederlanders continued to refuse to accept any blame for the theater's appalling condition, claiming that they had spent "significant amounts of money" to maintain the theater while 42DP officials struggled to get their act together.

All the while, Robertson was negotiating with the Nederlanders in hopes of persuading them to voluntarily surrender control of the New Amsterdam. She finally got the opening she needed in late 1991, when the Nederlander Organization breached its contract with the Industrial Development Agency. Complaining that his company already had sunk a total of $14 million into the New Amsterdam, Jimmy Nederlander stopped making the semiannual payment-in-lieu-of-taxes (PILOT) to the city, as required under the agreement. By the fall of 1992, Robertson had worked out a deal under which the city agreed to forgive the Nederlanders the $250,000 they owed the city in delinquent PILOT payments if they agreed to pay off the $2.6 million of principal remaining on the Industrial Development Agency bonds and surrender their rights to the New Amsterdam. The liberation of the theater from Nederlander control was "a major victory for the friends of the great Broadway theaters," said Landmarks Commission chairwoman Beckelman.

Cahan wanted to add the New Amsterdam to the New 42nd Street Inc.'s portfolio of theaters, but Robertson did not think that the not-for-profit group could afford to simultaneously carry through with its plans to renovate the Victory as a children's theater and make the emergency repairs the New Amsterdam needed. Through 42DP, the state pumped $1 million into the New Amsterdam to stabilize the building and prevent further damage. The roof was patched at last, windows and doors were sealed, a net was installed to catch plaster falling from the dome, and a giant gas-fired heater was installed in the orchestra pit to dry a decade's worth of moisture. Robertson even sent workers up on the New Amsterdam roof to shovel the snow that accumulated during what was one of the worst winters in the city's modern history. "If we had not been looking after the theater in the winter of 1992–93, the damage would have been many times worse than it was," she said. The rescue of the New Amsterdam was more timely even than Robertson realized, for the theater was about to excite the ambitions of America's biggest entertainment company.

Like many a baby boomer reared in New York, Michael Eisner carried fond memories of 42nd Street with him into adulthood. He had first visited Times Square at a tender age, attending Broadway shows with his parents. As a teenager in the late 1950s, Michael ventured forth on his own from the family's posh Park Avenue digs to take in double features at the grand but grungy New Amsterdam. "Afterwards, my friends and I would walk over and play arcade games at Fascination on Broadway and 47th Street," Eisner recalled. "It was a more innocent time, when Times Square was still safe and fun."

The theater-smitten Eisner wrote plays in college—bad ones, by all accounts—but went on to make his mark in Hollywood as a talented television and movie producer. Eisner was forty-two years old when he was named chief executive of the Walt Disney Company in 1984. Over time Eisner would prove a deeply flawed, imperious sort of executive, but in the 1980s he delivered big-time for Disney shareholders, as his energy and creativity powered one of the great corporate turnarounds in the history of American business. The company's annual revenues soared to $5.8 billion, from $1.5 billion, during Eisner's first six years on the job, driving a sevenfold rise in Disney's stock.

After refurbishing the coastal gold mines known as Disneyland and Disney World, Eisner yearned to build a new theme park or two of his own but was leery of taking business away from the company's established attractions. The question, in short, was whether America was big enough to support a third Disney theme park. Eisner's answer, at first, was no, and so he looked overseas, to Europe. In 1987, Disney signed a partnership agreement with the government of France to build a huge theme park on the outskirts of Paris. Its planning and construction were a debacle from beginning to end, and the hundreds of millions of dollars in cost overruns weren't the half of it. Even the American press lambasted Disney for its brash and overbearing manner in its dealings with the French, who were famously resentful of American "cultural imperialism" long before Eisner arrived to instruct them in "the Disney Way." At home, Disney long had been a lightning rod for cultural controversy. But it was not until 1992, the year that Euro Disney opened (it soon was renamed Disneyland Paris) that an epithet fashioned from the company name entered the *Collins Concise English Dictionary*. "*Disneyfication:* The process by which historical places are transformed into trivial entertainment for tourists."

Walt Disney's troubles in launching new theme parks in Paris and in suburban Washington, D.C., gave added urgency to its search for smaller-scale growth opportunities. Long before Eisner's hiring, the company had begun pondering a move into Broadway theater. And why not? Disney already was a prolific producer of live shows at its theme parks. But much as Eisner loved the theater, he was leery of the business of theater. "If you produce a movie, it can open in as many as three or four thousand theaters across the country. Even if it performs poorly, it has other lives on video, cable, network television, and overseas," the CEO reasoned. "By contrast, if you produce a full-scale Broadway musical—at a cost not all that much less than a midrange movie—it can close in a single night, forever."

In the late 1980s, Carl Weisbrod had tried a couple of times to interest Disney in restoring a 42nd Street theater but got nowhere. "They were totally unresponsive," Weisbrod recalled. "Eisner said he wasn't interested in bringing his company to New York and his decision was final." Marian Heiskell, a longtime friend of the Eisner family who had known Michael since he was in short pants, fared no better. Over dinner one night in Los Angeles, Heiskell explained her work with the New 42 and urged Eisner to get involved. Afterward, "he sent two or three people to check out the street," Heiskell recalled. "He then wrote a lovely letter to me saying he was sorry but 42nd Street just wasn't in Disney's cards." The architect Robert Stern also took it upon himself to lobby Eisner on behalf of 42nd Street's theaters. "He would have none of it. He'd say, 'Ten years from now, maybe,'" recalled Stern, who had designed a host of buildings for Disney and been rewarded in 1991 with a seat on its board of directors. "I guess you could say it was a New Yorker's reluctance to believe that anything good could happen to something that had been ruined."

Eisner's resistance began softening with the release of *Beauty and the Beast* in late 1991. The film went on to become the highest-grossing animated movie of all time (establishing a box office record that soon would be topped by Disney's own *Aladdin* and then by *The Lion King*), and the first animated feature ever nominated for an Oscar for best picture. Yes, stage musicals were riskier than films, but now every kid in America was enthralled with the beauteous Belle and her sensitive monster. Did someone say "brand extension"? By the end of 1992, Eisner had blessed the formation of Walt Disney Theatrical Productions within Disney Studios. The plan was to open the stage version of *Beauty and the Beast* in Houston and then bring it to Broadway, for, as Eisner acknowledged, "To be a really legitimate theater producer, you have to be in New York."

One afternoon in March 1993, Eisner joined Stern in his New York office to go over the drawings for a project in Florida. They began talking instead about Disney's plans to import *Beauty and the Beast* to New York and the difficulty of finding a Broadway house suitable for big-budget musicals that wasn't already tied up by Andrew Lloyd Webber or one of his ilk. Eisner asked for the latest news on 42nd Street. Within twenty minutes, Stern's assistants had assembled a model of the theater block. Intrigued, the CEO toured the New Amsterdam the next morning with his wife and two teenage sons, as well as Stern and Cahan, who was subbing for the vacationing Robertson. "We could see water leaking from the roof, birds nesting in the ceiling, puddles mingled with rubble on the floor. The interior was badly gutted," Eisner recalled. "Still, the theater's remarkable detailing remained in ghostlike form—its Art Nouveau decor, Wagnerian friezes, and allegorical murals. The once lavish grandeur of this building was easy to visualize, even in its dilapidated state. By the time we left, I felt excited."

The negotiations between Disney and representatives of 42DP commenced at once but would drag on tortuously for a year and a half— continuing long after *Beauty and the Beast* had triumphantly opened in the spring of 1994 at the Palace Theater on Broadway and 47th Street. The basic problem was that Disney was far more valuable to 42DP than the New Amsterdam was to Disney, and everyone knew it. Eisner certainly understood that he held the negotiating advantage and pressed it past the point of absurdity. In essence, the company wanted the New Amsterdam not only free of charge but free of risk. The more that the state and city offered, the more Disney demanded. Robertson committed to subsidizing the restoration of the New Amsterdam to Broadway standards, but then Disney wanted 42DP to underwrite a host of premium finishing touches, including a magnificent stage curtain decorated with mouse ears.

Before Disney came along, 42DP had attracted nibbles from other major entertainment companies, but none of these worthies came close to matching Walt Disney's financial muscle or its commercial credibility. True, Disneyland Paris was off to a horrendous start. But Disney was still defined by the triumph of Disney World, a theme park of theme parks that Eisner had inherited but expanded significantly. By an ever-widening margin, Disney World was the world's largest pure tourist destination, with more hotel rooms than New York City, Los Angeles, or Chicago. When word of Disney's interest in 42nd Street leaked to the press in mid-1993, Disney's recent setbacks were forgotten, in the United States at least, as its tarnished image was cleansed by media hype. The irony in the pairing of pop culture's mouse-eared icon of clean family fun and America's most infamously debauched block was irresistible to stand-up comics and op-ed pundits alike. But for all the jokes at Disney's expense, the consensus view was that if any company could make 42DP work, it was the Mouse House. The headlines practically wrote themselves: "A Prince Charming? Disney and the City Find Each Other," "Disney's Magic Wand," "Disney Leads Cinderella Transformation of 42nd Street."

The aggressiveness that Disney displayed in negotiating its entry onto 42nd Street was rooted not only in the institutional arrogance of a company accustomed to imposing its will on governments but also in uncertainty and self-doubt. A number of Disney executives thought that the company had no business setting foot on the Deuce, no matter how sweet a deal it could cut for itself. The city—especially the big city—was foreign territory to the Disney Company. Its forte was the creation of insular utopias of leisure and fantasy that occupied the urban periphery and offered escape from the city's messy realities. As one architecture critic put it, "The highly regulated, completely synthetic vision [of Disney theme parks] provides a simplified, sanitized experience that stands in for the more undisciplined complexities of the city." In building Disney World, the company amassed 27,000 acres near Orlando—an area twice the size of Manhattan—and extracted concessions from the government of Florida that went far beyond the usual tax breaks. In essence, the state legislature authorized Disney to act as a municipal government unto itself, with control over zoning, taxation, and environmental regulation within Disney World, a sovereign commercial state within a state.

When it was first presented with the New Amsterdam opportunity, Disney's reflex was to attempt to gain dominion over the entire theater block of 42nd Street and gate it, forgetting that 180,000 commuters were passing through the Port Authority Bus Terminal every weekday. "We do have some genetic instincts," conceded Peter Rummell, chairman of the Disney unit responsible for real estate development, including theme parks. "The question in these urban environments really becomes, 'Is there a way you can have enough control?' Because we are control freaks."

Disney's impulse to turn the Deuce in its entirety into a themed attraction was grounded in the same underlying premise as was 42DP—namely, that piecemeal, one-theater-at-a-time redevelopment of the block was likely to fail. The prospect of restoring the wreck of the New Amsterdam was daunting enough for Disney, which was not well versed in historic renovation and feared a headlong tumble down the "black hole" of cost overruns. But it was the dire condition of the rest of the block that really scared the California company. Not long after Eisner's guided tour of the Deuce, he sent an underling back alone with a video camera to document the street's malevolence. "It was the brand risk," one Disney exec later admitted. "We were terrified that we would go forward and there would be some unspeakably horrible act on 42nd Street." But after much internal debate, the Disney brain trust realized that attempting to reinvent a chunk of Midtown Manhattan in Uncle Walt's image was a fool's errand. "You don't do that on 42nd Street," said David Malmuth, the Disney executive directly responsible for the New Amsterdam venture. "It's a *public* place."

On December 30, 1993, the last day of the David Dinkins administration, Deputy Mayor Barry Sullivan signed a vaguely worded "memorandum of understanding" with Disney on a metal detector at City

Hall's front door as he was leaving for the last time. Eisner insisted that this preliminary agreement to subsidize the restoration of the New Amsterdam be kept confidential in hopes of currying favor with Republican Rudolph Giuliani, by letting the incoming mayor make the big announcement. In February, Disney's CEO appeared at a press conference with Giuliani and Governor Cuomo to belatedly announce the memorandum of understanding. In insisting that the press conference be held at City Hall, Giuliani defied the longstanding protocol that joint announcements by the governor and the mayor take place in the governor's Midtown office or at a neutral site. Cuomo, who'd been championing the redevelopment of 42nd Street for a dozen years, was incensed at Giuliani's effrontery but gloweringly played along rather than risk spooking Disney.

Despite all the hoopla, Disney still was a long way from signing a binding agreement. The memorandum of understanding was a Swiss cheese of loopholes allowing Eisner easy exit if the negotiations did not unfold to his liking. In truth, it was little more than a publicity stunt but was quite effective as such. The mere fact of Disney's interest in the Deuce drained much of the lingering skepticism from press coverage of 42DP and piqued the deal-making interest of other entertainment companies. The most notable of them were Tussaud's Group Ltd., proprietors of the world-famous Madame Tussaud's wax museums, and the movie theater chain American Multi-Cinema Entertainment, a Kansas City–based concern that was the country's largest distributor of Disney films.

Tussaud's Group had been pondering a move onto 42nd Street since 1991, well before Walt Disney came on the scene. In fact, the London-based parent of Tussaud's had helped attract Disney to the area by putting together a demographic analysis that documented the Deuce's latent tourist allure. The Tussaud Group's original plan was to buy One Times Square, the former Times Tower, and make it over into a $55 million high-tech entertainment complex. Robertson courted Tussaud's avidly and by the end of 1994 was ready to offer the London-based company a subsidy to clinch the deal. All Tussaud's had to do was buy the half-vacant building at a bankruptcy auction. But the Wall Street investment bank Lehman Brothers put in a surprise bid of $27.5 million, topping Tussaud's by $10 million. The wax museum folks beat a hasty retreat, furious that 42DP had not condemned One Times Square on its behalf.

Headquartered in Kansas City, AMC did not own a single screen in New York City. In early 1994, it stepped forward with a bold $53 million plan to build a twenty-nine-screen movie theater on the south side of 42nd. Robertson loved the idea of a giant movie complex. "To me, movies were always the key because we were trying to create a populist entertainment center," Robertson recalled. Movies, or at least certain kinds of movies, were more likely than the legitimate theater to draw blacks and Hispanic to the new 42nd Street and to ring the cash register all day, not just at night. Robertson hammered out an agreement with AMC, but the Giuliani administration would not okay it, despite Robertson's pleas and protests. "AMC would have done anything to do a deal," she recalled, "but the city just would not do one." Like Tussaud's Group, AMC went away hopping mad—but at the city, not the state. "If they want the damn block done, somebody's got to step up and say, 'Go,'" an AMC executive complained.

Mayor Giuliani and Clay Lifflander, the city's economic development chief, were averse to the idea of movies on 42nd Street and did not see why AMC should be subsidized, in any event. The underlying problem, though, was that 42DP offended the new administration's compulsion for complete control. It took particular offense at the independence of the New 42 Inc. The charitable group not only had a self-perpetuating board appointed by Governor Cuomo but also was entitled to keep all of the rental income from the six theaters that it had acquired under long-term lease from the city. The notion of dismantling the New 42 was the subject of many high-level meetings at City Hall in 1994. In the end, the Giulianistas were not willing to take the political risk of mounting a frontal assault on a not-for-profit group building a children's theater— and chaired by a Sulzberger, no less. But the administration did vex the New 42, mainly by refusing to sign off on the budget that it had to submit to the city annually for review, slowing the progress of the Victory's remodeling.

For Robertson, coping with Giuliani's intransigence was bad enough, but George Pataki's upset victory over Mario Cuomo in the election of November 1994, posed a more direct threat, given that she and the 42DP staff were state employees. Pataki, an upstate lawyer and former small-town mayor, had not taken an official position on the 42nd Street project during his campaign. But it would not have come as a surprise if the new Republican governor de-emphasized or perhaps even killed his Democratic predecessor's pet project in favor of his own initiatives. Disney executives were sufficiently alarmed to join with Robertson in an increasingly frantic attempt to reach a definitive agreement before Cuomo's term expired at midnight on December 31, 1994.

After working virtually nonstop from December 28 through December 30, a deal finally was struck. The transaction was tightly wrapped in legal and financial complications, but its essence was this: the state would make a $26 million capital investment in the New Amsterdam in the form of a subsidized loan to Disney, which would invest $8 million in equity. Taking into account a 20 percent federal historical tax credit, the company's net investment would be less than $3 million. Disney did not get everything it wanted. It would have to pay for its own mouse-eared curtains, for one thing. Most important, Disney was unable to purchase the New Amsterdam outright, settling for a forty-nine-year lease. All Robertson needed to do to seal the deal was to settle a few details with Disney. Her boss, Vince Tese, already had signed the papers but urged her to wait until she had heard from Charles Gargano, his successor as UDC chairman. Why hold a gun to Pataki's head when there was a chance he might actually support both the Disney deal and 42DP?

On December 31, Robertson sat in her office with aide Wendy Leventer awaiting Gargano's phone call as city workers began boarding up the storefronts along Broadway to protect them from the New Year's Eve revelers who soon would descend on Times Square. When the telephone finally rang in midafternoon, the two women nearly jumped out of their skins. Robertson picked up the receiver but heard only static. Gargano finally called at about 4:20 P.M. with a terse message. "You can go ahead and sign the deal," Gargano said. As soon as Robertson hung up, she and Leventer dashed for the front door. "Just as they were putting up the last piece of plywood, out we go," Leventer recalled. They made it crosstown to the offices of 42DP's lawyers, who had Disney executives waiting on a conference call to put the finishing touches on an agreement.

The eleventh-hour pact with Disney left the company two last outs. It could withdraw if the estimates for the renovation work topped $29 million. (The final estimates came in at $38 million, but Disney decided to stay in anyway.) Also, by July 15, 1995, two more "nationally recognized and reputable" entertainment companies had to sign letters of intent to occupy at least 35,000 square feet on 42nd Street. Ironically, it was Robertson who had suggested this second proviso to force the issue of

42nd's fate politically, reasoning that "no politician wanted to be the one to lose Disney."

Not long after Disney and the state had come to terms, Tussaud's executives decided to give it another go. Still furious at Robertson for refusing to condemn One Times Square, Tussaud's executives approached the city directly in tandem with the prolific developer Forest City Ratner. For all their complaints about the subsidies that the state had offered AMC, Lifflander and Dyson now granted a hefty twenty-year tax abatement to a $200 million retail and entertainment complex that Forest City would fashion from the Harris, Liberty, and Empire theaters. The mayor's office did not inform the state of the negotiations for five weeks, or until it had struck a deal with Forest City and the Tussaud's Group, which was looking to put $30 million into a wax museum. "The city sent us an agreement and said we had to sign it at once," recalled Robertson, who expected Gargano to pitch a fit. Instead, UDC's chairman suggested a quid pro quo, which Robertson delivered to the city. "We said, 'We'll take Tussaud's, if you take AMC," she recalled. On this basis, the deal finally was done. After city and state officials shook hands, Forest City Ratner amended its plans to include AMC, which planned to invest $25 million in a 5,000-seat multiplex.

On the morning of July 20, 1995, city officials erected a makeshift stage in front of the New Amsterdam and hastily assembled a media kit of press releases. On the front of a folder recycled from another press event, a strip of black tape was placed over the name of ex-Governor Cuomo. Eisner could not attend but phoned in from his corporate jet. "This is really going to happen," he said. "Even I'm surprised." Pataki and Giuliani both delivered self-congratulatory speeches, but it was a jubilant Rebecca Robertson who best summed up the moment. "The future of 42nd Street has arrived," she said.

The signing of Walt Disney, Tussaud's Group, and AMC brought the redevelopment of the theater block of 42nd to the tipping point. "It's like a snowball coming down a hill," said Andrew Tansley, Tussaud's executive director. "Now, the question is not, 'Is it going to happen?' But rather, 'Can you keep up as it happens?'" Redevelopment officials promptly condemned the western end of the theater block, inflating 42DP's property acquisition bill to almost $400 million. The final roster of 42nd Street evictees included fifteen video stores, six peep shows, five porn movie theaters, eight sex paraphernalia shops, four action film houses, two hairdressers, twenty-five lawyers, twelve fast-food restaurants, ten artists, two sporting goods stores, two newspapers, one hatter, one television studio, one joke store, one boxing gym, one pimp, and one sadomasochist therapist.

From 1995 to 2001, about $4 billion in private funds was invested in a two-square-block area that had not seen any significant capital investment since the 1920s. Not since the first half dozen of its theaters were built in the first few years of the twentieth century had 42nd Street bustled and boomed to the extent that it did in the last few years of the century. Every building within 42DP's boundaries was demolished, except for six historic theaters, the old Times Tower, and the Hotel Carter. The Deuce had been a street with a sky, as befitted an urban wilderness. But now redevelopment projected 42nd Street into Manhattan's skyline for the first time. Four huge office towers were indeed erected one after the other at the Crossroads of the World and a forty-five-story Westin luxury hotel sprouted at the block's Eighth Avenue end. The merchandise mart was not built, but the 42DP master plan was implemented in most every other essential particular a good decade and a half after it was drawn up. Yet the final chapter of the story of 42nd Street's reinvention contained innumerable twists and turns. In the most remarkable of them, the first of the four office towers—the Condé Nast Building—was erected not by the long-suffering George Klein, but by his and 42DP's archnemesis, Douglas Durst.

As the Manhattan property market showed the first flickering signs of revival in 1995, Durst, who now was running the Durst Organization, decided to try to get the jump on rival developers by building a new office tower in Midtown. The developer had lambasted the city and state for attaching hefty tax breaks to the office sites 42DP awarded to Klein and his money partner, Prudential Insurance. But thanks to these subsidies, there was no better place in all Manhattan for Durst to locate his new skyscraper than the Crossroads of the World—especially because the Durst Organization still owned "back" parcels adjacent to the largest of the four 42DP office sites. "Yes, it's ironic, but we didn't put the tax breaks in place," Durst acknowledged after he had made his move to supplant Klein. "If they're there, we'll use them."

Through an intermediary, Durst gingerly approached Klein, who agreed to a meeting. When Klein refused to consider selling the rights to any part of the 42nd Street site, Durst made his pitch directly to Prudential, which still controlled the purse strings in its joint venture with Klein's Park Tower Realty. The Pru was no more enamored of Durst than was Klein, but the insurer's management had grown wary of real estate investment in general and of 42nd Street in particular. The negotiations between Durst and the Pru were arduous and broke off entirely several times. Robertson's suspicions complicated matters. The state had to approve of any transfer of 42DP development rights to Durst, and Robertson just did not trust her old antagonist. Was this just another of the developer's ploys to undermine 42DP? She insisted that Durst guarantee in writing that he would immediately break ground on an office tower, even if he had not signed an anchor tenant to a lease. Durst assured Robertson that he had every hope of building expeditiously, but refused to commit to building "on spec." In the end, resentment and mistrust of Durst was no match for Charles Gargano's desire to press on. "I didn't care what happened in the past," the UDC chief declared. "I was looking for a fresh start."

Durst paid $75 million for the largest of the four office tower sites without having to guarantee construction. His architects designed an energy-efficient, environmentally correct "green" tower that came in eleven stories shorter than the fifty-eight-story colossus that was to have anchored Times Square Center and also incorporated setbacks and other density-alleviating features of the sort that Klein had defiantly shunned. With much effort and an assist from the Giuliani administration, Durst signed a glamorous name tenant for the building—Condé Nast Publications, publisher of *Vanity Fair, Vogue,* the *New Yorker, GQ,* and many other glossy magazines. Some $11 million in city tax breaks helped Condé Nast executives overcome their leeriness of moving to Times Square. Seymour Durst died at age seventy-nine in mid-1996, just before ground was broken on the $450 million Condé Nast Building (also known as Four Times Square), which was the largest of the Durst Organization's ten office towers and one of its most profitable. "I think Seymour would be very happy and proud at how it's turned out," Douglas said.

After coming to terms with Durst, Prudential Insurance sold off the three remaining office sites to major developers in separate transactions totaling about $462 million, leaving its partnership with Klein with a slim profit over its sunk cost of $435 million. "I don't think Prudential ever had a sophisticated idea of the project or the location," said Carl Weisbrod, who had headed the city's economic development office after he stepped down as 42DP's president. "They got in for the wrong reasons and got out for the wrong reasons, too." The few million dollars that came Klein's way provided little solace to the developer, whose lost shot at real estate's big time was memorialized in a final outpouring of humiliating headlines: "Developer Klein Goes Quietly into NY Night," "George Klein Out in the Cold." Weisbrod was not unsympathetic. "With George, it really was a Greek tragedy in how his dream ended up a nightmare," Weisbrod said. "But like Prudential, from soup to nuts he lacked a feel for Times Square."

Today, West 42nd houses many more corporate offices than it ever did in its heyday, including the national headquarters of accounting giant Ernst & Young and the mega law firm Skadden Arps Slate Meagher Flom. But the street—and all of Times Square—is noteworthy for its concentration of media and entertainment companies à la Condé Nast. Both MTV and ABC-TV opened glass-walled television studios on the Square that periodically attract large crowds on the sidewalk outside. Three Times Square, a thirty-two-story tower across Broadway from the Condé Nast Building, is the American headquarters of Reuters, a London-based company that is one of the world's largest news and financial information companies. SFX made the beautifully refurbished Candler Building its new headquarters, occupying the twenty-four-story building in its entirety, except for the capacious McDonald's branch on its ground floor. America's largest provider of live entertainment, SFX controls 120 venues, including legitimate theaters, arenas, concert halls, and racetracks. In 2000, SFX was acquired by Clear Channel Communications, which operates the country's largest chain of radio stations. There could be no more appropriate home for SFX than 42nd Street, America's first national capital of live entertainment.

Among them, the four new office towers at the Crossroads accounted for $2.4 billion, or 60 percent, of the $4 billion invested in 42nd Street's redevelopment. A mere $107 million was invested in fixing up the old theaters. But just as Robertson had envisioned during the dark days of the early 1990s, it was the restoration of the theater to 42nd Street that catalyzed the street's transformation. The state's deal with Disney was critical, but it was the New 42nd Street Inc. that led the way in its gutsy transformation of Hammerstein's Theatre Republic into the city's first performing arts center for children. Right from its opening on December 11, 1995, the 500-seat New Victory attracted both large audiences and large corporate donations that made a ticket to its appealingly diverse shows one of the great entertainment bargains in the city.

The New Victory's was the only lit marquee on 42nd Street for nearly two years, or until the New Amsterdam reopened in late 1997. Eliminating every trace of the heavy damage done during the Nederlanders' tenancy, Walt Disney restored 42nd Street's grandest theater to a condition very closely approximating its original splendor. Disney's first Broadway musical, *Beauty and the Beast,* had been an almost slavishly exact translation of the movie to the stage—and a huge box office hit. In choosing to open the New Amsterdam with an adaptation of *The Lion King,* Disney's biggest-grossing film ever, the company seemed to be reading from the same script. But to direct, Disney hired Julie Taymor, an avant-garde dramatist, and let her have her way. "I told them I wanted to go for elegance, not cute," Taymor said. An arresting fusion of middlebrow storytelling and experimental design, Taymor's creation won the most laudatory reviews Disney had received in decades and also eclipsed *Beauty and the Beast* at the box office. As of late 2003, *The Lion King* still was playing to full houses.

Three additional playhouses opened over the next few years. The American Airlines Roundabout Theater was the old Selwyn Theater remodeled and reduced in size by a third. American Airlines paid $8.5 million for the naming rights to the 740-seat theater, which is home to the Roundabout Theater Company, a not-for-profit troupe graduated to Broadway. Livent Inc., North America's largest theatrical producer, combined two of the old playhouses—the Lyric and the Apollo—into a new 820-seat venue suitable for lavish musicals, just like the New Amsterdam. Ford Motor Company paid Livent a hefty sum to put its name on the new theater, the Ford Center for the Performing Arts. In 1998, less than a year after the Ford Center opened, Livent imploded in an accounting scandal that resulted in fraud charges against Garth Drabinsky, its chief executive officer, and others. SFX acquired the Ford Center, which scored a big hit in 2001 with a revival of David Merrick's *42nd Street.*

During the remodeling of the Selwyn, the six-story office building attached to it collapsed, as did the facade of the theater. The facade was restored, but in place of the vanished building the New 42nd Street Inc.

erected a ten-story, glass-enclosed structure called the New 42nd Street Studios. A 199-seat theater for experimental productions—the Duke on 42nd Street—was constructed on the ground floor, and most of the rest of the space was given over to rehearsal studios. Auditions for the revival of Merrick's musical were held here, inspiring Cora Cahan to epiphany. "There were 250 girls in tights and tap shoes in a building called the New 42nd Street Studios auditioning for a show called *42nd Street* that was going to play in a New 42nd Street theater," said the New 42nd's executive director. "It felt like I was in some unreal world."

As recently as the late 1980s, only the wildest optimist would have predicted that 42nd Street's ravaged theater block would be home to five functioning playhouses by 2000. Even so, as an exercise in theater preservation, 42DP was only modestly successful. The Ford Center carefully preserved many elements of the old Lyric and Apollo, but for all intents and purposes it was a new venue. The old Harris Theater was incorporated into the lobby of Madame Tussaud's wax museum, and the Liberty Theater vanished into a new Hilton hotel. AMC won approval to use the Empire Theater as the lobby for its new twenty-five-screen multiplex. The problem was that the old theater was about 170 feet east of where the movie theater was supposed to be. In an uncharacteristic display of grit, the Landmarks Preservation Commission refused to allow Forest City Ratner to disassemble the Empire. So the contractor hoisted the 3,700-ton theater onto metal rails and gingerly towed it down 42nd to the AMC site. Directly across the street from the Tussaud's/AMC complex, Tishman Realty & Construction built a rival entertainment— E Walk—that contained a thirteen-screen Sony multiplex and a cavernous games arcade.

Try as they might, Robertson, Heiskell, and Cahan could not find an acceptable tenant for the Times Square Theater, which was still available for lease in 2003. Warner Leroy, the owner of Tavern on the Green and other plush restaurants, wanted to turn the theater into a theme restaurant with floating gondolas, but he was unable to secure financing for what might well have been the latter-day equivalent of the old 42nd Street lobster palace, Murray's Roman Gardens.

By decade's end, the riptide of rising property values created by redevelopment of the old theater block had rolled west all the way to Tenth Avenue, to Theater Row and Manhattan Plaza. "The fact that the Seventh-to-Eighth block is no longer a festering sore, rippling its ugliness east and west, is creating a pressure toward more redevelopment," observed Fred Papert, feisty as ever and eager to capitalize on the changing dynamics of 42nd Street real estate. Papert's Forty-Second Street Development Corp. joined with Playwrights Horizons and a surprising newcomer to 42nd Street—the Shubert Organization—to put all those dilapidated Maidman tenements out of their misery at last and usher Theater Row upscale.

Demolition began in the spring of 2000, and within two years the rebuilding of Theater Row was essentially complete. With $12 million of its own money and another $3 million kicked in by the developer on the project, the Brodsky Organization, 42nd Street Development built a five-story building at 410–412 West 42nd containing five new theaters: an 88-seat house (the Lion) for low-budget showcases; three 99-seat theaters (the Kirk, the Beckett, and the Clurman) for more advanced work; and a 199-seat theater (the Acorn) for full-fledged productions. Meanwhile, at 422 West 42nd the Shubert Organization put a 499-seat theater into the base of a new forty-one-story luxury apartment building with a distinctive purplish and cream-striped "zebra" design. Called the Little Shubert, this was an Off Broadway "transfer" house (for productions theoretically on their way to Broadway). The impetus for this expansion of the Shubert empire came not from Gerry Schoenfeld but from Rebecca Robertson, who took a real estate development position with the Shubert Organization after resigning as president of 42DP in 1997.

On July 2, 2001, Playwrights Horizons held a party at 416 West 42nd Street to commemorate its twenty-six years of residence in the former Maidman Playhouse on the eve of its demolition. Bob Moss, Playwrights Horizons' founder, came down from Syracuse, where he was happily ensconced as the artistic director of Syracuse Stage, to participate. It was a bittersweet affair, attended by hundreds of playwrights, actors, and technicians, who marked up the crumbling walls of the theater with lines from their favorite shows and nostalgic graffiti: "Does anyone have change for a food stamp?" and "For a good time call 564-1235," the theater's number. The name of every show Playwrights had performed on 42nd Street was read aloud and highlights from such especially memorable productions as *Boo Hoo, Floyd Collins,* and *March of the Falsettos* were reenacted.

Moss, now sixty-seven years old, was as cheery and pragmatic as ever. In impromptu remarks delivered in the tiny upstairs studio theater, the Neil Armstrong of the new 42nd Street skipped lightly over the distant past, speaking mainly about the new opportunities he saw opening to Playwrights Horizons in the five-story, $24 million theater that soon would arise on this site. Later, though, as he mingled with old friends and colleagues on the main stage downstairs, Moss quietly asserted his and Playwrights Horizons claim to a 42nd Street legacy. "Theater Row is a David and Goliath story. It wasn't that we were such a great success, but that we did what we set out to do in the face of such skepticism," he said. "I never spoke about the economic value to the neighborhood of what we were doing. It never occurred to me. We didn't realize what we were doing. But if we had not built Theater Row, I don't think Rebecca, Cora [Cahan], and their gang would have had the conviction to do what they did on their block."

The redevelopment project greatly diminished, but did not eliminate, the porn business on 42nd Street. Despite a relentless smut-busting crusade by the Giuliani administration, Richard Basciano's Show World continued to operate, along with a half dozen lesser adult establishments along Eighth Avenue just outside the 42DP zone. Giuliani declared war on porn in 1998, after the New York State court of appeals upheld a 1995 zoning law that prohibited porn stores, topless clubs, and X-rated movie theaters from locating within five hundred feet of a church, school, or residential building. The city soon shut down nearly one-half of the city's 144 sex establishments, but not Show World, which exploited a loophole in the zoning law that allowed an adult store to remain open if it limited its sex-oriented material to 40 percent of floor space. Basciano loaded up on martial arts and wrestling videos, stopped offering live sex shows altogether, and leased space to a series of Off Off Broadway theater groups, filmmakers, and artists. In mid-1999, the Giuliani administration won a court order allowing it to shut down Show World on the grounds that it was the center of a fencing operation dealing in stolen camcorders and videocassette recorders. However, it turned out that the ring was operating not out of Show World but from a nearby storefront leased from Basciano, who promptly evicted the man. Show World reopened after three weeks and gradually restocked its shelves with hard-core videos and magazines as a series of court rulings put Mayor Giuliani and his smut-busters on the defensive. Michael Bloomberg, who succeeded Giuliani in 2002, seemed disinclined to mess with Basciano.

Peep-O-Rama, the last porn shop on West 42nd Street per se, was closed in July 2002, not by the city but by its new landlord, Douglas Durst. Peep-O-Rama occupied the ground floor of 121 West 42nd Street, a run-down little building that lay just east of the 42DP zone and smack in the middle of a site that the Durst Organization had painstakingly assembled for its planned 42nd Street encore: a 2.1 million-square-foot, $1 billion behemoth of an office tower that would fill the eastern two-thirds of the block occupied by the Condé Nast Building.

Similarly, the New York Times Co. doomed a couple of the surviving porn shops along Eighth Avenue in deciding to build a new fifty-two-story headquarters between 41st and 40th Streets, directly across from the Port Authority Bus Terminal on what was to have been the site of 42DP's merchandise mart. The *Times* was only moving three blocks from the massive fourteen-story white-brick building on 43rd Street that it had occupied ever since vacating the Times Tower in 1913. But to cinch the deal, the city granted the *Times* $29 million in tax breaks, and the state through 42DP obligingly condemned eleven properties, forcing some fifty-five businesses to move out in 2002 and 2003. The *Times* was expected to move into its new home in 2005, exactly 100 years after the city fathers had renamed Long Acre Square in honor of Adolf S. Och's newspaper.

Epilogue

Over the decades, many a New York governor and New York City mayor predicted the revival of 42nd Street and Times Square. However, the confidence avowed in all their fulsome rhetoric combined could not equal the conviction that one Edward L. Woodyard, a screenwriter from Armonk, New York, demonstrated through the theoretically simple act of making a hotel reservation in 1983.

Woodyard, whose wife was about to have a baby, was on the telephone with his brother-in-law, trying to figure out when the newborn would graduate from high school. "I went, 'Holy cow, I know the millennium doesn't start till 2001, Arthur Clarke and all that, but the party is when all those zeroes turn out, so let's have a big blowout when the zeroes turn over,'" Woodyard recalled. "And then I said, 'The only place to be in the world is Times Square.'" Woodyard feared that the only hotels still operating in Times Square were the kind that charged by the hour. But then he remembered that Marriott Corp. was building a big hotel on Broadway at 44th Street—right in the heart of Times Square. The hotel's foundation was only half finished, but Woodyard called Marriott's 800 number and tried to reserve a suite for December 31, 1999—sixteen years in the future. The screenwriter's call was batted around the Marriott bureaucracy until he finally got the ear of an executive vice president at corporate headquarters in Maryland. "Sure, we'll take the reservation," the man said. Woodyard got his suite and Marriott threw in two adjoining bedrooms for free.

Woodyard's faith and foresight were amply rewarded. He and his son Christopher, whose impending birth had inspired the hotel reservation, enjoyed a forty-fourth-floor ringside seat on the grandest of all of Times Square's ninety-five New Year's Eve celebrations. People had started gathering a few days before the ball was to drop, arriving in great swarming shoals from the New York suburbs, from every state in America, and from many foreign lands. By midday on December 30, Broadway's sidewalks were gridlocked from 42nd Street up to 52nd Street. That night the New York Police Department closed off fifty blocks of Midtown to traffic, but neither the barriers nor the sleet that began to fall in the wee hours slowed the massive influx. By the time the midnight countdown began in New York, 1.5 million to 2 million people were massed in the corridor between Sixth and Eighth Avenues, extending from 42nd Street all the way up to Central Park, and a global television audience of about 1 billion was tuned in. Waterford Crystal had designed a new high-tech crystal ball for the occasion; at 1,070 pounds, it was twice the size of its predecessor and a whole lot more pyrotechnic. The perfectly timed completion of the ball's descent down the seventy-seven-foot pole atop One Times Square touched off a fearsome roar. Up in his forty-fourth-floor perch, Woodyard was enraptured. "I was almost speechless," he said later. "I don't have words for it." He tried four anyway: "Spectacular. Phenomenal. Overpowering. Wow."

Billed as "Times Square 2000: The Global Celebration at the Crossroads of the World," the millennial celebration centered at 42nd Street and Broadway lived up to its own hype. This was no small achievement, considering the sorry state of the New Year's tradition when Ed Woodyard made his leap of faith. The glitter ball had kept its tightly scheduled appointment with gravity every year since Adolph Ochs had introduced the stunt in 1906 except two: in 1943 and 1944, the trough of World War II, the climactic moment had been marked by recorded chimes and a moment of silence. However, by the early 1980s attendance had dwindled markedly as New Year's Eve in New York in general and in Times Square in particular, as *Newsday* observed, had "degenerated into a besotted bacchanalia marked by pickpockets and robberies."

In today's cyber-ruled age, it was astounding that any *place*, much less one as culturally ancient as Times Square, had commanded center stage at the dawn of the millennium. Times Square is no longer necessary in many of the ways that it once was, as Paul Goldberger has noted in the *New Yorker*: "You don't have to get your news off the zipper sign, you don't have to get your entertainment on Broadway, and you certainly don't have to gather on the streets when something big happens, as people did on V-J Day." Yet Times Square's renascent popularity was affirmed daily (albeit on a much smaller scale) as this epochal New Year's Eve receded into the past. The crowds did thin after the terrorist attacks of September 11, 2001, but not for long. In 2002, a record 20 million people passed through Times Square proper, nearly twice as many as in the average year of the 1980s. The city widened the pavements to accommodate the expanded pedestrian flow, and still the sidewalks remain gridlocked much of the time, forcing the tardy and the impatient to take their chances walking in the street. In 2003, no less than in 1923, 42nd Street's intersection with Broadway and Seventh Avenue deserves the appellation the "Crossroads of the World." As New York cabdriver Elas Dieye, a native of Senegal, puts it: "It doesn't matter if you make it to Paris or London. You are not satisfied until you make it to Times Square, New York."

Even at the low ebb of Times Square's popularity in the 1970s and 1980s, no other area of the city was nearly as alluring to out-of-towners as Times Square. As a tourist hub, the Square has the unique advantage of acting as the Broadway theater's open-air foyer, as the long lines at the TKTS discount ticket booth on 47th Street make plain every afternoon. Times Square also is a prime tourist attraction in its own right and has been ever since advertisers began encasing it within towering banks of billboards and electronic signs early in the previous century. Advertising is pervasive today in ways that would have astounded Ochs, and yet no place in America comes close to matching the razzle-dazzle of Times Square's incessant, Godzilla-scale salesmanship, now updated to incorporate the latest in video and computer technology. As a rule, the latest generation of the oversize signs and billboards may suffer in comparison to the artistry of the classics of the 1940s and 1950s, but they are more numerous and luminous than ever before. Times Square's one-of-a-kind light show casts an appealingly paradoxical high-tech glow over the antique industry that is the Broadway theater, with its age-old theaters, middle-aged audiences, and penchant for revivals.

Over the last fifteen years, developers have invested big money to enhance Times Square's appeal to tourists and corporate tenants alike. First came the big Marriott Hotel where Woodyard spent New Year's Eve, followed by a host of themed restaurants and megastores offering what one skeptic characterized as "a wholesome and, on the whole, ingeniously engineered version of the famously carnivalesque atmosphere of the seedy Times Square of generations past." Toys R Us even put a five-story Ferris wheel in the lobby of the huge outlet (which the company touted as "the largest toy store in the world") it opened on Broadway at 44th Street. Most of these glitzy retail attractions occupied the lower floors of the new skyscrapers that had arisen along Broadway and Seventh Avenue, replacing scores of derelict low-rise buildings in which pornography, prostitution, and other socially malignant enterprises long had flourished.

The city heavily subsidized the redevelopment of Times Square by passing out tax breaks to developers and tenants, but did not resort to the mass condemnations and other draconian urban renewal methods used on 42nd Street. The architects of 42nd Street's remaking continue to argue that government had had no choice but to intervene massively in the twisted economy of the Deuce. In their view, privately led, piecemeal development of the sort that had occurred in the upper reaches of Times Square never would have happened along the length of 42nd Street because of its higher levels of porn infestation, on one hand, and its extreme fragmentation of property ownership, on the other. (The 42DP project area encompassed parcels held by more than seventy different owners.) The counterargument, as articulated most forcefully by the Durst family, was that it was the looming threat of condemnation itself that had retarded development.

If 42nd Street had been left to its own devices, would business have committed substantial capital to its improvement after fifty years of disinvestment and neglect as the adjoining blocks of Times Square began to revive in the late 1980s? Probably. Clearly, though, once the city and state effectively had sentenced the Deuce to death by concocting the 42nd Street Development Project, government was obliged to press forward as expeditiously as possible. Had the Koch administration not turned against the City at 42nd Street, the street's remaking likely would have been completed by the mid-1980s. Self-serving political maneuvering was as much to blame for 42DP's hazardously protracted gestation as were forces beyond government's control. The project was afflicted by no less than three extended downturns in the property market, the last of which came with the recession of 2001 to 2003.

By the end of 2003, the redevelopment was best characterized as a qualified success economically. No longer was 42nd Street Midtown's economic dead zone; it had been integrated into the city's economy, radiating financial benefits to businesses and property owners throughout an area of many square blocks. However, there remained a patchwork quality to 42nd Street's revival. There were notable successes, to be sure. Both the New Amsterdam and the Ford Center for the Performing Arts were thriving as hosts to long-running musicals. Despite a lofty admission price, Madame Tussaud's wax museum was packing them in. The twenty-five-screen AMC Empire had established itself as the highest-grossing movie complex in America, and the smaller Sony multiplex across the street was not far behind. The cavernous, brightly lit McDonald's in the lower floors of the Candler Building (which had been cleverly designed to resemble the backstage area of a Broadway theater) ranked among the burger chain's five most profitable operations in the country. But for most restaurants and stores that were not tourist destinations in themselves, the new 42nd Street was a disappointment. It looked as well-scrubbed and safe and tourist-friendly as did Times Square proper and yet many of the out-of-towners who thronged Broadway never bothered to turn the corner and make their way down the refurbished theater block. Thousands of commuters were still coursing down 42nd Street every weekday headed to or from the Port Authority Bus Terminal, but the street's lineup of overly familiar national chain stores and restaurants tempted far too few of them into stopping, just as its refurbished theaters enticed too few of the 250,000 workers in all those shiny new office towers into sticking around after hours.

In transplanting a particularly glitzy version of shopping-mall theme-park culture from the suburbs into the heart of the big city, the redevelopers of the theater district enhanced its tourist appeal at the cost of disappointing and even alienating many New Yorkers. To be sure, local residents were best able to appreciate redevelopment's accomplishments. In a city that has blithely swept many an architectural treasure into the waste bin over the years, the restoration of the New Amsterdam, arguably New York's finest theater, and the Victory, its oldest theater, is no small matter. The project also inspired private interests to restore two historically important 42nd Street buildings that lay outside its boundaries: the Candler and the old Knickerbocker Hotel. And the resurgence of tourism and theater patronage along Broadway redounds to the economic benefit of the whole city, which needs all the financial help it can get. But for many if not most New Yorkers, a Times Square and 42nd Street lined with ESPN Zones, Chevy's, Disney Stores, and the like and swarming with tourists is perhaps an even less appealing destination than was the Deuce, which at least was intensely, bizarrely itself.

The old Times Square was the last great preserve of quirky, time-warp New York. For better or worse, its idiosyncrasies were the product of an economic decline that lasted for many decades, far longer than a market economy usually allows. It had to vanish, for ruin is the inevitable outcome of decline. There certainly is no turning back the clock now. Hubert's Museum is not going to be revived, nor is Murray's Roman Gardens, Minsky's, or the Automat. But one can only hope that with the passing of time the irresistible force of entropy will create a place for the unfamiliar and the unexpected on 42nd Street, making it again as distinctive and as quintessentially New York a place as it was in 1910, 1930, 1950, 1970, or even 1980, for that matter.

Notes

Overture

3   "I wasn't naked . . .": Morton Minsky and Milt Machlin, *Minsky's Burlesque*, 144.

4   "Times Square has all the mystique . . .": "Lurid but Profitable 42d Street Hopes to Survive New Cleanup," *New York Times*, 3/26/66.

6   "The struggle to reclaim . . .": Michael Sorkin, *Variations on a Theme Park*, xv.

6   "That's the magic of the place . . .": David W. Dunlap, "Reviving a True Classic on West 42nd Street," *New York Times*, 8/14/94.

Fathers of Times Square

9   "In his heyday . . .": Freddie Stockdale, *Emperors of Song*, 90.

9   The review of *Kohinoor* by James Huneker is quoted in William Morrison, "Oscar Hammerstein I: The Man Who Invented Times Square," *Marquee*, first quarter 1983, 3.

10   awarded thirty-eight patents: Hugh Fadin, *Getting to Know Him*, 7.

10   "Members of the family . . .": Vincent Sheean, *Oscar Hammerstein I*, xvii.

10   "Because of his determination . . .": John F. Carroll, "Oscar Hammer-
          stein I: 1895 to 1915," 5–6.

11   "a conically shaped topper . . .": Sheean, xviii.

12   "Any tobacconist who refuses . . .": Charles Mathes, *The Hammersteins
          of New York*, 1.

13   "Crowds throng the sidewalks . . .": James D. McCabe Jr., *New York by
          Sunlight and Gaslight*, 153, 155.

13   Road company numbers: Margaret Knapp, "A Historical Study of the
          Legitimate Playhouses on West Forty-Second Street Between Seventh
          and Eighth Avenues in New York City," 13.

13   "was a street of legend . . .": Lloyd Morris, *Incredible New York*, 182.

13   "With an unexpectedly sure . . .": Stockdale, 100.

14   "When I get through with you . . .": Morrison.

15   "most elegant display-case for feminine beauty": Morris, 189.

16   Details of *The Prodigal Daughter:* Knapp, 24–26.

17   "Historically, the center of the city . . .": William R. Taylor's introduc-
          tion to *Inventing Times Square*, xxv.

17   The politics of New York subway construction: Clifton Hood, *722 Miles*,
          56–71.

18   "My theater will make a place . . .": Sheean, 83.

19   "There was a tremendous uproar . . .": Ibid., 91. Theodore Roosevelt,
          then police commissioner of New York, decided to see for himself what
          all the fuss was about. He bought a ticket and was delighted to discover
          that one of the Olympia's risqué tableaux had been copied from a paint-
          ing hanging in his own library. Roosevelt "considered the whole act
          'artistic' and quite evidently enjoyed it"—no doubt to Hammerstein's
          chagrin.

19   "Hammerstein's originality . . .": Ibid., 95.

19   "It was a little after 10 o'clock . . .": Carroll, 84–5.

19   Hammerstein's explanation to the "bewildered bucolics . . .": Anthony
          Slide, *Selected Vaudeville Criticism*, 47.

20   "I am in receipt . . ." and "I have lost all . . .": Sheean, 97–8.

20   "You see those old shacks . . .": Ibid., 99.

21   "He encountered flat opposition at first . . .": Ibid., 101.

21   "We had no money . . .": Morrison.

21   "I have named my theater . . .": Fadin, 8.

22   "simply, and no doubt truthfully . . .": Carroll, 115.

23   "The roof was a wonderful . . .": Loney Haskell, "The Corner: Reminis-
          cences of Hammerstein's Victoria," pt. 1, *New Yorker*, 12/13/30.

23   "Realizing that its main . . .": Knapp, 81.

24 "He told the publisher . . .": Gerald W. Johnson, *An Honorable Titan*, 202.

24 "founded upon a rock": Sarah Bradford and Carl W. Condit, *Rise of the New York Skyscraper: 1865–1913*, 312.

25 "The brilliant illumination . . .": Meyer Berger, *The Story of the New York Times*, 149–50.

25 "The tower makes the building . . .": Susan Tifft and Alex Jones, *The Trust*, 72.

25 "The new building loomed up . . .": Berger, 151.

25 "No station on our route . . .": W. G. Rogers and Mildred Weston, *Carnival Crossroads;* 77–8.

26 "very likely the name . . .": Ibid., 79.

26 Subway statistics: Hood, 114–15.

27 "A final burst of fireworks . . .": Berger, 155.

The Great White Way: Pleasure Zone Supreme

29 "a bit of a Tartar . . .": Brooks McNamara, *The Shuberts of Broadway*, 25.

29 "the master of mediocrity . . .": Brooks Atkinson, *Broadway*, 45.

30 "The New Amsterdam . . .": Nicholas Van Hoogstraten, *Lost Broadway Theaters*, 73.

31 "even his hair looked . . .": Foster Hirsch, *The Boys from Syracuse*, 33.

32 "From their rooms . . .": Margaret Knapp, "A Historical Study of the Legitimate Playhouses on West Forty-Second Street Between Seventh and Eighth Avenues in New York City," 135–6.

33 "His shameless flag-waving . . .": Atkinson, 111–12.

33 Erlanger's conversation with Cohan: Ward Morehouse, *Yankee Prince*, 84.

33 Erlanger's showdown with the Shuberts: Jerry Stagg, *The Brothers Shubert*, 70.

34 "America really took a female . . .": Eve Golden, "Julian Eltinge: The Queen of Old Broadway," *TheaterWeek*, 7/31/95.

34 "Women went into ecstasy . . .": John Holusha, "A Theater's Muses Rescued," *New York Times*, 3/24/00.

34 "For the obese theater lovers . . .": Van Hoogstraten, 147.

34 "I lead a life . . .": Vincent Sheean, *Oscar Hammerstein I*, 121.

35 Lew Fields was one half of the celebrated Jewish comedy duo Weber and Fields, which had made its Broadway debut at the Olympia. Ham-

merstein also had booked them into the Victoria. In 1904, Fields broke up the act to go it alone. With Hammerstein's encouragement, Fields formed his own stock company of musical comedy players and took up what proved to be brief residence in the Lew M. Fields Theater.

35   "Vaudeville audiences across . . .": John Carroll, "Oscar Hammerstein I: 1895 to 1915," 239.

35   "Albee was the owner . . .": John F. Dimeglio, *Vaudeville U.S.A.*, 25.

36   First obscenity bust on 42nd Street: Knapp, 37.

36   Keith and Hammerstein both realized that their "contract" never would have withstood the scrutiny of a court. In effect, their pact was nothing more than a gentleman's agreement.

37   "If E. F. Albee owned . . .": Abel Green and Joe Lurie, *Show Biz*, 17.

37   "Whenever he had engaged . . .": Anna Marble Pollock, "Notes," *New York Times*, 12/2/34.

38   "That grand old showcase . . .": Buster Keaton with Charles Samuels, *My Wonderful World of Slapstick*, 68–9.

38   "When the Karno company . . .": Lillian Ross, *Moments with Chaplin*, 20.

39   "As I came off . . .": Will Rogers, *The Autobiography of Will Rogers*, 32.

39   "We have never produced another . . .": Ibid., 31.

39   Houdini's East River publicity stunt: Harold Kellock, *Houdini*, 232. Houdini could pick any lock, usually with a piece of metal hidden in his mouth. Although the box looked solid enough to pass any inspection, one of its boards was attached by short screws that Houdini was able to remove with his fingers and wriggle through.

40   "Houdini always described . . .": Ibid., 234.

40   "drawing power was more important . . .": Loney Haskell, "The Corner: Reminiscences of Hammerstein's Victoria," pt. 2, *New Yorker*, 12/20/30.

40   "In a sense, Oscar . . .": Ibid., pt. 1, *New Yorker*, 12/13/30.

40   "They'll have to *kill* someone . . .": Green and Lurie, 18.

41   Willie's court artist hype: Ibid., 21–2.

41   "Reggie and I . . .": Sheean, xvii.

42   "Broadway from 34th to 47th . . .": Stephen Jenkins, *The Greatest Street in the World*, 256. By most accounts, O. J. Gude, a shrewd advertising man nicknamed "the Napoleon of Publicity," coined "the Great White Way" in 1901. Fortunately, he neglected to copyright the slogan.

42   "The phrase '42nd Street . . .": Atkinson, 18.

42   "The celebration of New Year's . . .": Jenkins, 269.

42   "Demand for tables . . .": George Rector, *The Girl from Rector's*, 113–14.

43   "I never dreamed . . .": Derek Wilson, *The Astors: 1763–1992*, 205.

43   "Wall Street financiers, industrial . . .": Lloyd Morris, *Incredible New York*, 259.

44   "The Astor's interiors . . .": Robert A. M. Stern, Gregory Gilmartin, and John Montague, *New York 1900*, 269.

44   A favorite drinking sport at Knickerbocker's bar was the spinning of yarns about *Old King Cole*. According to the most popular tale, the artist depicted His Royal Highness as a flatulent monarch surrounded by royal attendants attempting in vain to hide their amusement. Parrish insisted that "when I painted it my thoughts were 100 percent pure."

44   Belasco at Shanley's: *Where and How to Dine in New York*, 62.

45   "A Broadway restaurant must . . .": Lewis A. Erenberg, *Steppin' Out*, 44.

45   Description of Murray's: "Murray's Roman Gardens," *New York Plaisance* 1 (1908), 47–48; and Rem Koolhaus, *Delirious New York*, 82–4.

46   "They even have lights . . .": Julian Street, "Lobster Palace Society," *Everybody's Magazine* 22 (May 1910).

46   "was the great Bohemian place . . .": Evander Berry Wall, *Neither Pest Nor Puritan*, 35.

46   "I found Broadway . . .": Rector, 3.

47   "Like Sherry's and . . .": Ibid., 155, 157.

47   "When Diamond Jim . . .": Ibid., 15.

47   Diamond Jim's gustatory exploits: Ibid., 16–20.

48   "These restaurants were artfully . . .": Morris, 261.

49   "at this writing, is the newest . . .": Street.

Flo Ziegfeld and the Cult of the Chorus Girl

50   "It was somewhat of a letdown . . .": Charlie Chaplin, *My Autobiography*, 119, 121.

51   "frequented by all classes . . .": Timothy Gilfoyle, "Policing of Sexuality," in *Reinventing Times Square*, ed. William R. Taylor, 303.

52   The hapless Osgood: Ibid., 306.

52   "Broadway was the avenue . . .": Laurence Seneleck, "Private Parts in Public Places," in *Reinventing Times Square*, 331.

53   "Numerous colored women . . .": Gilfoyle, 302.

53   "More than any figure . . ." and Nevell quote: Lois Banner, *American Beauty*, 180.

53   "the fire that provides . . .": Allen Churchill, *The Great White Way: A Recreation of Broadway's Golden Era of Theatrical Entertainment*, 8.

54   "Outside the stage door . . .": Evelyn Nesbit, *Prodigal Days*, 59.

54   "Girls who can stand in line . . .": Theodore Dreiser, *Sister Carrie*, 439–42.

55   "A girl my age . . .": Nesbit, 19.

56   "supping at Rector's . . .": Ibid., 24.

56   For accounts of Nesbit's seduction by White: Suzannah Lessard, *The Architect of Desire*, 277–91; and Nesbit's own *Prodigal Days*.

57   "It was loads of fun . . .": Nesbit, 47–8.

57   "hatred of Stanford White . . .": Ibid.

58   "*Florodora* beauties sing . . .": Lessard, 291.

58   "His passage to his table . . .": Michael M. Mooney, *Evelyn Nesbit and Stanford White*, 224.

59   "She was dressed . . .": John F. Carroll, "Oscar Hammerstein I: 1895 to 1915," 165.

60   "Though he and [Oscar] Hammerstein . . .": Nesbit, 266.

60   "In my life . . .": Vincent Sheean, "Oscar Hammerstein I," 338.

61   "Arthur tried to keep . . .": Loney Haskell, "The Corner," pt. 2, *New Yorker*, 12/30/30.

61   "The customary crowd . . .": Carroll, 271.

62   The Candler was built by Asa Candler, one of the founders of the Coca-Cola Co.

64   "Even the Strand . . .": Ben M. Hall, *Best Remaining Seats*, 51.

64   Opening night at the Rialto: Ibid., 50–51.

65   Architectural description of the Rialto: Ibid., 51.

65   "utterly devoid of intellect . . .": Charles Higham, *Ziegfeld*, 233.

66   "twangy, whiny voice . . .": Herbert G. Goldman, *Fanny Brice*, 43.

67   "It was like nitro . . .": Eve Golden, *Anna Held and the Birth of Ziegfeld's Broadway*, 22.

68   "merely a dim satellite . . .": Ibid., 111.

68   The cast of *The Follies of 1907* included May McKenzie, a chorus girl who had befriended Evelyn Nesbit and testified at length at Thaw's trial.

69   "Tall blondes with complexions . . .": J. P. McEvoy, *Show Girl*, 6.

69   "Deliciously robotic creatures . . .": Ralph Blumenthal, *The Stork Club*, 90.

69   "There are those today . . .": Marjorie Farnsworth, *The Ziegfeld Follies*, 81.

69   "Even if I had known . . .": Richard Ziegfeld and Paulette Ziegfeld, *The Ziegfeld Touch*, 56.

70   "I have a natural knack . . .": Ibid., 59.

70   "Half the comedians . . .": Ann Corio, *This Was Burlesque*, 64.

71   Golf at the New Amsterdam: Simon Louvish, *The Man on the Flying Trapeze*, 204–5. In a second version of the golf story, Fields said that he had first said "My, what a beautiful horse" and finally arrived by trial and error at camel. "I experimented night after night to find out what animal was the funniest," he said. "The funniest thing about comedy is you never know why people laugh."

71   Ziegfeld's fear of dwarves: Higham, 158–9.

72   "cartoonist working in the flesh": Barbara W. Grossman, *Funny Woman*, 99.

72   Brice's sidewalk contract display: Ibid., 39.

72   Brice's version of "My Man": Goldman, 104; and Higham, 144–5.

Last Suppers and Final Curtains

74   "In 1912, prostitution . . .": Timothy Gilfoyle, "Policing of Sexuality," in *Reinventing Times Square*, ed. William R. Taylor, 311.

74   "less open vice . . .": Ibid.

74   Throughout the city, brothels were replaced in the mid-1910s by "call houses"—cheap apartments rented by prostitutes. No longer allowed to work hotels and restaurants, hookers relied on bellboys, waiters, and taxicab drivers to steer johns their way. In Times Square especially, many prostitutes now operated out of taxicabs, charging $5 for their favors and $3 for the cab. As one hotel clerk put it, taxis were "nothing but floating whorehouses." Ibid., 312.

74   "Never before had . . .": Lloyd Morris, *Incredible New York*, 318.

74   "feverish, festive . . .": Ibid., 163.

75   "I speak of the last years . . .": George Rector, *The Girl from Rector's*, 205.

75   "It was a booze . . .": Ibid., 212.

75   "Do not wiggle . . .": David Nasaw, *Going Out*, 106.

76   "It sounds silly . . .": Mr. and Mrs. Vernon Castle, *Modern Dancing*, 47.

76   "Nowadays we dance . . .": Morris, 321.

76   "The opening night . . .": Irene Castle, *My Husband*, 57–8.

77   "short on wit . . .": Stephen Burge Johnson, *The Roof Gardens of Broadway Theatres, 1883–1942*, 152.

77   "It was dangerous . . .": Stanley Walker, *The Night Club Era*, 79.

78   "Pep speakers and patriotic . . .": Ibid., 81.

78   "There was a weird aroma . . .": Rector, 214.

78   "New Yorkers crowded . . .": Morris, 294.

79   "We can't go on . . .": Lewis Erenberg, "Impresarios of Broadway Night Life," in *Reinventing Times Square*, ed. William R. Taylor, 165.

79   "Ask the big hotels . . .": Andrew Sinclair, *Prohibition, the Era of Excess*, 232.

79   A guide to Midtown Manhattan observed ruefully in 1925 that the Knickerbocker "is so completely an office structure that it is a safe wager not one in 500,000 who pass it ever recall the crowded lobby where swains met lassies back in 1915." The public would not regain access to *Old King Cole* until 1935, when it was installed over the bar of the St. Regis Hotel, a posh Astor-owned establishment on 56th Street off Fifth Avenue.

80   "dancing, a sort of show . . .": Walker, 78–80.

80   Number of New York speakeasies: Sinclair, 230–1.

80   "knew little about cooking . . .": Walker, 83.

81   "you saw throngs . . .": Morris, 333.

81   "Hundreds of thousands . . .": J. George Fredericks, *Adventuring in New York*, 38.

82   Broadway statistics, 1920s: Jack Poggi, *Theater in America*, 46–7.

82   *Kosher Kitty Kelly:* Margaret Knapp, "A Historical Study of the Legitimate Playhouse on West Forty-Second Street Between Seventh and Eighth Avenues in New York City," 325.

83   "I may be wrong . . .": Brooks Atkinson, *Broadway*, 321.

83   "I'd never seen anything . . .": Richard Ziegfeld and Paulette Ziegfeld, *The Ziegfeld Touch*, 98.

83   *Follies* competitors: Randolph Carter, *The World of Flo Ziegfeld*, 101–9.

84   Escalating revue nudity: Stephen M. Vallilo, "Broadway Revues in the Teens and Twenties: Smut and Slime?"

84   "He kept strands of . . .": Charles Higham, *Ziegfeld*, 153.

84   Publicity stunts: Ibid., 155.

85   "The baring of breasts . . .": Carter, 105.

85   "to pass on the moral . . .": Laurence Senelik, "Private Parts in Public Places," in *Reinventing Times Square*, ed. William R. Taylor, 334.

86   "Bowery museums . . .": Luc Sante, *Low Life*, 99.

86   "After the theater . . .": William Ballantine, *Wild Tigers & Tame Fleas*, 252.

87   "Everyone had fistfuls . . .": Carter, 148.

88   Decline in theater weeks: Poggi, 49–50.

88   The *Abie's* bonanza: Ibid., 63.

88   72 percent failure rate: Knapp, 334–5.

89   *Ten Commandments* at the Criterion: William Leach, "Introductory Essay (Commercial Aesthetics)," *Reinventing Times Square,* ed. William R. Taylor, 237.

89   "The overheated air . . .": Dennis Sharp, *The Picture Palace and Other Buildings for the Movies.*

90   241 West 42nd: Knapp, 352–3.

91   Before deciding on 42nd Street, McGraw-Hill considered preleasing a big chunk of what would become the city's largest building upon its completion in 1931, the Empire State Building.

91   "looks as if [it] were cut . . .": Eric P. Nash, *Manhattan Skyscrapers,* 81.

The Grind House Phoenix

94   The Automat's Depression bonanza: Daniel Cohen, "For Food Both Cold and Hot, Put Your Nickels in the Slot," *Smithsonian,* 1/86. The first Automat in New York City opened in 1912 on Broadway at 46th Street and was an immediate sensation. The Times Square Automat held its own amid the dazzle of the theater district with a stained-glass front window thirty feet high artfully backlit to display the name AUTOMAT framed by garlands of fruits and flowers. Times Square was "a dream location. . . . Besides the after-theater crowd, the boarding houses and cheap hotels that lined the side streets assured it a three-meal-a-day clientele of theater hands, clerks and blue-collar workers."

94   "has degenerated into something . . .": Stanley Walker, *The Night Club Years,* 203.

94   "shooting galleries, bowling . . .": Ward Morehouse, *Matinee Tomorrow,* 260.

95   Ripley's Odditorium: "A Cleanup on the Square?" *Newsweek,* 4/18/66.

95   "Every other door in the block . . .": Helen Worden, *Here Is New York,* 25–6.

97   "the most elegant burlesque theater . . .": Gypsy Rose Lee, *Gypsy: A Memoir,* 251.

97   "natural on 42nd Street . . .": *Variety,* 10/27/31, 35.

98   "As a self-appointed champion . . .": "The Personal History of a Self-Made Man," *New York Times,* 7/14/40.

99   "Let 'em sue": "Exhibitors Dare Big Stars to Sue," *New York Post,* 5/5/38.

99   "The place was bristling . . .": Arthur L. Mayer, *Merely Colossal,* 167.

100   "The new Rialto will be . . .": Arthur L. Mayer, "A New Deal for the Forgotten Man," *New York Times*, 12/20/36.

100   "to glorify the American ghoul": Mayer, *Merely Colossal*, 170.

101   "labored over the copy . . .": E. J. Kahn Jr., "Boffos and Bustos," *New Yorker*, 12/9/74.

101   "Handicapped by weak . . .": Mayer, *Merely Colossal*, 176.

101   "I should have changed . . .": Michael Mok, "Hurrah for Horror! Down with Sex!" *New York Post*, 2/18/37.

101   "Our seats are probably . . .": Ibid.

101   "ushers were instructed to steer . . .": David Nasaw, *Going Out*, 236–7.

102   "attracted many patrons . . .": Mayer, *Merely Colossal*, 179.

102   "Word passed around . . .": "Tear Gas Empties Movie in 42d St.,"*New York Times*, 10/11/36.

102   "excessively vulgar, gossipy . . .": J. B Kaufman, "Movie Musicals Turn a Corner at 42nd Street," *American Cinematographer*, May 1994.

102   "Its title alone . . .": Rocco Fumento, introduction to Rian James and James Seymour, *42nd Street* screenplay, 13.

103   "hardboiled musical": J. Hoberman, *42nd Street*, 19.

103   "You're going out a youngster . . .": James and Seymour, 182.

103   "a production number so spectacular . . .": Kaufman.

103   "This time I'll sock . . .": James and Seymour, 64.

103   "Two hundred people . . .": Ibid., 182.

103   "Forty-second Street! . . .": Ibid., 141–2.

104   The progress of the 42nd Street Special: Hoberman, 32–3.

105   "If the gods had descended . . .": Ibid.

105   "While variety became vaudeville . . .": Irving Ziedman, *The American Burlesque Show*, 13.

106   "occupational disease . . .": Ibid., 42.

107   "just rotten, with parts . . .": Margaret Knapp, "A Historical Study of the Legitimate Playhouses on West Forty-Second Street Between Seventh and Eighth Avenues in New York City," 380–1.

107   "The notoriety given . . .": Ziedman, 169.

108   "The chorus girls were dressed . . .": Lee, 252–3.

108   "The remarkable thing . . .": Ibid., 97.

109   "Her music, 'Hold That Tiger' . . .": Ann Corio, *This Was Burlesque*, 90–2.

109   "As far as he was concerned . . .": Morton Minsky and Milt Machlin, *Minsky's Burlesque*, 101.

110   "When I say the theater contained . . .": Ibid., 197.

110   "There were still traces . . .": Lee, 255.

110   "a hoodlum element . . .": Brooks McNamara, "The Entertainment District at the End of the Thirties," in *Reinventing Times Square,* ed. William R. Taylor, 181.

111   "the almost universal idea . . .": Stanley Buder, "Forty-Second Street at the Crossroads: A History of Broadway to Eighth Avenue," in "West 42nd Street: The Bright Light Zone," ed. William Kornblum, 69.

111   "I was stone broke . . .": Herbert Huncke, *Guilty of Everything,* 43–4.

112   "By and large . . .": Milton Bracker, "Life on W. 42nd St.: A Study in Decay," *New York Times,* 3/14/60.

112   "Billy's new Broadway neighbors . . .": Minsky and Machlin, 97.

113   "This is the randiest story . . .": Corio, 134.

114   "Witnesses at the clean-up . . .": Minsky and Machlin, 108.

114   License Commissioner James F. Geraghty was no friend of burlesque, but he rose to the defense of Hubert's Museum and its headliner, Professor Heckler's Flea Circus, when the 42nd Street Property Owners' lawyer cast aspersions on them during the hearings. When the dime museum's license came up for renewal later that year, Geraghty praised it as "one of the most marvelous exhibitions in the city," even endorsing Doraldina, the double-gaited wonder, whose contortions some considered suggestive.

114   La Guardia's "puritanical streak . . .": Lawrence Elliott, *Little Flower,* 221–2.

115   "I'll open up with burlesque . . .": "New Burlesque on 42nd Street Barred," *New York Times,* 6/27/34.

115   "By the time I joined . . .": Lee, 256.

115   "No female shall be permitted . . .": Minsky and Machlin, 139.

116   "tend to corrupt . . .": "7 Chorus Girls Arrested in 42d St. Theater Raid," *New York Herald Tribune,* 11/17/34.

116   "I often thought . . .": Minsky and Machlin, 195–6.

116   "The lack of imagination . . .": 277.

116   "This is the beginning . . .": Ibid.

116   "If the audience couldn't . . .": Ibid., 281.

116   "The Bishop—any Bishop . . .": "The Eltinge Show," *New York Times,* 4/23/42.

Birth of the Cool: Hipster 42nd Street

118   "to go to Times Square . . .": Jill Stone, *Times Square,* 119.

119   "They had had repeated warnings . . .": "Moss Denies Licenses to 2 'Follies' Houses," *New York Times,* 2/1/42.

119   Brandts' development plans: "Brandt's Skyscraper or Hotel Planned for 42d–43d St., N.Y., Plot," *Variety* 6/12/46.

119   "Inside the theater . . .": Will Friedwald, *Sinatra! The Song Is You,* 124.

119   "He loved observing . . .": Patricia Bosworth, *Marlon Brando,* 50.

120   "In the early forties . . .": Woody Allen, "Playing It Again," *New York,* 4/6/98.

120   Wilson's 42nd Street tour: Earl Wilson, "42nd Street Badly Maligned; Its Fleas Are Lively," *New York Post,* 5/1/44.

121   "boomtown similar to . . ." and "How could you stop . . .": Stanley Buder, "Forty-Second Street at the Crossroads: A History of Broadway to Eighth Avenue," in "West 42nd Street: The Bright Light Zone," ed. William Kornblum, 71.

121   "Girlie" magazines: Frederick S. Lane III, *Obscene Profits,* 23.

121   "to make very abrupt . . .": Tennessee Williams, *Memoirs,* 53.

122   V-J Day: *Century in Times Square* (from the archives of the *New York Times*), 27; Stone, 126–7.

123   Coney Island attendance: David Nasaw, *Going Out,* 243.

123   In the spring of 1957, the disc jockey–cum–promoter Alan Freed brought the first of a series of all-star revues to the Paramount, breaking all of its previous attendance records.

123   "What was formerly a man's castle . . .": Arthur Mayer, *Merely Colossal,* 249.

124   "Goodbye to Ghouls . . .": E. J. Kahn Jr., "Boffos and Bustos," *New Yorker,* 12/9/74. Mayer never claimed to be prescient about television's impact on 42nd Street. Basically, he sold the Rialto because he had grown bored with the grinder scene as he shifted focus to the importation and distribution of European art house films like De Sica's *The Bicycle Thief* and Renoir's *The Lower Depths.*

124   "After World War II . . .": Kenneth L. Jackson, *Crabgrass Frontier.*

124   "These days the audiences run . . .": William Ballantine, *Wild Tigers & Tame Fleas,* 252–3.

125   "finest first-run . . .": Brandt Theaters file, New York Public Library for the Performing Arts.

125   "I used to rush down there . . .": Phillip Lopate, "42nd Street, You Ain't No Sodom," *New York Times,* 3/8/79.

126   "Back when I was out of my head . . .": Kevin Thomas, "A Long Wait, a Long Road for Hubert Selby's 'Last Exit,'" *Los Angeles Times*, 5/26/90.

126   "Westerns were particularly popular . . .": Marc Eliot, *Down 42nd Street*, 101–2.

126   Apocalyptic sales patter: Farnsworth Fowle, "'Giftshops' Baiting Tourist Trap Here," *New York Times*, 7/26/53; and "Broadway Blues," *New York Times*, 7/30/53.

127   "a neonized jungle . . .": Ballantine, 229.

127   "hanging around Bickford's . . .": Barry Gifford and Lawrence Lee, *Jack's Book*, 39.

127   "timeless room . . .": Steven Watson, *The Birth of the Beat Generation*, 76.

128   Kerouac and "beat": Herbert Huncke, *Guilty of Everything*, 72.

128   "Huncke appeared to us . . .": Tom Clark, *Jack Kerouac*, 71.

128   "As far as I know . . .": Herbert Huncke, *The Evening Sun Turned Crimson*, 8.

128   "I was always quick . . .": Huncke, *Guilty of Everything*, 43.

128   "I didn't mind being known . . .": Ibid., 44.

129   "Talking is my stock . . .": Watson, 72.

129   "the greatest storyteller I know . . .": Ibid., 74.

129   "huddled in coats . . .": Huncke, *The Evening Sun Turned Crimson*, 70–1.

130   "He had walked up and down . . .": Ibid., 80–1.

130   "my immediate reaction . . .": Ibid., 77.

130   "easily the city's most exciting . . .": Gore Vidal, *Palimpsest*, 101–2.

130   "There were really people that lived . . .": Gifford and Lee, 53–5.

131   Huncke and Dexter Gordon: Jerome Poynton, "Biographical Sketch," in *The Herbert Huncke Reader*, ed. Benjamin G. Schafer, xxii.

131   "Orson Welles's *Touch of Evil* . . .": Eliot, 101.

132   "His opponents would change . . .": www.ishipress.com/flease.htm.

132   "Forty-second Street was dangerous . . .": Patricia Bosworth, *Diane Arbus*, 166.

132   "When she first approached the freaks . . .": Ibid., 167.

133   "believed so totally in his fakery . . . studiously ignore us": Ibid., 167–8.

133   "drive the honky-tonks . . .": Charles G. Bennett, "Plan Board Seeks Times Sq. Clean-Up," *New York Times*, 11/11/53. Also, "Times Sq. Arcade Ban Protested," *New York Herald Tribune*, 11/12/53; and "Curb on Arcades in Times Sq. Voted," *New York Times*, 12/24/53.

133   McCaffrey's crackdown on the grinders: "Hearing Is Slated on Film Displays," *New York Times*, 10/7/54; "42d St. Movies to Adopt Curbs on

Lobby and Marquee Displays," *New York Times*, 10/9/54; and "42d Street Movies Bow to Good Taste," *New York Times*, 10/23/54.

133   "New York entered the postwar . . .": Roger Starr, *The Rise and Fall of New York City*, 113.

134   Times Square crackdown: "125 Seized in Times Square in a Drive on Undesirables," *New York Times*, 7/31/54; and "23 More Undesirables Are Seized in Times Square as Round-Up Spreads," *New York Times*, 8/1/54.

135   *Nights of Horror: Burke v. Kingsley Books*, 208 Misc. 150; 142 N.Y.S.2d 735. See also James Jackson, *The Smut Peddlers*, 96–9.

135   "all publications teaching lust . . .": Paul Crowell, "Ban on Crime-Inciting 'Comic' Ordered Sought in Court by City," *New York Times*, 9/9/54.

135   City's legal tussles with Kingsley and Times Square Book Bazaar: "Sale of a Crime Book Is Blocked as City Takes 5 Sellers to Court," *New York Times*, 9/11/54; and "2 Bookshops Accept Ban," *New York Times*, 9/18/54.

135   "indisputably pornographic . . .": "Court Upholds Ban on 'Obscene' Book," *New York Times*, 4/28/56.

135   *Roth v. United States:* Lane, 25–6.

Milking an Ugly Cow: Speculating on Redevelopment

138   Snibbe's scheme: Don Ross, "A Dream for a 'Clean' W. 42d St," *New York Herald Tribune*, 11/14/62.

Snibbe's was one of several 42nd Street redevelopment schemes floated in the early 1960s. The novelist Herman Wouk, whose book *The Caine Mutiny* had morphed into a hit play, urged the city to form a New York Theatre Authority as a vehicle for rehabbing Broadway theaters being used as "second-rate movie houses" and television studios. The authority would operate on a not-for-profit basis, making theaters available for commercial productions "under a special economic arrangement in which all parties in the theatre—dramatists, directors, producers, players, stagehands, and so forth—would accept reduced economic benefits." Reduced productions costs would translate to lower ticket prices, the novelist added. "The idea is to have more plays on Broadway at a lower cost to entrepreneurs, backers and audience, thus enabling shows to survive without being colossal smashes." At the same time, the city as a whole would benefit from the restoration to legitimate use of haphazardly maintained playhouses on run-down streets, Wouk continued. In particular, "the Theatre Authority could be the means for the long-overdue restoration of 42nd Street to its old status as one of the most attractive and famous streets in the world." (Herman Wouk, "Proposal for Renewal," *New York Times*, 9/10/61).

There was no denying the validity of Wouk's view that the Broadway theater was a vital cog in the tourism industry or that tourism, in turn, was a critical component of New York City's economy. Nor was there any doubt that Broadway desperately needed help: the number of new productions had declined from eighty-one in the 1950–51 season to a mere forty-eight in 1960–61, as Broadway lost ground not only to television but also to the smaller "Off Broadway" theaters now proliferating throughout Manhattan. It was certainly possible that Wouk's scheme would have breathed some desperately needed creativity into Broadway while boosting attendance. But its principal effect would have been to greatly expand productive capacity in an industry hurting for lack of demand. Would U.S. Steel react to loss of market share by reopening factories closed in the 1930s? The question was not how much it would cost to recast 42nd Street's grind houses in legitimate form, but whether anything short of the demise of television and the movies could restore Broadway to the popularity it enjoyed in the 1920s.

The January 1962 issue of *Show* magazine carried a widely read article by Henry Hope Reed Jr. and Gay Talese proposing that 42nd Street's ten movie grinders be converted back to use as playhouses. This would be "a relatively easy and inexpensive project," they argued. "While a new theater would cost, according to experts, in the neighborhood of three million dollars, this amount could probably convert all ten theaters along Forty-second, and New York would suddenly restore to that street some of the former grandeur of Ziegfeld and Barrymore. . . . If legitimates reopened on Forty-second Street, respectable people would populate the area and better restaurants and shops would replace the pizza parlors, obscene book shops, and shooting galleries that are there now."

For their part, the Brandts continued to yearn for the respectability that only the legitimate theater could confer, but had abandoned all hope of a 42nd Street theater revival. Harry Brandt told *Show*'s reporters that "he could turn his seven movie houses back into legitimates 'tomorrow,' if he wished. But he doesn't. He is making too much money from the grind-houses, which operate eighteen hours a day, which have none of the financial risks of legitimates, and which don't ever house flops." For his part, Max Cohen huffily rejected Talese's suggestion that he take the lead in reviving 42nd Street. "No, I won't convert these back to legits," he said from behind the bulletproof door of his office above the New Amsterdam. "What for? Three hundred thousand people a week are catered to on this street." (Henry Hope Reed Jr. and Gay Talese, "42nd St.," *Show*, 1/62.)

138   "People come from as far away . . .": "What a Drag," *Newsweek*, 12/31/62.

139   "Rube, they can't clean up . . .": Ibid.

139   "looks down on Times Square . . .": Ibid.

139   "I was so busy looking . . .": Muriel Fischer, "Realty Man Still Has Faith in 'Gem' of Playhouse," *New York World–Telegram and Sun*, 2/10/60.

140   Maidman held on to the Harris for only a year, selling out to its lease-holders, the Max Cohen family, owners of the New Amsterdam. See "Candler Property Taken by Maidman," *New York Times*, 3/7/50; and "Sales-Lease Closed on Harris Theatre," *New York Times*, 8/7/52.

140   "I've walked 1,000 miles . . .": Alden Whitman, "To Durst, This Is a Time for Caution," *New York Times*, 11/30/69.

141   "This was one of my father's . . .": Douglas Durst interview by author, 7/16/01.

141   "automatic" parking garage: "8-Story Garage Will Run Itself," *New York Times*, 10/3/60; and "Automated Parking Demonstrated Here," *New York Times*, 12/14/61.

142   Motel City: "400-Room Motel Is Planned for West Side," *New York Times*, 5/21/58.

142   "a somewhat successful attempt . . .": Robert A. M. Stern, Thomas Mellins, and David Fishman, *New York 1960*, 438.

142   Tenth Avenue motel: "Ground Broken for 10th Ave. Hotel," *New York Times*, 8/2/60.

142   "mushrooming vacation haven": "Riviera Congress Motor Inn Opens on West 41st Street," *Real Estate Record and Guide*, 2/3/62.

142   The 42nd Street motel vogue peaked in 1962, with the opening of the 426-room Sheraton Motor Inn at Twelfth Avenue. Designed by Morris Lapidus, of Miami Beach fame, the Sheraton was twenty stories tall and a luxury hotel in all but name, with a rooftop swimming pool offering panoramic views and a restaurant with revolving banquettes and waitresses in white top hats and black net stockings—a "startlingly classy pioneer in a somewhat déclassé neighborhood." ("Big Motel," *New Yorker*, 7/21/62.)

142   Conversion of Congress Riviera to drug facility: Martin Tolchin, "State Buys Motel as Addict Center," *New York Times*, 3/18/67.

143   "a kind of Atlantic City–on–Hudson touch": Gay Talese, "Motel Row on West Side Is Atlantic City–on–Hudson," *New York Times*, 8/26/63.

143   "While Broadway turns every leaf . . .": *New York Times*, 11/27/60.

143   "return the beautiful American showgirl . . .": "Memories," *New York Times*, 1/31/60.

143   "If the off-Broadway movement . . .": Muriel Fischer, "Realty Man Still Has Faith in 'Gem' of Playhouse," *New York World–Telegram and Sun*, 2/10/60.

143   "At least they loved my theater . . .": Ibid.

144   "It was what we call . . .": Olim interview by author 6/28/01.

144   "We didn't get any business . . .": Melvin Maddocks, "Maidman Ventures Far Afield," *Christian Science Monitor*, 12/28/62.

144   "It may be premature . . .": Lewis Funke, "News of the Rialto: Blueprints," *New York Times*, 11/27/60.

144   "The small theaters don't pay . . .": "Disenchanted Maidman," *New York Herald Tribune*, 8/16/63.

145   "arguing that the coming West . . .": Susan E. Tifft and Alex S. Jones, *The Trust*, 343–4.

145   Douglas Leigh biography: Tama Starr and Edward Hayman, *Signs and Wonders*, 104–7; and Douglas Martin, "Douglas Leigh, the Man Who Lit up Broadway, Dies at 92," *New York Times*, 12/16/99.

146   "We will eventually reidentify . . .": "Times Tower Sold for Exhibit Hall," *New York Times*, 3/16/61.

146   Fire damage: "2 Firemen Killed in Times Sq. Blaze," *New York Times*, 11/23/61; and "Third Body Found in Times Sq. Fire," *New York Times*, 11/24/61.

146   Sale to Allied Chemical: Don Ross, "Catalyst to Uplift Times Square—Chemistry Museum in the Tower," *New York Herald Tribune*, 4/17/63.

146   "Let's face it . . .": Gerd Wilcke, "Personality: A Move That Involves a Risk," *New York Times*, 11/7/65.

146   "We will be the showcase . . .": Ibid.

147   Allied's renovation: Thomas W. Ennis, "Allied Chemical Plans Showcase," *New York Times*, 10/27/63.

147   "The Times Tower was never . . .": Ada Louise Huxtable, "Architecture: How to Kill a City," *New York Times*, 5/15/63.

147   The Heidelberg was graced by one of the most famous of Times Square's early moving signs, a thirty-foot kitten chasing a silken spool of thread on behalf of the Corticelli Silk Company. But Corticelli's spectacular was the Heidelberg's first and last major sign. The building was only partially visible from Times Square proper, obscured by the taller

Times Tower, and advertisers could not be convinced that the pedestrians on 42nd Street would notice signs blinking eight to eighteen stories directly above their heads.

148   The Heidelberg and its transformation: Frank Farrell, "Anybody Need a 13-Story Tower?" *New York World Journal Tribune*, 12/18/66; and Christopher Gray, "The Heidelberg, a Times Sq. Tower That Couldn't," *New York Times*, 4/26/98.

148   Maidman's auto display plan: "Times Sq. Building to Become Huge Glass Showcase for Autos," *New York Times*, 4/28/64.

148   "It's an ugly cow . . .": "Lurid but Profitable 42d Street Hopes to Survive New Cleanup," *New York Times*, 3/26/66.

148   Bingo's new ventures: "Bingo Brandt's 'Class Sex' Cellar as Mate for His One-Theme Rialto," *Variety*, 4/10/68.

148   "It's probably the highest rent area . . .": "Lurid but Profitable 42d Street Hopes to Survive New Cleanup," *New York Times*, 3/26/66.

149   Lindsay's perfect dive: Vincent J. Cannato, *The Ungovernable City*, 64.

149   "to raise the quality of life . . . soul, an intellect, and style": Roger Starr, *The Rise and Fall of New York City*, 22–3.

150   For a photograph of Vliet as Jo, see the *Syracuse Post Standard*, 11/14/14. Her performance in *The Governor's Lady* is described in "Scrubbing as a Fine Art," *Chicago Record Herald*, 10/12/13. Belasco had taken Vliet aside during the New York rehearsals of the road show production of *The Governor's Lady*. "Study that scrubwoman down at Child's," said the producer, referring to an inexpensive chain restaurant on Broadway, just around the corner from the Belasco Theater. "Watch her every motion." Vliet apparently listened well, for her performance was hailed for its verisimilitude.

150   "In her time . . .": Nat Hentoff, *A Political Life: The Education of John V. Lindsay*, 51–2.

150   It took all the self-restraint that the Drama Desk, the Broadway writers' group, could muster to wait until early 1967 to present the mayor with its highest award for his "outstanding contributions to the American theater." (Louis Calta, "Theater Writers Honor the Mayor," *New York Times*, 4/22/67.)

151   "designing cities without . . .": Paul Goldberger, *New York Times*, 1/28/75.

151   "the design conscience . . .": Steven V. Roberts, "Report Urges Drastic Changes in City's Approach to Planning," *New York Times*, 2/8/67.

151   "That was a breakthrough . . .": William Robbins, "Revival Comes to Broadway," *New York Times*, 1/20/68.

152   "The theaters in the Broadway . . .": Jonathan Barnett, *Urban Design as Public Policy*, 19.

153   For a detailed account of the UDG's dealings with the Minskoffs, see Ibid., 16–21.

153   "those run-down movie houses on 42nd Street": John Sibley, "Board of Estimate Approves Measure to Encourage Theater Construction," *New York Times*, 12/8/67.

153   In addition to the Minskoff, the special theater district designation led to the building of two Circle in the Square theaters at the base of a single skyscraper at 51st and Broadway, and the American Place Theater on 44th and Sixth Avenue.

153   "You'll be seeing new buildings . . .": Richard Reeves, "Lindsay Outlines Program to Improve City in 1969," *New York Times*, 12/30/68.

154   Robertson bio: "Innovative Planner: Jacquelin Taylor Robertson," *New York Times*, 1/29/75.

154   "Silver Tongue": Bardel interview by author, 6/28/01.

154   "Lindsay was unhappy . . .": Elliott interview by author, 7/18/00.

155   "John Lindsay was a man . . .": Basini interview by author, 5/22/01.

155   "One day I said to this guy . . .": Ibid.

155   "the seedy side . . . 'My, my, Jacquelin'": Robertson interview by author, 9/27/00.

156   "He started laughing at me . . .": Basini interview by author, 5/22/01.

Marty Hodas and the Rise of XXX

158   "I'm not a religious man . . .": William Sherman, "That 42d St. Porno? Well, Meet the King," *Daily News*, 12/11/72.

158   "It's the most fascinating thing . . .": Hodas interview by author, 5/15/01.

158   "I was never arrested . . .": Ibid.

158   "No living creature . . .": *Senior Echoes* yearbook, 1949, Franklin K. Lane High School. Hodas's entry says that he belonged to the science club, swimming team, and cafeteria squad, and won a math award.

159   Joey Gallo and jukebox racketeering: Jay Maeder, "Nickels and Dimes Jukeboxes," *Daily News*, 3/9/01; and Daniel Goddard, *Joey*, 38–53.

160   "I was making about $100 a week . . .": Hodas interview by author, 6/21/01.

160   "They didn't give a shit . . . you can like them": Ibid.

160   "I came across a lot of people . . .": Ibid.

161   "I thought, 'Wow! . . .'": Ibid.

161   "Because so many of the boys . . .": David Nasaw, *Going Out*, 154.

162   "They all said the same thing . . .": Hodas interview by author, 6/21/01.

162   "install in the New York City . . .": Letter dated 6/9/67 from Louis A. Baldo, chief of License Issuance Division, Department of Licenses, to Martin J. Hodas, president of Island Amusement Co. Copy provided author by Hodas.

162   "Holy shit! . . .": Carreras interview by author, 7/12/01.

163   "I was as amazed as anybody . . .": Hodas interview by author, 6/21/01.

163   "They all told me the same thing . . .": Ibid.

164   "In those days . . .": Ibid.

164   "I didn't really want it to happen . . .": Hodas interview by author, 7/3/01.

164   "short films are the finest . . .": Richard F. Shepard, "Peep Shows Have New Nude Look," *New York Times*, 6/9/69.

165   "Book store proprietors . . .": Ibid.

166   The Pucciarelli family in Times Square: Testimony of Victor Pucciarelli before the New York State Commission of Investigation, *An Investigation of Racketeer Infiltration of the Sex-Oriented Materials Industry in New York City*, October 1970, vol. I, pp. 111–99. See also the commission's final report, pp. 205–14.

166   "Joe was not only connected . . .": Hodas interview by author, 7/12/01.

166   Brocchini was killed in May 1976: Selwyn Raab and Nathaniel Sheppard Jr., "Mobsters Skim New York Sex Industry Profits," *New York Times*, 7/27/77.

166   "Then my cousin . . .": Hodas interview by author, 7/12/01.

167   "The next night . . .": Bob Greene, "The Hood in Our Neighborhood," *Newsday*, 12/24/65.

167   Hodas's confrontation with Genova: New York State Commission of Investigation, testimony of Arthur Volgarino, 436–37, and Robert Genova, 456–61.

167   "Now began, you could say . . .": Hodas interview by author, 7/3/01.

167   "Hodas has for years been paying off . . . business deal": William Sherman, "Mafia Declares War, but Porn King Survives," *Daily News*, 12/13/72.

168   "who knew Hodas well . . . he was a killer": William Sherman, *Times Square*, 26.

168   "He told me . . .": Hodas interview by author, 7/3/01.

168   Peep show machine numbers: New York State Commission of Investigation, testimony of Ralph Russo, 28–34.

169   "Don't ask me where they came from . . .": Sherman, *Times Square*, 24.

169   Doubling of adult bookstores: Edward Benes, "Organized Crime Tied to Sex Materials, Shows," *Daily News*, 10/20/70.

169   "from a familiar landscape . . .": Susan Brownmiller, *In Our Time*, 296.

169   Live sex establishments: Michael T. Kaufman, "Live Sex 'Exhibitions' Present Problem Here," *New York Times*, 10/2/70.

170   "It was all authentic . . .": Hodas interview by author, 7/12/01.

171   "its style an anachronistic hangover . . .": Peter Whittaker, *The American Way of Sex*, 10.

171   Elimination of licensing requirement: Ken McKenna, "The Return of the Real Massage," *Daily News*, 9/28/73.

171   Reregulation of massage parlors: John Darnton, "Council Curbs Gas Tanks and the 'Massage Parlors,' " *New York Times*, 3/2/73; and "Licensed Masseurs Sue City to Exempt Them in New Law," *New York Times*, 4/17/73.

171   Yellow Pages parlor count: " 'Massage' Places Face Crackdown," *New York Times*, 9/19/72.

171   Traits of the Times Square parlors: William Sherman, *Times Square*, 64.

171   "There was just too much action . . .": Schwartz interview by author, 9/22/99.

172   "Things got really bad . . .": Durst interview by author, 7/16/01.

172   "These guys who had seen . . .": Ibid.

172   Lindsay's crackdown: Murray Schumach, "Sex Exploitation Spreading Here," *New York Times*, 7/1//71.

172   Formation of Midtown South and North: Gail Sheehy, "Cleaning Up Hell's Bedroom," *New York*, 11/13/72.

173   NYPD's dubious smut-busting tactics: Ibid.; and Schwartz interview by author.

173   "You'd better get down here . . .": Sheehy.

173   Peep show licensing: *City of NY v. 1487 Amusement Corp.*, Defendant's Motion, 9/20/76, p. 16A, 74 Civ 3095; and Ralph Blumenthal, "Ten Peep Shows Seeking Permits," *New York Times*, 12/13/72. In a letter to the editor of the *Times*, published 10/7/72, Hodas accused the NYPD of "a reign of terror and injustice" against the peep show industry. "At this point," he wrote, "the issue is not whether peep shows are good or bad; the issue is that when one man's constitutional rights are denied, then the rights of all are in jeopardy."

174   Sohn's analysis: New York State Commission of Investigation, *An Investigation of Racketeer Infiltration of the Sex-Oriented Materials Industry in New York City*, 243. Also, "Peep-Show Producer Is Called Evader of Federal Income Tax," *New York Times*, 10/22/70.

175   "I couldn't for the life of me . . .": Hodas interview by author, 7/12/01.

175   Firebombing of the Palace and French Model Studio: Lacey Fosburg, "'Massage Parlor' Bombing Laid to Hodas and 2 Others," *New York Times*, 7/14/73. See also Mike Pearl and Larry Kleinman, "'Porno King' Charged in Firebombings," *New York Post*, 7/13/73.

175   Arson trial verdicts: Nathaniel Sheppard Jr., "Hodas Is Cleared in Two Bombings," *New York Times*, 12/22/73; and Ellen Fleysher, "Sex Parlor King Cleared of Arson," *Daily News*, 12/22/73.

175   "It was the first night . . .": Hodas interview by author, 7/12/01.

176   "Would I do it over . . .": Manny Topol, "Adventures in the Peep Trade," *Newsday*, 9/29/74.

176   "I just decided that's enough . . .": Hodas interview by author, 7/12/01.

176   East Coast's dubious financials: *United States of America v. Martin J. Hodas and Herbert J. Levin*, 75 Crim. 295, U.S. District Court, Southern District of New York.

176   "seemed somber but not surprised": Arnold H. Lubasch, "A Pornographer Is Convicted of Evading $65,000 in Taxes," *New York Times*, 7/25/75.

176   "Your Honor . . .": Hodas to Judge Metzner, 12/20/75, *United States of America v. Martin J. Hodas and Herbert J. Levin*.

176   "We were the Band-Aid . . .": Schwartz interview by author, 9/22/99.

177   "We have . . . very little street enforcement . . .": Selwyn Raab, "Police Functions Hard Hit as Layoffs Curb Activity," *New York Times*, 7/14/75.

177   "We did not want a riot . . .": Schwartz interview by author, 9/22/99.

177   "I stood on that corner . . .": William Kornblum, ed., "West 42nd Street: The Bright Light Zone," 128.

177   "These were big heavy gangs . . . drank very well, too": McGarry interview by Czerina Patel, 11/6/00. In his youth, Cadillac had been a pimp in Harlem but had drifted into alcoholism. Malcolm X refers to him in his 1964 autobiography: "The world's most unlikely pimp was 'Cadillac' Drake. He was shiny baldheaded, built like a football; he used to call his huge belly 'the chippies playground.' Cadillac had a string of about a dozen of the stringiest, scrawniest, black and white prostitutes in Harlem. Afternoons around the bar, the old-timers who knew Cadillac well enough would tease him about how women who looked like his made enough to feed themselves, let alone him. He'd roar with laughter right along with us; I can hear him now, 'Bad-looking women work harder.' "

178   "perhaps the most heavily policed . . .": Alan Sagner to Paul B. Mott Jr., 1/18/78, archives of the Port Authority of New York and New Jersey.

178   "Every day I'd see some businessman . . .": Marc Eliot, *Down 42nd Street*, 147.

178   "The strolls cover regularly traveled routes . . .": Kornblum, 137.

179   "only when conditions are propitious . . .": Ibid., 27–8.

179   "Weather was terrible . . .": Ibid., 28–9.

Bob Moss and Fred Papert: Urban Moonwalkers

181   "When I go to 42nd Street . . .": "My New York: Wendy Wasserstein," *New York*, 12/18–25/00.

181   "I had no intention of staying . . .": Moss interview by author, 7/20/00.

182   "They should rename 42nd Street . . .": Mason interview by author, 6/7/01.

182   "In the second act . . .": Moss interview by author, 10/12/00.

182   Moss bio: Don Dust, "Backstage Boss," *Newark Evening News*, 2/21/66; Theodore Gross, "Will Bob Moss Become the Next Joe Papp?" *Village Voice*, 11/1/76; and Mimi Torchin, "Now We Are Ten," *Other Stages*, 11/20/80.

183   "It sounds hokey . . .": Moss interview by author, 10/12/00.

183   "All of Bob's friends . . .": Pressman interview by author, 7/11/01.

184   "It was very corny . . .": Keating interview by author, 1/24/01.

184   "Then we're going to have to give . . .": Moss interview by author, 10/12/00.

185   "legit theater groups . . .": "Realtor Irving Maidman Offering Movie Theatres for Legit Rental," *Variety*, 11/30/72.

185   "I've spent so much money . . .": Ralph Blumenthal, "Maidman Discovers Sex Shows Still Operating at His Properties," *New York Times*, 11/29/72.

185   "My view was that 42nd . . .": Pressman interview by author, 7/11/01.

186   "the sickening stench of urine . . .": Gene Nye, *Behind the Port Authority*, self-published novel, 5/5/99, 3. Provided to the author by Nye.

186   "It was like the aftermath . . .": Hackin interview by author, 11/14/00.

187   "It was utterly audacious . . .": Moss interview by author, 7/20/00.

187   "There are some funny parts . . .": Alzado interview by author, 6/5/01.

187   While preparing for the February 15 opening of *Bogotá*, Moss and his assistant Kathleen Chalfant settled into PH's new office on the third floor of 440 West 42nd. The previous tenant was the militant Jewish Defense League, which had left the windows painted over in black and

the walls pockmarked with what appeared to be bullet holes. The JDL had relocated to the second floor, just below Playwrights Horizons. Chalfant, whose duties as PH's production coordinator consisted mainly of running the office, amused herself by spying on the FBI agents who kept the JDL under sporadic surveillance from a parked car across the street. The agents, on the other hand, no doubt enjoyed watching her clamber up 440's rickety fire escape in her skirt and high-heeled boots on those mornings that she forgot to bring the front-door key. It also fell to Chalfant to placate the burly men in ill-fitting suits who showed up one day to recommend that PH avail itself of their garbage collection services. "In my naïveté, I had no idea that they might be dangerous," Chalfant said. "I told them, 'No, it's OK. We've got it under control.' I guess I just seemed so loony that they went away."

188   "One lady got so upset . . .": Gill interview by author, 8/4/00.

188   "I thought, 'Wait a minute . . .": Moss interview by author, 7/20/00.

189   "We were all very young . . .": Nye interview by author, 8/10/00.

189   "I guess I wasn't bright enough . . .": Chalfant interview by author, 7/3/00.

189   "She was this grand lady . . .": Nye interview by author, 8/10/00.

189   "Victoria's Secret let out . . . have a conscience": Nye, *Behind the Port Authority*, 12–14.

190   "I think Bob was embarrassed . . .": Keating interview by author, 1/24/01.

190   "We came here because . . .": Robert Moss, "A Bouquet or Two for Times Square," *New York Times*, 1/9/75.

190   "The way to clean up . . .": Bruce Buckley, "Theatre Manager Has Dream for 42nd," *Chelsea Clinton News*, 10/9/75. Also, Dick Brass, "Their Words to Joints Is 'Take It Off,'" *Daily News*, 7/25/76.

190   The 42nd Street Gang budgets: undated, Ford Foundation archives, Grant 78–318.

191   "Everybody wanted to hear . . .": Moss interview by author, 6/12/01.

191   "I don't want to be rude . . .": Moss interview by author, 10/12/00; and Levy interview by author, 7/12/00.

192   "They got along right away . . .": Basini interview by author, 5/22/01.

192   Papert bio: Papert interview by author, 1/8/99.

193   "an extremely likable smoothie . . .": George Lois, *George, Be Careful*, 45.

193   "Fred's selling quality . . .": Koenig interview by author, 12/24/99.

193   "I'm racking this thing up . . .": Papert interview by author, 1/8/99.

193 "In the end . . .": Ibid. On Papert, Koenig, Lois, see "Agency in Embryo," *Madison Avenue*, 2/60; Philip N. Schuyler, "Papert, Koenig & Lois Is Talk of 'Mad Ave.,'" *Editor and Publisher*, 8/5/61; and Stephen Mahoney, "How to Get Ahead in Advertising, and Maybe Stay There," *Fortune*, 11/62.

194 "I think the life I made . . .": Papert interview by author, 1/14/00.

194 "While she had a good . . .": Barwick interview by author, 8/7/01.

195 "My sister remembers . . .": Papert interview by author, 1/8/99.

195 "Jackie was game . . .": Ibid.

195 "I think Fred began . . .": Stanicki interview by author, 1/12/00.

196 "It was obvious . . . again in my life": Levy interview by author, 7/12/00.

196 "We didn't have all that much . . .": Davidson interview by author, 1/31/01.

197 "The Corporation would take on . . .": 42nd Street Development Corp., "What's a Nice Girl Like Estelle Parsons Doing in a Massage Parlor on 42nd Street?" 4.

197 "Fred did have some credibility . . .": Gill interview by author, 8/4/00.

197 "Port Authority paid . . .": Papert interview by author, 1/8/99.

198 "The building's immediate environment . . .": John R. White of James D. Landaueer Assoc. to Robert L Walters of McGraw-Hill, 1/25/74, McGraw-Hill archives.

199 "I had a huge fight . . .": Moss interview by author, 7/20/00.

199 Premature dismantling of sign: Egan interview by author, 6/25/01.

199 "Pretty soon, we'll have six . . . sooner": Theodore Gross, "Will Bob Moss Become the Next Joe Papp?" *Village Voice*, 11/1/76. Also, Dick Brass, "Happy Ending Plays on 42d St.," *Daily News*, 6/11/76; and Charles Kaiser, "Actors Move in at 42d St. Theater," *New York Times*, 6/11/76.

Turning the Corner in Hell's Kitchen

201 Durst's sale to Ravitch: "Apartment Developer Buys a Block on 42d Street," *New York Times*, 1/6/74.

201 Ravitch bio: Tom Shachtman, *Skyscraper Dreams*, 82, 105, 248–51.

201 Manhattan Plaza's design and amenities: Paul Goldberger, "Manhattan Plaza: Quality Housing to Upgrade 42d St.," *New York Times*, 8/19/74; and Glenn Fowler, "Builders Hope to Lure Richer Tenants to Project," *New York Times*, 8/19/74.

202 "red brick elephant": "Red Elephant and the 15% Solution," *New York Times*, 2/27/77.

202 "one of the more frighteningly spectacular . . .": Francis X. Clines, "A White Elephant Struggling to Be a Show Horse," *New York Times*, 3/1/77.

202 Manhattan Plaza's financial woes: Joseph P. Fried, "Just How City Will Utilize Manhattan Plaza Is Unclear," *New York Times*, 1/15/77.

203 The Section 8 solution: Joseph P. Fried, "Times Sq. Housing Project Poses a Problem for City," *New York Times*, 5/29/75.

203 "such a hullabaloo . . . his limited partners": Transcript of Starr interview, 7/9/86, 22–23, Manhattan Plaza Project, Columbia University Oral History Research Office.

203 "We had a very bitter argument . . .": Ibid. A much milder version of Starr and Ravitch's dispute played out in the press. See Joseph P. Fried, "Manhattan Plaza Is Focus of Dispute for High Stakes," *New York Times*, 8/20/75.

204 "would not be perceived . . .": Transcript of Rose interview, 10/29/86, 11, Manhattan Plaza Project.

204 Rose's idea and reactions to it: Paul Goldberger, "Performers May Get W. 42d St. Housing," *New York Times*, 8/2/76; "Plan to Rent Apartments on 42d St. to Theater People Draws Criticism," *New York Times*, 10/29/76; and Joseph P. Fried, "Plan to Rent W. 42d Street Housing to Performers Still Being Debated," *New York Times*, 11/21/76.

204 "When they heard . . .": Ibid., p. 13.

204 "forty-year, $400-million mistake": Molly Ivins, "Housing for Actors Under Final Study," *New York Times*, 12/12/76.

205 Ravitch's anger: Durst interview by author, 7/16/01.

205 "Miss Fox . . . wear your collar": Transcript of Kirk interview, 11/4/86, 108, Manhattan Plaza Project.

205 "You have all sorts of people . . .": Rose interview, 25.

205 Manhattan Plaza's residence requirements: John Wark, "Performers Queuing up to Audition for an Apartment," *New York Times*, 7/10/77; and Nancy I. Ross, "Manhattan Plaza: SRO for Performers," *Washington Post*, 7/23/77.

206 $7 million subsidy: David Bird, "For Some Theater People, Home Is Low-Cost Luxury," *New York Times*, 9/14/79.

206 "It was so damned expensive . . .": Starr transcript, 34–5.

206 "like a country club . . .": Anne E. Kornblut, "Real 'Seinfeld' Kramer's Real Job—Playing Himself," *Daily News*, 1/27/96.

206 "All of us like to think . . .": Kirk transcript, 313.

207   Founding of Midtown Enforcement: Baumgarten had to labor long and hard to obtain federal funding. See "City Seeking $1.7 Million for Times Sq. Smut Fight," *New York Times*, 3/2/75; and "Mayor Pressing Midtown Cleanup," *New York Times*, 1/13/76.

207   "I am not a moralist . . .": Baumgarten interview by author, 5/16/01.

207   "Under the law . . .": Daly interview by author, 2/8/99.

208   Decline in sex establishments: Office of Midtown Enforcement, *Annual Report (1985)*, 23.

208   "Bob was one of the few cons . . .": Daly interview by author, 2/8/99.

209   "I gravitated right back . . .": Paul Sloan, "Bob Brown's Street Life," *Newsday*, 5/25/89.

209   The story of Brown's criminal career was told in great detail by Croswell Bowen, "A Flight into Custody," pts. 1 and 2, *New Yorker*, 11/1/52 and 11/8/52.

209   "There's always some character . . .": Sloan.

209   "We needed a better understanding . . .": Weisbrod interview by author, 11/12/02.

210   "My senses alert me . . .": Sloan.

210   Manhattan Plaza ceremony: Judith Cummings, "42d St. Theater Row Dedicated As Rundown West Side Looks Up," *New York Times*, 5/14/78. Also Anthony Mancini, "Miracle on 42 St.," *Soho Weekly News*, 5/25/78.

210   "Marilyn, I'm real . . .": Moss interview by author, 10/12/00.

210   Moss's encounter with Maidman: Ibid. Had Maidman read the February 1978 issue of the theater magazine *After Dark*, he probably would not have bothered asking Moss for a favor. Moss was quoted describing Maidman as "one of the great slumlords of this city. He may say he's a philanthropist, but it begins at 5 P.M. in his hometown. But from 9 A.M. to 5 P.M. he will suck the blood out of your veins."

211   "We paid no cash . . .": Papert interview by author, 1/8/99.

211   Financing of Theater Row: Forty-Second Street Development, "The Theater Row Story," 78–9, in the Theater Row file at the New York Library for the Performing Arts.

211   "When I was first assigned . . . celebrity card": Travis interview by author, 11/6/00.

212   The Papert–UDC sale and leaseback: "The Theatre Row Story," 75–6. The net result of this transaction was that Forty-Second Street Development would have to pay the UDC 50 percent of any profits from Theater Row in lieu of real estate taxes—which was not really much of a concession, since the project was not-for-profit anyway. However, the city

did require Papert to pay off about \$118,000 in past-due property taxes on the Theater Row properties.

212 Conflicts with UDC, including punch-out: Sy Syna, "Strapped-for-Funds Theatre Row Needs Angels with Checks," *The Wisdoms Child*, May 14–20, 1979.

212 "Nothing less than completely . . .": Richard Goldstein, "The Fate of Theatre Row," *Village Voice*, 4/22/81.

213 "We were all disappointed . . .": Southern interview by author, 9/14/00.

213 For details on the Theater Row tenant companies, see Glenn M. Loney, "The 42nd Street Redevelopment," *Theatre Crafts*, 9/79.

213 Financial woes of member companies: Don Nelsen, "For Theater Row, Mixed Reviews," *Daily News*, 3/23/81; Syna; and Goldstein.

213 "A number of people thought . . .": Moss interview by author, 10/12/00.

214 "I have exactly the wrong . . .": Papert interview by author, 1/8/99.

214 "I don't think I ever trusted . . .": Nye interview by author, 8/10/00.

214 Demise of West Side Airlines Terminal: David Bird, "Plan to Close Airlines Terminal Is Seen Adding Blight to Area," *New York Times*, 8/12/72.

214 For details on Theater Row II, see G. Gerald Fraser, "West 42d St. Theater Row Begins \$9.6 Million Phase 2," *New York Times*, 10/9/80; and "Theater Row Project Finished with Flourish," *New York Times*, 5/26/82. Also, Sally Dixon Weiner, "Theater Row: A Tale of Theater and of Real Estate," *Dramatists Guild Quarterly*, spring 1991, 18–23.

214 Troop B stable: William G. Blair, "Mounted Police Unit Getting New Stables Nearer Theaters," *New York Times*, 4/8/82.

215 "They're like locusts . . ." and menacing of Nahas: "Influx of Transvestite Prostitutes Plaguing Manhattan Plaza Area," *New York Times*, 9/2/79.

215 "You don't see transvestites . . .": Transcript of Hunnings interview, 7/7/86, 21, Manhattan Plaza Project.

216 "Real estate values are improving . . .": Murray Schumach, "Manhattan Plaza: Small-Town Neighbors in a Blasé City," *New York Times*, 2/2/78.

The Theater Preservation Follies

217 *42nd Street* as campy artifact: J. Hoberman, *42nd Street*, 72.

217 "gave life to the clichés . . .": Pauline Kael, *5000 Nights at the Movies*, 73.

217 Merrick's musical was the second one to have been inspired by the

film *42nd Street*. In 1966, Café Cino in Greenwich Village presented a forty-five-minute pastiche called *Dames at Sea or Golddiggers Afloat*. Future star Bernadette Peters played Ruby, an aspiring actress from Utah who steps off the bus and instantly becomes "the toast of New York, a star of Broadway and the sweetheart of the navy" (J. Hoberman, 73).

218 "to muster all his reserves . . .": Cliff Jahr, " '42nd Street' Log—the Making of a Hit," *New York Times*, 9/7/80.

219 "Gower had no notion . . .": Ibid.

219 "A snake was loose . . .": Ibid.

219 "The All Singing All Dancing . . .": Howard Kissel, *David Merrick, The Abominable Showman*, 15.

219 "bursting to tell someone . . .": Ibid., 19–20.

220 "As he sings a reprise . . .": Jack Kroll, "Lullaby of Broadway," *Newsweek*, 9/8/80.

220 "I'm sorry to have to report . . . Bring it in!": Kissel, 20–1.

220 "final display of blazing . . .": Frank Rich, *Hot Seat*, 31–3.

220 "In thirteen hours . . .": Kissel, 23.

220 "the most thrillingly atavistic . . .": Kroll.

221 "architecturally . . . one of the finest . . .": Roberta Brandes Gratz, *The Living City*, 349–50.

221 "Implicit in the beginning . . .": Roberta Brandes Gratz, "Save the Helen Hayes," *New York*, 11/19/79.

222 "We had to preserve *everything*": Lynne B. Sagalyn, *Times Square Roulette*, 128.

222 "Anybody who knew anything . . . ": Stanicki interview by author, 1/12/00.

222 The best source of detailed information about the City at 42nd Street is a 96-page booklet entitled *42nd Street*. It was produced by the project's sponsors and completed in July 1978. The booklet is on file in the Rockefeller Center Archives.

223 "The problem was that the theaters . . .": Weinstein interview by author, 8/6/00.

223 "[Imagine] one long, continuous peel . . .": Marc Eliot, *Down 42nd Street*.

224 42nd Street valuations and square footage: New York City Department of City Planning and Public Development Corp., "42nd Street Development Project: A Discussion Document," 2/10/81, 16.

225 "There was general agreement . . .": Notes of Forty-Second Street Development Corp. meeting at the Ford Foundation, 2/16/78, Grant 78-318, Ford Foundation archives.

225   "an ambitious, expensive, and potentially risky . . .": City Planning
        Commission memorandum, Robert F. Wagner Jr. to Edward I. Koch,
        "42nd Street—'Cityscape,'" 12/6/78.

225   Koch's critique of the City at 42nd Street: Paul Goldberger, "A New
        Plan for West 42d St.," *New York Times*, 1/31/79; and James Carberry
        and Daniel Hertzberg, "New York Plans Renewal of Sleazy Times
        Square, but the Planning Stage Is About as Far as It Gets," *Wall Street
        Journal*, 8/20/80.

225   "Forty-second Street was once famous . . .": William D. Hartley, "A
        Happy Step Backward for Times Square," *U.S. News & World Report*,
        9/27/82.

226   "Our plan was Neronian . . .": William J. Stern, "The Unexpected
        Lessons of Times Square's Comeback," *City Journal*, autumn 1999.

226   "one of the best medium-sized theaters . . .": Paul Goldberger, "New
        York's Newest Theater Is Quite Old," *New York Times*, 2/22/79. For
        more on the conversion of the Apollo and the Lyric, see "Broadway Re-
        vives Two Theaters," *Business Week*, 10/16/78.

227   "The principal impetus . . .": Michiko Kakutani, "Rialto to Reopen
        Feb. 7 as Legitimate Theater," *New York Times*, 1/15/80.

228   "They're not . . .": Frank Prial, "Can 42nd Street Regain Its Showbiz
        Glamour?" *New York Times*, 4/18/82.

228   "We do not intend . . .": Ralph Blumenthal, "A Times Square Revival?"
        New York Times, 12/27/81. Robert Brandt gave vent to his dissatisfac-
        tion with 42DP in two lengthy letters to the editor published in the
        Times: "When Outsiders Offer to Revamp Times Square," 2/4/80; and
        "How to Kill a Tourist Attraction," 8/4/80.

228   "the people who brought 42nd Street to its knees": Owen Moritz, "Ap-
        ple Sauce," *Daily News*, 10/26/88.

229   "No producer wants a theater . . .": "Future's in Doubt," *New York
        Times*, 10/17/79.

229   David Merrick considered the New Apollo in his search for a venue for
        42nd Street but valued the Winter Garden's much larger and more mod-
        ern auditorium over the PR benefit of opening his musical on its name-
        sake street. When *42nd Street* was revived in 2001, it would indeed
        play on 42nd Street, in a new theater created by merging the old Apollo
        and the Lyric.

229   "a wholly ridiculous show . . .": Rich, 103.

230   "We can change the theater again . . .": "Apollo Going Back to Films,"
        New York Times, 9/29/83.

230   agenda of "class-displacement . . .": Sagalyn, 85, 87.

230   "postcard fu . . . *Friday the 13th*": John Tierney, "Era Ends as Times Square Drops Slashers for Shakespeare," *New York Times*, 1/24/91.

231   "Ever since I could cut . . . He bled and bled": Mark Jacobson, "Times Square: The Meanest Street in America," *Rolling Stone*, 8/6/81.

231   "Jay was up to speed . . .": Ibid.

232   ". . . a genre freak's paradise . . .": Mark Jacobson, "A Film Freak's Plea: Nationalize 42nd Street!" *Village Voice*, 1/6/75.

232   "If the city is really interested . . . City Planning Commission": Jacobson, "Times Square."

234   "worn-out seats . . . ": Eric Konigsberg, "Jimmy Nederlander's Endless Run," *New York*, 5/31/99.

235   "This is a structurally sound . . .": Bruce Chadwick, "Theater's Curtain to Rise by Fall," *Daily News*, 6/2/82.

235   "Jimmy kept saying . . .": Prudon interview by author, 7/3/02.

235   "The construction of that building . . .": Morgan interview by author, 5/2/02.

235   *New Amsterdam Follies:* Samuel G. Freedman, "Weintraub Buys Interest in Nederlander Theater," *New York Times*, 9/26/85.

236   "is exactly what we were looking for . . .": Eleanor Blau, "Revival on 42d Street: New Amsterdam Roof," *New York Times*, 5/11/83.

236   "The Nederlanders produce shows . . .": Prudon interview.

Down and Dirty on the Deuce

238   "blanket Canada with pornography": "Pornography Dealer Pleads Guilty to Shipping Lewd Tapes," *New York Times*, 12/9/84.

238   "I don't want to have anything . . .": Martin Gottlieb, "Pornography's Plight Hits Times Square," *New York Times*, 10/5/86.

238   "We did sometimes cite him . . .": Daly interview by author, 2/8/99.

239   In addition to Show World Center, Basciano's Times Square holdings included Show Follies, Show Center, Show Place de Paris, Les Gals, Joy, the Pussycat Showcase, and Movieplex 42.

239   "The difference between Richie . . .": Amy interview by author, 6/3/00.

239   "Basciano was a very, very nice guy . . .": Hodas interview by author, 7/3/01.

239   "a spasm of moral outrage . . . almost friendship": Robertson interview by author, 3/5/98.

239   On Nick Basciano, see "Nicholas J. Basciano, Former Professional Boxer," *Baltimore Sun*, 11/11/91; and "In Memory of Nick 'Bass' Basciano," Maryland Boxing Hall of Fame.

240   "He was one hell of a fighter . . .": Levy interview by Anneliese Gaeta, 6/8/01.

240   Basciano's coupon scam: *United States of America v. Richard C. Basciano*, U.S. District Court for Maryland, criminal case 27428. Also Theodore W. Hendricks, "Fraud Charged in Coupon Racket," *Baltimore Sun*, 8/31/68; and "Coupon Scheme Nets $750 Fine," *Baltimore Sun*, 2/2/68.

240   "They got to know each other . . .": Hershman interview by author, 5/8/01.

240   "the worst criminal case . . .": Andy Wallace, "Center City Speculator Sam Rappaport Dies," *Philadelphia Inquirer*, 9/7/94.

241   "Complaints of neighbors . . .": Ibid. For more on Rappaport, see Susan Caba, "Where the Other Half Lived: The Late Developer Sam Rappaport's Estate Is for Sale, Marked Down to $1.3 Million," *Philadelphia Inquirer*, 10/29/85.

241   "What I'd heard . . .": Daly interview.

242   Basciano's bookstores: See *Coast Holding Corp., 1487 Amusement Corp., 101 Book Center, Inc., et al. v. Brick Management Corp.*, Supreme Court of the State of New York, County of New York, Index 379/83, Basciano deposition.

242   "discriminatory tactics totally unjustified . . .": Ibid.

242   "When Show World opened . . .": Hodas interview.

243   Di Bernardo bio: Linda Di Bernardo, ex-wife, interview by author, 6/22/01.

243   On Star Distributing: New York State Commission of Investigation, *An Investigation of Racketeer Infiltration of the Sex-Oriented Materials Industry in New York* (1970), 214–17. Also, Deposition of Theodore Rothstein (2/10/87) in Estate of Robert Di Bernardo, Surrogate's Court County of Nassau, File 244378; and Selwyn Raab and Nathaniel Sheppard Jr., "Mobsters Skim New York City Sex Industry Profits," *New York Times*, 7/27/77.

243   DB as Mafia porn boss: U.S. Department of Justice, Attorney General's Commission on Pornography, *Final Report* (July 1986), 1062, 1066, and 1078–80. See also appendix 5, U.S. Department of Justice, *Organized Crime Involvement in Pornography*, 1214, 1218, 1221, 1226, 1223, and 1237.

243   "a brilliant, wealthy guy": Peter Maas, *Underboss*, 230.

243   DB's daily commute: Howard Blum, *Gangland*, 151. For more on DB's personality and lifestyle, see the depositions of Lori Kunen (8/15/86

and 2/10/87), Theodore Rothstein (2/10/87 and 4/30/87), Jay W. Rosen (3/12/87 and 9/10/92), and Linda Di Bernardo (4/10/87) in the Matter of Estate of Robert Di Bernardo, Surrogate's Court, County of Nassau, File 244378.

244   "DB was always a real gentleman . . .": Mouw interview by author, 10/20/99.

244   "DB is our messenger . . .": Maas, 197.

244   "worried about DB . . .": Mouw interview.

244   "I sent the girl in my office . . .": Maas, 217–18.

244   "They made some inquiries . . .": Mouw interview.

245   "These businesses may not be saleable . . .": Robert D. Baron to Patrick Castelluccio, 5/24/88, in the Matter of Estate of Robert Di Bernardo, Surrogate's Court, County of Nassau, File 244378. Baron assigned values to DB's interests in sixteen properties or companies jointly held with Basciano: Big Applies Cinemas ($7,000), 21 Video Corp. ($3,000), 942 Market Street ($1,300), 113 Video ($250), NTE Productions ($2,500), 777 8th Ave. ($500), 1900 Dellin ($100), 670 8th Ave. ($100), Charley's Dream ($2,000), 210 West 42nd St. ($1,800), 259 West 42nd St. ($750), 57 North 13th Street ($2,500), C & F Merchandising, Coral Assoc., Four Keys Enterprises, and Brighton Inc.

245   "Street kids start their day . . .": Marie P. Bresnahan, "Taking It to the Streets: Outreach to Youth in Times Square," in ed., *Sex, Scams, and Street Life,* ed. Robert P. McNamara.

246   "I found myself . . .": Bruce Ritter, *Covenant House: Lifeline to the Streets,* 52.

246   "I said to the local community . . .": Ibid., 53.

247   "My staff is forbidden . . .": "State Help Solves Dispute on Times Square Youth Center," *New York Times,* 9/16/79. Also E. J. Dionne Jr., "An Oasis for Runaway Teen-Agers Appears in a Pornographic Desert," *New York Times,* 4/2/77.

247   "I went out again about two . . .": Ritter, 58.

248   "He who touches pitch . . .": Ibid., 66.

248   "My heart rejoiced . . .": Ibid., 88.

248   Leasing the Congress Riviera: "State Help Solves Dispute on Times Square Youth Center."

249   "a simmering antagonism . . .": Charles M. Sennott, *Broken Covenant,* 148.

249   Homeless statistics: Kenneth Jackson, ed., *The Encyclopedia of New York,* 553.

250   "It's got to be one of the rottenest places . . .": Maureen Dowd, "Childhood in 'Hell': Growing Up in Times Sq.," *New York Times,* 6/25/84.

250   "there were children everywhere . . .": Ibid.

250   Truong's self-made legend: Deposition of Tran Dinh Truong (6/4/01), *76 Corp. d/b/a Club New York v. Alphonse Hotel Corp.*, Supreme Court of New York, Index. 603203/01; and Complaint, *Alphonse Hotel Corp., d/b/a The Hotel Carter and Tran Dinh Truong v. Tho Tran, Oanh-Nguyen, Mt. Fuji Japanese Restaurant and Sushi Bar,* Supreme Court of New York, Index 02104331.

251   "First of all, there weren't any soldiers . . .": Seth Faison, "Clashing Stories of 4 Ships and a Disputed Heroism," *New York Times,* 7/5/94.

251   Truong's hotel purchases: Michael Goodwin, "Vietnamese Buys Two Hotels, Seeks More," *New York Times,* 4/23/78.

251   "He just bleeds these places . . .": Seth Faison and Jo Thomas, "Empire of Hotels Riddled with Crime and Drugs," *New York Times,* 7/6/94.

251   Ritter's purchase of Times Square Motor Hotel: "Plans to Buy Times Sq. Hotel Prompts Debate," *New York Times,* 10/14/84.

252   "I'm trapped": Winston Williams, "Investment Sours for a Times Sq. Shelter," *New York Times,* 3/17/87.

252   "Don't let that collar fool you . . .": Sennott, 213.

252   City's planned purchase of Times Square Motor Hotel: Josh Barbanel, "New York City Seeks to Acquire Times Sq. Hotel," *New York Times,* 11/17/87.

252   Ritter's sale of hotel: Dennis Hevesi, "Covenant House Sells a Times Square Hotel," *New York Times,* 1/3/88. See also Scott Ladd, "City to Condemn Disputed Hotel," *Newsday,* 1/7/88.

253   Truong's takeover of the Times Square: Sara Rimer, "Despite Pledge, Homeless Still in Hotel," *New York Times,* 11/11/89.

252   The Times Square's woeful condition: Ibid.

253   Two hundred bags of garbage: Lisa W. Fordero, "Overnight Transformation at Midtown Welfare Hotel," *New York Times,* 1/14/90.

254   "The only difference . . .": Michael Pye, "Cleansing the Deuce," *Independent,* 8/12/80.

254   "Those big hotels . . .": Faison and Thomas.

Midtown's Dead Zone

255   "It was a miracle . . .": Carter Weisman, "Brave New Times Square," *New York,* 4/2/84.

256   "became a valued liaison . . .": Jonathan Greenberg, "How to Make It Big in New York Real Estate," *Forbes,* 10/18/84.

256   "at the very top . . .": Edward Koch, *Mayor*, 289.

256   "The mere act of hiring . . .": Paul Goldberger, "499 Park, the Intent Is Serious," *New York Times*, 2/12/81.

257   "A total feeling has to be engendered . . .": Weisman.

257   "We're giving Times Square . . .": Ibid.

257   "one would have to rename the square . . .": *New York Times*, 3/3/84.

258   "exceptionally repellent . . .": Lynne B. Sagalyn, *Times Square Roulette*, 223.

259   "Light up the street! . . .": James Bennet, "Vibrancy to Vacancy: Remaking the Deuce," *New York Times*, 8/9/92.

259   "City, I don't have nothing . . .": Ibid.

259   A. J. Liebling, *The Honest Rainmaker*, 7–8.

259   "time has not made invalid . . .": L. R. Shannon and Betsy Wade, "Last Days of the Newspaper Saloon," *Columbia Journalism Review*, July/August 1992.

259   "It all stinks . . .": Michelle Conlin, unpublished article for a Columbia University journalism class, 12/93. Provided courtesy of Conlin.

260   Franklin's 42nd Street peregrinations: Joe Franklin interview by author, 7/16/01.

260   "It has a quality . . . unfair to bums": William Whitworth, "Broadway Joe," *New Yorker*, 5/22/71.

261   "They would cut your pants . . .": Franklin interview.

261   "I am a liar for hire . . .": Andrew Maykuth, "The Man Who Would Save Times Square from Respectability," *Philadelphia Inquirer*, 12/30/91.

261   "The public likes to come here . . .": John Tierney, "Extra!! 'Liar for Hire' Evicted!!" *New York Times*, 11/6/91.

262   "Oblivious to the natural cycles . . .": Seymour Durst, "Times Square: The Big Con," *Newsday*, 2/26/88.

262   "Despite having soaked up taxpayer dollars . . .": Carl Weisbrod, "42nd Street Landlords: Greed Inc.," *New York Times*, 6/17/89.

262   "Champion of Midtown Laissez-Faire": Alan S. Oser, "Seymour B. Durst: The Champion of Midtown Laissez-Faire," *New York Times*, 8/30/92.

262   "Karl Marx government . . .": Associated Press, "Developer Vents Spleen on Page One," 7/8/91.

263   "The idea was not so much . . .": Douglas Durst interview by author, 7/19/02.

263   "Rebecca was very up-front . . .": Carl Weisbrod interview by author, 11/12/02.

263   "I'm a technocrat . . .": Rebecca Robertson interview by author, 8/9/02.

264   "No one cared . . .": Ibid.

265   Stern's scenarios are contained in New York State Urban Development Corp., "Report Finds 42nd Street Theaters Historic Yet Adaptable," 10/20/88. Under the most capital-intensive of Stern's scenarios, the Selwyn was to be shrunk to 699 seats and used for intimate dramas. The office building where the Selwyn brothers once had their offices and in which several of the Brandts still toiled would be transformed into a theater rehearsal studio with a new glass facade resembling an unbuilt 1927 design by Josef Urban, Ziegfeld's favorite designer. Times Square would present state-of-the-art Imax and other media productions while the Victory would be used for opera and classical musical performances. The Lyric and the Apollo would be combined into a 2,500-seat arena suitable for three-ring circuses, ice-skating, magic shows, or concerts. A 1,000-seat, glass-enclosed restaurant would be constructed over the restored auditorium and connected to an old-fashioned roof garden atop the Victory.

265   "From Tap Dance to Redford . . .": Harry Berkowitz, "From Tap Dance to Redford, Everyone Wants 42nd St.," *Newsday,* 5/11/89.

266   "The line was that we interviewed . . .": Robertson interview.

266   "Carl was brilliant . . .": Ibid.

267   ". . . a good soul . . .": Donald Kennedy interview by author, 7/17/00.

268   "I didn't know anything . . .": Sagalyn, 289.

268   "Marian twisted arms . . .": Robertson interview.

268   "We thought we could buy . . .": Ibid.

268   "Durst made a better offer . . .": Robert Brandt interview by author, 8/24/00.

268   Durst's theater plans: Harry Berkowitz, "Durst to Reopen Theater," *Newsday,* 5/10/89; and Barbara Selvin, "Durst's Anti-Plan Plan for a New Times Square," *Newsday,"* 10/26/89. In 1991, Durst commissioned a theater study by LucasArts Entertainment entitled "42nd Street Entertainment Concepts."

269   "As an evocation of ghostliness . . .": Thomas M. Disch, *Nation,* 3/19/90. See also Mel Gussow, "Lead Role for a Theater, with the Audience on Stage," *New York Times,* 2/20/90; and Robert Brustein, "Theater," *New Republic,* 3/26/90.

269   En Garde Arts and its 42nd Street adventures: Mervyn Rothstein, "A New Show In and About a Theater with a Past," *New York Times,* 2/16/90; and Ben Pesner, "Where the Underworld Can Meet the Elite," *Theater Week,* 2/26/90.

269   "It was the most amazing thing . . .": Robert Hewison, "Evoking the Ghosts of the Theatre Past," *Times* (London), 3/11/90.

270   "The early pictures are almost painfully nostalgic . . .": Erika Munk, "What Have We Become?" *Village Voice*, 3/6/90.

270   "I have a very strong feeling . . .": Roger Morgan interview by author, 5/2/02.

270   Condemnation ruling: Richard Levine, "State Acquires Most of Times Square Project Site," *New York Times*, 4/19/90; and Neil Barsky, "Times Square Reclamation Plan Gains as the State Takes Title to 34 Properties," *Wall Street Journal*, 4/19/90.

270   ". . . get-it-moving phase . . .": Barbara Selvin, "New Boss on 42nd St.," *Newsday*, 4/26/90.

271   "They *stole* those theaters from us": Durst interview.

271   "Good luck to her . . .": Selvin.

271   "All I meant . . .": Durst interview.

271   "We got through it . . .": Robertson interview.

271   "I took the box . . .": Ibid.

271   "He made about 500 trips": Franklin interview.

272   "was absolutely determined . . .": Robertson interview.

272   Falk's move: Rick Hampson, "Lights Dim for New York City's West 42nd Street Redevelopment Project," *Los Angeles Times*, 9/20/92.

272   "It doesn't make sense . . .": David W. Dunlap, "Long Delay Likely in Rebuilding Plan for Times Square," *New York Times*, 8/3/92.

272   "Are office buildings economically viable . . .": Seymour B. Durst, "Times Square: We Told You So," *Newsday*, 8/11/92.

Rebecca's Magic Wand

274   "We're not going to do anything . . .": Mervyn Rothstein, "Empty Theaters Bring Concerts to Broadway," *New York Times*, 5/24/89.

275   "The fallacy in their thinking . . .": Theo Prudon interview by author, 7/3/02.

275   "I remember having my breath . . .": Douglas Durst interview by author, 7/18/02. Years later, after the hatchet had been well and truly buried, Doug Durst told Rebecca Robertson that in 1989 he had given serious thought to acquiring the New Amsterdam from the Nederlanders and adding it to his portfolio of 42nd Street theaters. This brought Robertson up short. "That would have caused us real problems, if Durst had got a blocking position with the New Amsterdam," she said (Rebecca Robertson interview by author, 8/9/02).

275   "I said nothing of the kind . . .": Robert Neuwirth, "Amsterdam Theater Falling Down," *Village Voice*, 10/2/90.

275   Citations ignored: Department of Buildings, C146113 (10/3/90) and 34047227 (12/5/90), archives of the New York City Landmarks Preservation Commission.

276   "The deterioration must be stopped": Laurie Beckelman to Robert Nederlander, 2/21/91, Landmarks Preservation Commission archives.

276   "Despite repeated requests . . .": Beckelman to Nederlander, 5/6/91, Landmarks Preservation Commission archives.

276   "significant amounts of money": David W. Dunlap, "Reviving a True Classic on West 42d Street," *New York Times*, 8/14/94.

276   Robertson's deal with the Nederlanders: New York State Urban Development Corp. press release, "New York State Acquires 42nd Street's Historic New Amsterdam Theatre," 9/9/92.

276   "a major victory . . .": David W. Dunlap, "State Acquires Landmark Theater to Salvage While It Still Can," *New York Times*, 9/10/92.

277   "If we had not been looking . . .": Robertson interview.

277   "Afterwards, my friends and I . . .": Michael Eisner, *Work in Progress*, 236.

278   *Collins Concise English Dictionary* adds *Disneyfication:* Tom Shields, "Whipping Boy," *Herald* (Glasgow), 7/17/92.

278   "If you produce a movie . . .": Eisner, 253.

278   "They were totally unresponsive . . .": Marc Eliot, *Down 42nd Street*, 244.

278   "he sent two or three people . . .": Ibid., 243.

279   "I guess you could say . . .": David Henry, "Landing Disney on 42nd; Personal Connections Lured Eisner to City," *Newsday*, 2/4/94.

279   "To be a really legitimate . . .": Alan Finder, "A Prince Charming? Disney and the City Find Each Other," *New York Times*, 6/10/95.

279   "We could see water leaking . . .": Eisner, 257.

279   On *Beauty and the Beast:* Alex Witchel, "Is Disney the Newest Broadway Baby?" *New York Times*, 4/17/94; and Patrick Pacheco, "Disney's Broadway Gamble," *Newsday*, 4/10/94.

280   Disney headlines: Lynne B. Sagalyn, *Times Square Roulette*, 343.

280   "The highly regulated . . .": Michael Sorkin, *Variations on a Theme Park*, 208.

281   "We do have some genetic instincts . . .": Frank Rose, "Can Walt Disney Tame 42nd Street?" *Fortune*, 6/24/96.

281   "You don't do that . . .": Sagalyn, 346.

283   "To me, movies were always . . .": Rebecca Robertson interview by author, 3/5/98.

283   "AMC would have done anything . . .": Robertson interview, 8/9/02.

283   "If they want the damn block . . .": Charles V. Bagli, "Disney Dream Gang Mugs New York City," *New York Observer,* 5/22/95.

284   "You can go ahead . . .": Wendy Leventer interview by author, 8/9/02.

285   "no politician wanted . . .": Robertson interview, 8/9/02.

285   "The city sent us an agreement . . .": Ibid.

285   "This is really going to happen . . .": Brett Pulley, "Companies Reach Deal for Renewal in Heart of 42d Street," *New York Times,* 7/21/95.

285   "The future of 42nd Street has arrived": Ibid.

285   "It's like a snowball . . .": Anthony Bianco, "A Star Is Reborn," *Business Week,* 7/8/96.

286    $4 billion in capital investment: Sagalyn, 605.

286   "Yes, it's ironic . . .": Charles V. Bagli, "Times Square Reversal: George Klein Seethes as Doug Durst Moves In," *New York Observer,* 11/27/95.

287   "I didn't care . . . ": Bernice Miles Lucchese, "Durst Melts NYC Office Development Freeze," *Commercial Property News,* 6/16/96.

287   "I think Seymour . . .": Douglas Durst interview by author, 7/19/02.

288   "I don't think Prudential . . .": Carl Weisbrod interview by author, 11/12/02.

288   "With George, it really was a Greek tragedy . . .": Ibid.

289   The New Victory's ticket prices ranged from $15 to $25. But a $25 annual membership bought tickets to four shows, reducing the average cost to $8.57 per ticket.

289   "I told them I wanted . . .": Richard Zoglin, "The Lion King: A Different Breed of Cats," *Time,* 7/28/97.

290   "There were 250 girls . . .": Robin Pogrebin, "From Naughty and Bawdy to Stars Reborn," *New York Times,* 12/11/00.

290   "The fact that the Seventh-to-Eighth block . . .": Rick Lyman, "As the Great White Way Turns a Corner," *New York Times,* 5/8/98.

291   On the remaking of Theater Row: Jesse Martin, "The Upscale March of the New Theater Row," *New York Times,* 11/21/02.

292   "Theater Row is a David and Goliath story . . .": Robert Moss interview by author, 7/2/01.

292   Show World's closure: Anthony Ramirez, "After Eluding Past Attempts, Show World Is Closed Down," *New York Times,* 5/28/99; and Larry McShane, "Still Standing: Times Square's Bawdiest Joint," Associated Press, 7/5/99.

292   On the Giuliani porn crackdown: Dan Barry, "With John Wayne and Sushi, Sex Shops Survive a Cleanup," *New York Times,* 1/1/01; and Richard Perez-Pena, "City Too Zealous on X-Rated Shops, State Court Rules," *New York Times,* 11/21/99.

293   For details of the *Times'* deal with the city and state: Charles V. Bagli, "Investor Takes Step to Halt New Tower for the Times," *New York Times,* 7/25/02; and David W. Dunlap, "Blight to Some Is Home to Others," *New York Times,* 10/25/01.

Epilogue

294   Woodyard's New Year's story: James Barron, "The Year 2000: The Hyperbole; A Countdown Worth the Wait vs. a Big Ho-Hum," *New York Times,* 1/2/00. For New Year's Eve coverage generally, see Robert D. McFadden, "1/1/00, From Bali to Broadway," *New York Times,* 1/1/00; and Jane Gross, "1/1/00: At the Crossroads," *New York Times,* 1/1/00.

295   "degenerated into a besotted . . .": Mary Voboril, "Countdown to Y2K; Forget the Clock—the New Year Doesn't Begin Until the Ball Drops in Times Square," *Newsday,* 12/22/99.

296   "You don't have to get your news . . .": Paul Goldberger, "Extra! Extra! Newshounds Exit!" *New Yorker,* 11/29/99.

296   "It doesn't matter if you make it to Paris . . .": Charlie LeDuff, "The Heart of a Battered City Pulses On," *New York Times,* 6/2/02.

297   "a wholesome and, on the whole . . .": James Traub, "The Dursts Have Odd Properties," *New York Times,* 10/6/02.

Selected Bibliography

Alexander, H. M. *Strip Tease*. New York: Knight Publishers, 1938.

Atkinson, Brooks. *Broadway*. New York: Macmillan, 1970.

Austin, Ernesto, et al. "The City." Graduate School of Management and Urban Professions, New School for Social Research, 1979.

Bagli, Charles V. "Times Square Reversal: George Klein Seethes as Doug Durst Moves In." *New York Observer*, 11/27/95.

Ballantine, William. *Wild Tigers & Tame Fleas*. New York: Rinehart, 1958.

Banner, Lois. *American Beauty*. New York: Alfred A. Knopf, 1983.

Barber, Rowland. *The Night They Raided Minsky's*. New York: Simon and Schuster, 1960.

Barnett, Jonathan. *Urban Design as Public Policy*. New York: Architectural Record Books, 1974.

Belle, John, and Maxinne Lieghton. *Grand Central: Gateway to a Million Lives*. New York: W. W. Norton, 2000.

Bennet, James. "Vibrancy to Vacancy: Remaking the Deuce." *New York Times*, 8/9/92.

Berger, Meyer. *The Story of the New York Times*. New York: Simon and Schuster, 1951.

Berman, Marshall. "Signs of the Times: The Lure of Times Square." *Dissent* 44 (fall 1997).

Bianco, Anthony. "A Star Is Reborn." *Business Week,* 7/8/96.

Bloom, Ken. *Broadway: An Encyclopedic Guide to the History, People, and Places of Times Square.* New York: Facts on File, 1991.

Blumenthal, Ralph. *The Stork Club.* Boston: Little, Brown & Co., 2000.

———. "A Times Square Revival?" *New York Times,* 12/27/81.

Bosworth, Patricia. *Marlon Brando.* New York: Viking, 2001.

Bracker, Milton. "Life on W. 42nd St.: A Study in Decay," *New York Times,* 3/14/60.

Brownmiller, Susan. *In Our Time.* New York: Dial Press, 1999.

Burlingame, Roger. *Endless Frontiers: The Story of McGraw-Hill.* New York: McGraw-Hill, 1959.

Cannato, Vincent J. *The Ungovernable City.* New York: Basic Books, 2001.

Carroll, John F. "Oscar Hammerstein I: 1895 to 1915." Ph.D. diss., City University of New York, 1998.

Carter, Paul. *The Twenties in America.* New York: Crowell, 1968.

Carter, Randolph. *The World of Flo Ziegfeld.* New York: Praeger, 1974.

Castle, Irene. *My Husband.* New York: Scribner, 1919.

Chaplin, Charlie. *My Autobiography.* London: Bodley Head, 1964.

Churchill, Allen. *The Great White Way: A Recreation of Broadway's Golden Era of Theatrical Entertainment.* New York: Dutton, 1962.

Cohen, Daniel. "For Food Both Cold and Hot, Put Your Nickels in the Slot." *Smithsonian,* 1/86.

Cohn, Nik. *The Heart of the World.* New York: Random House, 1993.

Corio, Ann. *This Was Burlesque.* New York: Grosset & Dunlap, 1968.

Corry, John. "The Selling of Sex: A Look Through a Solemn Sodom." *New York Times,* 10/10/72.

Delany, Samuel. *Times Square Red, Times Square Blue.* New York: New York University Press, 1999.

Dimeglio, John F. *Vaudeville U.S.A.* Bowling Green, Ohio: Bowling Green University Popular Press, 1973.

Doig, Jameson. *Empire on the Hudson.* New York: Columbia University Press, 2001.

Dowd, Maureen. "Childhood in 'Hell': Growing Up in Times Sq." *New York Times,* 6/25/84.

Dreiser, Theodore, *Sister Carries.* New York: Doubleday, 1997.

Dunlap, David. *On Broadway.* New York: Rizzoli International Publications, 1990.

———. "Reviving a True Classic on West 42d Street," *New York Times,* 8/14/94.

Eisner, Michael. *Work in Progress.* New York: Random House, 1998.

Eliot, Marc. *Down 42nd Street.* New York: Warner Books, 2001.

Elliott, Lawrence. *Little Flower.* New York: Morrow, 1983.

Erenberg, Lewis A. *Steppin' Out: New York Nightlife and the Transformation of American Culture, 1890–1930*. Westport, Conn.: Greenwood Press, 1981.

Estate of Robert Di Bernardo, Surrogate's Court, County of Nassau, File 244378.

Fadin, Hugh. *Getting to Know Him: A Biography of Oscar Hammerstein II*. New York: Random House, 1977.

Farnsworth, Marjorie. *The Ziegfeld Follies*. London: Peter Davies, 1956.

Ford, Luke. *A History of X*. Amherst, N.Y.: Prometheus Books, 1999.

Forty-Second Street Development Corp. "What's a Nice Girl Like Estelle Parsons Doing in a Massage Parlor on 42nd Street?" Undated.

Friedman, Alan Jay. *Tales of Times Square*. New York: Delacorte Press, 1986.

Friedwald, Will. *Sinatra! The Song Is You*. New York: Scribner, 1995.

Gabrielan, Randall. *Times Square and 42nd Street in Vintage Post Cards*. Charleston, S.C.: Arcadia Publishing, 2000.

Gifford, Barry, and Lawrence Lee. *Jack's Book: An Oral Biography of Jack Kerouac*. New York: St. Martin's Press, 1978.

Gilbert, Douglas. *American Vaudeville*. New York: Whittlesley House, 1940.

Gilmartin, Gregory F. *Shaping the City*. New York: Clarkson N. Potter Inc., 1995.

Goewey, Edwin A. "The Man Who Made Times Square." *Dance*, 1/29.

Goldberger, Paul. "Buck Rogers in Times Square." *New York Times Magazine*, 8/26/73.

———. "'Green Building' Is a White Elephant." *New York Times*, 11/3/73.

Golden, Eve. *Anna Held and the Birth of Ziegfeld's Broadway*. Lexington: University Press of Kentucky, 2000.

Goldman, Herbert G. *Fanny Brice*. New York: Oxford University Press, 1992.

Goldstein, Richard. "The Fate of Theatre Row." *Village Voice*, 4/22/81.

Gottlieb, Martin. "Pornography's Plight Hits Times Square." *New York Times*, 10/5/86.

Gratz, Roberta Brandes. *The Living City*. New York: Simon & Schuster, 1989.

Greenberg, Jonathan. "How to Make It Big in New York Real Estate." *Forbes*, 10/18/84.

Gross, Theodore. "Will Bob Moss Become the Next Joe Papp?" *Village Voice*, 11/1/76.

Grossman, Barbara W. *Funny Woman*. Bloomington, Ind.: Indiana University Press, 1991.

Hall, Ben M. *The Best Remaining Seats*. New York: C. N. Potter, 1961.

Haskell, Loney. "The Corner: Reminiscences of Hammerstein's Victoria." Pts. 1 and 2. *New Yorker*, 12/13/30, 12/20/30.

Henderson, Mary C. *The City and the Theatre*. Clifton, N.J.: J. T. White, 1973.

———. *The New Amsterdam*. New York: Hyperion, 1997.

Hentoff, Nat. *A Political Life: The Education of John V. Lindsay*. New York: Alfred A. Knopf, 1969.

Hiassen, Carl. *Team Rodent: How Disney Devours the World*. New York: Ballantine Publishing Group, 1998.

Higham, Charles. *Ziegfeld*. Chicago: H. Regnery Co., 1972.

Hirsch, Foster. *The Boys from Syracuse*. Carbondale, Ill.: Southern Illinois University Press, 1998.

Hiss, Tony. *The Experience of Place*. New York: Alfred A. Knopf, 1990.

Hoberman, J. *42nd Street*. London: BFI Publishing, 1993.

Hood, Clifton. *722 Miles: The Building of the Subways and How They Transformed New York*. New York: Simon and Schuster, 1993.

Hopkins, Carol. "The Unsinkable Joey & Harry." *Detroit Monthly*, 4/92.

Horsley, Carter B. "A Critical Time for the Old Theaters Along 42nd Street." *New York Times*, 6/19/77.

Huncke, Herbert. *The Evening Sun Turned Crimson*. Cherry Valley, N.Y.: Cherry Valley Editions, 1980.

———. *Guilty of Everything*. New York: Paragon House, 1990.

Jackson, James. *The Smut Peddlers*. New York: Avon Book Division, Hearst Corp., 1960.

Jackson, Kenneth L., ed. *The Encyclopedia of New York City*. New Haven: Yale University Press; New York: New-York Historical Society, 1995.

Jacobs, Jane. *The Death and Life of Great American Cities*. New York: Random House, 1961.

Jacobs, Laura. "Taking It *All* Off." *Vanity Fair*, 3/03.

Jacobson, Mark. "A Film Freak's Plea: Nationalize 42nd Street!" *Village Voice*, 1/6/75.

———. "Times Square: The Meanest Street in America." *Rolling Stone*, 8/6/81.

Jahr, Cliff. "'42nd Street' Log—The Making of a Hit." *New York Times*, 9/7/80.

James, Rian, and James Seymour. *42nd Street*. Introduction by Rocco Fumento. Madison, Wis.: Published for the Wisconsin Center for Film and Theater Research by University of Wisconsin Press, 1980.

Jenkins, Stephen. *The Greatest Street in the World*. New York: G. P. Putnam's Sons, 1911.

Johnson, Stephen Burge. *The Roof Gardens of Broadway Theatres, 1883–1942*. Ann Arbor, Mich.: UMI Research Press, 1985.

Kahn, E. J., Jr. "Boffos and Bustos." *New Yorker*, 12/9/74.

Kaufman, J. B. "Movie Musicals Turn a Corner at 42nd Street." *American Cinematographer*, May 1994.

Kellock, Harold. *Houdini*. New York: Harcourt, Brace & Co., 1929.

Kissel, Howard. *David Merrick, The Abominable Showman*. New York: Applause, 1993.

Knapp, Margaret, "A Historical Study of the Legitimate Playhouses on West Forty-Second Street Between Seventh and Eighth Avenues in New York City," Ph.D. diss., City University of New York, 1982.

Konigsberg, Eric. "Jimmy Nederlander's Endless Run." *New York*, 5/31/99.

Kornblum, William, ed. "West 42nd Street: The Bright Light Zone." Unpublished study, City University of New York, 1978.

Kuntsler, James Howard. *The Geography of Nowhere*. New York: Touchstone, 1993.

Landmarks Preservation Commission (New York City). *McGraw-Hill Building*. Designation List 127 LP-1050, 9/11/79.

Lane, Frederick S., III. *Obscene Profits*. New York: Routledge, 2000.

Lass, William. *Crossroads of the World: The Story of Times Square*. New York: Popular Library, 1965.

Lee, Gypsy Rose. *Gypsy: A Memoir*. New York: Harper, 1957.

Lessard, Suzannah. *The Architect of Desire*. New York: Dial Press, 1996.

Loney, Glenn. "Forty-Second Street Changes Its Tune." *After Dark*, 2/78.

Lyman, Rick. "As the Great White Way Turns a Corner." *New York Times*, 5/8/98.

Maas, Peter. *Underboss*. New York: HarperCollins Publishing, 1997.

Manhattan Plaza Project. Columbia University Oral History Research Office.

Mathes, Charles. *The Hammersteins of New York: 100 Years of Music and Theater*. Program notes for exhibition by the Library of the Performing Arts at Lincoln Center, 6/10/86–9/20/86.

Mayer, Arthur. *Merely Colossal*. New York: Simon & Schuster, 1953.

McCabe, James D., Jr., *New York by Sunlight and Gaslight*. New York: Greenwich House, 1984. Distributed by Crown Publishers.

McNamara, Brooks. *The Shuberts of Broadway*. New York: Oxford University Press, 1990.

McNamara, Robert P., ed. *Sex, Scams, and Street Life: The Sociology of New York City's Times Square*. Westport, Conn.: Praeger, 1995.

Minsky, Morton, and Milt Machlin. *Minsky's Burlesque*. New York: Arbor House, 1986.

Mollenkopf, John. "The 42nd Street Development Project and the Public Interest." *City Almanac* 18 (summer 1985).

Mooney, Michael McDonald. *Evelyn Nesbit and Stanford White*. New York: Morrow, 1976.

Morehouse, Ward. *George M. Cohan, Prince of the American Theater*. Philadelphia: J. B. Lippincott Company, 1943.

———. *Matinee Tomorrow*. New York: Whittlesey House, 1949.

Morris, Jan. *Manhattan '45*. New York: Oxford University Press, 1987.

Morris, Lloyd. *Incredible New York*. New York: Random House, 1951.

Morrison, William. "Oscar Hammerstein I: The Man Who Invented Times Square." *Marquee*, first quarter 1983.

Muschamp, Herbert. "42nd Street Plan: Be Bold or Begone!" *New York Times*, 9/19/93.

Nasaw, David. *Going Out: The Rise and Fall of Public Amusements*. New York: Basic Books, 1993.

Nesbit, Evelyn. *Prodigal Days*. New York: J. Messner, 1934.

Neuwirth, Robert. "Amsterdam Theater Falling Down." *Village Voice*, 10/2/90.

New York City Department of City Planning and Public Development Corp. "42nd Street Development Project: A Disclosure Document." 2/10/81.

New York State Commission of Investigation. *An Investigation of Racketeer Infiltration of the Sex-Oriented Materials Industry in New York City.*

New York State Select Committee on Crime. "Children, Pornography, and the Illicit Sex Industry." 11/14/77.

New York Times. The Century in Times Square. New York: Bishop Books, 1999.

O'Brien, Geoffrey. *The Times Square Story*. New York: W. W. Norton, 1998.

Office of Midtown Enforcement. "Annual Report." 1976, 1977, 1982–88.

———. "What Are They Now?" 1982.

Okrent, Daniel. *Great Fortune: The Epic of Rockefeller Center*. New York: Viking, 2003.

Oser, Alan S. "Seymour B. Durst: The Champion of Midtown Laissez-Faire." *New York Times*, 8/30/92.

Paneth, Philip. *Times Square: Crossroads of the World*. New York: Living Books, 1965.

Petersen, James R. *The Century of Sex*. New York: Grove Press, 1999.

Poggi, Jack. *Theater in America*. Ithaca, N.Y.: Cornell University Press, 1968.

Price, Richard. *Ladies' Man*. Boston: Houghton Mifflin, 1978.

Pye, Michael. "Cleansing the Deuce." *Independent*, 8/12/80.

Raab, Selwyn, and Nathaniel Sheppard Jr. "Mobsters Skim New York City Sex Industry Profits." *New York Times*, 7/27/77.

Rector, George. *The Girl from Rector's*. Garden City, N.Y.: Doubleday, Page & Co., 1927.

Reichl, Alexander J. *Reconstructing Times Square*. Lawrence, Kans.: University Press of Kansas, 1999.

Rich, Frank. *Hot Seat*. New York: Random House, 1998.

Ritter, Bruce. *Covenant House: Lifeline to the Streets*. New York: Doubleday, 1987.

Rogers, W. G., and Mildred Weston. *Carnival Crossroads*. Garden City, N.Y.: Doubleday, 1960.

Rogers, Will. *The Autobiography of Will Rogers*. New York: Lancer Books, 1949.

Rose, Frank. "Can Walt Disney Tame 42nd Street?" *Fortune*, 6/24/96.

Ross, Lillian. *Moments with Chaplin*. New York: Dodd, Mead, 1980.

Rothstein, Mervyn. "A New Show In and About a Theater with a Past." *New York Times*, 2/16/90.

Sagalyn, Lynne B. *Times Square Roulette*. Cambridge, Mass.: MIT Press, 2001.

Sanders, James. *Celluloid Skyline*. New York: Alfred A. Knopf, 2001.

Sandrow, Nahma, "Center-Stage Living, at Balcony Rents." *New York Times*, 6/9/02.

Sante, Luc. *Low Life*. New York: Farrar Straus Giroux, 1991.

Schrader, Paul. *Taxi Driver*. London: Faber and Faber, 1990.

Schur, Robert. "Manhattan Plaza: Old Style Ripoffs Are Still Alive and Well." In *Critical Perspectives on Housing*, edited by Rachel G. Brett, Chester Hartman, and Ann Meyerson. Philadelphia: Temple University Press, 1986.

Sennott, Charles M. *Broken Covenant*. New York: Simon and Schuster, 1992.

Shachtman, Tom. *Skyscraper Dreams*. Boston: Little, Brown, 1991.

Sharp, Dennis. *The Picture Palace and Other Buildings for the Movies*. New York: Praeger, 1969.

Sheean, Vincent. *Oscar Hammerstein I*. New York: Simon and Schuster, 1956.

Sheehy, Gail. "Cleaning Up Hell's Bedroom." *New York*, 11/13/72.

Shepard, Richard F. "Peep Shows Have New Nude Look." *New York Times*, 6/9/69.

Sherman, William. *Times Square*. New York: Bantam Books, 1980.

———."That 42d St. Porno? Well, Meet the King." *Daily News*, 12/11/72.

———. "The King Harvests Lush Pornfield." *Daily News*, 12/12/72.

———."Mafia Declares War, but Porn King Survives." *Daily News*, 2/13/72.

———. "Knights in Blue Crumbling Porn King's Castle." *Daily News*, 2/14/72.

Shulman, Alix Kates. *On the Stroll*. New York: Alfred A. Knopf, 1981.

Sinclair, Andrew. *Prohibition, the Era of Excess*. Boston: Little, Brown, 1962.

Slide, Anthony, ed. *Selected Vaudeville Criticism*. Metuchen, N.J.: Scarecrow Press, 1988.

Sloan, Paul. "Bob Brown's Street Life." *Newsday*, 5/25/89.

Sorkin, Michael, ed. *Variations on a Theme Park*. New York: Hill & Wang, 1992.

Stagg, Jerry. *The Brothers Shubert*. New York: Random House, 1968.

Starr, Roger. *The Rise and Fall of New York City*. New York: Basic Books, 1985.

Starr, Tama, and Edward Hayman. *Signs and Wonders*. New York: Doubleday/Currency, 1998.

Stern, Robert A.M., Gregory Gilmartin, and John Montague. *New York 1900*. New York: Rizzoli, 1983.

Stern, Robert A. M., Thomas Mellins, and David Fishman. *New York 1960*. New York: Monacelli Press, 1995.

Stern, William J. "The Unexpected Lessons of Times Square's Comeback." *City Journal*, autumn 1999.

Stockdale, Freddie. *Emperors of Song*. London: J. Murray, 1998.

Stone, Jill. *Times Square: A Pictorial History*. New York: Macmillan, 1982.

Stouman, Lou. *Times Square: 45 Years of Photography*. New York: Aperture, 1985.

Street, Julian. "Lobster Palace Society." *Everybody's Magazine* 22 (May 1910).

Talese, Gay. "42nd St.: How It Got That Way." *Show*, 12/61.

Talese, Gay, and Henry Hope Reed Jr. "42nd St.," *Show*, 1/62.

Taylor, William R., ed. *Inventing Times Square: Commerce and Culture at the Crossroads of the World*. New York: Russell Sage Foundation, 1991.

Tierney, John. "Era Ends as Times Square Drops Slashers for Shakespeare." *New York Times*, 1/24/91.

―――. "Extra!! 'Liar for Hire' Evicted!!" *New York Times*, 11/6/91.

Tifft, Susan, and Jones, Alex. *The Trust*. Boston: Little, Brown, 1999.

Timberlake, Craig. *The Life & Work of David Belasco, the Bishop of Broadway*. New York: Library Publishers, 1954.

Topol, Manny. "Adventures in the Peep Trade." *Newsday*, 9/29/74.

Torchin, Mimi. "Now We Are Ten." *Other Stages*, 11/20/80.

U.S. Department of Justice, Attorney General's Commission on Pornography. *Final Report*. July 1986.

Vallilo, Stephen M. "Broadway Revues in the Teens and Twenties: Smut and Slime?" *Drama Review* 25, no. 1 (March 1981).

Van Hoogstraten, Nicholas. *Lost Broadway Theaters*. New York: Princeton Architectural Press, 1991.

Walker, Stanley. *The Night Club Era*. New York: Blue Ribbon Books, 1933.

Wall, Evander Berry. *Neither Pest Nor Puritan*. New York: Dial Press, 1940.

Watson, Steven. *The Birth of the Beat Generation*. New York: Pantheon Books, 1995.

Weiner, Sally Dixon. "Theater Row: A Tale of Theater and of Real Estate." *Dramatists Guild Quarterly*, spring 1991.

Weisman, Carter. "Brave New Times Square." *New York*, 4/2/84.

Where and How to Dine in New York. New York: Lewis, Scribner, 1903.

Whittaker, Peter. *The American Way of Sex*. New York: Berkley Pub. Corp, 1974.

Whitworth, William. "Broadway Joe." *New Yorker*, 5/22/71.

Wilson, Earl. "42nd Street Badly Maligned; Its Fleas Are Lively." *New York Post*, 5/1/44.

Winter, William. *The Life of David Belasco*. New York: Moffat, Yard, 1918.

Worden, Helen. *Here Is New York*. New York: Doubleday, Doran & Co., 1939.

The WPA Guide to New York City. 1939. Reprint, New York: Pantheon Books, 1982.

Zabarkes, Arthur B. "An Environmental and Economic Survey of Times Square and Mid-Manhattan," unpublished paper.

Ziedman, Irving. *The American Burlesque Show.* New York: Hawthorn Books, 1967.

Ziegfeld, Richard, and Paulette Ziegfeld. *The Ziegfeld Touch.* New York: Harry N. Abrams, 1993.

Acknowledgments

Business Week, my longtime employer, has its offices on 49th Street and Sixth Avenue, on the eastern edge of Times Square. I had been away from the magazine for four years and was struck upon my return in 1996 by how dramatically the area had changed in my absence. In researching an article on Times Square's revival, I came to realize how little I really knew about the neighborhood in which I had worked since 1982. Through several interviews with Rebecca Robertson, the president of the 42nd Street Development Project, came the first glimmerings of understanding that 42nd Street was Times Square's most distinctive and historically important component. Robertson's enthusiasm for the story of 42nd Street was palpable—and contagious. I might not have decided to write this book had I not begun by seeing 42nd Street through her eyes.

I'd like to thank my agent, Esther Newberg, for her wise and energetic counsel. My editor, Henry Ferris, instantly grasped the idea of the book and continued to believe in it with only slightly fraying patience as I missed first one and then another delivery date. I owe a debt of gratitude as well to Steven Shepard, the editor of *Business Week*, for granting me a leave of absence and for graciously extending that leave.

I'm indebted to Terri Thompson of Columbia University for helping me find two highly capable and tireless research assistants, Czerina Patel and Anneliese Gaeta, without whom I no doubt would have missed another deadline. Ronnie Weil, a *Business Week* colleague, provided valuable advice on photo selection, and the talented freelancers Kevin Kwan and Naomi Ben-Shahar assembled the pictures.

Mary Kuntz, the senior editor with whom I work most closely at *Business Week*, read the manuscript and made many valuable suggestions. Special thanks to Mara Der Hovanesian for graciously participating in countless discussions of the book-in-progress and for giving the text an insightful final read-through when she wasn't feeling nearly her best.

INDEX